Contract Law in Cyprus

Contract Law in Cyprus

Natalia Charalampidou

This book was originally published as a monograph in the International Encyclopaedia of Laws/Contracts.

Founding Editor: Roger Blanpain
General Editor: Frank Hendrickx
Volume Editor: Jacques Herbots

Wolters Kluwer

Published by:
Kluwer Law International B.V.
PO Box 316
2400 AH Alphen aan den Rijn
The Netherlands
E-mail: international-sales@wolterskluwer.com
Website: www.wolterskluwer.com/en/solutions/kluwerlawinternational

Sold and distributed by:
Wolters Kluwer Legal & Regulatory U.S.
7201 McKinney Circle
Frederick, MD 21704
United States of America
E-mail: customer.service@wolterskluwer.com

ISBN 978-94-035-4225-6

e-Book: ISBN 978-94-035-4230-0
web-PDF: ISBN 978-94-035-4231-7

to the loving memory of my grandmother, Aristea

The Author

Natalia Charalampidou, a native of Thessaloniki (Greece), is teaching International Environmental and Energy Law at the Faculty of Law of the Democritus University of Thrace in Greece.

Natalia's areas of expertise include the Energy Charter Treaty, contaminated site investigation and remediation, environmental liability, solid and hazardous waste, environmental due diligence, energy compliance, prospection, research and exploitation of hydrocarbons, renewable electricity, unconventional energy sources and smart grids & cities. She is an author of the International Encyclopaedia of Laws contributing the Chapters on Energy, Environment and Contract Law in Cyprus.

Prior to focusing on academic research and teaching in 2012, Natalia had joined the corporate and dispute resolution teams of high-profile law firms in Cyprus and overseas and acquired treasured experience in stock-exchange regulations, the European company (Societas Europaea), due diligence, fraud, anti-money laundering and investment arbitration in the energy sector. For these compelling and captivating times, she is much grateful to the heads of the departments and all her colleagues. She has Diploma in Turkish Language, Institute for Balkan Studies (Greece), 2002; LLB, Democritus University of Thrace (Greece), 2003; LLM, University of Heidelberg, 2004. She is currently doing PhD, University of Heidelberg. She was admitted in the bars of Cyprus, 2006, and Thessaloniki (Greece), 2014. Her indicative list of publications include the monograph 'Environmental Law: The Implementation of Directives of the European Union in Cyprus' (in Greek) (Sakkoulas Publications, Athens, 2013); the following contributions in collective volumes, 'The Energy Charter Treaty' (in Greek) 23–48 in: K. Antonopoulos & H. Aroni (eds) 'Introduction to International Energy Law' (Nomiki Bibliothiki 2020); 'Renewable Energy' (in Greek) 173–188 in: K. Antonopoulos & H. Aroni (eds) 'Introduction to International Energy Law' (Nomiki Bibliothiki 2020); (co-author) 'Cyprus', in: C. Esplugues (ed.) 'Civil and Commercial Mediation in Europe' (Intersentia, Cambridge 2014) 103–124; the following journal publications, 'Pressing Measures in Perilous Times: The Investment Perspective' 18(2) TDM No. 2 (2021); 'Energy Corporations and Their Information Duties Towards State Authorities' 30(2) EEELR 62–71 (2021); 'The Islamic Revolution of 1979 in Iran and Oil Disputes' Mobil Oil and Government of Iran (in Greek), 23(4) Periballon & Dikaio

(Greek legal journal) 673–678 (2019); 'Smart Buildings: From Flat-Rates to Smart Metering' (in Greek), 23(4) Periballon & Dikaio 540–559 (2019); 'Supply of Fuels and Diesel Generators' *Lighthouse v. Timor-Leste* (in Greek), 2 (3) Periballon & Dikaio 511–520 (2019); 'International Energy Disputes That Arose from the Financial Crisis in Argentina (1999–2002)' *Pan American & BP v. Argentina* and *Total v. Argentina* (in Greek), 23(2) Periballon & Dikaio 350–360 (2019); 'International Energy Disputes That Arose from the Financial Crisis in Argentina (1999–2002)' *CMS v. Argentina* and *El Paso v. Argentina* (in Greek), 23(1) Periballon & Dikaio 142–168 (2019); 'Investment on Oil Refinery and Electricity Production Unit' *Plama v. Bulgaria* (in Greek), 22(4) Periballon & Dikaio 673–678 (2018); 'The Applicability of the Energy Charter Treaty' *Yukos Universal v. Russia* (in Greek), 22(3) Periballon & Dikaio 544–552 (2018); 'Issues of Environmental Damage from Oil Activities' *Chevron and Texaco v. Ecuador* (in Greek), 22(3) Periballon & Dikaio 536–544 (2018); 'Range of Disputes under the Energy Charter Treaty', 15(7) TDM (OGEL/TDM Special Issue with ArbitralWomen 'Strategic Considerations in Energy Disputes') No. 10 (2018); 'The Notion of Waste: An Overview of the Legislation on Waste' (in Greek), 22(2) Periballon & Dikaio 246–258 (2018); 'Greek Soil Law', 2 International Yearbook of Soil Law and Policy 245–276 (2017); 'Annulment of Adoption Orders due to Fraud and Perjury Before the Supreme Court of Cyprus' (in Greek), Epitheorisi Politikis Dikonomias (Greek legal journal) 177–186 (2013); 'European Protection of the Soil: The Struggle for Uniform Regulation' (in German), 8(4) Europarecht 593–611 (2011); 'The Protection of Land in Greece', 19(4) EEELR 160–174 (2010).

Table of Contents

Dedication 3

The Author 5

List of Abbreviations 15

Preface 19

General Introduction 21

§1. The General Background of the Country 21

§2. To What Legal Family (E.g., Common Law, French Legal Family, Islamic Law) Does Cyprus Law Belong? 22

§3. Is Primacy of Legislation a Characteristic of Cyprus System? 23

§4. The Position of the Judiciary 23

§5. Distinction Between Public Law and Private Law ('Administrative Contracts') 24

§6. Distinction Between Civil Law and Commercial Law ('Commercial Contracts') 24

Introduction to the Law of Contracts 25

§1. Definition of Contract 25

§2. Historical Background of the Law of Contracts 25

§3. Classification of Contracts 26

§4. Contract and Torts 26

§5. Contract and Quasi-Contract 30

§6. Contract and the Law of Property 30

§7. CONTRACT AND TRUST 30

§8. GOOD FAITH AND FAIR DEALING 31

§9. STYLE OF DRAFTING 32

§10. SOURCES OF THE LAW OF CONTRACTS 32

Part I. General Principles of the Law of Contracts 33

Chapter 1. Formation 33

§1. AGREEMENT AND QUID PRO QUO 33
I. Offer and Acceptance 33
II. Intention to Create Legal Relations 35
III. Consideration 37
A. Does This Requirement Exist in Your Legal System? 37
B. Gratuitous Promises 38
C. 'Natural Obligations' 38
IV. Modifications of the Contract 39

§2. FORMAL AND EVIDENTIAL REQUIREMENTS 39
I. Formal Requirements 39
II. Evidential Requirement: Proof 40
A. The Parol Evidence Rule 40
B. Function of the Notary 40
III. Burden of Proof 41

§3. LIABILITY AND NEGOTIATIONS 42
I. Precontractual Liability 42
II. Breakdown of Negotiations 42

Chapter 2. Conditions of Substantive Validity 43

§1. CAPACITY OF THE PARTIES 43

§2. DEFECTS OF CONSENT 44
I. Mistake 44
II. Misrepresentation 45
III. Improper Pressure 47
IV. Gross Disparity 52

§3. OTHER CONDITIONS OF VALIDITY 52
I. Existing and Licit Cause 52
II. Determined or Determinable, Possible and Licit Object 56
III. Illegality and Public Policy 56

A. Illicit Object or Consideration 57
1. Object Prohibited by Law 57
2. Object Defeating Provisions of Any Law 58
3. Fraudulent Object 59
4. Object Injuring a Third Person or Other Property 62
5. Immoral Object and Object Opposing to Public Policy 62
B. Illegality Due to Agreed Content 64
IV. Unenforceable Contracts 65

§4. The Consequences of a Defect of Consent or a Lack of Substantive Validity 66
I. Avoidance of the Contract: Nullity 66
II. Retroactive Effect of Avoidance or Nullity 67
III. Damages 67

Chapter 3. The Contents of a Contract 68

§1. The Different Clauses 68
I. Ascertaining of Express Terms 68
II. Implied Terms 68
III. Standard Terms and Exemption Clauses 69
IV. Penalty Clauses 70
V. Arbitration Clauses 70

§2. Interpretation 72

§3. Conditional Contracts 73

Chapter 4. Privity of Contract 75

§1. The Rule of Privity of Contract 75
I. Third Parties and the Contract 75
II. Contract for the Benefit of a Third Party 75

§2. Transfer of Contractual Rights 75

§3. The Special Case of a 'Subcontract', for Example, the (Nominated) Subcontractor in Building Contracts 76

§4. *Actio Pauliana* 76

Chapter 5. The Termination of the Contract 79

§1. Performance and Breach 79

§2. Impossibility, Frustration and Hardship: The 'Unforeseen' 81

§3. Discharge by Agreement 84

Chapter 6. Remedies 86

§1. General Provisions 86

§2. Specific Performance and Injunctions Astreinte 86

§3. Termination 87

§4. *Exceptio Non Adimpleti Contractus* 88

§5. Faulty Behaviour of the Debtor 89

§6. Limitation of Actions 90

§7. Damages and Exemption Clauses 90

§8. Restitution 96

Part II. Specific Contracts 99

Chapter 1. Agency 99

§1. Parties to Agency 99

§2. Formation of Agency 100

§3. Content of Agency 101

§4. The Parties' Duties and Responsibilities 101
I. Agent's Duty to Principal 101
II. Principal's Duty to Agent 103

§5. Agency and Third Persons 103

§6. Termination of Agency 105

Chapter 2. Bailment 107

§1. Parties to Bailment 107

§2. Formation of Bailment 108

§3. Content of Bailment 108

§4. The Parties' Duties and Responsibilities 109
I. Duties and Responsibilities of a Bailee 109
II. Duties and Responsibilities of a Bailor 110

§5. Bailment and Third Persons 111

§6. Termination of Bailment 112

Chapter 3. Gaming and Wagering 113

§1. Law on Betting 113

§2. Law on Operation and Control of Casinos 115

Chapter 4. Sale of Goods 118

§1. Parties to a Contract of Sale 118

§2. Formation of a Contract of Sale 119

§3. Content of a Contract of Sale 119

§4. The Parties' Duties and Responsibilities 122

§5. Contract of Sale and Third Persons 127

§6. Hire Purchase Agreements 128

§7. Financial Leasing 132

§8. Termination of a Contract of Sale 137

§9. Actions for Breach of Contract of Sale 138

Chapter 5. Building Contracts, Hire of Work and Skills 140

§1. Building Contracts 140

§2. Hire of Work and Skills 141
I. Statutory Provisions Applicable to All Contracts of Employment 141
II. Statutory Provisions on Protection of Specific Categories of Employees 145
III. Statutory Provisions on Protection from the Working Environment 148

Chapter 6. Lease, Commercial and Agricultural Leases 150

Chapter 7. Compromise Settlement 155

§1. Settlement 155

§2. Mediation Settlement 156

Chapter 8. Suretyship 159

§1. Parties to a Contract of Guarantee 159

§2. Formation of a Contract of Guarantee 159

§3. Content of a Contract of Guarantee 161

§4. The Parties' Duties and Responsibilities 162

§5. Contract of Guarantee and Third Persons 163

§6. Termination of a Contract of Guarantee 163

Chapter 9. Pledge 164

§1. Parties to Pledge 164

§2. Formation of Pledge 164

§3. Content of Pledge 165

§4. The Parties' Duties and Responsibilities 165

§5. Pledge and Third Persons 169

§6. Termination of Pledge 169

Chapter 10. Loans 170

Chapter 11. Contracts with the Government 172

§1. Parties to Public Procurement 174

§2. Rules on the Formation of Public Contracts 174

I. General Principles and Statutory Obligations 174

II. Available Procedures 175

III. Conduct of Procedure 179

IV. Criteria of Awarding Contracts 180

A. Necessary Conditions 180

B. Exclusion Criteria 181
C. Selection Criteria 186
V. The European Single Procurement Document 188
VI. Contract Award Criteria 189

§3. Content and Performance of Public Contracts 192

§4. Duties and Responsibilities of Economic Operators and Contracting Authorities 194

§5. Specific Provisions for Particular Procurement Regimes 196
I. Social and Other Services 196
II. Design Contracts 198
III. Procurement by Entities Operating in the Water, Energy, Transport and Postal Services Sectors 199
IV. Procurement by Entities Operating in the Defence and Security Sector 204

§6. Termination of Public Contracts 208

Chapter 12. Contract of Partnership 210

§1. Parties to Partnership 210

§2. Formation of Partnership 210

§3. Content of Partnership 213

§4. The Parties' Duties and Responsibilities 214

§5. Partnership and Third Persons 219

§6. Termination of Partnership 220

Chapter 13. Quasi-Contracts 224

§1. *Negotiorum Gestio* 224

§2. Enrichment Without Cause 224

§3. Money Paid but Not Due 227

Selected Bibliography 229

Table of Cases 231

Index 251

Table of Contents

List of Abbreviations

ABCA	Alberta Court of Appeal
ABQB	Alberta Court of Queen's Bench
AC	Law Reports, Appeal Cases (Third Series)
All ER	All England Law Reports
All ER Rep	All England Law Reports Reprint
App. Cas.	Law Reports, Appeal Cases (Second Series)
BCCA	British Columbia Court of Appeal
Cap. 62	Fraudulent Transfers Avoidance Law
Cap. 113	Companies Law
Cap. 116	Law on Partnerships
Cap. 148	Civil Wrongs
Cap. 149	Law of Contract
Cap. 154	Criminal Code
Cap. 161	Prevention of Corruption Law
Cap. 252	Mental Patients Law (now repealed)
Ch	Law Reports, Chancery Division (3rd Series)
Ch. D.	Law Reports, Chancery Division (2nd Series)
Cl. & F.	Clark & Finnelly's House of Lords Cases
CLR	Cyprus Law Reports
Com LR	Commercial Law Reports
Directive 89/391/EEC	Directive on the introduction of measures to encourage improvements in the safety and health of workers at work
Directive 92/85/EEC	Directive on the introduction of measures to encourage improvements in the safety and health at work of pregnant workers and workers who have recently given birth or are breastfeeding
Directive 98/58/EC	Directive on the approximation of the laws of the Member States relating to collective redundancies

List of Abbreviations

Directive 2006/54/EC	Directive on the implementation of the principle of equal opportunities and equal treatment of men and women in matters of employment and occupation
Directive 2008/52/EC	Directive on certain aspects of mediation in civil and commercial matters
Directive 2009/81/EC	Directive on the coordination of procedures for the award of certain works contracts, supply contracts and service contracts by contracting authorities or entities in the fields of defence and security
Directive 2012/18/EU	Directive on the control of major-accident hazards involving dangerous substances
Directive 2014/24/EU	Directive on public procurement
Directive 2014/25/EU	Directive on procurement by entities operating in the water, energy, transport and postal services sectors
ECR	European Court Reports
EU	European Union
ESPD	European Single Procurement Document
EWHC	England & Wales High Court (Administrative Court)
GPA	Agreement on Government Procurement
H & C	Hurlstone & Coltman's Exchequer Reports
J.I. B.L.	Journal of International Banking Law
JSC	Judgments of the Supreme Court of Cyprus
K.B.	Law Reports, King's Bench
Law No. 10(I)/94	Law on Sale of Goods
Law No. 23/1983	Law on Rent Control
Law No. 28(I)/2001	Law on Collective Redundancies
Law No. 37(I)/2019	Law on Betting
Law No. 73(I)/2016	Law on Public Procurement
Law No. 81(I)/2011	Law on Sale of Land (Specific Performance)
Law No. 89(I)/1996	Law on Safety at Work
Law No. 100(I)/1997	Law on Protection of Motherhood
Law No. 100(I)/2000	Law on Informing on the Terms of Employment Contract
Law No. 101/87	Law on International Commercial Arbitration
Law No. 124(I)/2015	Law on Operation and Control of Casinos
Law No. 140(I)/2016	Law on Procurement for Water, Energy, Transport and Postal Services
Law No. 159(I)/2012	Law on Certain Aspects of Mediation in Civil Matters
Law No. 173(I)/2011	Law on Procurement in Defence and Security

Law No. 177(I)/2002	Law on Equal Payment between Men and Women for the Same Employment or Employment of Same Value
Law No. 188(I)/2007	Law on Prevention and Combat of Money Laundering
Lloyd's Rep.	Lloyd's List Law Reports
LR (NSW) Eq	New South Wales Law Reports, Equity
LT	Law Times Reports
No.	Number
OG	Official Gazette of Cyprus
p.	Page
QB	Law Reports, Queen's Bench (3rd Series)
Regulations 347/2015	Regulations on Safety and Health at Work (Control of Major-Accident Hazards Involving Dangerous Substances)
RR	Revised Reports
TFEU	Treaty for the Functioning of the European Union
VAT	Value Added Tax
Ves. Jun.	Vesey Junior's Chancery Reports
Warsaw Convention	Convention for the Unification of Certain Rules Relating to International Carriage by Air of 12 Oct. 1929
WLR	Weekly Law Reports

List of Abbreviations

Preface

This monograph is an attempt to portray the basic provisions on Law of Contract in Cyprus, alongside highlighting its fine letters. Shedding light was not always successful in view of the limited case law and the unpublished *travaux préparatoires*, which were drafted and composed when Cyprus was a colony of the British Empire. Hence, the original text of the most statutes elaborated in this monograph is written in English. Effort was made to write this monograph from the perspective of colleagues, mainly practitioners, unfamiliar with the laws of Cyprus and interested in acquainting themselves therewith. Hopefully, the scope of particularly enabling practitioners having civil law education to effortlessly comprehend the principles and maxims ruling this national law, which is deeply affected by common law, was achieved. Issues of Public International Law affecting Cyprus have been not considered. Finally, in accordance with Article 3(1) of the Constitution of Cyprus, pursuant to which both the Greek and the Turkish language are the official languages of the Republic, most of the legal termini have been quoted in both Greek and Turkish, although usually the original statutory text is in English.

I was very fortunate to have eminent teachers, Prof Dr Mager, Prof Dr Dres. h.c. Hess, Prof Antonopoulos and acclaimed mentors. I am much grateful to them for being my paragons. Their example has impressed on me the importance of persistence, endurance, curiosity, empathy and generosity. I shall never forget Prof Dr Dres. h.c. Hess delivering an outstanding lecture on Civil Procedure Law, despite having a severe sore throat; Prof Huber weekly giving a four-hour lecture on Civil Law, although he was legally obliged to a merely three-hour one; or the crisp baklava offered to all colleagues willing to work on Saturday mornings. Equally, I cordially thank Prof Herbots and Mr Joeri Lauwers for entrusting me with the current monograph, the third on Cyprus law, as well as Mrs Suzanne Leppen and Ms Kavya of Kluwer Law International for their wonderful collaboration and brilliant support. Warmest thanks also need to be expressed to Prof Emilianides for the precious opportunities that he abundantly offered to me. This monograph, in its actual form, would have not been possible without my Turkish teacher, Mrs Paulina Makridou – Barnalidou. I am deeply indebted to her for not only acquainting us with the Turkish language but also introducing us to the enchanting culture (and cuisine!) through both captivating narratives and alluring journeys. In my turn, I thank my – past, current and future – students. They inspire me to research, teach and write. I thank most cordially my friends and family for being in my corner, especially when I am in solitude, devoted to researching, absorbed by penning, deprived of any sense of time. Love you guys![*]

written in Izmir, Istanbul and Thessaloniki
March 2018

* Disclaimer: The opinions expressed and arguments employed herein do not reflect the official views of Democritus University of Thrace.

General Introduction

§1. The General Background of the Country

1. Cyprus is an island in the Mediterranean Sea, south of Turkey and west of Syria.[1] Inhabited for more than 10,000 years, Cyprus stands at a cultural, linguistic and historic crossroads between Europe and Asia. Since ancient times it has been renowned for its mineral wealth, superb wines and natural beauty.[2] The Republic of Cyprus was established in 1960, after becoming independent from the British rule. Three years later tensions between the Greek Cypriot majority and the Turkish Cypriot minority lead to the deployment of United Nations peacekeepers in 1964. In 1974, a Greek Government-sponsored attempt to overthrow the elected president was met by military intervention from Turkey, which soon controlled more than a third of the island.[3] In 2004, Cyprus joined the European Union (EU) and later, in 2008, the Eurozone. Currently, Cyprus is in the process of joining the Schengen area.[4] The effect of the new political party 'Ego o Politis' (I the Citizen) that was launched in September 2017 by a Russian restauranteur and investor, who holds a Cypriot passport and speaks neither English nor Greek, and the co-founder of an online war-gaming company, is still unfolding. Its proclaimed scope of fighting graft and shrinking the island's bloated bureaucracy is met with concerns that it heralds more Russian intervention in Cypriot public life.[5]

2. In the past years Cyprus has enjoyed rapid economic recovery, including a rapidly improving labour market, which is expected to help accelerate the correction of excessive macroeconomic imbalances. Yet, the negative net international investment position highlights Cyprus' dependency on foreign financing sources and its vulnerability to shifts in international financial market sentiment. The key vulnerability of the banking sector is the high level of non-performing loans. Inefficiency in the justice system continues to affect contract enforcement and prompt

1. Central Intelligence Agency, *The World Factbook – Cyprus, Geography*. Available: https://www.cia.gov (last visited: 17 Mar. 2018).
2. H.W. Goult, D.W. Sather Hunt and J.S. Bowman, *Cyprus*, in: Encyclopaedia Britannica, last updated 13 Mar. 2018. Available: https://www.britannica.com/place/Cyprus (last visited: 17 Mar. 2018).
3. Central Intelligence Agency, *The World Factbook – Cyprus, Introduction*. Available: https://www.cia.gov (last visited: 17 Mar. 2018).
4. European Union, *EU countries in brief – Cyprus*. Available: https://europa.eu/european-union/about-eu/countries/member-countries/cyprus_en (last visited 17 Mar. 2018).
5. No author, *Taking Care of the Billionaires: A New Party for Cyprus's Russian Exiles and Expats*, The Economist, 14 Nov. 2017. Available: https://www.economist.com (last visited: 17 Mar. 2018).

resolution of civil and commercial cases. Turning to other key structural issues, labour market is improving, the education sector is modernized and key steps to reform the healthcare sector have been taken. Finally, enforcement of environmental regulation remains weak, whereas it is suggested that Cyprus tax rules are used by companies engaged in aggressive tax planning.[6]

§2. To What Legal Family (E.G., Common Law, French Legal Family, Islamic Law) Does Cyprus Law Belong?

3. Law in Cyprus belongs to the common law family, but for some exceptions in Administrative Law and Family Law. Yet even in these areas of law, which are influenced by the continental law system, the principle of precedent is firmly respected.[7] Precedent is considered to ensure the principle of certainty of the Law and Justice, which is an essential feature of the rule of law.[8] Common law is applicable in Cyprus in virtue of section 29(1)(c) of the Courts of Justice Law, which reads '[e]very court in the exercise of its civil or criminal jurisdiction shall apply the common law and the principles of equity save in so far as other provision has been or shall be made by any law made or becoming applicable under the Constitution or any law […] in so far as they are not inconsistent with, or contrary to the Constitution'. Hence, common law is applicable under the following conditions: (i) no other provision has been made by any law; (ii) common law is not inconsistent with, or contrary to the Constitution of Cyprus; and (iii) it is suitable for Cyprus, as the common law 'must be planted here as a living growth which can be pruned by judicial decision to suit local conditions'.[9]

4. Especially with reference to the law of contract, this is codified common law which is enacted in the Law of Contract[10] (hereinafter 'Cap. 149'). It should be noted here that due to historical reasons mention is made to statutes in Cyprus as chapters. Therefore, Cap. 149, a single chapter, regulates the Law of Contract; Cap. 154,[11] a single chapter, regulates Criminal Law; and Cap. 113,[12] a single chapter, regulates Companies Law.[13] In Cap. 149, the legislator expressly provided a general rule of construction. According to this rule, Cap. 149 is interpreted in accordance with the principles of legal interpretation obtaining in England, and expressions used in it are presumed, so far as is consistent with their context, and

6. European Commission, *Country Report Cyprus 2018*, SWD(2018)211 final of 7 Mar. 2018, pp. 1 et seq. Available: https://ec.europa.eu/ (last visited: 17 Mar. 2018).
7. *Re Makushin (No. 1)* 1(A) CLR 20 (2012); *Goouts v. Laouris a.o.* Supreme Court of Cyprus, Civil Appeal No. 319/08 of 7 Jul. 2014, not reported in CLR.
8. *Paulides v. Cyprus* 3 CLR 217 (1967); *Oikonomides v. Cyprus* 3(B) CLR 535 (1989).
9. *Paikkos v. Kontemeniotis* 1 CLR 50 (1989). On common law not being static: *Kem (Taxi) Ltd v. Tryphonos* 1 CLR 52 (1969), citing *Chic Fashions (West Wales) Ltd v. Jones* 2 WLR 201 (1968).
10. Contract of 1 Jan. 1931, Ch. 149 of the Laws, London, 1959 edition, as amended.
11. Criminal Code of 1 Jan. 1929, Ch. 154 of the Laws, London, 1959 edition, as amended.
12. Companies of 16 Feb. 1951, Ch. 113 of the Laws, London, 1959 edition, as amended.
13. *See* a mistype in: *Yukos Universal Limited (Isle of Man) v. The Russian Federation* (PCA Case No. AA 227) Final Award of 18 Jul. 2014, para. 229. Available: https://www.italaw.com (last visited: 17 Mar. 2018).

except as may be otherwise expressly provided, to be used with the meaning attaching to them in English law and are construed in accordance therewith.[14] In addition to said provision, the Supreme Court of Cyprus in a line of cases ruled that statutory provisions in local legislation, intended to codify the English common law, should be interpreted and construed in line with the common law which they purported to codify.[15]

§3. Is Primacy of Legislation a Characteristic of Cyprus System?

5. Generally, primacy of legislation is a characteristic of the legal system in Cyprus. When a matter is being especially regulated by the laws of Cyprus, neither the equity rules[16] nor the common law is applied.[17] Albeit the doctrine of necessity, which allowed for bending constitutional provisions and enacting legislation that is in a flexible relation to the Constitution in view of responding to restoration of public law and order and ensuring continuance of the state and its institutions, was established via case law and specifically through *Ibrahim and Others v. The Attorney General* CLR 195 (1964). Since then, this judgment, which among others reminds that the law of necessity was enshrined in Article 48 of the Weimar Constitution[18] and adopts the view that '[n]ecessity creates the law, it supersedes rules; and whatever is reasonable and just in such, cases, is likewise legal', is a pillar of the Constitution of Cyprus,[19] as it is irrefutable that exceptional circumstances exist on the island the last fifty-four years.

§4. The Position of the Judiciary

6. The judiciary both makes judgments and decrees law, in the sense of the principle of precedent being an inseparable aspect of the domestic law of Cyprus. Furthermore, the Supreme Court of Cyprus has the authority and the power to issue its procedural rules. Said double function reinforces the common law nature of the Cypriot legal system.

---

14. Section 2(1) Cap. 149.
15. *Vassiliou v. Vassiliou* 16 CLR 69; *The Universal Advertising and Publishing Agency v. Vouros* 19 CLR 87; *Marcou v. Michael* 19 CLR 282; *The Queen v. Haralambos Erodotou* 19 CLR 144; *Papadopoulou v. Polycarpou* 1 CLR 352 (1968).
16. *Christofides v. Kotzanastasi* 1 CLR 718 (1993).
17. Section 29(1)(c) of the Courts of Justice Law.
18. In this regard *see* a straightforward introduction: R. Sturm, *Die Weimarer Verfassung*, Bundeszentrale für politische Bildung, 1 Sep. 2009. Available: http://www.bpb.de/geschichte/deutsche-geschichte/grundgesetz-und-parlamentarischer-rat/39193/weimarer-verfassung (visited: 19 Mar. 2018).
19. *See* in this respect, M.M. Nikolatos, *Fifty Years since the Law of Necessity in Cyprus* (in Greek). Available: www.supremecourt.gov.cy (last visited 19 Mar. 2018).

§5. Distinction Between Public Law and Private Law ('Administrative Contracts')

7. Cyprus law, despite it being under the deep influence of common law, does distinguish between public law and private law. However, this distinction does not affect contracts made by the state. Statutory provisions on administrative contracts, in the sense of sections 54–62 of the Verwaltungsverfahrensgesetz of Germany regulating public contracts ('öffentlich-rechtliche Verträge') do not exist. Specifically, regarding procurement, the relevant EU legislation has been implemented in Cyprus, as elaborated below (*see* in this regard paragraphs 348 et seq. below).

§6. Distinction Between Civil Law and Commercial Law ('Commercial Contracts')

8. No statutory provision or law on commercial contracts exists under Cyprus law.

Introduction to the Law of Contracts

§1. Definition of Contract

9. Contract ('σύμβαση' in Greek, 'sözleşme' in Turkish) is an agreement enforceable by law.[20] Agreement ('συμφωνία' in Greek, 'anlaşma' in Turkish) is every promise and every act of promises, forming the consideration for each other.[21]

§2. Historical Background of the Law of Contracts

10. Current statutory codification of the law of contract came into force as Law No. 24 of 1930 in January 1931. Prior to that, the law in Cyprus governing a transaction of this nature was the Ottoman Civil Code known as the 'mejelle',[22] which was in force throughout the Ottoman Empire. In Cyprus, since the end of the nineteenth century and up until the enactment of Cap. 149, English distinguished and much-praised judges with a firm background in common law faced the challenge of applying Ottoman Law as modified by Cyprus Statute Law.[23]

11. Until today, the said code has remained much of a mystery.[24] Nonetheless, it suffices here to say that it was divided into sixteen books. The first book (Articles 2–100) set out the general principles. Some of the said principles, such as 'actus non facit reum, nisi mens sit rea', 'absoluta, sententia expositore non eget', 'injuria non excusat injuriam', 'necessitas quod cogit, defendit', 'optimus interpres rerum usus', 'sublato principali, tollitur adjunctum', 'acta exteriora indicant interiora secreta' and 'nemo contra factum suum venire potest', are not unknown to Roman law. The second book (Articles 101–403) described the contract of sale. The third book (Articles 404–611) prescribed the contract of lease. The third book (Articles 612–672) regulated suretyship. The fourth book (Articles 673–700) provided for assignment of debt. The fifth book (Articles 701–761) regulated pledge. The sixth book (Articles 762–832) described bailment. The seventh book (Articles 833–880) regulated donation. The eighth book (Articles 881–940) provided for unlawful appropriation. The ninth book (Articles 941–1044) regulated capacity to contract and sound mind. The tenth book set out (Articles 1045–1328) rights in personam on land, rules on neighbouring, rights on common things but no rights in rem on land, along with (Articles 1329–1448) rules on partnership. The eleventh book (Articles 1449–1530) enacted rules on agency. The twelfth book (Articles 1531–1571) prescribed compromise settlement. The thirteenth book (Articles 1572–1612) regulated confession in the sense of oral and written admission, whereas the fourteenth book (Articles 1613–1675) included provisions on civil procedure, including limitation of time, the

20. Section 2(2)(h) Cap. 149.
21. Section 2(2)(e) *ibid.*
22. *Papadopoulou v. Polycarpou* 1 CLR 352 (1968).
23. *Miltiades Mavrovouniotis v. Estate of Chrystalleni Ch. Nicolaidou* 14(1) CLR 272.
24. Y. Meron, *The Mejelle Tested by Its Application*, 5(2) I.L.R. 203 (1970).

fifteenth book (Articles 1676–1783) provisions on evidence and the sixteenth book (Articles 1784–1851) rules on judges, procedure, judgment, remedies and arbitration. Thus, the prevailing description of 'mejelle' as the Ottoman Civil Code is to some extent misleading, as it entailed, along with substantive law, elaborated procedural rules.

§3. Classification of Contracts

12. Contracts are classified under Cap. 149, which is a codification of common law principles and axioms. A general definition of contract is offered, along with definitions of bonds in customary form, indemnity, guarantee, bailment, pledge and agency, among others. Equally, specific provisions apply to specific contracts. However, this classification does not meet the standards of the Civil Code, *Bürgerliches Gesetzbuch,* of Germany. Cap. 149 lacks the elaborative structure, precision and mathematical approach of continental legislations. Rather, Cypriot statute and case law on contracts shall seem minimal, simple and philosophical with a particular focus on factual surrounding, to readers unfamiliar with common law. The interpretation of unspecified legal terms, such as 'reasonableness', is a legal matter, which is determined by courts. No guidance can be found in the statutes. Case law does offer some in the sense of attributing the meaning understood by ordinary people, but such guidance is blended closely with the factual surrounding of each case. Hence, the use thereof in a different set of events shall not always be successful.

§4. Contract and Torts

13. Contract and torts ('αστικά αδικήματα' in Greek, 'haksız fiiller' in Turkish) are not regulated in a single statute. They share neither common provisions on interpretation, nor general principles, nor damages. Contracts are regulated in Cap. 149, as already explained above. Torts are regulated in Civil Wrongs, Cap. 148.[25]

14. The structure of Cap. 148 is as follows. Part I (sections 2–3) provides for preliminary issues, those being interpretation and the right to remedy in respect of civil wrongs. Part II (sections 4–16) sets out rights and liabilities of certain persons. These include limitation of actions against certain persons in respect of civil wrongs, acts of state, bankrupts, corporate bodies, persons under the age of 18 years and under the age of 12 years, husband and wife, joint civil wrongdoers, liability for acts committed by other persons not being servants, master's liability for acts of his servants, when knowledge of agent or servant is knowledge of master, armed forces and liability or right in respect of not assignable civil wrong. Part III (sections 17–60) specifies civil wrongs and provides for defences to certain actions therefor. In particular, these are defamation, injurious falsehood, assault, false imprisonment, malicious prosecution, unlawfully causing breach of contract, passing off, fraud, unlawful detention, conversion, trespass to movable and immovable

25. Civil Wrongs of 1 Jan. 1933, Ch. 148 of the Laws, London, 1959 edition, as amended.

property, public and private nuisance, saving, interference with daylight, negligence, rights of action of certain persons in respect of act causing death of another, special defence that plaintiff voluntarily exposed himself to state of affairs causing civil wrong and special defence that act was done under an enactment. Part IV (sections 61–68) included miscellaneous provisions as to the recovery of remedies. More specifically these were compensation only to be recovered once, compensation not to be recoverable under both this law and Workmen's Compensation Law, no action to be brought on contract if compensation is awarded for civil wrong, recovery of contribution from joint civil wrongdoers, insurance not to be taken into account in assessing compensation, recovery of compensation for libel published in a newspaper, civil wrong which is also a crime, and limitation of action for civil wrongs. The last part, Part V, contains a single section on Cap. 148 not affecting any jurisdiction in admiralty vested in any Court in Cyprus, the provisions of any law as to claims against the government of Cyprus, the provisions of the Companies Law or the provisions of section 40 of the Civil Aviation Orders of 1952 and 1953.

15. In any event, both contractual and tortious claims can be brought forward in a single case, as in *Said Hamade v. Anthimos Demetriou.*[26] Plaintiff, in this case, claimed USD 253,674,000 for damages for the value of its cargo that was transported with the ship 'Ayii Anargiroi' (*Άγιοι Ανάργυροι* in original in the judgment), which had shank off the shores of Lebanon *en route* from Limassol to Beirut. Plaintiff had been asserting that the goods had been transported to the port of Limassol in order to be transported to Beirut. They further alleged that some of the defendants (defendants Nos 1–6), who had accepted to forward the goods to Beirut, were the ship's charterers. They further asserted that the rest of the defendants (defendants Nos 7–11) were owners or managers of the same ship under conditions that made them responsible for the cargo's loss. Moreover, they argued that the goods had been loaded in an incorrect manner and that the ship had been overloaded, in order to transfer all goods with a single journey. This, they alleged, caused the ship to sink. Finally, they asserted that: the Hague Rules were applicable; defendants were liable as carriers or common carriers, or as bailees of the cargo under Cap. 149; defendants had committed fraud, conspiracy and barratry under Cap. 148. On the basis of the evidence adduced by the parties, the Court made the following findings. The ship that had sunk was not a Cypriot one, as plaintiffs asserted, but a Panamanian ship belonging to the Panamanian company Ayii Anargyrii Shipping Co. S.A. A ship under the same name had been registered in Cyprus, but it had been deleted from the register after it was scrapped in Larnaca four years before the present incident. Regarding defendants Nos 1–6 neither a bill of lading nor an agreement was made between them and the plaintiffs. Therefore, the assertion that defendants Nos 1–6 were common carriers and/or bailees failed. In particular, with reference to the Hague Rules, the Court noted that, generally, these are applicable under Cap. 263,[27] where there is a bill of lading.[28] The claim that defendants Nos

26. *Said Hamade v. Anthimos Demetriou Ltd a.o.* 1 CLR 443 (1994).
27. Carriage of Goods by Sea Law of 4 Feb. 1927, Ch. 263 of the Laws, London, 1959 edition, as amended.

1–6 had committed fraud, conspiracy and barratry failed due to lack of proof. In truth, a witness for plaintiff had testified that the alleged payments of invoices and expenses for the journey had been made, but the lack of paper trail did not convince the Court. Turning to defendants Nos 7–11, the Court noted that defendant No. 7 had signed the bill of lading under its capacity as agent of the carrier. At the same time, this bill of lading foresaw that agents of the carrier do not bear any liability. Thus, defendant No. 7 could not bear any liability. Moreover, same bill of lading set out that a contract was made between the owners of the ship and the owners of the goods, the merchants. The Court further noted that it did not accept the plaintiff's evidence of respondents Nos 7–10 having been the ship's charterers. It was equally not convinced by the plaintiff's evidence with regard to defendants' Nos 7–10 having performed the alleged torts. It, therefore, dismissed the claims. Especially with reference to defendant No. 11, the Court dismissed the action, as he had not been served with any notices and pleadings.

16. Fraud ('απάτη' in Greek, 'hile' in Turkish), apart from being a defect of consent, a condition of validity of a contract (*see* in this regard paragraphs 80 et seq. below), is also a civil wrong. Section 36 Cap. 148 reads:

> Fraud consists of a false representation of fact, made with the knowledge that it is false, or without belief in its truth or recklessly, careless whether it be true or false, with intent that it shall be acted upon by the person deceived:
> Provided that no action shall be brought in respect of any such representation unless it was intended to and did deceive the plaintiff and has acted upon it and has thereby suffered damage:
> Provided also that no action shall be brought in respect of any such representation as to the character, conduct, credit, ability, trade or dealings of any person in order to obtain his credit, money or goods unless such representation is in writing and signed by the defendant himself.

17. In these cases, the paths of Cap. 149 and Cap. 148 run in parallel.[29] The prerequisites of the civil wrong of fraud are the following five: (1) a false representation of fact; (2) made with the knowledge that it is false, or without belief in its truth or recklessly, careless whether it be true or false; (3) with the intent that it shall be acted upon by the plaintiff; (4) plaintiff having acted on the false representation; and (5) plaintiff having suffered damage.[30]

18. However, no person recovers any compensation in respect of any breach of contract, or an obligation resembling those created by contract, if such breach also

28. *The Ship Dama v. Georghiades SA* 1 CLR 368 (1980), *Kounnas and Sons Ltd v. Zim* 1 CLR 181 (1966).
29. *Synergatiki Pistotiki Etaireia Konteas v. Nikos Larkos* 1 CLR 369 (1998).
30. *Antriani Haralambous v. Maria Haralambous* 1 CLR 1298 (2008), citing *Bradford Building Society v. Borders* 2 All ER 205 (1941).

constitutes a civil wrong and compensation or other relief has been awarded for such civil wrong by any Court to such person or to any person through whom such person claims.[31]

19. One more point, where the paths of Cap. 149 and Cap. 148 blend closely, is the following. Unlawfully causing breach of contract ('παράνομη πρόκληση άλλου σε παράβαση σύμβασης' in Greek, 'yasal olmayan yollardan sözleşmenin ihlalini sağlamak' in Turkish) constitutes a civil wrong. This is set out in section 34(1) of Cap. 148, which reads:

> [a]ny person who, otherwise than in furtherance of a strike or lockout in respect of a trade dispute within the trade or industry in respect of a trade dispute within the trade or industry in which the strikes or persons locking out are engaged, knowingly and without sufficient justification, causes any other person to break a legally binding contract with a third person, commits a civil wrong against such third person.

Case law clarified that the necessary conditions for this civil wrong are the following three. Respondent must have caused breach of contract made between two other persons that is still in force. Due to this breach, claimant must have suffered damage. Importantly, respondent must have acted, while knowing of the existence of the contract and without sufficient reasoning.[32] When these conditions are cumulative met, the Court may order exemplary damages ('τιμωρητικές αποζημιώσεις' in Greek, 'örnek niteliğinde zarar ziyan' in Turkish),[33] which have the same content as in common law.[34] Moreover, for the purposes of this civil wrong, the relationship created by marriage is not deemed to be a contract.[35]

20. Finally, noteworthy is section 3 of Cap. 148, which reads:

> [t]he matters of this Law hereinafter enumerated shall be civil wrongs, and subject to the provisions of this Law, any person who shall suffer any injury or damage by reason of any civil wrong committed in the Colony or within three miles of the coast thereof measured from low water mark shall be entitled to recover from the person committing or liable for such civil wrong the remedies which the Court has power to grant:
> Provided that an act which if repeated would not tend to establish an adverse claim or which is an act of which in the circumstances a person of ordinary sense and temper would not complain shall not be deemed to be a civil wrong.

31. Section 63 Cap. 148.
32. *xxx Zachariades v. Universal Life Insurance Ltd*, Civil Appeal No. 144/2013, Judgment of 16 Apr. 2019, not reported in CLR, citing *Xenophondos v. Anastasiadou* 4 JSC 578 (1974), *Torquay Hotel Co Ltd v. Cousins* 2 Ch. 106 (1969).
33. *Giannakis Erotokritou v. Eirinarhou Theodorou a.a.* 1 CLR 1800 (1997), citing *Constantinides v. Pitsillou a.a.* JSC 279 (1980).
34. *Giannakis Erotokritou v. Eirinarhou Theodorou a.a.* 1 CLR 1800 (1997), citing *Rookes v. Barnard* 1 All ER 367 (1964) and *Cassel & Co Ltd v. Broone* 1 All ER 801 (1972).
35. Section 34(2) Cap. 148.

It has been decided that this provision establishes the jurisdiction of the Courts of Cyprus in civil wrongs committed abroad, under the condition that the asserted civil wrong may form the base of an action also under the laws in force in the foreign country, where the alleged civil wrong was committed.[36] Thus, under specific circumstances, the Courts of Cyprus have the power to exercise extraterritorial jurisdiction.

§5. Contract and Quasi-Contract

21. Contracts and quasi-contracts ('σχέσεις που προσομοιάζουν με συμβατικές' in Greek, 'sözleşmenin doğurduğu ilişkilere benzer bazı ilişkiler' in Turkish) are both regulated in Cap. 149. Five provisions, sections 68–72 Cap. 149 and the relevant case law provide for quasi-contracts (*see* in this regard paragraphs 446 et seq. below).

§6. Contract and the Law of Property

22. Contracts are regulated in Cap. 149, as already explained above. They may only confer rights in personam. Rights in rem, especially in immovable property, is conferred by Law on Sale of Land[37] and Law on Mortgage of Land.[38]

§7. Contract and Trust

23. Trusts are regulated in Cap. 193,[39] a statute separate and distinct from Cap. 149. The notion trust ('εμπίστευμα' in Greek, 'tröst' in Turkish) and trustee ('επίτροπος εμπιστευμάτων' in Greek, 'mütevelli' in Turkish) extends to implied and constructive trusts as well as to cases where the trustee has a beneficial interest in the trust property, and to the duties incidental to the office of a personal representative, but do not include the duties of chargee.[40]

24. The structure of Cap. 193 is set out as follows. In Part I (sections 2–3), it regulates the application of the law and interpretation. In Part II (sections 4–11), this statute clarifies matters related to investments, including authorized investments,

36. *See* in this regard *The Ship Yayasan Satu v. Welsen Shipping Co. Ltd* 1 CLR 1115 (1998), referring to *Jupiter Electrical (Overseas) Ltd v. Savvas Costa Christides* 1 CLR 144 (1975).
37. Law on Sale of Land (Specific Performance) ('ο περί Πώλησης Ακινήτων (Ειδική Εκτέλεση) Νόμος') No. 81 of 2011, OG I(I) No. 4282 of 29 Apr. 2011, p. 672, as last amended by amending Law No. 48 of 2017, OG I(I) No. 4603 of 2 Jun. 2017, p. 407.
38. Law on Mortgage on Land (Temporary Provisions) ('ο περί Υποθηκεύσεως Ακινήτων (Προσωριναί) Διατάξεις Νόμος') No. 66 of 1977, OG I No. 1399 of 11 Nov. 1977, p. 1183, as last amended by amending Law No. 3 of 1979, OG I(I) No. 1496 of 18 Jan. 1979, p. 7.
39. Trustees of 1 Oct. 1955, Ch. 193 of the Laws, London, 1959 edition, as amended.
40. Section 3 of Cap. 193.

discretion of trustees, power to retain investment which has ceased to be authorized, investment in bearer securities, loans and investments by trustees not chargeable as breaches of trust, liability for loss by reason of improper investment, powers supplementary to powers of investment and power to deposit at bank and pay calls. Part III (sections 12–33) provides for the power of trustees for sale, as well as the power to give receipts, compound liabilities, raise money by sale and charge, including protection of purchasers and chargees, devolution of powers of trust, powers to insure, employ agents, concur with others and delegate trusts during absence abroad, indemnities, maintenance, advancement and protective trusts. Part IV (sections 34–39) sets out the conditions for appointment and discharge of trustees. Part V (sections 40–60) regulates the powers of the Court. More specifically, it foresees the power of the Court to appoint new trustees and his powers, the power to authorize remuneration, the vending orders, jurisdiction to make other orders, such as to authorize dealings with trust property, to give judgment in absence of a trustee, to charge costs on trust estate, to relieve trustee from personal liability and make beneficiary indemnity for breach of trust. Miscellaneous matters are regulated in Part VI (sections 61–65). These are trust estates not being affected by trustee becoming a convict, indemnity, effect of court order under the Administration of Estates Law,[41] Rules of Court and Administration of Estates Law remaining unaffected.

25. Further, Cyprus has recently ratified the Hague Convention on the Law Applicable to Trusts and on their Recognition.[42] Within this legal context, the term *trust* refers to the legal relationships created – *inter vivos* or on death – by a person, the settlor, when assets have been placed under the control of a trustee for the benefit of a beneficiary or for a specified purpose. Within the same context, a trust has the following characteristics: (a) the assets constitute a separate fund and are not a part of the trustee's own estate; (b) title to the trust assets stands in the name of the trustee or in the name of another person on behalf of the trustee; and (c) the trustee has the power and the duty, in respect of which he is accountable, to manage, employ or dispose of the assets in accordance with the terms of the trust and the special duties imposed upon him by law. Furthermore, the reservation by the settlor of certain rights and powers and the fact that the trustee may himself have rights as a beneficiary is not necessarily inconsistent with the existence of a trust.[43]

§8. Good Faith and Fair Dealing

26. Good faith is not a part of substantive law in Cyprus, with the exception of the fiduciary rights of trustees and among partners of a partnership. Even where parties have agreed to act in good faith during negotiations to a contract, they are not

41. Administration of Estates Law of 24 Aug. 1954, Ch. 189 of the Laws, London, 1959 edition, as amended.
42. Law on the Hague Convention on the Law Applicable to Trusts and on their Recognition (Ratification) ('ο περί της Σύμβασης της Χάγης περί του Νόμου που Εφαρμόζεται σε Εμπιστεύματα και περί της Αναγνώρισης Αυτών (Κυρωτικός) Νόμος') No. 4 of 2017, OG I(III) No. 4229 of 24 Feb. 2017, p. 17.
43. Table, Part I Art. 2 Law No. 4(III)/2017.

obliged to act in such a manner, as such an obligation lies contrary to the opposite sites of the parties during negotiations. In fact, it is accepted that, under commercial habit, parties usually make declarations which are not totally true, whereas such actions are not commercially improper.[44]

§9. Style of Drafting

27. Cap. 149, which contains the main provisions on contracts, is divided into thirteen parts, as described below. The first part (sections 1 and 2) contains the introductory provisions. The second part (sections 3–9) describes acceptance and revocation of offers. The third part (sections 10–30) sets out contracts, voidable contracts and void agreements. The fourth part (sections 31–36) provides for contingent contracts. The fifth part (sections 37–67) includes: contracts which must be performed; by whom contracts must be performed; time and place for performance; performance of reciprocal promises; appropriation of payments; and contracts that need not be performed. The sixth part (sections 68–72) regulates quasi-contracts. The seventh part (sections 73–75) prescribes the consequences of breach of contract. The eighth part (section 76) sets out specific performance of contracts. The ninth part (section 77) provides requirements of contracts relating to certain matters. The tenth part (sections 78–81) provides for bonds in customary form. The eleventh part (sections 82–105) prescribes indemnity and guarantee. The twelfth part (sections 106–141) sets out bailment and bailments of pledges. The thirteenth part (sections 142–198) writes on agencies and in particular on appointment and authority of agents, subagents, subagent's responsibility, ratification, revocation of authority, agent's duty to principal, principal's duty to agent and effect of agency on contracts and third persons.

§10. Sources of the Law of Contracts

28. Law of contracts has two primary sources: statutes, case law and naturally common law. *Travaux préparatoires*, when available, are usually simple and prompt and therefore of little help. However, when national statutes in fact implement European law, additional sources constitute the preparatory documentation of the implemented directive of the EU, along with any case law of the Court of Justice of the EU.

44. *See* in this respect *Walford v. Miles* 2 AC 128 (1992).

Part I. General Principles of the Law of Contracts

Chapter 1. Formation

§1. Agreement and Quid Pro Quo

I. Offer and Acceptance

29. Offer ('πρόταση' in Greek, 'önerim' in Turkish)[45] is said to be made, when one person signifies his willingness to do or to abstain from doing anything, with a view to obtaining the assent of that other to such act or abstinence.[46]

In accordance with common law, an offer contains both an objective and a subjective element. The objective element dictates that an offer must be specific, that being not ambiguous,[47] uncertain or inconclusive.[48] Statements, the meaning of which is not certain or capable of being made certain, do not qualify as an offer, as it can be derived from section 29 Cap. 149.

30. An offer may be made to an individual or to a specified group of persons or to the world at large, expressly, that being either by words or by conduct.[49,50] Along with an offer being put forward and hence a contract made on one particular note or memorandum formally signed, a contract may be found in a correspondence. In such a case, the whole of that which has passed between the parties must be taken into consideration. Especially where each letter is immediately followed by another

45. The terminology used in the original English text is *proposal* (ss 2(2)(a), 3 and 4(1) Cap. 149). Nevertheless, mention to *offer* shall be made in this monograph, in order to foster better understanding and avoid any misunderstandings.
46. Section 2(2)(a) Cap. 149.
47. *Raffles v. Wichehaus* 2 H. & C. 906; *Haji Kypri Constantinides and Sons v. The King's Advocate* 10 (1) CLR 29. Interestingly, at the time of this case law Cap. 149 was not enacted and the Ottoman Civil Code was in force.
48. *Scammell & Nephew Ltd v. Ouston* AC 251 (1941); *Kotsonia v. Photos Photiades Distributors Ltd* 1 CLR 670 (2012) quoting *Day Morris Associates v. Voyce* All ER (D) 368 (2003).
49. Section 3 Cap. 149.
50. *Georgiou v. Kypriakon Aerogrammon Ltd* 1C CLR 1794 (1998).

which suggests something else as a topic of further discussion, it has been ruled that it becomes most dangerous to draw a line after any particular letter.[51]

31. Communication of an offer is considered to be complete and therefore to exist when it comes to the knowledge of the person to whom it is made.[52] Revocation is possible. It is done by communication of notice of revocation by the offeror to the other party.[53] Further, it may be done at any time before the communication of its acceptance is complete as against the offeror, but not afterwards.[54]

32. Offer must be differentiated from invitation to treat. The relevant common law principles equally apply here.[55] Exhibiting alcoholic drinks on the shelves of the bar of a restaurant,[56] commercial advertisements[57] and notices of a public tender[58] have been held to qualify as an invitation to treat. This does not entail an obligation to accept any offer submitted to same,[59] whereas the following submission of an offer does not result in creating a legally binding contract.[60] The distinction between an offer and an invitation to treat is considered an issue of fact, which is judged objectively, regardless of the subjective intention of the parties.[61]

33. Acceptance ('αποδοχή' in Greek, 'kabül' in Turkish) needs to bear two qualities, that of being absolute and unqualified.[62] Communication of acceptance of an offer is deemed to be made by any act or omission of the party accepting by which he intends to communicate such acceptance or which has the effect of communicating it.[63] It is required to be expressed in some usual and reasonable manner, unless the proposal prescribes the manner in which it is to be accepted.[64] Acceptance of any consideration or performance of the conditions of an offer constitutes

51. *Biometal Ltd v. Hawaii Hotels Ltd* 1 CLR 281 (1998). Case law cited therein: *Hussey v. Horne-Payne* AC 311 (1879); *Bristol, Cardiff, and Swansea Aerated Bread Co. v. Maggs* 44 Ch. D. 616 (1890).
52. Section 4(1) Cap. 149.
53. Section 6(a) *ibid.*
54. Section 5, 1st sentence *ibid.*
55. *See* in this respect: *Partridhe v. Crittenden* 1 WLR 1204 (1968); *Pharmaceutical Society v. Boots* 1 QB 401 (1953); *Gibson v. Manchester City Council* 1 WLR 294 (1979); *Storer v. Manchester City Council* 1 WLR 1403 (1974).
56. *Chalhoub v. the Police* 2 CLR 153 (1988).
57. *Kostonia v. Photos Photiades Distributors Ltd* 1 CLR 670 (2012).
58. *Polycast Panels Ltd v. Alpha Trapeza Ltd* 1 CLR 1396 (2009).
59. *A. Panayides Contracting Ltd v. M & M Frangos Engineering & Contracting Ltd*, Supreme Court of Cyprus, Civil Appeal No. 301/2008, Judgment of 31 May 2012, not published in CLR.
60. *Georgiou v. Kypriakon Aerogrammon Ltd* 1C CLR 1794 (1998).
61. *Ibid.* Case law cited therein: *Smith v. Hughes* LR 6 QB 597 (1871); *McCutcheon v. David Macbrayne Ltd* 1 Lloyd's Rep. 16 (1964); *Centrovincial Estates plc v. Merchant Investors Assurance Co. Ltd* Com LR 158 (1983); *Whittaker v. Campbell* QB 318 (1984); *The Antclizo* 2 Lloyd's Rep. 130 (1987).
62. Section 7(a) Cap. 149.
63. Section 3 *ibid.*
64. Section 7(b) 1st sentence *ibid.*

acceptance of the proposal.[65] However, silence ('σιωπή' in Greek, 'susma' in Turkish) is an exception thereto. An offer may not set out that silence of the receiver shall be construed as acceptance. Neither may such silence be construed as acceptance. A further exception is paying the premium, especially with reference to insurance contracts. It has been ruled that a mere such action does not result in the completion of the agreement,[66] as acceptance of the offer, that being risk assuming of the insurance company, has to be separately proved.[67] Further to specific prescribed manner of acceptance, when this is not performed in such manner, the offeror may within a reasonable time after the acceptance is communicated to him, insist that his proposal shall be accepted in the prescribed manner.[68] Should he fail to do so, it is deemed that he accepted the acceptance.[69]

34. Communication of acceptance is considered to be complete and therefore to exist when it is put in a course of transmission to the offeror, so as to be out of the power of the acceptor, as against the offeror.[70,71] As against the acceptor, it is complete, when it comes to the knowledge of the offeror.[72] Revocation is possible. It is made at any time before the communication of the acceptance is complete as against the acceptor, but not afterwards.[73]

II. Intention to Create Legal Relations

35. Intention to create legal relations is an inseparable condition to the formation of a contract under the applicable law now in force,[74] as well as under the precedent one.[75] The intention of contracting parties towards the creation of rights and duties, which may be manifested directly or indirectly,[76] has to be mutual according to the rule *consensus ad idem*.[77] This rule may be elaborated through reference to common law, which dictates that a *consensus ad idem* on all essential terms speaks

65. Section 8 *ibid.*
66. *Silver Trust Commercial Ltd v. Genikes Asphalies Kyprou Ltd a.o.*, District Court of Limassol, Civil Case No. 4837/08, Judgment of 15 Apr. 2016, not published in CLR.
67. *Paschalis v. Proodeutikis Asphalistikis Etaireias Ltd* 1A CLR 69 (2008); *Prince v. Alico American Life Insurance Company* 1A CLR 280 (2005).
68. Section 7(b) 2nd sentence Cap. 149.
69. Section 7(b) 3rd sentence *ibid.*
70. Section 4(2)(a) *ibid.*
71. *Kolokasides v. Epitropis Ekpaideutikis Ypiresias* 4 CLR 1063 (1996).
72. Section 4(2)(b) Cap. 149.
73. Section 5 2nd sentence *ibid.*
74. *C. Malathouras & Sons Ltd v. Popular Insurance Company Ltd* 1 CLR 1233 (2004); *A. Panayides Contracting Ltd v. M&M Frangos Engineering & Contracting Ltd,* Supreme Court of Cyprus, Civil Appeal No. 301/2008, Judgment of 21 May 2012, not published in CLR.
75. *Najem Houry and Sons v. Ex-King Hussein* 1 CLR 49 (V13).
76. *Stylianides v. British American Insurance Co. Ltd* 1C CLR 1722 (2003).
77. *Haji Kypri Constantinides and Sons v. The King's Advocate* 10 (1) CLR 29; *Lambrianides a.o. v. The Electricity Authority of Cyprus* 1 CLR 466 (1968); *Klemke Mining Corporation v. Shell Canada Ltd* ABQB 176 (2007).

for mutuality of agreement, which lies at the root of any legally enforceable contract. Such a meeting of minds is affirmed, where it is clear to the objective reasonable bystander, in light of all the material facts, that the parties intended to contract and the essential terms of that contract can be determined with a reasonable degree of certainty.[78]

36. Depending on the manner of discussions, the persons performing these and the content of an agreement, intention to create legal relations may be absent. This is the case, when terms and content of a contract are discussed in a funny and cheerful manner, as well as when agreements are negotiated in a serious manner, but nevertheless between persons that are bond with family or social ties.[79] Intention to create legal relations is equally absent, when agreements are negotiated in a serious manner between persons not having any family or social ties, albeit it is agreed that the agreement shall not be legally binding, as the case is in gentlemen agreements or when it is explicitly agreed that a legally binding contract has to be penned.[80]

37. In addition to the above, further agreements demonstrating no intention to create legal relations with grave practical importance, are fictitious. In particular, it has been ruled that a leasing agreement for furniture was fictitious, as no furniture, which could have been the object of that contract, existed in the possession of the party of the same agreement, whereas to the contrary, the true scope thereof was to provide a loan to the purpose of investing in the stock exchange.[81] This structure had been used, due to the Central Bank of Cyprus prohibiting loans having such scope.[82] Necessary condition for such agreements is both parties to the contract have knowledge of it being fictitious.[83] The same has been ruled over a leasing agreement for heating and cooling appliances[84] as well as for a motor vehicle.[85] However, where the objects of the leasing contract were real, courts have rejected the suggestion of it being fictitious, regardless of the money being received with the aim to be invested in the stock exchange, a practice prohibited by the Central Bank of Cyprus.[86] Fictitious agreements are held to be void.[87] However, it is here suggested that under said circumstances, where admittedly *consensus ad idem* was

78. *Ron Ghitter Property Consultants Ltd v. Beaver Lumber Company Ltd* ABCA 221 (2003), citing *Scammell & Nephew Ltd v. Ouston* AC 251 (1941); *British Columbia (Minister of Transportation and Highways) v. Reon Management Services Inc* BCCA 679 (2001); *Langley Lo-Cost Builders Ltd v. 474835 BC Ltd* BCCA 365 (2000); *Anchorage Management Services Ltd v. 465404 BC Inc* BCCA 771 (1999).
79. *See* in this respect the common law rule established in *Balfour v. Balfour* 2 K.B. 571 (1919).
80. *Stylianides v. British American Insurance Co. Ltd* 1C CLR 1722 (2003), citing *Winn v. Bull* 7 Ch. D. 29 (1877); *Chillingworth v. Esche* 1 Ch. 97 (1924); *Riley v. Troll* 1 All ER 966 (1953); *Roland Preston & Partners v. Markheath Securities* 2 EGLR 23 (1988).
81. *Cyprus Popular Bank (Leasing) Ltd v. Michael* 1 CLR 41 (2012).
82. *Kastanos a.o. v. Cyprus Popular Bank (Leasing) Ltd* 1 CLR 1374 (2009).
83. *Solomou a.o. v. Marfin Popular Bank Public Co. Ltd* 1 CLR 36 (2011).
84. *Kastanos a.o. v. Cyprus Popular Bank (Leasing) Ltd* 1 CLR 1374 (2009).
85. *Cyprus Popular Bank (Leasing) Ltd v. Konstantinou a.o.* 1 CLR 1432 (2001); *Solomou a.o. v. Marfin Popular Bank Public Co. Ltd* 1 CLR 36 (2011).
86. *Atesli a.a. v. Bank of Cyprus Public Company Ltd* 1 CLR 2222 (2013).
87. *Cyprus Popular Bank (Leasing) Ltd v. Konstantinou a.a.* 1 CLR 2067 (2002); *Cyprus Popular Bank (Leasing) Ltd v. Michael* 1 CLR 41 (2012).

absent, an agreement was far from being concluded, let alone void. Hence, the mere promise constituted neither a contract nor an agreement. In any event, the courts have been dismissing claims based on said factual surroundings, even the ones raised on the legal grounds of obligation of person enjoying benefit of non-gratuitous act.[88] The reasoning rested with lack of proof of the relevant facts. Yet, it is not clear why giving money as a non-gratuitous act, a fact disputed by neither party, was not proved. The courts, following said lack of proof, ruled that persons receiving money under fictitious agreements are not obliged to return it.[89]

III. Consideration

A. Does This Requirement Exist in Your Legal System?

38. Consideration is a prerequisite to a contract under Cyprus law. Consideration ('αντιπαροχή' in Greek, 'karşılık' in Turkish) is statutorily defined as an act or abstinence performed at the desire of the promisor, that being when the promisee or any other person has done or abstained from doing, or does or abstains from doing, or promises to do or to abstain from doing, something.[90] This approach is not unusual under common law.[91]

39. From the said definition, it follows that consideration must be provided upon the demand of the offeror. In the event that a third party demands an aforementioned act or abstinence, this may not constitute consideration under Cyprus law. Yet again, consideration may be provided by the offeree or a third party,[92] in deviation from common law. In such an event, the third party merely contributes to the validity of the contract, an action that does not equal to acquiring any rights or duties. Solely the promisor and the promisee have legal rights arising from the contract.

40. With reference to time, consideration may be executory, executed or past,[93] the latter being one more deviation from common law.[94] Further, consideration needs to be: specific and not uncertain, such as a promise to pay compensation estimated in a manner which shall be deemed proper in the future; not legally impossible, such as a promise to relieve from a debt that has already been paid for; and not naturally impossible, such as an agreement to perform an act on a date already due. However, an act that the promisee promises to perform or abstain from, may not constitute a consideration, when he is already under a legal or contractual obligation to do so. It has been held that abandonment of a right to litigate is good consideration in law and this would be so even if his claim was not well founded

88. Section 70 Cap. 149.
89. *Kastanos a.o. v. Cyprus Popular Bank (Leasing) Ltd* 1 CLR 1374 (2009).
90. Section 2(2)(d) Cap. 149.
91. *See* in this respect *Dunlop Pneumatic Tyre Co Ltd v. Selfridge & Co Ltd* AC 847 (1915).
92. *Stylianides v. Hadjipiera* 1 CLR 1056 (1992); *Romanos v. Chrysanthou* 1 CLR 991 (1991).
93. *Raif v. Dervish* 1 CLR 158 (1971).
94. *Zervos a.o. v. Bank of Cyprus Public Company Ltd* 1 CLR 38 (2013); *Bank of Cyprus Public Company Ltd*, District Court of Nicosia, Civil Case No. 6394/04 of 2 Aug. 2013, not reported in CLR.

because what he abandoned was not his ultimate right or claim but his right to have the assistance of the court to determine and, if admitted or held good, to enforce it.[95]

B. Gratuitous Promises

41. Generally, an agreement made without consideration is void. Especially gratuitous promises are valid, as long as the following statutory conditions are fulfilled. The agreement must be expressed in writing and signed by the party to be charged therewith, along with being made on account of natural love and affection between parties standing in a near relation to each other.[96] The Greek translation further attributed the phrase 'near relation' to a close relative relation ('στενή συγγένεια').[97] Hence, it is safe to assume that gratuitous promises are likely to be ruled as valid only within one's close family. This was held to be true and valid between sisters,[98] mother and daughter,[99] grandmother and granddaughter,[100] grandfather and granddaughters,[101] uncles and nieces,[102] but not between first cousins.[103] Nevertheless, the Supreme Court – oddly – did not doubt the validity of donation of a shareholder to his company,[104] of a company to its shareholders,[105] or between directors of a company.[106] In addition, it has been ruled that the act of donation per se must be proved to be spontaneous and the result of the free will of the donator.[107] Irrationality of the donation may lead to the same being held void by the court.[108]

C. 'Natural Obligations'

42. Natural obligations do not exist in Law of Contract in Cyprus.

---

95. *Iosifakis a.o. v. Mohammed Abdul Ghani* 1 CLR 190 (1967).
96. Section 25(1)(a) Cap. 149.
97. The Turkish translation ('yekdiğerlerine olan') did not follow the spirit of the Greek one.
98. *Solomou v. Solomou a.o.* 1 CLR 1058 (2001).
99. *Charalambous v. Solomou* 1 CLR 1058 (2001); *Agrotou a.a. v. Agrotou*, Supreme Court of Cyprus, Civil Appeal No. 288/2010, Judgment of 31 May 2016, not published in CLR.
100. *Patatsou v. Hilmi a.a.*, Supreme Court of Cyprus, Civil Appeal No. 300/2011, Judgment of 31 May 2017, not published in CLR.
101. *Christoforou v. Christoforou* 1 CLR 1551 (1998).
102. *Demetriou a. o. v. Konstantinides a.a.* 1 CLR 1503 (2002); *Christophorou v. Iakovou* 1 CLR 33 (2002).
103. *Ellinopoulou v. Demetriades* 1 CLR 709 (1995).
104. *Roussos v. Cyprus* 3 CLR 517 (1996).
105. *Kefalas a.o. v. Cyprus* 3 CLR 1011 (1993).
106. *Vetalia Clothing Manufacturers Ltd v. Cyprus* 4 CLR 453 (2000).
107. *Christophorou v. Iakovou* 1 CLR 33 (2002), citing *Allcard v. Skinner* 35 Ch. D. 145 (1887).
108. *Sokratous v. Tsivanides* 1 CLR 1602 (1998).

IV. Modifications of the Contract

43. Modification, which includes substitution, rescission and alteration, of the original contract must comply with all conditions for making a contract, such as offer, acceptance and consideration.[109] Hence the aforementioned on formation equally apply here.

44. Substitution, that being novation, and rescission shall be discussed below in paragraph 143 under the chapter on termination of a contract.

45. A further form of contract modification, which shall be analysed here, is *collateral agreement*. This needs to fulfil all conditions for the formation of a contract. In addition, it is collateral to the original contract and must have the same object as the original agreement, but entail terms and conditions not stated in the original one.[110] It is considered to be an exception to the rule of prohibiting extrinsic evidence. It is applied, when the written contract entailing the agreement is not detailed and results in not revealing in full and with clarifying the parties' intention.[111] In the case establishing it, the oral reassurance by the first party about transferring the goods in its ship's hold was held to be a contractual promise, applicable as a collateral agreement, because it was given with the intention to convince the other party to transfer its goods with the first party's ship. In fact, the court declined to apply the written term of the contract, freeing the party from all liability, due to it being contrary to the collateral agreement and, if applied, it would frustrate the agreement.[112]

§2. Formal and Evidential Requirements

I. Formal Requirements

46. Neither contracts under seal nor solemn contracts exist under Cyprus law.

47. Specifically with regard to bill of lading, this is considered to be a mere receipt for the goods, stating the terms on which they were delivered to and received by the ship, and therefore excellent evidence of those terms. It does not constitute a contract, which has been made before the bill of lading was given.[113]

---

109. *Karaoli a.o. v. Laouri a.a.* 1 CLR 225 (2008).
110. *Solon Piitarides Developers Ltd a.o. v. Markoullis a.o.*, District Court of Famagusta, Civil Case No. 47/2008, Judgment of 30 Apr. 2015, not published in CLR.
111. *Marketventures Ltd v. Dikomites* 1 CLR 383 (2009).
112. *Muskita Aluminium Industries Ltd a.o. v. Alsako Aluminium Ltd a.o.* 1 CLR 1481 (2009), citing *J. Evans & Son (Portsmouth) Ltd v. Andrea Merzario Ltd* 2 All ER 930 (1976).
113. *Archangelos Domain Ltd v. Adriatica Societa per Azione di Navigatione* 1 CLR 439 (1978), citing *Leduc v. Ward* QBD 475 (1888).

II. Evidential Requirement: Proof

48. As a general rule, every court in Cyprus, in the exercise of its jurisdiction in any civil and criminal proceeding, shall apply so far as circumstances may permit, the law and rules of evidence as in force in England on 5 November 1914, save in so far as other provision is made in the Law on Evidence.[114]

A. The Parol Evidence Rule

49. Generally, a contract made in writing is itself the sole criterion of the intention of the parties that are bound by it. Parol evidence is not admissible to vary or contradict its terms.[115] Similarly, where a contract, not required by law to be in writing, purports to be contained in a document, which the court infers was not intended to express the whole agreement between the parties, proof may be given of any omitted or supplemental oral term, expressly or impliedly agreed between them before or at the time of executing the document, if it be not inconsistent with the documentary terms.[116] When an agreement is set out in writing, it is established that, as a general rule, extrinsic evidence ('εξωγενής μαρτυρία' in Greek, 'sözlü şahadet' in Turkish) may not contradict, amend, deduce or add terms to such contract. As an exception, such evidence may be accepted under specific conditions, such as failure to set out consideration in the document,[117] proving the validity of an agreement,[118] the actual nature of a transaction[119] and the ambiguous nature of the contracting parties.[120,121] Equally, when mutual mistake has entered into a contract parol evidence is allowed to be given of such mistake. Then, the court has the authority to rectify the written contract on parol evidence, so as to express the true agreement between the parties.[122]

B. Function of the Notary

50. In Cyprus, notary, as an office bearing public authority mission and interweaved with the proper application of the law familiar in the continental legal system (i.e., 'notaires' in France, 'Notar' in Germany, 'συμβολαιογράφοσ' in Greece, 'noter' in Turkey), does not exist. However, signatures and seals on documents are

114. Section 3 of the Evidence of 8 Aug. 1946, Ch. 9 of the Laws, London, 1959 edition, as amended.
115. *Eleni Christofides v. Moustafa Ahmet Aliye Kadis* 18 (1) CLR 1.
116. *Xenopoulos v. Thomas Nelson (Insurance) Ltd a.o.* 1 CLR 674 (1982), citing *Mercantile Bank of Sydney v. Taylor* AC 317 (1893).
117. *Polycarpou v. Polycarpou* 1 CLR 182 (1982).
118. *Mavrou v. Theodorou* 1 CLR 635 (1984).
119. *KYRIO (I.T.H.) Company v. Kassapi* 2 JSC 259 (1980); *Fuad Nadem El Djamal v. the Chief Customs Officer* 1 CLR 372 (1961).
120. *Loizidou v. Georgiou* 9 JSC 1219 (1973).
121. *Marketrends Finance Ltd v. Perdikou a.o.* 1 CLR 1042 (2006); *Papapetrou v. Laiki Factors Ltd*, Supreme Court of Cyprus, Civil Appeal No. 180/2010, Judgment of 20 Feb. 2015, not published in CLR.
122. *Eleni Christofides v. Moustafa Ahmet Aliye Kadis* 18 (1) CLR 1.

verified by certifying officers ('πιστοποιών υπάλληλος' in Greek, 'tasdik memurları' in Turkish). More specifically, certifying officers, who are appointed in specific prefectures by the Minister of Interior,[123] have the duty to certify that the signature and/or the seal subscribed or affixed to any document is the signature and/or the seal of a particular natural or legal person, upon request. Such certification shall be effected by inscribing upon the document a certificate in one of the statutory forms and by affixing thereto the seal of the certifying officer.[124] Signatures and seals may only be certified, under the requisites that the document is written legibly, continuously, and without erasure, interlineation, blank or interval.[125] A properly made certification has the legal effect of it being receivable as evidence of the facts thereby certified in all courts in Cyprus.[126]

III. Burden of Proof

51. Generally, each party bears the burden of proof of all assertions, arguments and allegations put forward by the same.[127] Statutory provisions in this regard are absent, but for one exception and some guidance may be deduced from case law. In particular, it has been ruled that the onus of proof in cases of claims based on mistake[128] lies on the party alleging same. Same applies to undue influence and fraud.[129] These cannot be presumed. The mere proof of the existence of a close relationship does not raise a presumption of undue influence sufficient to vitiate a gift by will.[130] Still, this is not applicable, when a special relationship between the parties exists.[131] Situations can raise a presumption of undue influence, which a defendant recipient has to rebut. Here, the donee shall have to prove that the transaction was completed by the donor only after full, free and informed thought about it.[132] This principle has been enshrined in section 16(3) Cap. 149, the only statutory provision on burden of proof in Law of Contracts.

---

123. Sections 3(1), 2 and 5 of the Law on Certifying Officers 'ο περί Πιστοποιούντων Υπαλλήλων Νόμος' No. 165 of 2012, OG I(I) No. 4368 of 30 Nov. 2012, p. 1795.
124. Section 6 *ibid.*
125. Section 8 *ibid.*
126. Section 9 *ibid.*
127. *Pittalis a.o. v. Ianira Enterprises Ltd a.o.* 1 CLR 814 (1997); *Papadopoulos v. Christophorou* 1 CLR 2004 (2002).
128. *Portsmouth v. Cyprus Inland Telecommunications Authority* 1 CLR 87 (1967).
129. *Mourtzinos v. 'Galaxias' a.o.* 1 CLR 80 (1997), citing *Bater v. Bater* 2 All ER 458 (1950); *Hornal v. Neuberger Products Ltd* 3 All ER 970 (1956); *Whitehouse v. Jordan a.a.* 1 All ER 650 (1980).
130. *Christopoulou a.o. v. Christopoulou* 1 CLR 437 (1971).
131. *Ioannou v. Charalambidou* 1 CLR 555 (1998).
132. *Patsalidou v. Kyriakides* 1 CLR 71 (1979), citing *Re Craig (Deceased)* Ch. 95 (1971); *Zamet v. Hyman* 3 All ER 933 (1961); *Lloyds Bank v. Bundy* 3 WLR 501 (1974). *See also Re Brocklehurst (deceased) Hall and Another v. Roberts* 1 All ER 767 (1978); *Socratous v. Sivitanides* 1 CLR 1602 (1998), citing *Aulesford (Earl) v. Morris* 8 Ch App 484 (1873).

52. Turning to damage, it has been held that compensation shall be awarded, even if damage or loss is not proved.[133] The court has the power to award reasonable compensation, but it shall only grant nominal damages if no evidence for damage or loss of the innocent party is furnished.[134]

53. No distinction between 'obligation of means' and 'obligation of result' exists under Cyprus law.

§3. LIABILITY AND NEGOTIATIONS

I. Precontractual Liability

54. Precontractual liability does not exist under Cyprus law.

II. Breakdown of Negotiations

55. Breakdown of negotiations unfolds no legal effects in Cyprus.

133. *Lambrianides a.o. v. Electricity Authority of Cyprus* 1 CLR 466 (1968).
134. *Mourtzinos v. 'Galaxias'* 1 CLR 80 (1997).

Chapter 2. Conditions of Substantive Validity

56. Central provision on conditions of substantive validity is section 10(1) Cap. 149, which provides '[a]ll agreements are contracts if they are made the free consent of parties competent to contract, for a lawful consideration and with a lawful object, and are not hereby expressly declared to be void, and may, subject to the provisions of this Law, be made in writing, or by word of mouth, or partly in writing and partly by word of mouth, or may be implied from the conduct of the parties'.

§1. Capacity of the Parties

57. Every person is competent to contract, who (a) is of sound mind and (b) is not disqualified from contracting by any Law.[135] It is further elaborated that a person is said to be of sound mind for the purpose of making a contract if, at the time when he makes it, he is capable of understanding it and of forming a rational judgment as to its effect upon his interests. A person who is usually of unsound mind, but occasionally of sound mind, may make a contract when he is of sound mind. A person who is usually of sound mind, but occasionally of unsound mind, may not make a contract when he is of unsound mind.[136] The court has actually found a person of sound mind at the time of making the disputed agreement, despite a court order adjudicating him a mental patient, which was at material time in force, and of him being temporarily discharged from the Patient Institute. The disputed agreement has held however to be void, due to violating a statutory provision, which was transferring control and disposition power over a mental patients' property to the District Court.[137,138] This law has been revoked in 1997.[139] Further, a person diagnosed with bipolar disorder, who had been hospitalized for over eighteen months, was held at the material time to be of sound mind due to her conduct, which did not indicate her being unaware of the nature and content of her action. The agreed consideration was equally taken into consideration. In view of lack of evidence proving it to be inconsistent with the then market value, it was decided that it did not offer any ground of the vendor being of unsound mind.[140]

135. Section 11(1) Cap. 149.
136. Section 12 *ibid.*
137. Section 27 Mental Patients of 29 May 1931, Ch. 252 of Laws, London, 1959 edition.
138. *Charalambous v. Krystallis* 1 CLR 656 (1984).
139. Section 42 of Law relating to Establishment and Operation of Psychiatric Centres for the Treatment of Mentally Ill Persons, to Safeguarding of their Rights and to Defining the Duties and Responsibilities of their Relatives ('Νόμος που Προνοεί για την Ίδρυση και Λειτουργία Ψυχιατρικών Κέντρων για τη Νοσηλεία Ψυχικά Ασθενών Προσώπων, τη Διασφάλιση των Δικαιωμάτων των Προσώπων αυτών και τον Καθορισμό των Καθηκόντων και Ευθυνών των Συγγενών') No. 77 of 1997, OG I(I) No. 3170 of 27 Jul. 1997, p. 1311, as last amended by amending Law No. 26 of 2007, OG I(I) No. 4116 of 9 Mar. 2007.
140. *Koropoulis v. Pelides*, Supreme Court of Cyprus, Civil Appeal No. 324/2009, Judgment of 14 Nov. 2014, not published in CLR.

58. With reference to persons, who have not attained the age of 18 years and are parties to a contract, the law in force in England for the time being relating to contracts to which such persons are parties shall apply.[141] In view of the words of the statute, which in themselves are precise and unambiguous, no doubt is left as to the intention of the legislature to render infants' agreements void, and not merely voidable.[142]

§2. Defects of Consent

I. Mistake

59. Mistake (in Greek 'πλάνη' in Turkish 'yanılgı') is a defect of consent, where both the parties to an agreement[143] are under a mistake as to a matter of fact essential to the agreement.[144] Such a matter of fact was decided to be the exact boundary of neighbouring plots in an agreement granting a right of way,[145] as well as the length of the plot in a sale agreement.[146] Mistake leads to the concluded agreement being void.[147]

60. However, an erroneous opinion as to the value of the thing which form the subject matter of the agreement is not to be deemed a mistake as to a matter of fact.[148] Equally, a contract caused by one of the parties to it being under a mistake as to a matter of fact[149] as well as a mistake as to any law in force in Cyprus have the same effect. Hence, they may not lead to an agreement being declared void by a court. An exception to the aforementioned is a mistake as to a law not in force in Cyprus, which has the same effect as a mistake of fact.[150]

61. Alongside mistake as a defect of consent, mention deserves the term mistake in section 72 Cap. 149, which regulates quasi-contracts and reads '[a] person to whom money has been paid, or anything delivered, by mistake or under coercion, must repay or return it'. Mistake in this statutory provision includes both a mistake of law and a mistake of fact.[151]

141. Section 11(1) 1st sentence Cap. 149.
142. *Papadopoulou v. Polycarpou* 1 CLR 352 (1968), citing s. 11 of the Indian Contract Act 1872 and *Mohori Bibee v. Dhurmodas Ghose* 19 Times Law Reports 295.
143. *Raptopoulos a.o. v. Alpha Bank Ltd*, Supreme Court of Cyprus, Civil Appeal No. 337/2011, Judgment of 11 Apr. 2017, not published in CLR.
144. Section 21(1) 1st sentence Cap. 149.
145. *Ioannou a.a. v. Siakalli a.o.* 1 CLR 1877 (2013).
146. *Theologou a.a. v. Ktimatikis Etaireias Nemesis Ltd* 1 CLR 407 (1998).
147. Section 21(1) 1st sentence Cap. 149.
148. Section 21(1) 2nd sentence *ibid.*
149. Section 22 *ibid.*
150. Section 21(2) *ibid.*
151. *Portsmouth v. Cyprus Inland Telecommunications Authority* 1 CLR 87 (1967), citing s. 72 Indian Contract Act 1878 and *Sir Shiba Prasad v. Maharaja Srish Chandra* AIR PC 297 (1949).

II. Misrepresentation

62. Misrepresentation ('ψευδής παράσταση' in Greek, 'yanıltma' in Turkish) is a defect of consent under Cyprus law. According to the statutory definition provided, '[m]isrepresentation includes: (a) the positive assertion not warranted by the information of the person making it, of that which is not true, though he believes it to be true; (b) any breach of duty, which without an intent to deceive, gains an advantage to the person committing it, or anyone claiming under him, by misleading another to his prejudice or to the prejudice of anyone claiming under him; (c) causing however innocently, a party to an agreement to make a mistake as to the substance of the thing which is the subject to the agreement'.[152] In practice, solely paragraph (a) is being applied by the courts in Cyprus, whereas paragraphs (b) and (c) are not. Misrepresentation leads to the concluded contract being voidable at the option of a party whose consent was so caused.[153] Same party, if he thinks fit, may insist that the contract shall be performed and that he shall be put in the position in which he would have been if the representation made had been true.[154] However, the concluded contract is not voidable, if the same party had the means of discovering the truth with ordinary diligence.[155] Lastly, a misrepresentation, which did not cause the consent to a contract of a party, to whom such misrepresentation was made, does not render a contract voidable.[156]

63. Misrepresentation was thoroughly analysed in *Nicolaides v. The Chartered Bank of Famagusta.*[157] The facts surrounding this case included a merchant (defendant No. 1), husband to Mrs Nicolaides (defendant No. 2, now appellant), opening a credit current account with the respondent and the wife signing the same contract as a guarantor. The wife was called to sign further guarantee as supplementary security due to no substantial payments to the said account, but without being interviewed or having met the responsible bank's manager. Further, supplementary agreements were signed not in presence of any bank's representative and statements of accounts were not sent to her as guarantor to said contract. It was further established that the bank misled the appellant on the fact that her husband was at the time of the signing of the further guarantee, already indebted to the bank in a considerable amount exceeding the future credit limit sought to be granted by the letters in question. At the same time, it was affirmed that it is the duty of the creditor not to mislead any prospective guarantor on a material substance. In said case, the fact that the husband was indebted in the sum of CYP 38,000 (approx. EUR 64,980) at the time the supplementary guarantee was obtained from the appellant was held to be a material circumstance for same. The court further answered negatively to the hypothetical question, whether the appellant would have entered into such guarantee if

---

152. Section 18 Cap. 149.
153. Section 19(1) *ibid.*
154. Section 19(2) *ibid.*
155. Section 19(3) *ibid.*
156. Section 19(4) *ibid.*
157. 1 CLR 56 (1966).

the non-disclosed fact had been disclosed to her. Lastly, the court held that creditors and bankers have to be more strict and careful when accepting as guarantor a wife for the husband's debt.[158]

64. A case involving a similar factual background is *Markidou v. Hellenic Bank Ltd.*[159] Husband acquired a loan from the bank, and the provided securities were a plot owned by the husband, which was mortgaged in favour of the bank, and the wife being a guarantor for the same loan. The wife purported that when signing the guarantee, the bank employee informed her that it was a typical procedure and she would suffer no consequences therefrom. The court was not convinced by the witness testimony of the guarantor and aligned with the one of the bank employee, who witnessed that he had properly informed her of all duties and responsibilities. In view of the lack of facts supporting an allegation of misrepresentation, it disregarded said claim and did not declare the contract void.[160]

65. In *Georgiou a.a. v. Alpha Concrete Ltd*,[161] the appellee entered into a contract with the appellants purchasing a complete undertaking of ready-mixed concrete, which consisted, among others, of land, buildings, equipment and machinery. However, it was later established that the machinery, the buildings and the service spaces were situated not on the purchased land, as the appellants had informed them, but within adjourning government land. This was held to be a misrepresentation by the appellants. It was further confirmed that when the innocent party omits the opportunity to discover the truth does not constitute an estoppel to claim restitution, as long as the innocent party, in this case the appellee, reasonably based its assumption on the misrepresentation of the contract party, in this case the appellants.[162]

66. In *Mountis v. Papachristophorou*,[163] claimants and other parties invested in the form of loans to the company Maxdata Holdings Ltd, following respondent's representations, according to which within eight months following the conclusion of the contracts the company would be listed in the Cyprus Stock Exchange and shares would be given to the investors. In case of failure, the loans would be returned to the creditors. It was held that the respondent made the following false representations regarding: his eligibility to register as holder of a big parcel of shares; Maxdata Holdings Ltd being the result of mergers; Maxdata Holdings Ltd

158. *Nicolaides v. The Chartered Bank of Famagusta* 1 CLR 56 (1966), citing *Chaplin & Co. Ltd v. Brammail* 1 K.B. 233 (1908); *London General Omnibus Company Ltd v. Holloway* 2 K.B. 72 (1912); *Lee a.a. v. Jones* English Reports 144 (1864); *Jean Mackenzie v. Royal Bank of Canada* AC 468 (1934).
159. 1 CLR 2069 (2001).
160. *Markidou v. Hellenic Bank Ltd* 1 CLR 2069 (2001). The Court declined to apply the following case law that was put forward by the appellant: *Barclays Bank Plc v. O'Brien a.a.* All ER 417 (1993); *Barclays Bank Plc v. Boulter a.a.* 4 All ER 513 (1994); *Royal Bank of Scotland v. Etridge* (No. 2) All ER 449 (2001).
161. 1 CLR 1049 (2009).
162. *Georgiou a.a. v. Alpha Concrete Ltd* (2009) 1 CLR 1049 (2009), citing *Redgrave v. Hurd* 20 Ch. D. 1 (1881); *Laurence v. Lexcourt Holdings Ltd* 1 WLR 1128 (1978).
163. 1 CLR 2637 (2012).

being a powerful company owning many immovable properties and listing a share of CYP 5 (EUR 8.55) at the Cyprus Stock Exchange. Said false representations were decisive for the claimant's consent to the concluded loans, whereas the claimants had no means of discovering the truth with ordinary diligence.[164]

67. In *Raptopoulos a.o. v. Alpha Bank Ltd,*[165] it was purported that a security, that being the pledge of shares belonging to a person personally guaranteeing for a loan, was the object of misrepresentation and hence the entire loan contract is voidable and thus should be declared void by the court. The court was not convinced and rejected the claim on two grounds, without examining whether the pledge of shares was misrepresented to the claimants. First, it noted that said pledge was not the only security to the loan, as a life insurance was assigned to the loan provider and the holder of said pledged shares along with another person had provided personal guarantee for the concluded loan. Second, the court held that the pledge of shares was not a fundamental or vital part of the contract. Hence, misrepresentation, even if true, could not lead to rescission.[166]

68. The term misrepresentation in section 18 Cap. 149 has the same meaning as the one in section 100 Cap. 149,[167] which regulates guarantee obtained by misrepresentation. This equally applies for the term misrepresentation in section 198 Cap. 149, which regulates misrepresentations made by agents acting in the course of their business for their principals, although this is a mere allegation resting on the plain meaning of the words used in said statutory provision and not affirmed by the court.

III. Improper Pressure

69. Improper pressure under Cyprus law may have the form of undue influence or coercion.

70. Undue influence ('ψυχική πίεση' in Greek, 'kötüye kullanılması' in Turkish), is a statutory defect of consent. A contract is said to be induced by undue influence where the relations subsisting between the parties are such that one of the parties is in a position to dominate the will of the other and uses that position to obtain an unfair advantage over the other.[168] The jurisdiction in relation to the exercise of undue influence is founded on the principle of correcting abuses of confidence and ought to be applied whatever may be the nature of the confidence reposed

164. *Mountis v. Papachristophorou* 1 CLR 2637 (2012).
165. Supreme Court of Cyprus, Civil Appeal No. 337/2011, Judgment of 11 Apr. 2017, not reported in CLR.
166. *Raptopoulos a.o. v. Alpha Bank Ltd* Civil Appeal No. 337/2011, Judgment of 11 Apr. 2017, not reported in CLR.
167. *Nicolaides v. The Chartered Bank of Famagusta* 1 CLR 56 (1966).
168. Section 16(1) Cap. 149.

or the relation of the parties between whom it has subsisted.[169] In addition, the courts have adopted the view that undue influence is some unfair and improper conduct, some coercion from outside, some overreaching, some form of cheating and generally, though not always, some personal advantage obtained by the guilty party.[170] The scope of undue influence is to ensure that no one should be allowed to maintain the profit that resulted from his illegal act.[171] It is further statutory defined that in particular and without prejudice to the generality of the foregoing principle, a person is deemed to be in a position to dominate the will of another (a) where he holds a real or apparent authority over the other, or where he stands in a fiduciary relation to the other, or (b) where he makes a contract with a person whose mental capacity is temporarily or permanently affected by reason of age, illness, or mental or bodily distress.[172] Where a person who is in a position to dominate the will of another enters into a contract with him, and the transaction appears, on the face of it or on the evidence adduced, to be unconscionable, the burden of proving such contract was not induced by undue influence shall lie upon the person in a position to dominate the will of the other.[173] The consequence of an agreement being caused by undue influence is that the agreement is a contract voidable at the option of the party whose consent was so caused.[174]

71. Undue influence was discussed in *Petrotim Ltd v. Itera International Energy LLC*,[175] a case involving trading unsecured debts. Petrotim Ltd was a Russian company dealing with oil trade and had deposited USD 23 million at the Russian Bank Inkombank, which had a branch in Cyprus. Itera International Energy LLC was an American limited liability company registered in Florida, USA. During the financial crisis of 1998, the licence of Inkombank was revoked by the Central Bank of the Russian Federation and by the Central Bank of Cyprus. The appellant purported that it contacted Alrosa and agreed to provide a loan of USD 10 million. It then gave the instruction to Inkombank to transfer USD 10 million to Alrosa's bank account, but the bank denied to do so. Rather, the bank suggested that the appellant pays USD 15 million to the appellee for a promissory note of the same value that it would later sell to Mellton Trading Ltd. Eight months later the appellant filed an action claiming that said agreement was the result of undue pressure. The appellee purported that it was acting as a guarantor for the company Tec Itera Rus. To this effect, it had agreed to issue a promissory note for USD 15 million that would be delivered to the appellee in exchange for transferring USD 15 million to the account of the appellee at Inkombank. Then Mellton Trading Ltd would buy said promissory note for the amount of USD 10.5 million. The Court noting the given commercial uncertainties, in view of the prohibition to withdraw money from Inkombank, which

169. *Patsalidou v. Kyriakides* 1 CLR 71 (1979); citing *Billage v. Southee* 9 Hare 534 (1852); *Lloyds Bank Ltd v. Bundy* 3 WLR 501 (1974). *See also Chloe Andrea Patatsou v. Ahmet Hilmi a.o.* Civil Appeal No. 300/2011, Judgment of 31 May 2017, not reported in CLR.
170. *Kefalas a.a. v. Nicola* 1 CLR 1226 (2000), citing *Allcard v. Scinner* 36 Ch. D. 145 (1887).
171. *Synergatiki Pistotiki Etaireia Agias Fylaksews v. Poulla a.a.* 1B CLR 961 (2004).
172. Section 16(2) Cap. 149.
173. Section 16(3) *ibid.*
174. Section 20(1) *ibid.*
175. 1 CLR 260 (2007).

existed prior to the conclusion of the agreement, and the lack of any positive actions by Itera as well as the absence of a relation between the parties, which could under circumstances suggest undue influence, dismissed the claim.[176]

72. In *Kefalas a.a. v. Nicola,*[177] the appellants agreed to provide care and anything necessary for a dignified life to the appellant for CYP 44,000 (EUR 75,240) and the house, in which she was living. One year later, the appellee filed a claim to annul the agreement due to undue pressure, along with fraud, misrepresentation, and unjust enrichment. The court accepted the appellee's version of events, which summarized as follows: the appellee was 72 years old, sick and bedridden due to an accident. Following said accident the appellant visited her and provided her with food and comfort. The same evening the appellant visited the appellee once more, this time with her husband. At that time the appellee had decided to go to a residential care home for the elderly, but the appellee and her husband were trying to talk her out of this and promised that they would take care of her if she would transfer to them her property. Said effort continued for one month while providing her with food and comfort. Among the arguments they used in their effort to persuade the appellee was that an acquaintance of them who resided at such a home suffered maltreatment and eventually died. They also promised that they would take her to doctors in Canada for her health problems. As soon as the appellee was convinced to trust the appellants with her care, they visited a lawyer, who prepared the documentation according to the appellants' instructions. The appellee, who could not read and write and did not receive independent advice from a lawyer,[178] executed the documentation and transferred her movable property by executing documentation brought to the lawyer's office by a bank officer. The appellee's house was transferred to the appellants without safeguarding the appellee's right to reside in it for as long as she lives. In view of said established facts, the court confirmed that a special relation of trust and confidence existed between the appellee and the appellants, that the latter dominated the will of the first. It therefore held that the agreement was voidable and declared it void.[179]

73. In *Christophorou v. Iakovou,*[180] the facts surrounding the case, which included donation of a plot and an elderly person, are quite similar and yet bear significant differences. In late 1993, the appellant appeared before the land registry with a general power of attorney requesting to transfer a plot of land from his uncle to him. The public servant declined to proceed with the request, as a special power of attorney was necessary for such a transfer. Thereafter, the appellant reappeared before the land registry with a special power of attorney and filed the same request

176. *Petrotim Ltd v. Itera International Energy LLC a.o.* 1 CLR 260 (2007), citing *Stavrou v. Demetriou* 1 CLR 304 (1991).
177. 1 CLR 1226 (2000).
178. Receiving independent legal advice functions against the claim of undue influence, as it was confirmed in *Sokratous v. Tsivanides* 1 CLR 1602 (1998).
179. *Kefalas a.a. v. Nicola* 1 CLR 1226 (2000), citing *Credit Lyonnais Bank Nederland NV v. Burch* 1 All ER 144 (1997); *Morely v. Loughnan* 1 Ch. D. 736 (1893); *Powell v. Powell* 1 ChD 243 (1900); *Inche Noriah v. Shaik Allie Bin Omar* All ER Rep 189 (1928).
180. 1 CLR 33 (2002).

that was then materialized. At this material time, the court was convinced following an expert testimony that the previous owner of the plot, who being the uncle of the appellant, could not communicate with his surroundings, was suffering from arteriosclerosis of the brain vessels, senility and Parkinson's disease. He could therefore not be held accountable for his actions. Following these facts, the court held that this person transferred the plot due to undue influence of the appellee and therefore the agreement was declared void.[181]

74. The case *Charalambous v. Aristotelous*[182] involved acquiring a lottery after the announcement of the winning numbers. In particular, at material time, the appellant entrusted a minor with running a small off-licence shop, which was selling lots among others. Lots were ordinarily being delivered by the appellee. On a particular day, the appellee called the minor, one or one and a half hour after the announcement of the winning numbers and asked her, whether any lots remained unsold. Following her positive response, he requested to be informed of the numbers. After being informed on this, he passed by and picked up the unsold lots. The court was satisfied that between the minor and the appellee a special bond existed, which caused the delivery of the winning lot. The above-described conduct of the appellee was estimated to be a form of indirect undue influence, which fell within the statutory notion set out in section 16(1) Cap. 149.[183]

75. In *Ioannou v. Charalambidou*,[184] appellant and appellee were married and parties to the disputed contract. Wife had had a love affair with a third party and revealed this to husband, who encouraged her to stop it and meet this third person for this reason on a specific day. In the evening of said day, husband and wife were invited for dinner at 8.00 pm at a friend's house. On the same day, wife returned to her home at about 11.00 pm and found her husband and parents waiting for her. Her parents, who were informed about the events by her husband, insulted her verbally and physically and encouraged her to put an end to the love affair until 3.00 am of the next day. Upon their departure, husband, who had remained silent during her parents' actions, started to verbally and physically insult her and abuse her. During this evening wife was deprived of sleep. Further, while husband held her at gunpoint, he threatened to kill her and her lover and demanded that she donates their home, which was her property, to him. In the morning, husband instructed her to put on her sunglasses and make-up in order to cover up the beating and look natural. They visited a lawyer, who was instructed by husband to prepare necessary documentation for the transfer of ownership of said property. Lawyer advised wife against transferring the property, but husband reminded wife of the events of the

181. *Christophorou v. Iakovou* 1 CLR 33 (2002), citing *Kefalas v. Nicola* 1 CLR 1226 (2000); *Allcard v. Skinner* 35 Ch. D. 145 (1887); *Sokratous v. Tsivanides* 1 CLR 1602 (1998).
182. 1 CLR 750 (2001).
183. *Charalambous v. Aristotelous* 1 CLR 750 (2001), citing *Foreman v. Great Western Railway* 38 LT 851 (1878); *Re D'Angiban* 15 Ch. D. 228 (1880); *Smally v. Smally* 1 Eq Cas Abr 283 (1700); *Watkins v. Vince* 2 Stark 368 (1818); *Burnard v. Haggis* 14 CBNS 45 (1863); *Allcard v. Skinner* 36 Ch. D. 145 (1877); *Tufton v. Sperni* 2 TLR 516 (1952); *Mutual Finance Ltd v. Wetton* 2 K.B. 389 (1937); *Bank of Credit and Commerce International SA v. Aboody* 1 QB 923 (1990).
184. 1 CLR 555 (1998).

previous night. Then wife yielded and agreed to the said donation. Following the conclusion of the contract, husband isolated wife at home and had the telephone disconnected and removed the battery from the vehicle, so that she would be unable to use it. Husband then encouraged her to visit Greece 'in order to think'. When she returned home, they had an argument and with a friends' help she was transferred to her parents' house, who were then informed of both the donation and the circumstances under which this happened. Parents then visited more than once husband on this matter and he kept on promising that he would transfer the property to wife's father, but failed to do so. The court affirmed that the aforementioned husband's actions constituted undue influence and declared the voidable contract to be void. The husband was ordered to leave the disputed house. In the event that he failed to do so, he was ordered to monthly pay the amount of CYP 150 (EUR 256) from the day that the judgment was rendered until he left property.[185]

76. Coercion ('εξαναγκασμός' in Greek, 'zorlama' in Turkish) is the committing or threatening to commit, any act forbidden by the Criminal Code, or any amendment thereof, or the unlawful detailing, or threatening to detain, any property, to the prejudice of any person whatever, with the intention of causing any person to enter into an agreement.[186] It is further specified, that it is immaterial whether the Criminal Code, or any amendment thereof, is or is not in force in the place where the coercion is employed.[187] In determining whether there was a coercion of will such that there was no true consent, it is material to enquire whether the person alleged to have been coerced did not protest; whether, at the time he was allegedly coerced into making the contract, he did or did not have an alternative course open to him such as an adequate legal remedy; whether he was independently advised; and whether after entering the contract he took steps to avoid it. All these matters are relevant in determining whether he acted voluntarily or not.[188] The statutory definition of coercion has been ruled not to include threats in commerce or trade. Yet these created the equity principle of economic duress or coercion on the grounds of *Universe Tankships v. ITF*.[189] This principle, as a principle of equity and not as a statutory provision, does apply in Cyprus, when free consent is absent.[190]

185. *Ioannou v. Charalambidou* 1 CLR 555 (1998), citing *Patsalidou v. Kyriakides* 1 CLR 71 (1979); *Bullock v. Lloyds Bank Ltd* Ch. 317 (1955); *Allcard v. Skinner* 36 Ch. D. 145 (1887); *Turner v. Collins* 7 Ch App 329 (1871); *Alexiadi v. Robinson* 2 F & F 679 (1861); *Morley v. Loughnan* 1 Ch. 736 (1893).
186. Section 15(1) Cap. 149.
187. Section 15(2) Cap. 149.
188. *Koutas v. Dimos Lefkosias* 1(E) CLR 516 (1989), citing *Maskell v. Horner* 3 K.B. 106 (1915).
189. *Universe Tankships Inc of Monrovia v. International Transport Workers' Federation* 2 All ER 67 (1982). *See also The 'Hoegh Apapa'* 2 Lloyd's Law Reports 9 (1983).
190. *To Ploio 'Panayia Myrtidiotissa' v. Sidiropoulou a.a.* 1 CLR 1000 (1998), citing *Koutas v. Dimos Lefkosias* 1(E) CLR 516 (1989).

77. Coercion is different from undue influence in the following manner. Undue influence need not amount to positive coercion; it is enough if it improperly induces one of the parties to do that which he would otherwise have been unwilling to do.[191]

IV. Gross Disparity

78. Gross disparity per se does not have any legal effect. It does, however, function as a presumption that the contract was made under undue influence.[192] It has been ruled that this presumption triggers in when the amount of donation is so great or the promises of the contract are so uneven that may not be justified by friendship, family relationship, charity or other usual.[193]

§3. Other Conditions of Validity

I. Existing and Licit Cause

79. An agreement constitutes a contract when the pursued cause is both possible in itself[194] and licit.[195]

80. Relevant to the cause of a contract and therefore its legality is fraud in the sense that it relates to acts being performed with the intent to deceive another party to a contract. According to the statutory definition, fraud ('απάτη' in Greek, 'hile' in Turkish) includes any of the following acts committed by a party to a contract, or with his connivance, or by his agent, with intent to deceive another party thereto or his agent, or to induce him to enter into the contract: (a) the suggestion, as to a fact, of that which is not true by one who does not believe it to be true; (b) the active concealment of a fact by one having knowledge or belief of the fact; (c) a promise made without any intention of performing it; (d) any other act fitted to deceive; (e) any such act or omission as the law specially declares to be fraudulent.[196] However, mere silence as to facts likely to affect the willingness of a person to enter into a contract is not fraud, unless the circumstances of the case are such that, regard being had to them, it is the duty of the person keeping silence to speak, or unless his silence is, in itself, equivalent to speech.[197] Furthermore, the high standard of

191. *Patsalidou v. Kyriakides* 1 CLR 71 (1979); citing *Baudains v. Richardson* AC 169 (1906); *Noriah v. Omar* AC 127 (1929).
192. *Synergatiki Pistotiki Etaireia Agias Fylaxeos v. Poulla a.a.* 1 CLR 961 (2004), citing *Poosathurai v. Kannappa Chettiar* LR 47 Ind. App. 1 (1919) and *National Westminster Bank plc v. Morgan* 1 All ER 821 (1985).
193. *Synergatiki Pistotiki Etaireia Agias Fylaxeos v. Poulla a.a.* 1 CLR 961 (2004), citing *Goldsworthy v. Brickell* Ch. 378 (1987).
194. *E contrario* from ss 36 and 56(1) Cap. 149.
195. Section 10(1) *ibid.*
196. Section 17(1) Cap. 149.
197. Section 17(2) *ibid.*

proof of fraud deserves mention, which actually exceeds the one usually required for claims in civil cases. The relevant English authorities[198] have been adopted in Cyprus.[199]

81. In *Fakonti v. Vryoni*,[200] the appellee was asked to come to a lawyer's office in order to sign a typical sales agreement related to the business between him and Mr Kakoutis, who frequently had friendly business relationships. The appellee signed the document without reading it, following confirmation that it was ready for execution, whereas its terms and conditions were dictated to the lawyer by Mr Kakoutis and the appellant. The executed agreement was actually a sales agreement between the appellee and the appellant regarding a plot of the appellee, a point of law that the appellee ignored, and one of the terms stated that the appellant received full consideration upon execution thereof, whereas in fact, he had received none. Upon establishing said facts as true facts, the court declared the agreement void due to fraud.[201]

82. The case *Antoniou v. Gestami & Co Ltd*,[202] where the allegation of fraud was declined, rested on the following factual surrounding. Appellee No. 2, accompanied by appellees Nos 3 and 4, visited the appellant at her home and made the following representations to her: (i) he had no interest in selling the disputed property, but for his commission; (ii) the disputed property would not be developed within the next ten to fifteen years; (iii) the amount of CYP 45,000 (EUR 76,950) offered by the buyers corresponded to the value of the disputed property; (iv) he wished the best for her; (v) she should not miss this opportunity, which was offered to her; (vi) she should trust him. Appellant had instructed neither appellee No. 2 nor appellee No. 5 with selling the disputed property. Rather appellee No. 2 had discovered that appellant had property for sale and he visited her on his own initiative with the purpose of convincing her to sell said property to appellee No. 1. Initially the appellant did not intend to sell her property, but following the aforementioned representations, she agreed to sell it for the amount of CYP 48,000 (EUR 82,080). The aforementioned events along with transfer of property to its new owner took place in April 1991. In March 1991 a confidential report was compiled by the local authorities, which suggested to change the classification of the disputed property into a build-up area. In October of the same year, the said report was approved by the competent Minister but was published two years later in 1993. From that time onwards, applications for building permits could be submitted to the competent authorities. At the material time, the value of the property was estimated to be CYP 50,000 (EUR 85,500), not far from the consideration paid for the disputed contract. The

198. *Bater v. Bater* 2 All ER 458 (1950); *Hornal v. Neuberger Products Ltd* 3 All ER 970 (1956); *Whitehouse v. Jordan a.a.* 1 All ER 650 (1980).
199. *Mourtzinos v. tou ploiou Galaxias a.o.* 1 CLR 80 (1997).
200. 1 CLR 1404 (2004).
201. *Fakonti v. Vryoni* 1 CLR 1404 (2004), citing *Polycarpou v. Polycarpou* 1 CLR 182 (1982).
202. 1 CLR 1070 (2002).

court having regard of this and all the evidence put forward concluded that the appellant failed to prove the claim of fraud and on these grounds, it dismissed the claim.[203]

83. In *Kallice Holding v. MTR*,[204] fraud and illicit object were affirmed. The claimants, a company registered in Liberia owning a ship, entered into a contract with the respondents, a company registered in Cyprus. The disputed contract of 18 January 1993, was executed in Nicosia and provided for chartering said ship for transporting iron from Ukraine to Hong Kong and China under the therein agreed terms and conditions. To the purpose of performing said contract, the ship approached the port Ust-Dunaysk for receiving the cargo, which was discovered to be defect due to iron being rusty. On this ground the claimants denied to receive a clean bill of lading. Their denial was bend when the respondents offered to provide compensation for any consequences they would suffer from signing the said bill and issued an indemnity. It covered any form of damage, loss or expenditure that the claimants would suffer as a result of the said bill, including legal fees. Issuing a clean bill of lading aimed mainly to safeguarding the conditions for receiving the letter of credit and the payment of the cargo rate. The ship arrived at Hong Kong on 28 March 1993 and on the next day it gave notice that the ship was ready to unload. The contract set out no specific time for unloading and hence this was held to be reasonable. It further provided USD 6,800 per day as compensation for demurrages. Despite the notification, unloading did not commence. Representatives of the receivers and of the P. & I. Club of the ship along with Inspector of the charterer inspected the cargo and following the completion of the inspection they filed an action for damages against the ship and/or the charter, breach of the contract to transfer goods, misrepresentations, breach of duties of bailees for reward or negligence in relation to upload and transfer the goods and issuing the bill of lading. On the same day the ship was arrested. Following negotiations between the parties, the claim was settled on 15 April 1993, which lead to the termination of the arrest and unloading of the cargo. The claimants then, on the ground of the executed indemnity, claimed legal expenses, unloading expenses, travel expenses of an officer of the ship's managers, inspection expenses and additional docking and attendance expenses. Additionally, they claimed compensation for demurrages from 28 March 1993 until 15 April 1993. In view of these facts, the court ruled that the disputed indemnity was void, in view of it being executed with the intention of defrauding third parties under the meaning of fraud in section 17 Cap. 149, as well as having an illegal object under section 23 Cap. 149.[205]

84. In *Moniati v. Neophytou*,[206] the appellee rented from the appellant an establishment for the operation of a pool bar. The appellant was aware of the intended operation of the establishment and encouraged the appellee to proceed with his

203. *Antoniou v. Gestami & Co Ltd* 1 CLR 1070 (2002), citing no case law.
204. *Kallice Holding Co Ltd v. MTR Metals (Overseas) Ltd* 1 CLR 1011 (2001).
205. *Ibid.*, citing: *Brown v. Percy Dalton Ltd* 2 All ER 844 (1957); *Holman v. Johnson* 1 Cowp 341 (1775).
206. *M. Moniati & Sons Ltd v. Neophytou* 1 CLR 1096 (2008).

plans. Mention deserves the term included in the contract, according to which a kitchen was included in the establishment. In reality, neither a kitchen nor related equipment was available. The appellee encountered problems from the initiation of its business, as the establishment was authorized to operate only as an open-air restaurant. The competent authorities upon enquiring the illegal operation of the establishment prohibited it and shut it down. The appellee then claimed damages from the appellant. The court accepted the reality put forward by the appellee and concluded that the aforementioned actions of the appellants constituted fraud and misrepresentations in the meaning of sections 17 and 18 Cap. 149.[207]

85. Selling of forged paintings was the issue in dispute in *Christodoulides v. Kymisi*.[208] The appellant sold consecutively sixteen paintings of famous Greek painters, which were falsely presented to be originals, for the amount of CYP 34,450 (EUR 58,909). Sold paintings were actually copies of the originals. The court did not dispute that these agreements were concluded under fraud.

86. Trading of illegal diamonds was discussed in *Christodoulou v. Vraets*.[209] The parties had agreed to purchase two packets of uncut diamonds from Angola for USD 3,106,200. The goods would be later transferred to Antwerp in Belgium for processing and selling. Profit, which was estimated to be four times the aforementioned amount of the expenses, would be distributed after selling the cut diamonds. The appellee deposited USD 856,000 at the account of the appellant, whereas the rest would be deposited by other persons. The appellee claimed that the whole business was illegal because the uncut diamonds would be illegally exported from Angola, due to them being bought in the black market. He further purported that the appellant was aware of the illegality of purchasing and transferring said diamonds. In view of these, the appellee suggested that the appellant could not claim anything due to his participation in the illegality. The court reached the conclusion that neither party was telling the whole truth. The appellant had the sole object of gaining profit and his narrative was only intended to mislead. He had neither any intention to fulfil his promise nor performed any purchase of diamonds. He aimed at deceiving the appellant and getting his money. The appellee was fully aware of the illegality of the transactions, but accepted to participate in view of the great profit. The court ruled that the law deprives a party involved in illegal actions of any remedy, whereas it applied the principle *ex turpi causa non oritur action*, reaffirming that no court will lend its aid to a man who founds his cause of action upon an immoral or illegal act.[210] In view of the illegality of the entire transaction, as unauthorized export of diamonds was a penal act under the law of Angola, the court did not grant any claim.[211]

---

207. *Ibid.*, citing no case law.
208. *Christodoulides v. Kymisi and Ekastica Kymisis Ltd* 1 CLR 635 (2009).
209. *Christodoulou and Lindsay v. Antonius H.F.M. Vraets* 1 CLR 802 (2009).
210. Citing *Holman v. Johnson* 1 Cowp 341 (1775).
211. *Christodoulou and Lindsay v. Antonius H.F.M. Vraets* 1 CLR 802 (2009), citing *Vandervell's Trusts (No. 2)* 3 All ER 205 (1974); *Drane v. Evangelou* 2 All ER 437 (1978); *Euro-Diam Ltd v. Bathurst*

II. Determined or Determinable, Possible and Licit Object

87. A contract is further required to have an object both licit and possible in itself. Generally, the object of a contract is deemed to be licit, but for some statutory exceptions,[212] which are set out below in paragraphs 89 et seq. Whether the agreed object is possible in itself, is a question to be evaluated on a case-by-case basis. Should this not be affirmed, the agreement is void,[213] as explained below in paragraphs 140 et seq.

88. Reasonable certainty as to the terms of the contract, in other words clarity of the essential terms of the contract, is one of the ingredients of a valid contract.[214] Agreements the meaning of which is not certain or capable of being made certain are void.[215] However, courts as a general rule are reluctant to reject a contract for uncertainty motivated by a desire to give effect to the bargain of the parties. They tend to uphold the agreement of the parties.[216] The test used in order to determine whether the terms of a contract are sufficiently certain to render the agreement enforceable is whether someone, genuinely seeking to discover its meaning, is able to do so.[217] In case *Oikonomou v. Ttofini*,[218] which included a dispute regarding a term in a dowry, the court decided that the wording of the disputed term was far from an ideal wording, on which the court could base any conclusions as to the matters agreed between the parties. The used wording was so incomprehensible and improper to deduce a final and precise meaning, that the court was unable to attribute to the parties any specific contractual intention. As a result, the court ruled that the disputed agreement was void.[219]

III. Illegality and Public Policy

89. An agreement may be illegal either on the ground of having an illicit object or consideration under sections 23 and 24 Cap. 149 or due to the agreed content under sections 26, 27, 28, 29, 30 and 36 Cap. 149. Violation of public policy may cause an agreement to be illicit under the first set of cases.

---

1 QB 1 (1990); *Howard v. Shirlstar Container Transport Ltd* 1 WLR 1292 (1990); *Tinsley v. Milligan* 1 AC 340 (1994); *Pitts v. Hunt* 1 QB 24 (1991); *Clunis v. Camden and Islington Health Authority* 3 All ER 180 (1998).

212. Section 23 Cap. 149.
213. Section 56(1) *ibid.*
214. *Saab a.a. v. The Holy Monastery of Ayios Neophytos* 1 CLR 499 (1982), citing *Horrocks v. Forray* 1 All ER 737 (1976).
215. Section 29 Cap. 149.
216. *Saab a.a. v. The Holy Monastery of Ayios Neophytos* 1 CLR 499 (1982), citing *Charles Clay & Sons Ltd v. B. R. Board* 1 All ER 1007 (1971).
217. *Ibid.*, citing *Brown v. Gould* 2 All ER 1505 (1971); *Bushwell Properties v. Vortex Properties* 2 All ER 283 (C.A.) (1976).
218. 1 CLR 436 (1993).
219. *Oikonomou v. Ttofini* 1 CLR 436 (1993).

A. *Illicit Object or Consideration*

90. The object of an agreement is illicit, when: (a) it is forbidden by law; or (b) is of such a nature that, if permitted, it would defeat the provisions of any law; or (c) is fraudulent; or (d) involves or implies injury to the person or property of another; or (e) the court regards it as immoral or opposed to public policy.[220] This section is a codification of the common law on the subject of illegal contracts.[221] Distinctive common characteristic of all cases of illegality codified in this section is the mutual intention of the parties to an agreement. In other words, both parties to an agreement aimed to the object of the same agreement, which under this statutory provision is illicit.[222]

91. The issues explained below on illicit object equally apply on consideration and may render it illicit.[223] Case law on this matter has been scarce. In *Iosifakis v. Ghani,*[224] consideration was not ruled to be illegal in on the ground that it involved registration of property in the name of an alien without the required consent of the competent authorities. This violation was considered a mere irregularity committed in the course of the performance of an otherwise legal contract.

92. As usual, a party claiming illegality as a defence is expected to set out in the pleadings the facts indicating the allegation, which it was put forward. However, in cases, where the court takes notice of manifest illegality either from the agreement itself or from the furnished evidence regarding said agreement, it has the authority to examine on its own motion, whether illegality exists, even if neither party purported it.[225]

1. Object Prohibited by Law

93. Prohibition by law[226] can be explicitly provided or deduced from law. When prohibition is explicitly provided by law, illegality of the agreement in question cannot be disputed. The agreement is tainted with illegality and cannot be executed by either party.[227] This applied in a case involving selling of animals, where no certificates of ownership of same were produced and it was ruled that this equally applies to: agreements for the sale of prohibited goods; agreements for the sale of goods without accompanying documents when the statute specifically said there

---

220. Section 23 Cap. 149.
221. *Mavromoustaki v. Yeroudes* 1 CLR 176 (1965).
222. *M. C.A. Hotels Ltd v. Sartas Ltd*, District Court of Larnaca, Civil Case No. 1662/04 of 29 Mar. 2007, not reported in CLR, citing *Agathocleous v. Lappa* 1 CLR 2202 (1998); *St. John Shipping Corporation v. Joseph Bank Ltd* 1 QB 267 (1957).
223. Section 23 Cap. 149.
224. *Iosifakis a.o. v. Ghani* 1 CLR 190 (1967).
225. *Ayia Napa Nissi Ltd a.o. v. Papamichail* 1 CLR 549 (1992); *Christou v. S.D. Clinic Co Ltd* 1 CLR 2039 (2000); *Michaelides a.o. v. Chatziirodotou* 1 CLR 1609 (2003).
226. Section 23(a) Cap. 149.
227. *Agathocleous a.a. v. Lappa* 1 CLR 2202 (1998).

must be accompanying documents; and agreements for work and labour done by persons who were prohibited from doing the whole of the work and labour for which they demanded recompense.[228] In this spirit, the court has heard cases,[229] where constructors agreed to build specific works, although they did not possess the necessary qualification under applicable law, that being the Law on Registration and Control of Constructors of Building and Technical Works. It decided that, under the circumstance of lacking the statutory authority to construct the agreed work, the agreements were illegal. It was also noted that both parties were aware of the illegality (*in pari delicto*) and made the agreement with the intention to evade statutory provisions. The claims for breach of agreement were dismissed. Equally, payments performed for services rendered without the statutory licence may not be deduced from the taxable income, as they were illegal.[230] Turning to the point of prohibition being deduced from law,[231] interpretation of law is vital to illegality on this ground. Laws aiming solely to the increase of state's revenue may not cause a contract to be held illicit.[232] However, laws aiming to consumers' protection[233] or to a scope of general policy, as most do, may lead, upon violation, to an agreement being void and unenforceable.[234]

2. Object Defeating Provisions of Any Law

94. The nature of an agreement's object can lead to it being illicit. In particular, when the object of an agreement is of such a nature that, if permitted, it would defeat the provisions of any law, it is illicit.[235] In this respect, it has been ruled that if an agreement is illegal at its inception, it must follow that any agreement which is founded on or is so directly connected with it and springs from it must also be illegal and void. If it were otherwise, then the provisions of the law might be easily evaded. And it must also be irrelevant that it forms no part of the original transaction or that it is itself innocuous.[236]

---

228. *Kanaris v. Tosoun* 1 CLR 637 (1969), citing *Anderson Ltd v. Daniel* 1 K.B. 138 (1924); *St. John Shipping Corporation v. Joseph Rank Ltd* 1 QB 267 (1957).
229. *Koropouli & Demetriou v. Abraham* 1 CLR 78 (1987); *Flecha Contracting Ltd v. M. C. Michael Development Ltd* 1(A) CLR 263 (2003); *Andreas Kasianos & Sons Ltd v. Filitsas D. Vasileiou Ltd* 1(B) CLR 1337 (2006).
230. *Zacharias Stavrou Zachariades Ltd v. Tax Department* 3 CLR 445 (2000).
231. Section 23(a) Cap. 149.
232. *Agathocleous a.a. v. Lappa* 1 CLR 2202 (1998), citing *Smith v. Mawhood* 14 M & W 452 (1845).
233. *G.M. Platritis & Co a.o. v. Computer Patent Annuities a.o.* 1 CLR 135 (1988).
234. *Agathocleous a.a. v. Lappa* 1 CLR 2202 (1998), citing *Cope v. Rowlands* 2 M & W 149 (1836).
235. Section 23(b) Cap. 149.
236. *Chr. Tornari & Co. & F. Vassiliades v. Savva* JSC 389 (1974), citing *Fisher v. Bridges* 3 E & B 642 (1834); *Jennings v. Hammond* 9 QB 225 (1882).

95. Mention deserves the tendency not to draw a strict line dividing this reason of illegality[237] from the one of prohibition by law,[238] already analysed above. Submitted claims and issued case law not unusually put them forward jointly and without distinction.[239]

3. Fraudulent Object

96. When an agreement's object is fraudulent, it becomes an illegal object.[240] This provision differentiates from section 17 Cap. 149, as the latter regulates issues related to a party to a contract aiming to defrauding the other party to the same contract. The provision explained here, provides for both parties to a contract having a common fraudulent object, which usually consists of defrauding a third party.

97. A special form of illicit cause pursued with a contract by both parties is that of money laundering. Money laundering is prohibited at national level,[241] throughout the EU, along with terrorist financing according to Article 1(2) Directive (EU) 2015/849[242] as well as at international level under the Vienna Convention[243] and the Palermo Convention.[244,245] Under the law of the EU '[t]he following conduct, when committed intentionally, [is] regarded as money laundering: (a) the conversion or transfer of property, knowing that such property is derived from criminal activity or from an act of participation in such activity, for the purpose of concealing or disguising the illicit origin of the property or of assisting any person who is involved in the commission of such an activity to evade the legal consequences of that person's action; (b) the concealment or disguise of the true nature, source, location, disposition, movement, rights with respect to, or ownership of, property, knowing that

237. Section 23(b) Cap. 149.
238. Section 23(a) *ibid.*
239. *Kanaris v. Tosoun* JSC 17 (1970); *D I Demades Sons Ltd v. Kaoullas a.a.* JSC 270 (1972); *Frangos v. Limited Liability Partnership 'Prasino Livadhi'* JSC 48 (1978); *Mosilioti v. Panayi a.a.* JSC 384 (1979).
240. Section 23(c) Cap. 149.
241. Section 4 Law on Prevention and Combat of Money Laundering ('ο περί της Παρεμπόδισης και Καταπολέμησης της Νομιμοποίησης Εσόδων από Παράνομες Δραστηριότητες Νόμος') No. 188 of 2007, OG I(I) No. 4154 of 31 Dec. 2007, p. 1715, as last amended by amending Law No. 158 of 2018, OG I(I) No. 4679 of 19 Dec. 2018.
242. Directive (EU) 2015/849 of the European Parliament and of the Council of 20 May 2015 on the prevention of the use of the financial system for the purposes of money laundering or terrorist financing, amending Regulation (EU) No. 648/2012 of the European Parliament and of the Council, and repealing Directive 2005/60/EC of the European Parliament and of the Council and Commission Directive 2006/70/EC, OJ L 141 of 5 Jun. 2015, p. 73, as last amended by Directive (EU) 2018/843 of the European Parliament and of the Council of 30 May 2018, OJ L 156 of 19 Jun. 2018, p. 43.
243. The United Nations Convention against Illicit Traffic in Narcotic Drugs and Psychotropic Substances 1988, UN Treaty Series, Vol. 1582, p. 95. It has been ratified by Cyprus on 25 May 1990.
244. The United Nations Convention against Transnational Organized Crime 2000, UN Treaty Series, Vol. 2225, p. 209. It has been ratified by Cyprus on 22 Apr. 2003.
245. *See also* Recommendation 3, International Standards on Combating Money Laundering and the Financing of Terrorism and Proliferation – The FATF Recommendations 2012 (updated October 2016).

such property is derived from criminal activity or from an act of participation in such an activity; (c) the acquisition, possession or use of property, knowing, at the time of receipt, that such property was derived from criminal activity or from an act of participation in such an activity; (d) participation in, association to commit, attempts to commit and aiding, abetting, facilitating and counselling the commission of any of the actions referred to in points (a), (b) and (c)'.[246]

98. In a case involving transferring money from the claimant's bank accounts without previous authorization from the Board of Directors, where an injunction was sought for bank accounts in Cyprus and in Singapore, money laundering was put forward as a defence by the respondents.[247] In particular, they alleged that agreements justifying the money's origin were illicit, as their object was money laundering. Thus, they purported that void agreements could not support a petition for injunction. The court took no regard of this allegation due to lack of evidence. It further had no doubt that the claimant came forward with clean hands. Thus, it granted the injunction.

99. In the case *Cyprus v. Yaacoub*,[248] money laundering was a small, but nevertheless vital part of the bigger picture. The factual surrounding of this case, which can realistically depict the extent to which money laundering and terrorist financing are interweaved, involved the following. The accused, who had a dual Lebanese and Swedish nationality, was arrested in Limassol on the basis of information about him belonging to a terrorist organization and planning terrorist attacks against Israelis or other European representations in Cyprus. He denied all accusations and purported that he had come to Cyprus solely for business. However, when police pointed out to him that he admitted to being at the Larnaca airport, watching the arrival of a flight from Israel, monitoring the vehicles used by the passengers to leave the airport and noted the vehicle licence plates, he replied 'I will explain you everything.' He then admitted to being a member of *Hizballah*, having been trained to the use of weapons and explosives, performing surveillance and making cover stories. *Hizballah* had sent him to various missions in Antalya (Turkey), Lyon (France) and Amsterdam (the Netherlands) mainly to deliver and receive objects and parcels. He had visited Cyprus six times in order to create a cover story, that of business activities, for the objects of the organization. *Hizballah* had instructed him to visit, photograph and map the Central Police Station, the old hospital in Limassol, the Traffic Police in Limassol and a hotel, along with enquiring on rending a warehouse, locating internet cafes without surveillance cameras, acquiring SIM cards, identifying possible *rendezvous* locations and locating *kosher* restaurants. He then admitted to receiving a monthly allowance of USD 600 from *Hizballah* since 2010, but declared that he does not agree with terrorism and that he would never participate to a terrorist attack, although he supports 'armed struggle for the liberation of Lebanon

246. Article 1(3) Directive (EU) 2015/849.
247. *Janissa Trading Ltd v. Tikhonov a.o.*, District Court of Paphos, Civil Case No. 214/16, Judgment of 12 Feb. 2016, not published in CLR.
248. *Cyprus v. Hossam Taleb Yaacoub*, District Court of Limassol, Criminal Case No. 17714/12, Judgment of 21 Mar. 2013, not published in CLR.

from Israel'. He purported that his actions merely consisted of 'collecting information on Jews, as [his] organisation does all over the world'.

100. Expert testimony provided that *Hizballah* Lebanon declared having as a scope the obliteration of Israel. This organization, which was designated wholly or partly as a foreign terrorist organization by many countries,[249] was also involved in money laundering and terrorism according to same testimony. In support of this specific mention of criminal and terrorist actions undertaken by *Hizballah* was made. Equally, the *modus operandus* used for the preparation of criminal and terrorist actions was portrayed. The expert expressed his expert opinion that the verified facts of this case strongly indicated that an attack was being prepared.

101. The ruling court accepted the most of the accused's testimony, but only a part of the expert testimony. More specifically, the court did accept the evidence on declarations, object and structure of *Hizballah*. However, it declined to take as true the information on *Hizballah* undertaking terrorist and suicide attacks, money laundering and assassinations, on the ground of this being hearsay evidence. The court refused to allow 'rumour' and 'suspicion of terrorism' to become evidence and disagreed with the estimation that an attack was being prepared. In any event, the court did accept that *Hizballah* constituted a criminal organization in view of the specific actions performed in Cyprus, for which no innocent excuse could be provided.

102. The ruling court found the defendant guilty of money laundering, participation to a criminal organization and participation and approval of committing a crime under sections 63A, 63B,[250] 247, 251 and 231 of Cap. 154. The accused was sentenced to four years for participation and approval of committing a crime. No

249. *See* in this respect: *U.S. Department of State*, Office of the Coordinator for Counterterrorism, Designation of *Kata'ib Hizballah*, 26 Jun. 2009. Available: https://www.state.gov/j/ct/rls/other/des/143209.htm (last visited: 20 Mar. 2018); Home Office, Policy Paper, Proscribed Terrorist Organisations, last updated 29 Sep. 2017. Available: https://www.gov.uk/government/publications/proscribed-terror-groups-or-organisations--2/proscribed-terrorist-groups-or-organisations-accessible-version#list-of-proscribed-international-terrorist-groups (last visited: 20 Mar. 2018). Furthermore, the EU has determined that the '*Hizballah Military Wing*' has been involved in terrorist acts and that it should be added to the list of persons, groups and entities whose funds, other financial assets or economic sources shall be frozen. Council Implementing Regulation (EU) No. 714/2013 of 25 Jul. 2013, OJ L 201 of 26 Jul. 2013, p. 10. This regulation has been since repealed and currently in force is Council Implementing Regulation (EU) 2019/24 of 8 Jan. 2019 implementing Art. 2(3) of Regulation (EC) No. 2580/2001 on specific restrictive measures directed against certain persons and entities with a view to combating terrorism, and repealing Implementing Regulation (EU) 2018/1071, OJ L 6 of 9 Jan. 2019, p. 2.

250. These have been enacted to the purpose of implementing 98/733/JHA: Joint action of 21 Dec. 1998 adopted by the Council on the basis of Art. K.3 of the Treaty on European Union, on making it a criminal offence to participate in a criminal organisation in the Member States of the European Union, OJ L 351 of 29 Dec. 1998, p. 1. This has been repealed by Council Framework Decision 2008/841/JHA of 24 Oct. 2008 on the fight against organised crime, OJ L 300 of 11 Nov. 2008, p. 42.

sentence was imposed for money laundering.[251] The Supreme Court of Cyprus upheld said judgment of the ruling court and the four-year imprisonment sentence.[252]

103. Alongside that, a dissenting opinion was expressed by a judge of the Supreme Court of Cyprus. It was suggested that evaluating whether the organization is a criminal one, may only be answered through evaluation of the organization's establishment and activity connected to committing offences. Thereafter, dissenting opinion would set aside the appealed judgment and evaluated the facts itself. Then it reached the conclusion that the actions performed in Cyprus, which in essence consisted of monitoring Israelis, did not prove beyond reasonable doubt and without the assistance of any assumptions that the aforementioned crimes would be committed. Dissenting opinion further added that the declared hatred of *Hizballah* against the people of Israel, which 'is not a crime or may not be per se convicted or even criticized, as it had to do with history and the memories of peoples', did not lead to a robust conclusion that the actions of the accused were preparation for any of the accused crimes. Thus, dissenting opinion found the conclusion of the District Court of Limassol false and suggested that said monitoring could take place for reasons other than the one accepted by the District Court. Albeit, no suggestion of such reason was proposed. The accused would, therefore, be acquitted of the conviction to participation and approval of committing a crime, according to the dissenting opinion.

4. Object Injuring a Third Person or Other Property

104. The object of an agreement involving or implying injury to the person or property of another is illicit.[253] This ground which renders the object of an agreement illicit is frequently quoted among the other grounds of illegality. However, no case law on this was issued until today by the courts in Cyprus. In view of this, as well as due to the clear and unequivocal wording of the provision, any analysis thereon is unnecessary.

5. Immoral Object and Object Opposing to Public Policy

105. When an agreement's object is immoral (in Greek 'αντίκειται στα χρηστά ήθη' in Turkish 'ahlâk dışı') or opposed to public policy (in Greek 'δημόσια

---

251. *Cyprus v. Hossam Taleb Yaacoub*, District Court of Limassol, Criminal Case No. 17714/12, Judgment of 28 Mar. 2013, not published in CLR.
252. *Hossam Taleb Yaacoub v. Cyprus,* Supreme Court of Cyprus, Criminal Appeal No. 72/2013, Judgment of 19 Mar. 2014, not published in CLR.
253. Section 23(d) Cap. 149.

πολιτική' in Turkish 'kamu siyaseti'), it is illicit.[254] This provision offers little certainty, as no further guidance regarding the meaning of morality or public policy is offered.

106. Case law affirmed that the view on public policy[255] in Cyprus aligns with the one in England. A service agreement by a public officer without permission of the competent authority was ruled to be illegal and thus void as opposed to public policy, alongside to infringement of statutory provisions and therefore forbidden by law.[256] Public policy was held to be that principle of the law which holds that no citizen lawfully do that which has a tendency to be injurious to the public, or against the public good, which may be termed, as it sometimes has been, the policy of the law, or public policy in relation to the administration of the law.[257] Public policy is perceived as a matter of public concern, that being a matter which pre-eminently affects the interests of the public.[258] In addition, it was noted that public policy is an unruly horse, and dangerous to ride. No evidence is given in these public policy cases. The court is to say, as a matter of law, that a matter is against public policy, and void. The question whether a particular agreement is contrary to public policy is a question of law.[259] Also, it was ruled that the doctrine of public policy should be involved only in clear cases, in which the harm to the public is substantially incontestable and does not depend upon the idiosyncratic inferences of a few judicial minds.[260]

107. Public policy, enshrined generally in Cyprus in section 23(e) Cap. 149, was further discussed in a case discussing enforcement of foreign judgment. In *Pilavachi v. International Chemical*,[261] it was affirmed that the principles of English public policy, which lead to refusal of enforcing a foreign acquired right, are equally applicable in Cyprus. A probable classification of cases are: (a) where the fundamental conceptions of English justice are disregarded; (b) where the English conceptions of morality are infringed; (c) where a transaction prejudices the interests of the United Kingdom or its good relations with foreign powers; and (d) where a foreign law or status offends the English conceptions of human liberty and freedom of

254. Section 23(e) *ibid.*
255. On public policy and immovable property being owned by Turkish-Cypriots *see Perihan Mustafa Korkut v. Georgiou* 1 CLR 905 (2008).
256. *Glamor Development Ltd v. Christodoulou* 1 CLR 444 (1984).
257. *Ibid.*, citing *Egerton v. Brownlow* All ER Rep. 970 (1843–1860).
258. *Panayiotou v. Solomou* 1 CLR 779 (1979).
259. *Glamor Development Ltd v. Christodoulou* 1 CLR 444 (1984), citing *Mogul Steamship Co v. McGregor, Gow & Co* AC 25 H.L (1982).
260. *Glamor Development Ltd v. Christodoulou* 1 CLR 444 (1984), citing *Fender v. Mildmay* 3 All ER 402 (1937).
261. *Pilavachi & Co Ltd v. International Chemical Co Ltd* 1 CLR 97 (1965).

action.[262] It was further ruled that public policy derives from statutory provisions.[263] Lastly, the practice of upholding agreements, which have been concluded between competent parties, was decided to be equally a matter of public policy.[264]

B. Illegality Due to Agreed Content

108. Along with the aforementioned codification of cases involving an illicit object rendering an agreement illicit, same outcome may be the result of the agreed content of an agreement. The relevant statutory provisions may be classified into three groups for the purpose of the present analysis. The first group relates to breach of human rights or, fundamental rights and freedoms, enshrined in the Constitution, the European Convention on Human Rights and the Charter of Fundamental Rights of the EU. The second group involves cases, where impossibility has been agreed, whereas the third group concerns matters of wager, a sub-matter of public moral if seen from a historical perspective of the time of the statute's enactment.

109. The first group's statutory prohibitions provide the following, in the order set out in the law. Every agreement in restraint of the marriage of any person is void.[265] Further, every agreement by which anyone is restrained from exercising a lawful profession, trade, or business of any kind, is to that extent void.[266] Equally, every agreement, by which any party thereto is restrained absolutely from enforcing his rights under or in respect of any contract, by the usual legal proceedings in the courts, or which limits the time within which he may thus enforce his rights, is void to that extent.[267]

110. Exceptions to the aforementioned restrictions are set out in the law. With reference to exercising profession, trade, or business of any kind, exceptions are foreseen. In particular, contracts not to carry on business of which goodwill is sold, are valid. The statutory provision reads that one who sells the goodwill of a business may agree with the buyer to refrain from carrying onto a similar business, within specified local limits, so long as the buyer or any person deriving title to the goodwill from him, carries on a like business therein, provided that such limits appear to the court reasonable, regard being had to the nature of the business.[268] In addition, contracts between partners prior to dissolution are also valid. It is foreseen that partners may, upon or in anticipation of a dissolution of the partnership, agree

262. *Ibid.*, citing *In re Macartney* 1 Ch. 522 (1921); *Huntington v. Attrill* AC 150 (1893); *Jacobson v. Frachon* 138 LT 386 (1928); *Scarpetta v. Lowenfeld* 27 TLR 509 (1911).
263. *Diaheiristiko Symvoulio Emporikis Sholis Mitsi Lethymou v. Petraki* 1 CLR 941 (1998); *Glamor Development v. Christodoulou* 1 CLR 444 (1984).
264. *Diaheiristiko Symvoulio Emporikis Sholis Mitsi Lethymou v. Petraki* 1 CLR 941 (1998); *Electromatic Const. v. Azov* 1 CLR 768 (1988).
265. Section 26 Cap. 149.
266. Section 27(1) *ibid.*
267. Section 28(1) *ibid.*
268. Section 27(2)(a) *ibid.*

that some or all of them will not carry on a business similar to that of the partnership within such local limits as are referred to above regarding selling goodwill.[269] Furthermore, contracts during continuance of partnership are equally valid. It is set out that partners may agree that someone or all of them will not carry on any business, other than that of the partnership, during the continuance of the partnership.[270] Lastly, arbitration clauses are not deemed to restrain legal proceedings[271] and are hence valid. Same applies to agreeing to refer to arbitration any question that has already arisen between the parties.[272]

111. Turning to the group of illicit agreements due to impossibility, uncertain agreements,[273] as already mentioned above, as well as agreements to do an act impossible in itself[274] are void. In addition and related to contingence, contingent agreements to do or not to do anything, if an impossible event happens, are void, whether the impossibility of the event is known or not to the parties to the agreement at the time when it is made.[275]

112. Lastly, agreements by way of wager are void. Furthermore, no legal proceedings may be brought for recovering anything alleged to be won on any wager or entrusted to any person to abide the result of any game or other uncertain event on which any wager is made.[276] The latter provision is identical with section 30 of the Indian Contract Act 1872 and closely similar to section 18 of the English Gaming Act 1845.[277] Yet, operation of betting services and casinos is a regulated and licit activity, as analysed below in paragraphs 205 et seq. below.

IV. Unenforceable Contracts

113. Agreements legally unenforceable are void.[278] Therefore, Law of Contract in Cyprus follows the common law approach, according to which the question of illegality in an agreement may arise in connection with its performance. Hence, an agreement may be unenforceable by the offending party, where illegality arises from the fact that the mode of performance adopted by the party performing it is in violation of some statute, even though the agreement as agreed upon between the parties was capable of being performed in a perfectly legal manner.[279] Equally adopted is the approach, that an agreement which is entered into with the object of committing an illegal act is unenforceable. The application of this principle depends upon

269. Section 27(2)(b) *ibid.*
270. Section 27(2)(c) *ibid.*
271. Section 28(2) *ibid.*
272. Section 28(3) *ibid.*
273. Section 29 *ibid.*
274. Section 56(1) *ibid.*
275. Section 36 *ibid.*
276. Section 30 *ibid.*
277. *Constantinou v. Panayi a.a.* 1 CLR 191 (1968).
278. Section 2(2)(g) Cap. 149.
279. *Kanaris v. Tosoun* 1 CLR 637 (1969), citing *Anderson Ltd v. Daniel* 1 K.B. 138 (1924).

proof of the intent, at the time the agreement was made, to break the law; if the intent is mutual the agreement is not enforceable at all, and, if unilateral, it is unenforceable at the suit of the party who is proved to have it.[280] Actually, the first principle is an offshoot of the second principle that a prohibited agreement will not be enforced. Furthermore, the law shall neither enforce the original illegal agreement nor will it allow the parties to enforce a security for the purchase money, which by the original bargain was tainted with illegality.[281]

§4. The Consequences of a Defect of Consent or a Lack of Substantive Validity

I. Avoidance of the Contract: Nullity

114. The provisions regarding age[282] as well as soundness of mind[283] provide for avoidance. In particular, the essence of these provisions lies in enabling a party under such disadvantage to avoid agreements to his detriment, where his disadvantage has been taken advantage of, by the other party.[284]

115. The consequence of a defect of consent depends on the precise defect. Mistake by both parties to the agreement in question leads to it being void.[285] Misrepresentation makes the agreement a voidable contract at the option of the party whose consent was so caused.[286] The same party may, if he thinks fit, insist that the contract shall be performed and that he shall be put in the position in which he would have been if the representations made had been true.[287] Undue influence makes the agreement a voidable contract at the option of the party whose consent was so caused.[288] Any such contract may be set aside either absolutely or, if the party who was entitled to avoid it has received any benefit thereunder, upon such terms and conditions as the court may seem just.[289] Lastly, coercion makes the agreement a voidable contract at the option of the party whose consent was so caused.[290]

116. Agreements lacking substantive validity may be void agreements or voidable contracts. The specific consequence depends on the precise defect, as explained above for defect of consent. When the pursued cause is illicit, the agreement is

---

280. *Ibid.*, citing *St. John Shipping Corporation v. Joseph Rank Ltd* 1 QB 267 (1957).
281. *Kanaris v. Tosoun* 1 CLR 637 (1969), citing *Fisher v. Bridges* 3 E & B 642 (1854).
282. Section 11 Cap. 149. *See Vartholomeou v. Kannaourou* 1 CLR 221 (1978), citing *Edwards v. Carter* AC 360 (1893); *Cornell v. Harrison a.a.* All ER Rep 1827 (1916–1917); *Carter v. Silber* 2 Ch. 278 (1892); *Savoy Overseers v. Art Union of London* AC 296 (1896); *Attorney-General v. Ellis* 2 QB 466 (1895).
283. Section 12 Cap. 149.
284. *Papadopoulou v. Polycarpou* 1 CLR 352 (1968).
285. Section 21(1) Cap. 149.
286. Section 19(1) *ibid.*
287. Section 19(2) *ibid.*
288. Section 20(1) *ibid.*
289. Section 20(2) *ibid.*
290. Section 19(1) *ibid.*

void.[291] Fraud makes the agreement a voidable contract at the option of the party whose consent was so caused.[292] The same party may, if he thinks fit, insist that the contract shall be performed and that he shall be put in the position in which he would have been if the representations made had been true.[293] Uncertain meaning of an agreement,[294] illicit[295] and impossible object,[296] as well as an impossible contingence,[297] an agreement restraining marriage[298] or unenforceability[299] constitute such agreement void. Especially agreements restraining from exercising a lawful profession, trade, or business of any kind, are void only to the extent that are affected by illegality.[300] This equally applies to agreements in restraint of access to the usual legal proceedings in the courts.[301]

II. Retroactive Effect of Avoidance or Nullity

117. An explicit provision on, whether the effect of avoidance or nullity is retroactive, is not foreseen in the statute. However, case law has affirmed *rescission ab initio* for agreements made by mistake, fraud or defect of consent.[302] Further, it follows from the provisions on returning advantages and benefits, which are explained below under paragraphs 164 and 165, that the effect is indeed retroactive. In addition, this conclusion is equally reached, when it is contemplated that, upon nullity of the contract, the legal ground for the provided advantages and benefits has lapsed, whereas the cause of nullity was existing already when the agreements were made. Hence, at no time a legal ground for acquiring advantages and benefits did exist.

III. Damages

118. Damages as a consequence of a defect of consent or lack of substantive validity are regulated by the general provisions on damages, those being sections 64, 65 and 75 Cap. 149, which are elaborated in paragraphs 170 et seq. below.

---

291. Section 23 Cap. 149. *See Syrimi v. Organismos Chrimatodotiseos Pagkypriaki Ltd* 1 CLR 1131 (2010).
292. Section 19(1) Cap. 149.
293. Section 19(2) *ibid.*
294. Section 29 *ibid.*
295. Section 23 *ibid.*
296. Section 56(1) and (2) *ibid.*
297. Section 36 *ibid.*
298. Section 26 *ibid.*
299. Section 2(2)(g) *ibid.*
300. Section 27(1) *ibid. See Kimon Tutorial Centre (Idiotika Frontistiria) Ltd v. Gabriel* 1 CLR 2069 (1998).
301. Section 28(1) Cap. 149.
302. *Metaxas Loizides Syrimis & Co a.o. v. L K Globalsoft Co Ltd* 1 CLR 54 (2007).

Chapter 3. The Contents of a Contract

§1. The Different Clauses

I. Ascertaining of Express Terms

119. Express terms ('σαφείς όροι' in Greek, 'açık şartları' in Turkish) in contracts are divided into two groups: conditions and warranties. Conditions ('ουσιώδεις όροι' in Greek, 'esaslı şart' in Turkish) relate to vital part(s) of a contract, violation of which gives to the innocent party the right to terminate the contract.[303] Especially time is considered a condition, in addition to it being explicitly agreed, where the nature or the surroundings of the contract suggest that time shall be precisely complied with. Furthermore, the innocent party may transform time into a condition, by providing a reasonable time for compliance.[304] Warranties ('απλοί όροι' in Greek, 'koşul' in Turkish) do not relate to vital part(s) of a contract. Upon violation they give to the innocent party the mere right to damages by the guilty one.[305]

II. Implied Terms

120. The notion 'implied terms' ('εξυπακουόμενοι όροι' in Greek, 'zımni şartları' in Turkish) is used in different senses. Sometimes it denotes some term, which does not depend on the actual intention of the parties but on a rule of Law. More often, however, it is some term, of which it can be predicted that 'it goes without saying', some term not expressed, but necessary to give to the transaction such business efficacy as the parties must have intended. Under no circumstances, may the court embark on a reconstruction of the agreement on equitable principles, or on a view of what the parties should, in the court's opinion, reasonably have contemplated.[306] This reaffirms that the terms of a contract are defined by the contracting parties. It is not for the court to replenish an imperfect contract.[307]

121. It has been ruled that in construing an express contract the court may imply a term or terms into the agreement if it is clear from the nature of the transaction that had the parties adverted to the situation they would have intended to incorporate such term into their agreement. The object of raising an implication from the presumed intention of the parties is to give to the transaction such efficacy as both parties must have intended that at all events it should have. But the general presumption is that the parties have expressed every material term which they intended

303. *Savva v. Laiki Asfalistiki Etaireia Ltd* 1(B) CLR 1609 (2009).
304. *George Charalambous Ltd v. Kalos Kafes Ltd a.o.* 1 CLR 199 (1997).
305. *Savva v. Laiki Asfalistiki Etaireia Ltd* 1(B) CLR 1609 (2009).
306. *Portsmouth v. Cyprus Inland Telecommunications Authority* 1 CLR 87 (1967), citing *Luxor (Eastbourne) Ltd a.o. v. Cooper* 1 All ER 33 (1941).
307. *Alpan Furnishings v. Demades* 1(E) CLR 170 (1989); *A. Athinodoros (Antiprosopeies) Asphalion Ltd v. Marketrends Financial Services Ltd* 1 CLR 1205 (2008).

should govern their agreement, whether oral or in writing; and no term should be implied if the contract is effective without the proposed term and capable of being fulfilled as it stands.[308]

122. In *Konteades v. Yusukjian,*[309] the building contract in question entailed a clause providing that orders for extras must be in writing, whereas orders for extras were given verbally. The defendant, who admittedly gave the verbal orders, declined payment on the ground of those not given in writing, as provided in the contract. It was decided that in such cases, it is open to the court to find, if there was an implied promise by the building owner that the work as ordered should be paid for as an extra, although the order is verbal instead of written as required by the contract. It would be a fraud on the part of the employer to have desired these alterations and additions to be made, to have stood and seen the expenditure going on upon them, to have taken the benefit of that expenditure, and to refuse payment on the ground that the expenditure was incurred without proper orders having been given for the purpose.[310] Thus, the Supreme Court of Cyprus upheld the judgment of the District Court ordering payment for extras, although relevant orders were given orally.[311]

III. Standard Terms and Exemption Clauses

123. Both statutes and case law are silent as to standard terms. Albeit laws regulating consumers' contracts provide for protection against unfair terms[312] and unfair business-to-consumer commercial practices in the internal market,[313] as well as ensuring consumer rights.[314]

---

308. *Portsmouth v. Cyprus Inland Telecommunications Authority* 1 CLR 87 (1967).
309. 15 (1) CLR 83.
310. *Konteades v. Yusukjian* 15 (1) CLR 83, citing *Hill v. South Staffordshire Railway* 12 LT Rep 63 (1865).
311. *Konteades v. Yusukjian* 15 (1) CLR 83.
312. Law on Abusive Terms in Consumer Contracts ('ο περί Καταχρηστικών Ρητρών σε Καταναλωτικές Συμβάσεις Νόμος') No. 93 of 1996, OG I(I) No. 3097 of 8 Nov. 1996, p. 476 (as last amended by amending Law No. 49 of 2016, OG I(I) No. 4563 of 22 Apr. 2016, p. 621) that implements Council Directive 93/13/EEC of 5 Apr. 1993 on unfair terms in consumer contracts OJ L 95 of 21 Apr. 1993, p. 29, as last amended by Directive 2011/83/EU of the European Parliament and of the Council of 25 Oct. 2011 on consumer rights, OJ L 304 of 22 Nov. 2011, p. 64. Further amendments have been proposed through Proposal for a Directive of the European Parliament and of the Council amending Council Directive 93/13/EEC of 5 Apr. 1993, Directive 98/6/EC of the European Parliament and of the Council, Directive 2005/29/EC of the European Parliament and of the Council and Directive 2011/83/EU of the European Parliament and of the Council as regards better enforcement and modernisation of EU consumer protection rules, COM(2018) 185 final of 11 Apr. 2018. Available: https://eur-lex.europa.eu.
313. Law on Unfair Business-to-Consumer Commercial Practices ('ο περί των Αθέμιτων Εμπορικών Πρακτικών των Επιχειρήσεων προς τους Καταναλωτές Νόμος') No. 103 of 2007, OG I(I) No. 4135 of 18 Jul. 2007, p. 886, as last amended by amending Law No. 135 of 2013, OG I(I) No. 4415 of 22 Nov. 2013, which implements Directive 2005/29/EC of the European Parliament and of the Council of 11 May 2005 concerning unfair business-to-consumer commercial practices in the internal market, OJ L 149 of 11 Jun. 2005, p. 22. Amendments to this directive have been proposed through COM(2018) 185 final (*see* in this regard n 312 above).
314. Law on Consumers Rights ('ο περί των Δικαιωμάτων των Καταναλωτών Νόμος') No. 133 of 2013, OG I(I) No. 4412 of 8 Nov. 2013, as last amended by amending Law No. 187 of 2017, OG

124. Scarce case law exists regarding exemption clauses. It is ruled that such clauses in insurance policies are construed with the utmost strictness.[315] Further, it has been decided that such clauses should be construed as not applying to a situation created by a fundamental breach of contract, whereas any doubt as regards to their construction must operate against the author of the document in which it is contained.[316]

IV. Penalty Clauses

125. Penalty clauses are regulated in section 74 Cap. 149 and are explained in paragraph 62 below. Here, it suffices to say this quantitative stipulation as to damages, which is stated in such a clause, merely sets the ceiling to the damages recoverable. It does not bind the court, which nevertheless has the discretion to award a reasonable amount.

V. Arbitration Clauses

126. No statutory provision regulates in any manner arbitration clauses. Yet, case law offers a vivid insight to domestic understanding of such clauses and to the effect they have. As a general rule, the court should if the circumstances allow lean in favour of giving effect to the arbitration clause to which the parties have agreed and sought to give effect to their intentions.[317] Albeit, courts in Cyprus have the discretion to trial a dispute despite it arising in connection to or from an agreed arbitration clause. To this end, courts in Cyprus take into consideration the location of evidence, the costs, any discomfort of the interested parties, proximity of substantive law of the foreign court, the country, to which the parties connect, whether the desire of the respondents to be bound by an exclusive foreign jurisdiction clause is true or merely procedural benefits are pursued.[318] And they do exercise this

I(I) No. 4633 of 22 Dec. 2017, p. 1262, which implements Directive 2011/83/EU of the European Parliament and of the Council of 25 Oct. 2011 on consumer rights, OJ L 304 of 22 Nov. 2011, p. 64, as last amended by Directive (EU) 2015/2302 of the European Parliament and of the Council of 25 Nov. 2015 on package travel and linked travel arrangements, amending Regulation (EC) No. 2006/2004 and Directive 2011/83/EU of the European Parliament and of the Council and repealing Council Directive 90/314/EEC, OJ L 326 of 11 Dec. 2015, p. 1. Further amendments have been proposed through COM(2018) 185 final (*see* in this regard n 312 above).

315. *Kyrillis Masouri & Bro v. the Employers' Liability Assurance Corporation Ltd* 1 CLR 517 (1969).

316. *Ioannis Kokkalos & Sons Ltd v. Karayiannis* 1 CLR 377 (1975).

317. *Yalta Sea Trade Port v. Emed Chartering Ltd a.o.* 1 CLR 7 (2001), citing *Astro Vendeor Compania Naviera S.A. v. Mabanaft GmbH* 2 Lloyd's Rep 267 (1970); *Paul Smith Ltd v. H & S. (International) Holdings Inc.* 2 Lloyd's Rep 127 (1991).

318. *Synergatiki Kentriki Trapeza Ltd v. The Ship 'Elegance' of Belize* 1 CLR 981 (2005), citing *The Eleftheria* 2 All ER 641 (1969); *The El Amria* 2 Lloyd's Reports 119 (1981); *The Sennar* 2 All ER 104 (1985); *Balkancarimpex Fto v. Leasco Ltd* 1 CLR 815 (1994).

discretion.[319] This not uncommon Cypriot practice refrains from giving effect to the parties' agreement not to litigate and to take part in a sui generis process.[320]

127. In *Oterom v. Christodoulides,*[321] the appellee filed a claim regarding salaries due and other remuneration with courts in Cyprus. The appellant filed an application for a stay and/or set aside of proceedings due to agreed arbitration, as the contract in question contained an arbitration clause, which provided that '[t]his agreement shall be governed by and construed in accordance with the Laws of Greece. Any dispute with respect to the interpretation or application of this agreement shall be finally settled by arbitration in accordance with the rules of conciliation and arbitration of the International Chamber of Commerce'. The ruling court decided that the afore-stated clause was vague, indefinite and general. Notwithstanding this, it further ruled that the dispute that had been brought before it did not constitute a 'dispute' within the meaning of the same clause. Thus, the application was rejected. Said findings of the ruling court were challenged before the appellate court. This court reaffirmed the first finding of the ruling court, as it ruled that the arbitration clause defines the procedural rules for the arbitration, but not the place of arbitration. No further reasoning was offered, and therefore it is not clear, why the appellate court disagrees with – the then Article 14 now – Article 18 of the ICC Rules of Arbitration. With regard to the second finding, the appellate court ruled that the wording 'any dispute' does not necessarily include any claim even if this derives from breaching the terms of a contract. For a 'dispute' to arise, it shall have to relate to the facts relevant to liability or the obligation, or the implications of such facts of law.[322] The court, without offering any further grounds or elaborations accepted that the notion of 'dispute' as explained here, did not include salaries and remunerations. Hence, the judgment of the ruling court was deemed to be correct and the appeal was rejected.

128. Nonetheless, in another case, a clause providing '[a]ny dispute or difference arising out of this contract or in connection therewith which cannot be amicably settled between the parties, shall be finally settled under the provisions of the Arbitration Law (Cap. 4) of the Republic of Cyprus' was deemed clear and accurate without any need for interpretation.[323]

---

319. *See* in this regard *Cyprus Phassouri Plantations Co. Ltd v. Adriatica di Navigazione SP of Venice* 1 CLR 290 (1985); *PT Kiani Kertas v. Interorient Navigation Company Ltd a.o.* 1 CLR 967 (1999).
320. Gary B. Born, 'Chapter 8: Effects and Enforcement of International Arbitration Agreements', in Gary B. Born (ed.), International Commercial Arbitration (2nd ed., Kluwer Law International 2014) pp. 1256 et seq.
321. *Oterom Ltd v. Christodoulides* 1 CLR 1081 (2002).
322. *Ibid.*, citing *Tradax v. Gueensea Marine Co* 1 CLR 559 (1986); *Steamer Shipping Co Ltd v. Sibyl Trading & Shipping Ltd* 1 CLR 106 (1996).
323. *Pell Frishmann Consultants Ltd v. Cyprus* 1 CLR 33 (2001).

§2. INTERPRETATION

129. Interpretation of a contract is a legal matter to be decided by the court.[324] It aims to crystallizing, of what was agreed between the parties in the specific contract, taking into consideration any other agreements reached prior to signing said contract.[325] In particular, it has been ruled that to some extent decisions on one contract may help by way of analogy or illustration in the decision of another contract. But however similar the contracts may appear, the decision as to each must depend on the consideration of the language of the particular contract, read in the light of the material circumstances of the parties in view of which the contract is made.[326] Prior negotiations, unilateral declarations and subjective intentions shall not be considered.[327] Equally, the manner of the parties after the contract was made shall not be evaluated for the purpose of illuminating its meaning or content.[328]

130. Interpretation tools may only be used, when the meaning of a term is inconclusive.[329] Even the creation of anomalies as such is not a reason for departing from the express provisions of a contract.[330] In the construction process, the first rule is that a term is understood within the context of the contract as a whole.[331] To this extent, the cause of the contract, as revealed by the contract in itself as a whole, is of paramount importance.[332] In fact, looking at the whole of the instrument, and seeing what one must regard, as its main purpose, one must reject words, indeed whole provisions, if they are inconsistent with what one assumes to be the main purpose of the contract.[333] Even the name given to a contract is not conclusive. Moreover, the nature of a contract depends upon the substance of the contract and not upon the name given thereto.[334] Witnesses or parties to a dispute may not define the meaning or the nature of a contract.[335] Only when a single or more blanks are noted in the contract or doubts regarding the correct interpretation are emerged, may extrinsic evidence ('εξωγενής μαρτυρία' in Greek, 'sözlü şahadet' in Turkish) be admissible

324. *Alexandrou v. Komodromou* (1997) 1 CLR 576; *Karaoli a.o. v. Laouri a.a.* 1 CLR 225 (2008).
325. *Lefkaritis a.o. v. Beach Hotels Ltd* 1 CLR 194 (2000).
326. *Ch.P.Th. Alexandrou Ltd v. Symvouliou Apoheteuseon Leukosias* 1 CLR 630 (1999), citing *Luxor v. Cooper* 1 All ER 33 (1941).
327. *Kyriakides v. Kyriakides* 1 CLR 76 (1976), citing *Prenn v. Simmonds* 3 All ER 237 (1971); *Theologou a.a. v. Ktimatikis Etaireias Nemesis Ltd* 1 CLR 407 (1998); *Zinonos a.o. v. Cyprus Popular Bank (Financing) Ltd* 1 CLR 927 (2002); *Karaoli a.o. v. Laouri a.a.* 1 CLR 225 (2008).
328. *Kyriakides v. Kyriakides* 1 CLR 76 (1976), citing *James Miller and Partners Ltd v. Whitworth Street Estates (Manchester) Ltd* 1 All ER 796 (1970); *Gort Processing Centre Ltd v. Cyprus* 1 CLR 442 (1997); *Amethyst Distributors Ltd v. Ieras Monis Kykkou* 1 CLR 199 (2011).
329. *Pell Frishmann Consultants Ltd v. Cyprus* 1A CLR 33 (2001).
330. *G.I.P. Constructions Ltd v. Assiotis* (1982) 1 CLR 535, citing *Stock v. Frank Jones* 1 All ER 948 (1978).
331. *Georgiki Etaireia D.G. Phoutas v. Etaireia Vasos, Emporoi Georgikon Proionton Ltd* 1 CLR 168 (1993).
332. *Karaoli a.o. v. Laouri a.a.* 1 CLR 225 (2008); *Lambrou v. Paraschou a.o.* 1 CLR 397 (1993).
333. *Alexandrou v. Komodromou a.a.* 1 CLR 576 (1997), citing *Glynn & Co v. Margetson* All ER Rep 693 (1891–1894).
334. *Papakleovoulou v. Elia a.a.* 1 CLR 222 (1972).
335. *Alexandrou v. Komodromou* 1 CLR 576 (1997).

before the court,[336] although such evidence may vary or add to the written instrument.[337] This test also applies in queries for the true nature of a transaction.[338]

131. The second rule relates to the intention of the parties. In view of the settled point of law that a document does reveal the intention of the contracting parties through the wording of thereof,[339] the court has the duty to confirm what the parties meant through the wording they chose and to apply the parties' intention, as this was expressed. The court may not proceed with guessing the parties' intention and replace the explicit intention with a fictive one.[340] However, having regard to the general principle of avoiding injustice and absurdity, any construction would, if possible, be rejected, which enabled a person to defeat or impair the obligation of his contract by his own act, or otherwise to profit by his own wrong.[341]

132. The third rule, which seems to contradict the aforementioned one, orders to attribute to the wording of the contract, the meaning attributed to such by ordinary reasonable men.[342]

133. Lastly, the commercial scope of a contract, as well as practice or customs established to a specific commercial activity or profession related to the specific contract, shall be taken into consideration.[343] In fact, it was held that the contract must be construed in the light of the course of business which was well known to the contracting parties in view of the state of affairs prevailing at the port of Famagusta, particularly during the month of May.[344]

§3. Conditional Contracts

134. Contingent contract ('σύμβαση υπό αίρεση' in Greek, 'koşula bağlı sözleşme' in Turkish) is a contract to do or not to do something, if some event, collateral to such contract, does or does not happen.[345] Contingent contracts may only be enforced by law, when the specific uncertain future event has happened. If the event becomes impossible, such contracts become void.[346]

---

336. *Georgiki Etaireia D.G. Phoutas v. Etaireia Vasos, Emporoi Georgikon Proionton Ltd* 1 CLR 168 (1993).
337. *Xenopoulos v. Thomas Nelson (Insurance) Ltd a.o.* 1 CLR 674 (1982).
338. *A.B.C. Ltd v. Koiliaris a.a.* 1 CLR 41 (1996).
339. *Lazouras v. Skyllouriotou* 1A CLR 168 (1992).
340. *Saab a.o. v. The Holy Monastery of Ayios Neophytos* 1 CLR 499 (1982); *Theocharous v. Pastelli* 1 CLR 240 (1993); *Oikonomou a.a. v. Ttofini a.a.* 1 CLR 436 (1993).
341. *Papadopoulou v. Polycarpou* 1 CLR 352 (1968), citing *Kish v. Taylor* 1 KB 625 (1911).
342. *Theologou a.a. v. Ktimatikis Etaireias Nemesis Ltd* 1 CLR 407 (1998); *Karaoli a.o. v. Laouri a.a.* 1 CLR 225 (2008).
343. *Georgiki Etaireia D.G. Phoutas v. Etaireia Vasos, Emporoi Georgikon Proionton Ltd* 1 CLR 168 (1993).
344. *Hellenic Lines v. Artemis Co Ltd* 1 CLR 139 (1969).
345. Section 31 Cap. 149.
346. Section 32 *ibid.*

135. The agreed contingence may consist of an uncertain future event or the action of a third party. These may be positive, in the meaning of them happening, or negative, in the meaning of them not happening. If the agreed contingence is a negative uncertain future event, the contingent contract may only be enforced, when the happening of that event becomes impossible.[347] If the agreed contingence is a positive uncertain future event within a fixed time and this does not take place within the set time frame or becomes impossible, then the contingent agreement is void.[348] Should the agreed contingence be a negative uncertain future event within a fixed time, the contingent contract may be enforced by law, when the fixed time expires and the event has not happened. This equally applies, when it becomes certain that such event will not happen.[349] Lastly, if the agreed event is impossible, the contingent agreement is void, regardless of the impossibility of the event being known or unknown to the parties of the agreement at the time when it was made.[350]

136. Turning to contingence being the way in which a third party will act, the following is foreseen in the law. A contract entailing such a contingence at an unspecified time is considered to become impossible when such person does anything which renders it impossible that he should so act within any definite time, or otherwise than under further contingencies.[351] Such contingence may be the acceptance of a specific bank to finance a transaction,[352] the securing, by the appellants of the agency of a group of companies in Portugal,[353] or the approval of the competent authority.[354]

347. Section 33 *ibid.*
348. Section 35(1) *ibid.*
349. Section 35(2) *ibid.*
350. Section 36 *ibid.*
351. Section 34 *ibid.*
352. *Cyprus Import Corporation Ltd v. Kaisis* 1 CLR 16 (1974).
353. *Courtis a.a. v. Iasonides* 1 CLR 83 (1972).
354. *Molivo Ltd a.a. v. Hudaverdi Mustafa Hudaverdi a.a.* 1 CLR 278 (2013).

Chapter 4. Privity of Contract

§1. The Rule of Privity of Contract

I. Third Parties and the Contract

137. The parties to an agreement, and solely these parties, enjoy rights from said agreement; third persons may not claim any rights, due to absence of the privity of contract.[355] If privity of contract is not found, claims based thereon are dismissed.[356] Hence, a person who is not party to a contract may not raise a claim regarding the same contract,[357] be added as a co-defendant,[358] or be a respondent in such a claim.[359] The rule of *res inter alios acta alteri nocere non debet* was held to be applicable in Cyprus.[360] Yet, it is acceptable that one of the parties to the agreement may be the nominee or trustee of the third person and therefore the trust's beneficiaries can take the benefit of the contract.[361]

II. Contract for the Benefit of a Third Party

138. An exception to the rule of privity of contract is when an agent is engaged for making a contract.[362] Agency ('αντιπροσωπεία' in Greek, 'vekillik' in Turkish) is a specific contract, thoroughly regulated in sections 142–198 Cap. 149. Furthermore, a quasi-contract to the benefit of a third party may be made. In particular, it is set out that a person who is interested in the payment of money which another is bound by law to pay, and who therefore pays it, is entitled to be reimbursed by the other.[363]

§2. Transfer of Contractual Rights

139. A statutory provision settling distinctly the assignment of rights is absent. However, relevant case law has been issued, recognizing that the routes of assignment ('εκχώρηση' in Greek, 'temlik' in Turkish) lie in equity.[364] In *Chrysostomou v. G.S. Chalkousi & Sons*,[365] assignment of debt was discussed. It was held that a

355. *Kallice Holding Co. Ltd v. MTR Metals (Overseas) Ltd* (No. 2) 1B CLR 946 (1996).
356. *U Drive Company Ltd v. Panayi a.a.* 1 CLR 544 (1980); *Kourris v. Alpo Ltd a.o.* 1 CLR 217 (1981).
357. *Pirillou v. Konnari* 1 CLR 1153 (2000).
358. *Sonco Canning Ltd v. 'Adriatica' (Societe Per Azioni Di Navigazione)* 1 CLR 127 (1973); *Cyprus Trading Corporation Ltd v. ZIM Israel Navigation Co. Ltd a.a.* 1 CLR 1335 (2000).
359. *U Drive Company Ltd v. Efstathios Panayi a.a.* 1 CLR 544 (1980).
360. *Merkis v. Intertobacco (Cyprus) Ltd* 1 CLR 1091 (2003).
361. *Pirillou v. Konnari* 1 CLR 1153 (2000), citing *In re Empress Engineering Company* 16 Ch. D. 125.
362. *Eurogal Surveys Ltd v. D. Trade International Ltd*, Civil Appeal No. 348/2009 of 17 Oct. 2014, not reported in CLR.
363. Section 69 Cap. 149.
364. *Louka v. Eurolife Ltd* 1 CLR 1524 (2009).
365. 1 CLR 10 (1978).

debt is a legal chose in action and it was accepted that there could be an equitable assignment of a legal chose in action without having any particular form because equity looks to the intent rather than the form.[366] In *Markidou v. Kiliaris a.a.*,[367] the issue of assigning rights under a contract for the sale of land was decided. Although a single case of assignment of rights under a contract for the sale of land was not found, the court was not convinced not to apply the general principle of equitable assignment in such contracts. It continued holding that the rights acquired under a contract for the sale of land are personal, due to a contract for the sale of land not creating rights in rem. Hence, as such, these rights are prima facie assignable. It also clarified, that no specific form is required to effect an assignment, as form is never significant in equity. It lastly, affirmed that the judicial trend is towards extending the class of rights assignable in equity.[368] An agreement to assign a legal chose was reaffirmed in *Fetokakis a.a. v. Cyprus Trading Corporation Plc*.[369]

§3. The Special Case of a 'Subcontract', for Example, the (Nominated) Subcontractor in Building Contracts

140. Subcontracts are regulated in a specific manner neither by statutes nor by case law save for some exceptions in contracts with the government that are explained below (*see* in this respect paragraphs 339 et seq.).

§4. *Actio Pauliana*

141. A legal instrument bearing the characteristics of an *actio pauliana* is regulated not in Cap. 149, but rather in the Fraudulent Transfers of Property Made to Hinder Creditors[370] (hereinafter 'Cap. 62'). The intention of this enactment is to prevent fraud, or rather to prevent creditors being injured by the fraud of debtors and it must be construed to give effect to that intention, so far as possible.[371]

142. According to the main statutory provision, every gift, sale, pledge, mortgage or other transfer or disposal of any movable or immovable property made by any person with the intent to hinder or delay his creditors or any of them in recovering from him, his or their debts shall be deemed to be fraudulent and shall be invalid as against such creditor or creditors. Notwithstanding any such gift, sale,

---

366. *Chrysostomou v. G.S. Chalkousi & Sons* 1 CLR 10 (1978), citing *Inland Revenue Commissioners v. Electric and Musical Industries Ltd* 1 All ER 120 (1949); *Gorringe v. Irwell India Rubber and Gutta Percha Works* 34 Ch. D. 128 (1886).
367. 1 CLR 392 (1983).
368. *Markidou v. Kiliaris a.a.* 1 CLR 392 (1983), citing *Trendtex Trading corpn.v. Credit Suisse* 3 All ER 721 (1980).
369. *Fetokakis a.a. v. Cyprus Trading Corporation Plc*, Joined Civil Appeals Nos. 328/2010 and 431/2011 of 31 Mar. 2017, not reported in CLR, citing *Three Rivers DC v. Bank of England* 4 All ER 312 (1995).
370. Fraudulent Transfers Avoidance of 24 Apr. 1886, Ch. 62 of the Laws, London, 1959 edition, as amended.
371. *Christodoulides v. Mehmed Pasha* 10 (1) CLR 82.

pledge, mortgage or other transfer or disposal, the property purported to be transferred or otherwise dealt with may be seized and sold in satisfaction of any judgment debt due from the person making such gift, sale, pledge, mortgage or other transfer or disposal.[372] The meaning of 'transfer' ('μεταβίβαση' in Greek, 'devredilme' in Turkish) was elaborated in *Savides v. Haji Stavrinou.*[373] It was ruled that the term transfer is possible to be used in a wide sense to cover every part of a dealing from the first offer to final registration of the accepted offer and cannot refer to registration of immovable property only. Furthermore, it was established that the law had a wide scope addressing in general acts done between parties. The term 'property' ('περιουσία' in Greek, 'mal' in Turkish) describes rights under contract, which have a value and can be sold, and refers to such, which can be transferred or assigned gratis.[374] Necessary prerequisite for avoiding a contract deemed fraudulent under Cap. 62 is that the purchaser, mortgagee, transferee or assignee, as the case may be, is shown to have accepted it with knowledge that such transaction was made with the intent to delay or defraud his creditors.[375] The crucial time for ascertaining the existence or non-existence of fraud, good faith and valuable consideration is the time of execution.[376]

143. Any transfer or disposal of property deemed to be fraudulent under the aforementioned, may be set aside by an order of the court, following an application by any judgment creditor.[377] Such a creditor is any person to whom the debtor is actually indebted as well as any competent authority lawfully putting into execution any judgment given against the debtor, and every person, in whom the property of the debtor or the right to sell and dispose of it shall either by his own act or by operation of law become vested for the common benefit of all the persons to whom he is indebted.[378] The creditor, who applies for such avoidance, must be the one who was intended at the time of the transfer to be delayed or hindered in recovering his debt from the transferor. Cap. 62 does not provide a remedy for a 'subsequent creditor', that being a creditor who was not in the contemplation of the debtor at the time of the fraudulent transfer.[379] No regard shall be taken of whether the act in question was made before or after the commencement of an action or other proceeding wherein the right to recover the debt has been established.[380]

144. The onus of proof when a relative is involved in the transaction is specially regulated by the law. In particular, when a transfer or assignment of any property is made to any parent, spouse, child, brother or sister of the transferor or assignor, the onus of proving that such transfer or assignment was bona fide rests upon both the

372. Section 3(1) Cap. 62.
373. *Savides v. Haji Stavrinou, Haji Sava and Yannadji* 13 (1) CLR 29.
374. *Christodoulides v. Mehmed Pasha* 10 (1) CLR 82.
375. Section 3(3) Cap. 62.
376. *Kotsara v. The Official Receiver and Registrar, Trustee in Bankruptcy* 1 CLR 119 (1966).
377. Section 4 Cap. 62.
378. Section 2 *ibid.*
379. *Lymperopoulou v. Christodoulou a.o.* 22 (1) CLR 184; *Pampos Zenios Trading Ltd a.o. v. Hadjipavlou & Ios Ltd a.o.* 1C CLR 2322 (2011); *Tziepra v. Savva a.a.* 1 CLR 2410 (2013).
380. Section 4 Cap. 62.

transferor or assignor and the person to whom such transfer or assignment was made, provided that no exchange for money, for other property of equivalent value or for good consideration took place.[381]

381. Section 3(2) *ibid.*

Chapter 5. The Termination of the Contract

§1. Performance and Breach

145. Parties to a contract must either perform or offer to perform their respective promises, save for such performance being dispensed with or excused under law.[382] In case of joint promisors, unless a contrary intention appears by the contract, all such persons during their joint lives bear the statutory obligation to fulfil the promise.[383] Release of a joint promisor by the promisee does not discharge the other joint promisors; neither does it free the joint promisor so released from responsibility to the others.[384] Promises are to be performed by the promisor himself if it appears from the nature of the case that this was the intention of the parties. In other cases, the promisor or his representatives may employ a competent person to perform it.[385] If the promisee accepts performance from a third person, he is then deprived of his right to proceed with enforcement against the promisor.[386]

146. In case of death of promisors before performance, promises bind their representatives, unless a contrary intention appears from the contract.[387] Under the same condition, that being lack of intention to the contrary, when two or more persons have made a joint promise, after the death of any of them, his representative jointly with the survivor or survivors must fulfil the promise. After the death of last survivor this obligation binds the representatives of all jointly.[388]

147. Joint promisees have the right to claim performance during their joint lives, unless a contrary intention appears from the contract. Under the same condition, after the death of any of them, this right rests with the representative of such deceased person jointly with the survivors, whereas after the death of the last survivor, with the representatives of all jointly.[389]

148. Time of performance may be specified in a contract. Where this is not the case and no application ('όχληση' in Greek, 'başvurulmak' in Turkish) by the promisee is necessary, the engagement must be performed within reasonable time ('εύλογος χρόνος' in Greek, 'makul bir süre' in Turkish). The question '*what is a reasonable time*' is, in each particular time, a question of fact.[390] When the day of performing the promise has been agreed and no application by the promisee is required, the promisor may perform it at any time during the usual hours of business on such day and at the place at which the promise ought to be performed.[391]

382. Section 37(1) Cap. 149.
383. Section 42 *ibid.*
384. Section 44 *ibid.*
385. Section 40 *ibid.*
386. Section 41 *ibid.*
387. Section 37(2) *ibid.*
388. Section 42 *ibid.*
389. Section 45 *ibid.*
390. Section 46 *ibid.*
391. Section 47 *ibid.*

When both days has been agreed and an application is necessary, the promisee has the duty to apply for performance at a proper ('κατάλληλος' in Greek, 'uygun' in Turkish) place and within the usual hours of business. The question '*what is a proper time and place*' is, in each particular case, a question of fact.[392] Same applies when no place of performance has been agreed.[393] Finally, the performance of any promise may be made in any manner and at any time, which the promisee prescribes or sanctions.[394]

149. Fundamental breach ('θεμελιώδης παραβίαση' in Greek, 'esaslı ihlal' in Turkish) of contract, which is different and distinct from breach of a condition of contract, is a breach that shatters the foundations of the contract.[395] A breach is of this nature if, having regard to the contract as a whole, the promise that has been violated is of major as distinct from minor importance.[396] The object of the contract becomes totally different than the one originally agreed.[397] This results in giving to the innocent party the right to terminate the contract and claim damages.[398]

150. The doctrine of anticipatory breach of contract has been settled by case law, adopting the doctrine of common law.[399] It relates to contracts that are to be performed on a future date and one of the parties repudiates the contract by showing that he does not intend to perform it. In such an event, the other party is entitled to sue him for breach of contract without having to wait for the time fixed for performance and is absolved from further performance of his own part of the contract. Where the innocent party does sue without waiting for the time fixed for performance, the contract is terminated.[400] Still, the innocent party may wait till the time for performance arrives and then sue[401] or claim special performance.[402] In other cases, the Courts have found that anticipatory breach of contract is nothing more

392. Section 48 *ibid.*
393. Section 49 *ibid.*
394. Section 50 *ibid.*
395. *Bauer v. Diogenis Erodotou & Yioi Ltd* 1 CLR 325 (1994), citing *Smeaton Hanscomb & Co. Ltd v. Sassoon I. Setty Son & Co. (No. 1)*, 1 WLR 1468 (1953); *Panasoft AE v. Xenos Travel Ltd*, District Court of Nicosia Action No. 4828/2005, Judgment of 28 Feb. 2011, not reported in CLR; *Chrystalla Stylianoudes v. Sportking Limited*, District Court of Limassol Action No. 4569/11, Judgment of 12 Sep. 2012, not reported in CLR.
396. *Myroforas John Seago v. Thoma Athanasiou and another*, District Court of Larnaca, Action No. 1730/2005, Judgment of 19 Sep. 2007, not reported in CLR.
397. *Euaggelos Charalambous v. Yiannaki Lysioti* 1 CLR 409 (1991). Also *Bauer v. Diogenis Erodotou & Yioi Ltd* 1 CLR 325 (1994), citing *Smeaton Hanscomb & Co. Ltd v. Sassoon I. Setty Son & Co. (No. 1)* 1 WLR 1468 (1953), and *Xenos Travel Ltd v. Panasoft AE*, Supreme Court of Cyprus, Civil Appeal No. 116/2011, Judgment of 21 Feb. 2017, not reported in CLR, citing *Suisse Atlantique Societe D'armement Maritime SA v. N V Rotterdamsche Kolen Centrale* 2 All ER 61 (1966).
398. *Bauer v. Diogenis Erodotou & Yioi Ltd* 1 CLR 325 (1994).
399. Cypriot case law has been referring to *Johnstone v. Milling*, 16 Q.B.D. 460 (1886), *Hochster v. De la Tour* 22 L.J. (Q.B.) 455 (1853), *Frost v. Knight* Law Rep. 7 Ex. 111 (1872), *Heyman and another v. Darwins, Limited* AC 356 (1942), *Garnac Grain Co., Inc. v. H.M.F. Faure and Fairclough, Ltd and Bunge Corporation* 2 All ER 353 (1967).
400. *Tams Beit v. Elias Ioanni Papa and another* 1 CLR 172 (1971).
401. *Efthymiou v. M. & T.H. Petrou & Sons Developers Ltd*, District Court of Ammochostos Action No. 98/2010, Judgment of 9 Mar. 2018, not published in CLR.

than a violation of a contract, which is performed with an action, omission or conduct that takes place before the time fixed in the same contract as the time of the contract's fulfilment.[403] Finally, it has been found that anticipatory breach is treated as a cause for action and therefore may not be used by a defendant as a defence to the action for breach of promise.[404]

§2. Impossibility, Frustration and Hardship: The 'Unforeseen'

151. Impossibility may be initial or appear after the contract is concluded. With reference to initial impossibility, it is provided that an agreement to do an act impossible in itself is void.[405] This provision lays down the law in the same way as in England. It speaks of something, which is impossible inherently or by its very nature and no one can obviously be directed to perform such an act.[406] Knowledge of the impossibility by one of the parties affects the consequences of an agreed impossible act. It is set out that, where one person has promised to do something which he knew, or, with reasonable diligence, might have known, and which the promisee did not know to be impossible or unlawful, such promisor must make compensation to such promisee sustains through the non-performance of the promise.[407]

152. With reference to act becoming impossible after a contract is concluded, the following is foreseen in the statute. A contract to do an act which, after the contract is made, becomes impossible, becomes void when the act becomes impossible.[408] Source of this provision is the correlated provision in Indian Contract Law and therefore the meaning of frustration under English law is of little help to the literal application of this provision.[409] The word impossible has not been used here in the sense of physical or literal impossibility. The performance of an act may not be literally impossible but it may be impracticable and useless from the point of view of the object and purpose which, the parties had in view, and if an untoward event or change of circumstances totally upsets the very foundation upon which the parties rested their bargain, it can very well be said that the promisor found it impossible

402. *Christodoulou v. C.H.R. Othonos Homes Ltd*, District Court of Paphos Action No. 3291/2010, Judgment of 30 Aug. 2019, not published in CLR, citing *Leniana Tourist Services Ltd v. Andrea Chr. Karpaspi & Yioi (Biomihania) Ltd* 1 CLR 75 (1991).

403. *Neophytos Neophytou v. Elma Holdings Ltd* 1 CLR 1807 (2013). This approach has also been adopted in *Christodoulou v. C.H.R. Othonos Homes Ltd*, District Court of Paphos Action No. 3291/2010, Judgment of 30 Aug. 2019, not published in CLR.

404. *Theodorou v. Sekkeris* 1 CLR 337 (1971).

405. Section 56(1) Cap. 149.

406. *Xenophontos v. Tyrimou* 1 CLR 23 (1984), citing *Satyabrata Ghose v. Mugneeram Bangur and co.* SCR 31 (1954), of the Supreme Court in India. *See also Maison Jenny Limited v. Krashias Footwear Industry Limited* 1 CLR 1156 (2002) and *Fadil Izzet v. Kypriaki Et. Apothikeusis Petreleoeidon Ltd* 1(A) CLR 11 (2009).

407. Section 56(3) Cap. 149.

408. Section 56(2) *ibid.*

409. *Maison Jenny Ltd v. Krashias Footwear Industry Ltd* 1 CLR 1156 (2002).

to do the act which he promised to do.[410] It has been ruled that a court applies either the statutory rule concerning impossibility of performance contained in said provision or the English doctrine of an implied term. In order that a supervening impossibility of performance should excuse the non-performance of a contract, the underlying principle for not enforcing the contract is the same. This principle orders that the occurrence itself may yet be of a character and an extent so sweeping that the foundation of what the parties are deemed to have had in contemplation had disappeared and the contract itself has vanished with that foundation. This spirit of the English law is to be followed. Section 56(2) Cap. 149 only applies to an impossibility which destroys the foundation of the contract.[411] It is furthermore noted that frustration is not to be lightly held to have occurred. It is useful within its proper limits. For example, disappointed expectations do not lead to frustration, or a contract is not frustrated because its performance has become more onerous.[412] The doctrine of frustration comes into play when a contract becomes impossible of performance, after it is made, on account of circumstances beyond the control of parties or the change in circumstances makes the performance of the contract impossible.[413] Hardship or inconvenience or material loss itself does not call the principle of frustration into play.[414] Frustration terminates automatically the contract at the time that the event causing it took place and no right of the parties to choose may be put forward.[415]

153. One form of the unforeseen that takes place following the conclusion of a contract, is force majeure. It has not found its way into statutory provisions, but rather it is shaped by case law. Force majeure ('ανωτέρα βία' in Greek, 'doğal afet veya bir çatışma' in Turkish) has been explained as 'an accidental and unforeseeable event that is beside the human factor and could not reasonably be foreseen'.[416] Furthermore, the courts of Cyprus have adopted the approach of the Supreme Court of Greece that found that force majeure occurs when a random and unforeseen event takes place which could not have been avoided even if measures of outmost diligence and prudence had been taken. Events falling within a commercial activity and its sphere of risk do not qualify as force majeure, as such events, according to the common experience, could have been considered possible and therefore, adequate

---

410. *Xenophontos v. Tyrimou* 1 CLR 23 (1984), citing *Satyabrata Ghose v. Mugneeram Bangur and co.* SCR 31 (1954), of the Supreme Court in India.
411. *Vincent Della Tolla v. Kyriakides* 20 (1) CLR 89, citing *Tamplin S.S. Co. v. The Anglo Mexican Petroleum Products Co* 2 AC 397 (1916).
412. *Xenophontos v. Tyrimou* 1 CLR 23 (1984).
413. *Kier (Cyprus) Ltd v. Trenco Construction Ltd* 1 CLR 30 (1981).
414. *Xenophontos v. Tyrimou* 1 CLR 23 (1984), citing *Denny, Mott & Dickson, Ltd v. James B. Fraser & Co. Ltd* 1 All ER 678 (1944).
415. *A.N. Stasis Estates Co Ltd v. Waldner a.a.* 1 CLR 250 (1998); *Izzet v. Kypriaki Etaireia Apothukeusis Petrelaioeidon Ltd* 1 CLR 11 (2009).
416. *Gerolemou and another v. Giovani Developers Ltd and others*, District Court of Ammohostos Civil Action No. 801/2012, Judgment of 8 Jan. 2018 not published in CLR, citing *Greenock v. Caledonian Ry* (1917) A.C. 556; *Orlando Development Ltd v. Lante Enterprises Ltd*, District Court of Larnaca Civil Case No. 871/2011, Judgment of 30 Nov. 2018, not published in CLR.

preparations could have been made.[417] Further, it has been found that force majeure coincides with act of God,[418] which stands for the appearance of forces of nature that no human foreseeability could handle, the possibility of their occurrence similarly no human prudence could have expected.[419] Act of God has been also specified as 'the operation of uncontrollable natural forces, such as earthquake, flood, storm or lighting, which could not happen by the intervention of man'.[420] Noteworthy is that the notion of act of God also appears in tort. In the apposite statutory provision it is set out that in any action brought in respect of any negligence, it shall be a defence, notwithstanding that the defendant was negligent that the damage was due to the happening of some extraordinary natural occurrence which a reasonable person would not have anticipated and the consequences of which could not have been avoided by the exercise of reasonable care.[421]

154. Should a force majeure occur, the relevant provisions as agreed by the parties are applicable.[422] In the event of a disagreement between the parties, force majeure may only be used as a defence before a court. The party raising this defence bears the burden of establishing the alleged facts that purportedly constitute force majeure. Furthermore, he has to prove that same facts impeded him from complying with his contractual obligations or caused the delay in the compliance, as the case may be. He also has to prove that non-performance was beyond his control and that he could not mitigate the events or their consequences.[423] Generally, the courts are unwilling to accept such a defence; it is recognized only in the event of extreme conditions and exceptionally unforeseeable circumstances.[424]

155. Returning to the statutory provisions, it is stated that where illegality involves reciprocal promises to do things legal and other illegal things, the set of promises referring to legal promises is a contract. The set of promises relating to illegal things is not. It is merely a void agreement.[425] This provision has been frequently applied to contracts providing for interest higher than the lawful one. Interest has been set to mean the return or compensation for the use or retention by one

---

417. *Gerolemou and another v. Giovani Developers Ltd and others*, District Court of Ammohostos Civil Action No. 801/2012, Judgment of 8 Jan. 2018 not published in CLR, citing *unknown v. unknown* Supreme Court of Greece (Areios Pagos) Civil Case No. 172/2013, Judgment of 8 Jan. 2013, unpublished.
418. *Gray and another v. Demari Kronos Ltd*, District Court of Ammochostos, Civil Case No. 748/2009, Judgment of 16 Jun. 2014, not published in CLR; *Cyprus Cinema & Theatre Co. Ltd. v. Christodoulos Karmiotis* 1 CLR 42 (1967).
419. *Sokraotus v. Emenby Company Ltd*, District Court of Limassol, Civil Case No. 1534/2012, Judgement of 7 Sep. 2018, not published in CLR.
420. *Cyprus Cinema & Theatre Co. Ltd. v. Christodoulos Karmiotis* 1 CLR 42 (1967).
421. Section 56(b) Cap. 148. *See also Markitsis v. Thanos Hotels Ltd* 1 CLR 449 (2005), citing *Tennent v. Earl of Glascow* 2 Macq. (H.I.) 22 (1864); *Neophytou and others v. Ttaba* 1 CLR 1352 (2012).
422. *Ellinas and others v. Zartarian*, Court of Rent Control of Nicosia, Case No. E209/2011, Judgment of 19 Oct 2015, not published in CLR.
423. *Chrineste Holdings Ltd v. Zavos Race-City Co. Ltd*, District Court of Limassol, Civil Case No. 5905/2011, Judgment of 29 Jun. 2018, not published in CLR.
424. *Tomaridou-Eliadou v. Dimou Paphou*, District Court of Paphos, Civil Case No. 3093/2007, Judgment of 28 Jul. 2011, not published in CLR.
425. Section 57 Cap. 149.

person of a sum of money belonging to or owned to another.[426] Such contracts are not void agreements or contrary to public policy.[427] The settled approach thereto is to generally treat the contract legally valid, while prohibiting the excessive interest, in the sense of the latter being a set of illegal promises.[428] Finally, in the case of an alternative promise ('διαζευκτική υπόσχεση' in Greek, 'şıklı sözveri' in Turkish), where one branch of which is legal and the other illegal, the legal branch alone can be enforced.[429]

§3. Discharge by Agreement

156. Discharge can occur by agreement to a new contract or to dispense performance of promise. In particular, the law sets out that if the parties to a contract agree to substitute a new contract for it, or to rescind or alter it, the original contract need not be performed.[430] This provision enshrines novation, an English principle, which is equally in force in Cyprus. Novation ('αντικατάσταση' in Greek, 'borcun nakli' in Turkish) is a transaction by which, with the consent of all the parties concerned, a new contract is substituted for one that has already been made. The new contract may be between the original parties or between different parties.[431] Similarly, the promises undertaken with the new contract need not be the same as the ones undertaken through the substituted contract. Neither is it necessary that the new contract has exactly the same terms with the substituted one.[432] However, endorsement of the original contract which was void ab initio and could not have any effect does not constitute novation.[433] The same provision equally endorses rectification ('διόρθωση' in Greek, 'düzeltilme' in Turkish). Rectification is interweaved with mistake, both a unilateral and a bilateral.[434] More specifically, when a single party alleges mistake and requests rectification, it must produce convincing proof not only that the document to be rectified was not in accordance with the parties' true intentions at the time of its execution, but also that the document in its proposed form does not accord to their intentions.[435] Only in such cases can evidence regarding

426. *Turkish Bank of Nicosia Ltd v. Cukurova a.o.* 1 CLR 233 (1977).
427. *Antoniadou v. Laiki Kypriaki Trapeza (Chrimatodotiseis) Ltd* 1(A) CLR 530 (2003); *Ioannou a.a. v. Laiki Kypriaki Trapeza (Chrimatodotiseis) Ltd* 1 CLR 91 (2011).
428. *Bank of Cyprus v. Coudounaris Fund Products Ltd a.a.* 1 CLR 641 (1995); *Neophytou v. Kyriakides (No. 3)* 1 CLR 299 (1999).
429. Section 58 Cap. 149.
430. Section 62 *ibid.*
431. *Bank of Cyprus a.o. v. Coudounaris Food Productions Ltd a.o.* 1 CLR 641 (1995).
432. *Hellenic Bank Ltd v. Polydorides a.o.* 1 CLR 68 (1993).
433. *Demetriou v. Andorkas* 21 (1) CLR 187.
434. *Kokkinos v. Pissarides* 1 CLR 967 (1995).
435. *Oxynou v. Nikolaides a.o.* 1 CLR 351 (2001), citing *Thomas Bates & Son v. Wyndhams Ltd* 1 WLR 505 (1981).

subjective factors be furnished and considered.[436] Finally, rectification presupposes an agreement, though not necessarily a binding contract, between the parties, to the instrument to be rectified.[437]

157. Lastly, every promisee may dispense with or remit, wholly or in part, the performance of the promise made to him. He further has the ability to extend the time for such performance or even accept instead of if any satisfaction which he thinks fit.[438]

436. *Theologou v. Ktimatikis Etaireias Nemesis Ltd* 1 CLR 407 (1998), citing *ICS v. West Bromwich BS* 1 All ER 98 (1998).
437. *Stylianou a.o. v. Papacleovoulou a.a.* 1 CLR 542 (1982).
438. Section 63 Cap. 149.

Chapter 6. Remedies

§1. General Provisions

158. Remedies for breach of contract as well as for defects of consent of validity include specific performance, termination, *exceptio non adimpleti contractus*, damages and restitution, as explained below. Albeit, general provisions on remedies are absent.

§2. Specific Performance and Injunctions Astreinte

159. Specific performance of contracts is regulated in Cap. 149. In particular, it is set out that contracts are capable of being specifically enforced by a court of law when the statutory conditions are fulfilled. Said conditions are validity of the contract in question, which is expressed in writing[439] and signed at the end thereof by the party to be charged therewith, as long as the court considers, having regard to all circumstances, that the enforcement of specific performance of the contract would not be unreasonable ('παράλογη' in Greek, 'mantıksız' in Turkish) or otherwise inequitable ('ανεπιεικής' in Greek, 'herhangi başka bir biçimde adaletsiz' in Turkish) or impracticable ('πρακτικά ανεφάρμοστη' in Greek, 'olanaksız' in Turkish).[440] A contract agreed partly in writing and partly orally may not be specifically enforced.[441]

160. This provision codifies the principles of English law of equity regarding specific performance.[442] The remedy of said performance is personal, special and extraordinary in its character. The court has a discretion to grant such remedy while exercising its discretion on fixed principles in accordance with the previous authorities and in a judicial manner. In addition, the court may refuse to enforce a contract due to the conduct of the plaintiff, such as delay, acquiescence, breach on his part, or some other circumstance outside the contract, or because of the contract itself, i.e., on the ground of misdescription.[443] With reference to third persons, as a general principle, they may not join a judicial request for its enforcement. However, should such third person acquire property that was previously objected of a contract, he can be ordered to transfer this property to its lawful owner, under the condition that said third person had knowledge of that contract. If the same third person bought this property without any knowledge of said contract, no such order may be issued.[444] In the event of requesting to enforce a lease contract, it is important to note that according to settled case law, such specific performance shall only be

439. *Gregoriou a.a. v. Christoforou a.a.* 1 CLR 248 (1995).
440. Section 76(1) Cap. 149.
441. *Christofides v. Kotzanaggasi* 1 CLR 718 (1993).
442. *Xenopoulos v. Makrides* 1 CLR 488 (1969); *HadjiYannis v. Attorney-General* 1 CLR 32 (1970); *Trifonides v. Alpan (Taki) Bros* 1 CLR 224 (1988).
443. *HadjiYannis v. The Attorney General* 1 CLR 32 (1970).
444. *Apaisioti v. Rayia* 1 CLR 882 (1993), citing *Taylor v. Stibbert* 2 Ves 437 (1794); *Potter v. Sanders* 6 Hare 1 (1846).

ordered if the term has not expired.[445] Whether there is delay in the prosecution of the judicial proceedings, shall not be taken into consideration.[446]

161. Contracts for the sale of land underlie the procedure of specific performance set out in the Sale of Land (Specific Performance) Law,[447] which is an equitable remedy.[448] Specific performance of a land sale contract requested on the premises of Cap. 149 is dismissed by courts.[449] Under the Sale of Land (Specific Performance) Law, a contract may be submitted for specific performance, as long as this contract in its written form has been deposited with the land registry of the competent local authority within six months of it having been made.[450] A contract for the sale of land prior to said deposit merely confers personal rights or rights in personam, that is rights against the counter-contracting party, in the event of breach.[451] It does not give any rights over the land. An estate in land may accrue from adherence to the provisions of this law.[452] Same law further prescribes that any condition in such a contract prohibiting said deposit with the competent authorities is void *ab initio*.[453]

162. Joint promises ('κοινή υπόσχεση' in Greek, 'ortaklaşa sözveri' in Turkish) deserve special mention. Such promises may at the request of the promisee be compelled to be performed in full by one or more of such joint promisors, save for express agreement to the contrary.[454] Similarly, and under the same reservation, each of two or more joint promisors may compel every other joint promisor to contribute equally with himself to the performance of the promise.[455] Should any joint promisor make default in his contribution, the remaining ones bear equally the loss arising therefrom.[456]

163. There is no equivalent in Cypriot law to *Astreinte*, which is available in some civil law jurisdictions.

§3. TERMINATION

164. Contracts can be terminated as a remedy for defects of consent and improper fulfilment of validity conditions due to them being either voidable or void

---

445. *Trifonides v. Alpan (Taki Bros) Ltd a.a.* 1 CLR 224 (1988), citing *De Brassac v. Martyn* 9 LT 287 (1863).
446. *Trifonides v. Alpan (Taki Bros) Ltd a.a.* 1 CLR 224 (1988).
447. Section 76(2) Cap. 149.
448. *Xenopoulos v. Makridi* 1 CLR 488 (1969).
449. *See* in this respect *Eleni Andrea Avgousti v. Niovi Papadamou a.a.* 1 CLR 66 (1968); *Xenopoulos v. Makrides* 1 CLR 488 (1969); *Erotokritou v. Theodorou a.a.* 1(C) CLR 1800 (1997).
450. Section 3(1)(a), (b) and (c) Law No. 81(I)/2011.
451. *Markidou v. Kiliaris a.a.* 1 CLR 392 (1983).
452. *Ibid.*, citing *Property Discount Corpn. v. Lyon Group* 1 All ER 33 (1980).
453. Section 3(2) Law No. 81(I)/2011.
454. Section 43(1) Cap. 149.
455. Section 43(2) *ibid.*
456. Section 43(3) *ibid.*

agreements, according to the aforementioned. For the sake of clarity, it is here stated that, when a party of a contract, at whose option it is voidable, rescinds it, the other party thereto need not perform any promise therein contained in which he is promisor.[457]

§4. *Exceptio Non Adimpleti Contractus*

165. *Exception non adimpleti contractus* is a principle applicable in Cyprus. The precise conditions and legal consequences depend upon whether the contract in question contains reciprocal promises or time is a condition agreed in a contract.

166. Where reciprocal promises ('αμοιβαίες υποσχέσεις' in Greek, 'karşılıklı sözveriler' in Turkish) have been agreed in a contract, the law foresees for the order of their performance, as well as for consequences of failure of proper performance. If simultaneous performance is agreed, no promisor need perform his promise unless the promisee is ready and willing ('έτοιμος και πρόθυμος' in Greek, 'hazır ve istekli' in Turkish) to perform his reciprocal promise.[458] Further, it is provided that, where the order in which said promises are to be performed is expressly fixed by the contract, they must be performed in that order. If this is not the case, they shall be performed in that order, which the nature of the transaction requires.[459] It is also provided that, when in the same contracts one party prevents the other from performing his promise, the contract becomes voidable at the option of the party so prevented. The latter party is entitled to compensation ('αποζημίωση' in Greek, 'tazminat' in Turkish) from the other party for any loss ('ζημιά' in Greek, 'zarar veya ziyan' in Turkish) which he may sustain in consequence of the non-performance of the contract.[460] Moreover, when one of the reciprocal promises cannot be performed, and the promisor of the other promise fails to perform it, such promisor cannot claim the performance of the reciprocal promise. Rather, he is statutory obliged to compensate ('αποζημίωση' in Greek, 'tazmin' in Turkish) the other party to the contract for any loss ('ζημιά' in Greek, 'zarar ziyanı da' in Turkish) which such other party may sustain by the non-performance of the contract. The same applies when the performance of one of the reciprocal promises cannot be claimed till the other has been performed.[461]

167. Specific provisions refer to contracts where time is bound to the promise. In particular, where a party to a contract promises to do a certain thing at or before specified times and fails to timely do any such thing, the contract becomes voidable at the option of the promisee, under the condition that time was intended to be of

457. Section 64 *ibid.*
458. Section 51 *ibid. See Hadjiantoni v. Matsis* 1 CLR 260 (1979).
459. Section 52 Cap. 149.
460. Section 53 *ibid.*
461. Section 54 *ibid.*

the essence thereof.[462] In same set of events, when the promisee accepts performance of promise at any other time after the contract has become voidable, he cannot claim compensation for any loss caused by the non-performance, unless upon accepting such performance, he gives a notice of his intention to the promisor.[463] Alternatively, if parties did not agree to time of performance being of essence, the promisee is entitled to compensation from the promisor for any loss occasioned to him by such failure, whereas the contract does not become voidable.[464] From the aforementioned, it can be deduced that time is not of the essence of contract. It has been ruled that equity has superseded the common law rule that contractual stipulations affecting payment are of the essence of the agreement. Now the rule is that time stipulations for the payment of the purchase price are not of the essence of the agreement unless they are so declared to be for reasons mutually in the contemplation of the contracting parties.[465]

§5. Faulty Behaviour of the Debtor

168. Neglect ('παράλειψη' in Greek, 'red' in Turkish) or refusal ('άρνηση' in Greek, 'ihmal' in Turkish) to afford the promisor reasonable facilities ('εύλογες διευκολύνσεις' in Greek, 'makul ölçüde kolaylık' in Turkish) for the performance of his promise by the promisee leads to the promisor being excused as to any non-performance caused thereby.[466] Similar effect has the refusal to accept an offer of performance. In particular, it is provided that where a promisor has made such an offer to the promisee and the latter does not accept it, the promisor is not responsible for non-performance, nor does he thereby lose his rights under the contract.[467] However, for the promisor to be excused in this manner, such an offer must fulfil the following conditions: it must be unconditional; it must be made at a proper time and place, and under such circumstances that the person to whom is made is able and willing there and then to do the whole of what he is bound by his promise to do; if the offer is an offer to deliver anything to the promisee, the promisee must have reasonable ('εύλογη' in Greek, 'makûl' in Turkish) opportunity of seeing that the thing offered is the thing which the promisor is bound by his promise to deliver.[468] Finally, it is clarified that an offer to one of several joint promisees has the same legal consequences as an offer to all of them.[469]

169. Mention deserves the fact that faulty behaviour of the debtor does not affect the calculation of damages. It has been ruled that mere moral culpability of the party

462. Section 55(1) *ibid. See Melaisi v. M & M Georgiki Eteria* 1 CLR 748 (1979).
463. Section 55(3) Cap. 149.
464. Section 55(2) *ibid.*
465. *Papargyrou v. Michaelides*, Supreme Court of Cyprus, Civil Appeal No. 215/2010, Judgment of 27 Sep. 2016, not published in CLR, citing *Paraskeva a.o. v. Lantas* 1 CLR 285 (1988); *Melaisi v. M & M Georgiki Eteria* 1 CLR 748 (1979); *Smith v. Hamilton* 2 All ER 928 (1950).
466. Section 67 Cap. 149.
467. Section 38(1) *ibid.*
468. Section 38(2) *ibid.*
469. Section 38(3) *ibid.*

failing to comply with his contractual obligations is not a good ground for departing from the normal basis on which damages are awarded.[470]

§6. Limitation of Actions

170. The events of 1963 and the 'abnormal situation' that followed triggered the enactment of the Law on Suspension of Limitation.[471] This prescribed that the period, during which the 'abnormal situation' would last, that being 21 December 1963 onwards, shall be regarded as a suspension period and would not count as a limitation period.[472] In 2002 the 'abnormal situation' was renamed as 'degraded situation'.[473] Clarity over the issues of limitation ('παραγραφή' in Greek, 'zamanaşımı' in Turkish) was offered only in 2012, as the legislation issued elucidated that actions may be filed within six years from the date on which the cause of action accrued, but for two exceptions. Contracts related to remuneration of lawyers, doctors, dentists, architects and other freelancers, must be filed within three years. Also, contracts of loans, where repayment on a specific date was not agreed or notice of the promisee was not agreed to be a condition for repayment, issuing a written application for repayment by the promisee to the promisor is a condition for the initiation of the limitation period.[474]

171. Alongside limitation, another principle encountered in common law countries that has time as its principal ingredient is the doctrine of promissory estoppel. According to settled case law, the doctrine of promissory estoppel, where by his words or conduct one party to a transaction makes to the other a promise or assurance which is intended to affect the legal relations between them and the other party acts upon it, altering his position to his detriment, the party making the promise or assurance will not be permitted to act inconsistently with it. This is the gist of equity.[475]

§7. Damages and Exemption Clauses

172. When a contract has been broken, the party who suffers by such breach is entitled to receive, from the party who has broken the contract, compensation for any loss or damage ('απώλεια ή ζημιά' in Greek, 'zarar ve ziyan' in Turkish) caused

---

470. *Dryades a.a. v. Kalispera* 1 CLR 881 (1998), citing *A.G. v. Blake* 1 All ER 933 (1998).
471. Law on Suspension of Limitation ('ο περί Αναστολής της Παραγραφής Νόμος') No. 57 of 1964, OG I No. 363 of 30 Oct. 1964, p. 545, as last amended by amending Law No. 110 of 2002, OG I(I) No. 3621 of 12 Jul. 2002.
472. Section 3 Law No. 57/1964.
473. *See* the last amending law n. 464.
474. Article 7(1), (2) and (3) of the Law on Limitation of Actionable Rights ('ο περί Παραγραφής Αγώγιμων Δικαιωμάτων Νόμος') No. 66 of 2012, OG I(I) No. 4336 of 31 May 2012, p. 757, as last amended by amending Law No. 150 of 2017, OG I(I) No. 4624 of 27 Oct. 2017, p. 1057.
475. *HadjiYannis v. The Attorney-General of the Republic* 1 CLR 32 (1970), citing *Central London Property Trust Ltd v. High Trees House Ltd* K.B. 130 (1947). *See also Attorney-General of the Republic v. Etaireia Technikon Ergon Ltd* 1 CLR 94 (1993).

to him thereby, which naturally arose in the usual course of things from such breach, or which the parties knew, when they made the contract, to be likely to result from the breach of it. Yet, such compensation is not given for any remote ('απομακρυσμένη' in Greek, 'uzak' in Turkish) and indirect ('έμμεση' in Greek, 'dolaylı' in Turkish) loss or damage sustained by reason of the breach.[476] This provision codifies the rule of *Hadley v. Baxendale*.[477] Crucial in this regard are the terms loss or damage, which have been clarified by case law in alignment to English law. It has been held that damage usually refers to a changed physical state, whereas its precise definition depends upon the context of the word or words used, although generally speaking, damage requires some altered state, the relevant alteration being harmful in the commercial context.[478] Should the innocent party make use of said statutory right and claim damages, the contract is terminated, however not *ab initio*.[479] Further, it is provided that a person who rightly ('νομίμως' in Greek, 'haklı' in Turkish) rescinds a contract is entitled to compensation for any damage which he has sustained through the non-fulfilment of the contract.[480] This section, which is related to sections 64 and 65 Cap. 149,[481] establishes the right of a party that annuls an agreement on statutory grounds, to claim damages due to rescission of same.[482]

173. In particular in cases where the innocent party is a company, it is noted that no cause of action vests in the shareholder. Solely the company acquires causes of action for breaches of contract, which damage the same.[483] This approach is consistent with the rule laid down in *Foss v. Harbottle*,[484] which has been adopted by Courts in Cyprus,[485] as well as with the prohibition of double recovery.[486] Importantly, the Courts in Cyprus allow for the exception of derivative actions,

---

476. Section 73(1) Cap. 149.
477. *Kolokasides v. Michael Theodosiou Ltd* 1 CLR 1671 (1997); *XXX Georgiades and Tahudomi Ltd and XXX Theodotou*, District Court of Larnaca Action No. 2008/2011, Judgment of 25 Apr. 2019, not published in CLR.
478. *G.K. Theonell Building & Construction Ltd v. AIG Cyprus Limited*, District Court of Limassol Action No. 2743/2013, Judgment of 7 Mar. 2017, not published in CLR, citing *Pilkington United Kingdom Limited v. CGU Insurance Plc* EWCA Civ 23 (2004).
479. *Metaxas Loizides Syrimis & Co., and others v. L.K. Globalsoft Com. Ltd* 1 CLR 54 (2007), citing *Katafygiotis v. Chrysostomis* 1 CLR 1746 (1997); *Andris Spanou v. Christinas Vasileiou a.o.*, District Court of Larnaca Action No. 3522/2012, Judgment of 22 Jan. 2018, not published in CLR.
480. Section 75 Cap. 149.
481. *Pantziari v. Aquarian Container Lines Ltd a.o.* 1 CLR 748 (1993).
482. *Komodromou v. A.Th. Shikkis Motors Ltd a.a.* 1 CLR 481 (1999); *Metaxas Loizides Syrimis & Co a.a. v. L.K. Globalsoft Com. Ltd* 1 CLR 54 (2007).
483. *Litonor Financial Ltd v. R.G.I. Residential Holdings Ltd*, District Court of Nicosia Action No. 3073/2014, Judgment of 29 Dec. 2016, not published in CLR, citing *Prudential Assurance Ltd v. Newman Industries Ltd & Others* (No. 2) Ch. 204 (1982).
484. *Foss v. Harbottle* 67 ER 189 (1843); *see also Edwards v. Halliwell* 2 All ER 1064 (1950).
485. *Georgiou v. Berriman*, District Court of Larnaca Action Nos 418/2015, 419/2015, 420/2015, Judgment of 5 Aug. 2019, not published in CLR; *Aimilios Thoma and others v. Iacovos Eliades* 1 CLR 1263 (2006).
486. *Litonor Financial Ltd v. R.G.I. Residential Holdings Ltd*, District Court of Nicosia Action No. 3073/2014, Judgment of 29 Dec. 2016, not published in CLR, citing *Peak Hotels And Resorts Limited v. Tarek Investments Limited* EWHC 3048 (2015).

meaning that a shareholder is able to sue when the management of the company fraudulently prevents an action from being raised.[487]

174. Especially with regard to void agreements, under which any person has received any advantage ('όφελος' in Greek, 'yarar' in Turkish), same person is statutory obliged to make compensation for it, or alternatively restore it ('αποκαταστήσει' in Greek, 'geri vermek' in Turkish).[488] The obligation to pay compensation under this section is quite different from a claim under the contract itself and the two cannot coexist.[489] In *Papadopoulou v. Polycarpou*,[490] which set aside the sale and transfer of land at the request of the appellant due to her being a minor at material time, the appellant was ordered to pay compensation to the respondent according to section 65 Cap. 149, as she had received an advantage under the agreement discovered to be void. In *Ali Selim v. The Heirs of Emete Filo Ali*,[491] the court refused to apply this section, as the claimant failed to show that the respondent had received an advantage, which was considered the first essential for the application thereof. This approach was equally adopted in the most recent case of *Salgrove v. Amro*.[492] However, the courts have been reluctant to apply section 65 Cap. 149 on fictitious contracts, while putting forward that the agreement was not just legally void, but also in itself non-existence and therefore no facts were available to enable the application of any statutory provision or legal principle.[493] However, this reasoning fails to address the matter of fact that money did exchange hands without legal cause, in view of the non-existence of the agreement.

175. The general principle that underlies the assessment of damages is that of reinstatement, meaning that the aim is to restore the innocent party to the position he would be but for the breach, so far as money can do it.[494] Said principle runs in parallel to a second one, according to which in estimating the loss or damage arising from a breach of contract, the means which existed of remedying the inconvenience caused by the non-performance of the contract must be taken into account.[495] In this regard, the courts have been found that the plaintiff must take all

---

487. *Litonor Financial Ltd v. R.G.I. Residential Holdings Ltd*, District Court of Nicosia Action No. 3073/2014, Judgment of 29 Dec. 2016, not published in CLR.
488. Section 65 Cap. 149.
489. *Kier (Cyprus) Ltd v. Trenco Constructions Ltd* 1 CLR 30 (1981).
490. *Papadopoulou v. Polycarpou* 1 CLR 352 (1968).
491. CLR 143 (V17).
492. *Salgrove Properties Inc v. Amro Consultants Ltd a.o.* 1 CLR 2171 (2012).
493. *Kastanos a.o. v. Cyprus Popular Bank (Financing) Ltd* 1 CLR 1374 (2009).
494. *George Charalambous Ltd v. Kalos Kafes Ltd* 1 CLR 199 (1997), citing *Saab and Another v. Holy Monastery Ay. Neophytos* 1 CLR 499 (1982), as well as *Johnson v. Agnew* 1 All ER 883 (1979); *Capital Tour (Cyprus) Ltd and D & CH Travel & Tours Ltd v. Gesoma Estates Ltd*, District Court of Famagusta Action No. 703/2011, Judgment of 25 Jul. 2018, not published in CLR; *Men Mar Ltd v. CLP Catering Ltd*, District Court of Larnaca Action Nos 891/06 & 874/06, Judgment of 1 Dec. 2011, not published in CLR.
495. Section 73(3) Cap. 149.

reasonable measures for remedying the inconvenience caused, at the greatest possible extend.[496] The defendant bears the burden of proof of the plaintiff not having taken all appropriate measures for damage mitigation.[497] The method for assessing reinstatement, which is usually followed by the Courts in Cyprus, is that of comparing the situation of the innocent party at the present day, that being after the breach of the contract, to the fictitious one, which would have existed, had the breach not occurred. The difference is the calculation of damages for the innocent party. For example, in the case *Fairways (Limassol) Ltd v. A. Petsa & Yioi Ltd*,[498] a contract party repudiated the contract of purchasing eleven vehicles for the agreed remuneration causing the innocent party to negotiate with other companies the purchase of vehicles. The Supreme Court accepted that the additional money that the innocent party paid for the purchase of the vehicles was the proper method for calculating damages.[499] The innocent party is free to claim, restitution aside, loss of profit (also loss of bargain) or reliance loss, but not all three in order to avoid double recovery, although restitution and reliance loss possibly overlap.[500] The leading authority for loss of profit is *Philippou Ltd. v. Josephy Hoyle*.[501,502] There it was held that loss of profit as a rule is not recoverable, save for exceptional cases where the seller is held liable for such loss of profits or expenses under the sub-sale when his liability is based on the contemplation of the parties of the consequences of a breach the contract which depends on the knowledge, actual or imputed of the seller at the time of the contract.[503] It has been also held that loss of profit depends on whether, as result of the – actual or according to the natural course of things – knowledge of the relevant facts,[504] it is deemed that loss of specific profit was reasonably foreseen and therefore considered by the contract parties as a serious possibility or real danger at the time that the contract was done. When the innocent party claims reliance loss or wasted expenditure, he incurs expense before entering the contract, but in the expectation that if such a contract is made, the expenditure will be needed to enable him to perform the contract and that he will be able to

496. *Ktimatiki Etaireia Hadjikyriakou Demosia Ltd v. A. & Chr. Agapiou Imports Ltd and others*, District Court of Nicosia Action No. 6408/2006, Judgment of 4 Oct. 2012, not published in CLR, citing *Ramez Karanouh v. Maros Agapiou and another* 1(E) CLR 377 (1989); *Annita Pantziari v. Aquarian Container Lines Ltd and another* 1 CLR 748 (1993).

497. *Pattis v. Pari*, District Court of Nicosia Action No. 60/2015, Judgment of 18 Oct. 2017, not published in CLR, citing *Centra (Holdings) Ltd v. Reuters Ltd* 1(A) CLR 298 (1999); *Eraclis Michaelides Ltd v. G & C. Exhaust Systems Ltd* 1(A) CLR 500 (2001).

498. *Fairways (Limassol) Ltd v. A. Petsa & Yioi Ltd* 1B CLR 1387 (2000).

499. *P.A. Panagoulas Trading Ltd v. Aggelas Oikonomidou*, District Court of Paphos Action No. 144/2011, Judgment of 3 Oct. 2017, not published in CLR.

500. *Kalisperas v. Dryadi* 1 CLR 867 (1998); *Firippis v. Elvimag Ltd*, District Court of Nicosia Action No. 1661/04, Judgment of 10 Apr. 2006, not published in CLR; *Georgios Ppatsia and another v. K. & M. (Famagusta) Developers & Constructions Ltd*, District Court of Famagusta, Action No. 634/10, Judgment of 24 May 2011, not published in CLR.

501. *Philippou Ltd v. Josephy Hoyle and Son Ltd* 1 CLR 625 (1982).

502. *Veniera Navigation Co. Ltd v. Sertina Shipping Co. Ltd* 1 CLR 742 (1985).

503. *Philippou Ltd v. Josephy Hoyle and Son Ltd* 1 CLR 625 (1982).

504. *MARCEGAGLIA SpA and another v. m/v VYSOKOGORSK*, Naval Court of Cyprus, Naval Action No. 31/2013, Judgment of 25 Sep. 2017, not published in CLR, citing *Hadjikypris and others v. Sanifix Agencies Ltd and others* 1 CLR 447 (1993).

recoup the expenditure from the benefit of the defendant's performance of that contract or from the profits he expects to make from the activity in question.[505]

176. Special damages ('ειδικές αποζημιώσεις' in Greek, 'özel tazminat' in Turkish) deserve special mention. These are the ones that will not infer from the nature of the act as the law and are exceptional in their character. They do not follow in ordinary course. Thus, they must be claimed specially and proved strictly, meaning that furnished proof must be specific, clear, admissible[506] and positive.[507] The details of special damages must be provided by the party claiming those,[508] that being usually the plaintiff, not necessarily due to an unusual nature of loss, but because the plaintiff, as the party having the advantage of basing his claim on precise calculation, must give to the defendant access to the facts that make this calculation possible.[509] When the party is unable to prove special damages, he may claim general damages ('γενικές αποζημιώσεις' in Greek, 'genel tazminat' in Turkish). These embrace all kinds of loss that need not be specified by the plaintiff in the pleadings, in order for relevant proof to be allowed,[510] are assessed by the Court,[511] and they may include damages that are concluded or inferred in favour of the plaintiff; thus, precluding the defendant from claiming that he has been surprised during the trial.[512]

177. Turning to the time of quantification, this is the date of breach because the damage suffered by the innocent party crystallizes naturally on that day. What is natural in a given situation is a matter of logical and common sense. Albeit, this basic principle has exceptions, as in common law there is no restriction to the choice of time at which damages should be assessed. Exceptionally, damages may be assessed at a subsequent date, if the justice of the case so necessitates. This could be the case when the breach becomes known, but a party cannot shape his position

505. *A. Panayides Contracting Ltd v. M & M Frangos Engineering & Contracting Ltd* 1 CLR 1136 (2012); *Firippis v. Elvimag Ltd*, District Court of Nicosia Action No. 1661/04, Judgment of 10 Apr. 2006, not published in CLR.
506. *Demetris Souglis and another v. Elias Papadopoulos and another*, District Court of Limassol Action No. 4390/2009, Judgment of 24 Jun. 2015, not published in CLR, citing *Papakokkinou v. Kanther* 1 CLR 65 (1982); *Kakoullou v. Kakoulli* 1 CLR 355 (1985); *Kounouna and others v. Kostas Kyriakou & Yios Ltd and others* 1(C) CLR 2126 (2001).
507. *Demosthenous and another v. Unicars Limited and another*, District Court of Limassol Action No. 5488/2009, Judgment of 9 Aug. 2019, not published in CLR, citing *Eracleous v. Pitrou* 1 CLR 239 (1994).
508. *Pirillos v. Roupinettas Konnari* 1(B) CLR 1153 (2000); *Bakeview Properties Ltd and XXX XXX Charalambous*, District Court of Limassol Action No. 2642/12, Judgment of 18 Sep. 2019, not published in CLR.
509. *Demosthenous and another v. Unicars Limited and another*, District Court of Limassol Action No. 5488/2009, Judgment of 9 Aug. 2019, not published in CLR, citing *Perestrello e Companhia Limitada v. United Paint Co Ltd* 1 WLR 570 (1969).
510. *Magdalene Theodoulou Kalogerou v. A. Zakheos Estates Ltd*, District Court of Famagusta Action No. 411/2002, Judgment of 21 Jun. 2006, not published in CLR.
511. *Bakeview Properties Ltd v. Charalambous*, District Court of Limassol Action No. 2642/2012, Judgment of 18 Sep. 2019, not published in CLR.
512. *Magdalene Theodoulou Kalogerou v. A. Zakheos Estates Ltd*, District Court of Famagusta Action No. 411/2002, Judgment of 21 Jun. 2006, not published in CLR.

accordingly and guide his affairs subject to that reality due to him being prevented by objective considerations.[513] Where for example a party persists for good cause to have the contract enforced, notwithstanding the breach, as it often happens where a party is seeking the specific enforcement of the contract, there is valid ground for assessing damages as at a subsequent date. Here, the damage crystallizes when specific performance is refused in the exercise of the court's discretion.[514]

178. With reference to exemption clauses, it has been held that one can rely on an exemption clause only if such an exemption clause does not come outside the contract. The exemption clause must be within the four corners of the contract, not to be contrary to the main object and intent of the contract and of its intention.[515] Moreover, the Courts of Cyprus have adopted the view that an exception or limitation clause should not be given effect if it is either unreasonable per se or unreasonable as applied to the circumstances of a given case.[516] Further, they have held that an exemption clause did not relieve respondents from breaches of their specific contractual obligations, which moreover constituted the cornerstones of the agreement. No contractual provision could relieve the defendants from the consequences of failing to fulfil the obligations that it imposed.[517] The ensuing general principles have been distilled by case law: (a) exemption clauses providing for exclusion of liability of a contract party for non-fulfilment or violation of the contractual obligations are to be approached strictly, and in case of doubt as to their scope, they are to be interpreted against the party invoking them; (b) provision which foresees the exemption of a contracting party from an obligation related to the foundations of an agreement lacks the power to relieve him from liability for breach; and (c) in order to exempt a person from liability for negligence, the exemption should be clear on the face of the contract.[518]

179. Regarding stipulations by way of penalty ('ποινική ρήτρα' in Greek, 'para cezası kabilinden bir koşul' in Turkish) agreed in a contract, the following is set out in the law. Upon breach of the same contract, the party complaining of the breach

513. *Markidou v. Kiliaris a.a.* 1 CLR 392 (1983), citing *Saab a.a. v. Holy Monastery Ay. Neophytos* 1 CLR 499 (1982).
514. *Dryades a.a. v. Kalispera* 1 CLR 881 (1998), citing *Saab a.a. v. Holy Monastery Ay. Neophytos* 1 CLR 499 (1982).
515. *Photo-Staff Consultants Ltd v. Michael Geades and others*, District Court of Nicosia Action No. 645/1977, Judgment of 19 May 1980, not published in CLR, citing *lderslade v. Hendon Laundry Ltd* QB Div 149 (1945).
516. *Kypio (I.T.H.) Company v. Ioannis Kassapi and another*, District Court of Larnaca Action No. 1138/1977, Judgment of 29 Mar. 1979, not published in CLR, citing *Levison v. Patent Steam Carpet Cleaning* 3 All ER 498 (1977).
517. *Stefanos & Andreas Cold Stores Trading Ltd v. Etaireias Anapsyktikon KEAN Ltd* 1 CLR 2335 (1998). *See also Nikolas Genethliou and another v. G. Kofteros Industries Ltd*, District Court of Nicosia Action No. 1060/2011, Judgment of 5 Sep. 2017, not published in CLR.
518. *Ibid.*, citing *Ioannis Kokkalos & Sons Ltd v. Nicos Karayiannis* 1 CLR 377 (1975); *Aristotelous v. General Insurance Co.* 1 CLR 582 (1981); and *Bauer v. Diogenis Erodotou & Yioi Ltd* 1 CLR 325 (1994). *See also Eliza Christodoulou v. Christos Papadopoulos & Yioi Ltd*, District Court of Paphos Action No. 1040/2011, Judgment of 5 Apr. 2016, not published in CLR; *Trapeza Kyprou Dimosia Etaireia Ltd v. K&M Famagusta Developers and Constructions Ltd*, District Court of Larnaca-Famagusta Action No. 736/2012, Judgment of 22 Sep. 2016, not published in CLR.

is entitled, whether or not actual damage or loss is proved to have been caused thereby, to receive from the party who has broken the contract reasonable ('εύλογη' in Greek, 'makul' in Turkish) compensation not exceeding the penalty stipulated for. The same applies if a sum is named in the contract as the amount to be paid in case of such breach. A stipulation for increased interest from the date of default may be a stipulation by way of penalty.[519] This provision was intended to eliminate the distinction in English law between liquidated damages and penalties.[520] This quantitative stipulation as to damages sets the ceiling to the damages recoverable,[521] and aside from that, it is not binding for the court. In fact the court only has regard thereto, when it considers it to be a true effort to determine the damage that the innocent party shall suffer due to breach of contract.[522] Penalty was discussed in a case involving a contract providing for the marriage of two individuals, daughter and son of the parties.[523] Along with this promise the contract in question provided for a penalty stipulation and a provision for transfer of certain properties to the same individuals within one month from the date thereof. Due to refusal of one of the individuals to marry the other, breach of contract was held and therefore penalty damages were awarded. However, court refused to grant specific performance.

180. Punitive or exemplary ('τιμωρητικές ή παραδειγματικές' in Greek, 'cezai veya örnek niteliğinde' in Turkish) damages are not awarded for breach of contract. Such remedies are only available for civil wrongs.[524] They constitute a special category of damages aiming to punish respondent for willingly committing an offence or to teach him or her that committing an offence is not accepted.[525]

§8. Restitution

181. Generally, upon rescission of a contract the parties shall, so far as possible, be restored to their pre-contract position.[526] More specifically, a party to a contract, that according to his allegation is voidable, is obliged to restore any benefit ('όφελος' in Greek, 'yarar' in Turkish) that he might have received thereunder, so far as may be to the person from whom such benefit was received upon rescission

519. Section 74(1) Cap. 149. *See Lambrianides a.o. v. The Electrical Authority of Cyprus* 1 CLR 466 (1968).
520. *Panayiotou v. Island Beach Development Ltd* 1 CLR 623 (1985), citing *Iordanou v. Anyftos* 1 CLR 97 (1958); *Tseriotis v. Christodoulou* 19 CLR 216.
521. *Markidou v. Kiliaris a.a.* 1 CLR 392 (1983).
522. *Damtsas a.o. v. Ouzounian M. Sultanian and Company (Cars) Ltd*, Supreme Court, Civil Action No. 133/11, Judgment of 24 Mar. 2016, not reported in CLR, citing *Charalambous a.o. v. Liberty Life* 1 CLR 1739 (2011); *Panayiotou v. Island Development Ltd* 1 CLR 623 (1985); *Panagiasis a.o. v. Spyros Stavrinides Chemicals Ltd* 1 CLR 232 (1993).
523. *Maltezou a.a. v. Louka a.a.* 16 CLR 88.
524. *Erotokritou v. Theodorou* 1(C) CLR 1800 (1997).
525. *Papakokkinou v. Kanther* 1 CLR 65 (1982).
526. *Paraskeva a.o. v. Lantas* 1 CLR 285 (1988); *Stavrou v. Demetriou* 1 CLR 304 (1991); *Pantziari v. Aquarian Container Lines Ltd a.o.* 1 CLR 748 (1993).

thereof.[527] Rescission of such contract is communicated and revoked in the same manner, and subject to the same rules, as the ones applicable to communication and revocation of a proposal.[528] Turning to void agreements, upon becoming void or discovering them to be void, any advantage ('όφελος' in Greek, 'yarar' in Turkish) thereunder has to be restored ('αποκαταστήσει' in Greek, 'geri vermek' in Turkish) or alternatively compensated.[529] The basis of this section is the doctrine of *restitio in integrum*. It does not make a new contract between the parties but only provides for restitution of the advantage taken by a party under the contract. It is not wider in scope than the English doctrine of restitution. Such restitutionary remedy, as quasi-contractual, only arise where the original agreement is put to an end.[530]

182. In *Kier (Cyprus) Ltd v. Trenco Constructions Ltd*,[531] an agreement of 3 May 1972, which provided for building two blocks of flats at Kyrenia, gave rise to the dispute. The court accepted that due to the events of 1974 impossibility of performance was due to changes in circumstances beyond the control of the parties in the meaning of section 56(2) Cap. 149. Therefrom followed that the grounds for restitution under section 65 Cap. 149 were available and it upheld the judgment of the District Court.[532]

527. Section 64 Cap. 149.
528. Section 66 *ibid.*
529. Section 65 *ibid.*
530. *Kier (Cyprus) Ltd v. Trenco Constructions Ltd* 1 CLR 30 (1981).
531. 1 CLR 30 (1981).
532. *Kier (Cyprus) Ltd v. Trenco Constructions Ltd* 1 CLR 30 (1981).

Part II. Specific Contracts

Chapter 1. Agency

183. Agency, which is regulated in Cap. 149, has to be differentiated from apparent or ostensible authority ('φαινόμενη εξουσιοδότηση' in Greek, 'görünürdeki yetkisi' in Turkish), which has its roots in estoppel. This is part of Cyprus law according to section 29 of Law on Courts of 1960.[533] Ostensible or apparent authority is the authority of an agent as it appears to others. It often coincides with actual authority, but sometimes it exceeds actual authority.[534] It is a legal relationship between the principal and a third party, which is created on the basis of representations of the principal towards the third party with the intention of the third party to act upon it. The issue represented is that the agent has the authority to make, on behalf of the principal, a contract belonging within the width of his apparent authority in order to abide the principal to the promise to fulfil any obligations imposed on him from such an agreement. The form of such a representation may vary, having as the most usual one the conduct of the principal, meaning the principal allowing the agent to act in the manner that he does, with reference to handing business relationships with third parties.[535] The legal effect thereof is that the principal due to these representations may not deny the commitment that was established in such a way, when a third party based on this representation, makes actions unfavourable to himself or even differentiates his position.[536]

§1. Parties to Agency

184. Parties to an agency are an agent ('αντιπρόσωπος' in Greek, 'vekil' in Turkish) and the principal ('αντιπροσωπευόμενος' in Greek, 'müvekkil' in Turkish). Agent is a person employed to do any act for another or to represent another

533. *Paikkos v. Kontemeniotis* 1 CLR 50 (1989); *Marketventures Ltd v. Kallika* 1 CLR 48 (2010).
534. *Liopetri Transport Co. v. Constantinou* 1 CLR 424 (1971), citing *Hely-Hutchinson v. Brayhead Ltd a.a.* 3 All ER 98 (1967). *See also Stylianou v. Iliada Hotels Ltd*, District Court of Famagusta, Joint Civil Case Nos. 1293/2010 and 1294/2010, Judgment of 8 Jun. 2015, not published in CLR.
535. *Alpha Bank Cyprus Ltd v. Miller a.a.*, District Court of Paphos, Civil Case No. 2014/2008, Judgment of 31 Oct. 2017, not published in CLR, citing *Freeman and Lockyer v. Buckhurst Properties* All ER 630 (1964); *ING Re (UK) Ltd v. R & V Versicherung AG* All ER (Comm) 870 (2006).
536. *Filiki Asfalistiki Etaireia Ltd v. Dimitri* (1999) 1 CLR 551; *Marketventures Ltd v. Kallika* 1 CLR 48 (2010).

in dealings with third parties.[537] Any person, including legal persons,[538] may become an agent, but for persons, who are not competent to contract, so as to be responsible to his principal according to the provisions in that behalf herein contained.[539] An agent can be employed by any person who is competent to contract.[540] Principal is the person for whom an act is done by the agent, or who is represented by same.[541]

185. Under circumstances of such appointment being lawful, a subagent ('υποκατάστατος αντιπρόσωπος' in Greek, 'ikinci vekil' in Turkish) is a person competent to contract, employed by, and acting under the control of, the original agent in the business of the agency.[542] Proper appointment of subagent is negatively provided, as the statutory provision states that an agent may not lawfully employ another to perform acts which he has expressly or impliedly undertaken to perform personally, unless by the ordinary custom of trade a subagent may, or, from the nature of the agency, a subagent must be employed.[543]

186. Appointment of a subagent, must be separated from appointing an (additional) agent in the following case. An agent, holding an express or implied authority to name another person to act for the principal in the business of the agency, is statutory empowered to name another person accordingly. Such person is an agent of the principal for such part of the business of the agency as is entrusted to him, and not a subagent.[544]

§2. Formation of Agency

187. Due to agency being a special form of contract, the aforementioned on formation of contract equally apply here. However, under the explicit statutory provision, to the creation of agency, no consideration is necessary.[545] Further, the authority of an agent may be expressed or implied.[546] It is deemed to be expressed, when it is given by words spoken or written, whereas it is implied, when it is to be inferred from the circumstances of the case. All things spoken or written or the ordinary course of dealing may be accounted circumstances of the case.[547]

---

537. Section 142 Cap. 149. *See* in this respect *General Attorney v. G.T.P. Electrical Products Ltd* 1 CLR 2326 (1998); *Christopher Scottis Ltd a.a. v. Scottish & Newcastle International Ltd a.a.*, Supreme Court of Cyprus, Civil Appeal No. 179/2011, Judgment of 20 Sep. 2017, not published in CLR.
538. *Lindos Constructions Ltd v. Dieufthintis Tmimatos Kinonikon Asfaliseon* 1 CLR 17 (1993).
539. Section 144 Cap. 149.
540. Section 143 *ibid.*
541. Section 142 *ibid.*
542. Section 151 *ibid.*
543. Section 150 *ibid.*
544. Section 154 *ibid.*
545. Section 145 *ibid.*
546. Section 146 *ibid.*
547. Section 147 *ibid.*

§3. Content of Agency

188. An agent is given an authority to do an act set out in the agreed authority.[548] He is further statutory empowered to do every lawful thing which is necessary to do such act. This also applies to authority to carry on a business.[549] In cases of emergency, an agent has the authority to do all such acts for the purpose of protecting his principal from loss as would be done by a person of ordinary prudence, in his own case, under similar circumstances.[550]

189. When acts are done without authority, ratification ('έγκριση' in Greek, 'onaylama' in Turkish) may follow. A principal may choose to ratify or to disown such acts done by an agent or subagent, as long as these are performed without his knowledge or authority.[551] Ratification may be expressed or implied in the conduct of the person on whose behalf the acts are done.[552] If a principal chooses to ratify such acts, the same effects will follow, as if they had been performed by his authority,[553] save for subjecting a third person to damages or terminating any right or interest of a third person.[554] Ratification has effect to the whole of the transaction, of which such act formed a part.[555] However, ratification fails, when the principal's knowledge of the facts of the case is materially defective.[556]

§4. The Parties' Duties and Responsibilities

I. Agent's Duty to Principal

190. It is the agent's statutory duty to conduct the business of his principal according to the directions given by the principal,[557] or, in the absence of any such directions, according to the custom which prevails in doing business of the same kind at the place where the agent conducts such business. When the agent acts otherwise, if any loss be sustained, he must make it good to his principal, and, if any profit accrues, he must account for it.[558] Especially on the required skill and diligence, an agent is bound to conduct the agency with as much skill as is generally possessed by persons engaged in a similar business, unless the principal has notice of his want thereof. Furthermore, the agent is always bound to act with reasonable

548. *Protopappa v. Protopappa a.a.* 1 CLR 1329 (2002).
549. Section 148 Cap. 149.
550. Section 149 *ibid.*
551. Section 156 *ibid. See* in this respect *Pourikkos v. Savva a.o.* 1 CLR 507 (1991); *Spyrou a.a. v. Kosta Kyriakou & Sons Ltd a.o.* 1 CLR 663 (1992).
552. Section 157 Cap. 149.
553. Section 156 *ibid.*
554. Section 160 *ibid.*
555. Section 159 *ibid.*
556. Section 158 *ibid.*
557. *Cyprus Popular Bank Public Co. Ltd v. Otis Elevators (Cyprus) Ltd*, Supreme Court of Cyprus, Civil Appeal No. 371/2009, Judgment of 16 Feb. 2015, not published in CLR.
558. Section 171 Cap. 149.

diligence, and to use such skill as he possesses,[559] whereas he is in a fiduciary position towards the principal.[560] It is equally his duty to make compensation to his principal in respect of the direct consequences of his own neglect want of skill or misconduct. Exceptions thereto are loss or damage indirectly or remotely caused by such neglect, want of skill or misconduct.[561] An agent is also bound to render proper accounts to his principal on demand, as well as to use all reasonable diligence in communicating with his principal and in seeking to obtain his instruction.[562]

191. Should an agent deal on his own account in the business of the agency, the principal enjoys certain statutory rights. In particular, if, in such a case, the agent has not obtained the consent of his principal and acquainted him with all material circumstances which have come to his own knowledge on the subject, the principal may repudiate the transaction, as long as one of the following conditions is fulfilled. The first one is any material fact being dishonestly concealed from him by the agent. The second condition is dealings of the agent having been disadvantageous to him.[563] Parallel to the aforementioned, a further statutory right of the principal is claiming from the agent any benefit, which may have resulted to him from the transaction done in his account without the principal's knowledge.[564]

192. The agent's duty in selecting a subagent for his principal is to do so by exercising the same amount of discretion as a man of ordinary prudence would exercise in his own case. If he does not fail to do so, he is not responsible to the principal for the acts or negligence of the agent so selected.[565]

193. The responsibility related to a subagent depends on whether the same subagent is properly appointed. When this is true, the principal is, so far as regards third persons, represented by the subagent, and is bound by and responsible for his acts, as if he were an agent originally appointed by the principal.[566] Also, the agent is responsible to the principal for the acts of the subagent,[567] whereas the subagent is responsible for his acts to the agent, but not to the principal, except in case of fraud or wilful wrong.[568] However, when the appointment was not proper, the agent stands towards such subagent in the relation of a principal to an agent and is responsible for his acts both to the principal and to third persons. The principal is not represented by or responsible for the acts of the not properly appointed subagent, nor is this person responsible to the principal.[569]

---

559. Section 172 *ibid.*
560. *Iakovou a.a. v. Zapri* 1 CLR 926 (2008); *Agrotou a.a. v. Agrotou*, Supreme Court of Cyprus, Civil Appeal No. 288/2010, Judgment of 31 May 2016, not published in CLR.
561. Section 172 Cap. 149.
562. Sections 173 and 174 *ibid.*
563. Section 175 *ibid.*
564. Section 176 *ibid.*
565. Section 155 *ibid.*
566. Section 152(1) *ibid.*
567. Section 152(2) *ibid.*
568. Section 152(3) *ibid.*
569. Section 153 *ibid.*

194. The agent also bears the statutory duty to pay to his principal all sums received on his account.[570] At the same time, he has the right to retain out of such sums, all moneys due to himself in respect of advances made or expenses properly incurred by him in conducting such business, and also such remuneration as may be payable to him for acting as agent.[571] He is further entitled to retain goods, papers and other property of the principal received by him, until the amount due to himself for commission, disbursements and services in respect of the same has been paid or accounted for to him, save for any contrary contract.[572] Agent's remuneration becomes due upon completion of the agreed act, save for any special contract. Nevertheless, an agent may detain moneys received by him on account of goods sold earlier than that, that being before the whole of the good consigned to him for sale may is sold, or before the sale is actually complete.[573] In any event, an agent guilty of misconduct in the business of the agency is not entitled to any remuneration in respect of that part of the business that he has misconducted.[574]

II. Principal's Duty to Agent

195. The principal has the duty to indemnify the agent against the consequences of all lawful acts done by such agent in exercise of the authority conferred upon him.[575] The same duty applies to acts having caused an injury to the rights of third persons but done in good faith.[576] If, however, the act agreed to be done by way of agency is a criminal one, the principal is not liable to the agent to indemnify him against the consequences of that act.[577] Lastly, the principal bears the duty to make compensation to his agent in respect of injury caused to such agent by the principal's neglect or want of skill.[578]

§5. Agency and Third Persons

196. Evidently, contracts entered into through an agent, along with obligations arising from acts done by an agent, may be enforced in the same manner, as if they had been entered into and done by the principal in person. They shall equally have the same legal consequences.[579] In the event that an agent acts beyond his authorization, the part done within authorization is binding. This rule applies only under

570. Section 178 *ibid. See* in this respect *Prolific Insurance Consultants Ltd v. Liberty Life Insurance Public Co Ltd* 1 CLR 1069 (2010).
571. Section 177 Cap. 149.
572. Section 181 *ibid.*
573. Section 179 *ibid.*
574. Section 180 *ibid.*
575. Section 182 *ibid.*
576. Section 183 *ibid.*
577. Section 184 *ibid.*
578. Section 185 *ibid.*
579. Section 186 *ibid.*

the condition that the act done within authorization can be separated from the part done without.[580] If said condition is not fulfilled, the principal is not bound to recognize the transaction.[581]

197. The agent may, generally, not personally enforce contracts entered into by him on behalf of his principal. He is equally not bound by them.[582] Exceptions thereto are the following cases: (a) where the contract is made by an agent for the sale or purchase of goods for a merchant resident abroad; (b) where the agent does not disclose the name of his principal;[583] and (c) where the principal, though disclosed, cannot be sued.[584] Further exceptions may be agreed in a contract.[585]

198. Any notice given to the agent, as between the principal and third parties, has the same legal consequence as if it had been given to the principal, provided it is given in the course of the business transacted by him for the principal. Said rule applies to information obtained by the agent as well.[586]

199. Turning to contracts made by two agents, where one of them neither knows nor has a reason to suspect that the other is an agent, his principal may require the performance of the contract. However, the other contracting party has, as against the principal, the same rights as he would have had as against the agent of the agent had been principal.[587] Should the principal disclose himself before the contract is completed, the other party may refuse to fulfil the contract. For this option to take effect, this other party has to show that, if he had known who was the principal in the contract, or if he had known that the agent was not a principal, he would not have entered the contract.[588] In the similar event of making a contract with a person, neither knowing nor having reasonable ground to suspect that the other party is an agent, the principal can only obtain performance of the contract, which is subject to the rights and obligations subsisting between the agent and the other party to the contract.[589]

---

580. Section 187 *ibid.*
581. Section 188 *ibid.*
582. Section 190(1) *ibid. See* in this respect *Thunder Shipping Co Ltd v. Lloyd Triestino, Di.Nav.S.p.A.* 1 CLR 135 (1984); *Kypriaki Epitropi Sitiron v. Zako Ltd* 1 CLR 1046 (1990); *Eurogal Surveys Ltd v. D Trade International Ltd*, Supreme Court of Cyprus, Civil Appeal No. 348/2009, Judgment of 17 Oct. 2014, not published in CLR.
583. *Yiannakouri a.a. (No. 3) v. Cyprus Sea Cruises (Limassol) Ltd* 1 CLR 397 (1965); *Georgiades v. Bernoulli Trading Co. Ltd* 1 CLR 629 (1994); *Evaggelides v. Kosma a.a.* 1 CLR 932 (1998); *Tecoma Travel & Tours Ltd v. Basos Ioannou Ltd* 1 CLR 399 (2007).
584. Section 190(2) Cap. 149.
585. Section 190(1) *ibid.*
586. Section 189 *ibid. See* in this respect *Isseyegh v. Cyprus* 4 CLR 956 (1992); *Sergidou v. Dimos Lefkosias a.a.* 4 CLR 211 (1993).
587. Section 191(1) Cap. 149.
588. Section 191(2) *ibid.*
589. Section 192 *ibid.*

200. Parties contracting with an agent, in cases of the agent being personally liable, may hold liable him, his principal or both of them.[590] Nevertheless, where both agent and principal bear liability, contracting parties have the duty to abide to any relevant representations made. In particular, parties, who have made a contract with an agent and induced him to act upon the belief that only the principal will be held liable, may not afterwards hold the agent liable. Equally, the same parties, who induced the principal to act upon the belief that only the agent will be held liable, may not afterwards hold the principal liable.[591] Especially, when a company is acting as an agent, this might trigger piercing its corporate veil.[592]

201. The last set of provisions relates to pretended agents, misrepresentation and fraud. A pretended agent inducing a third person to deal with him as agent of another is liable to compensate the other in respect of any loss or damage which he has incurred by so dealing, of his alleged principal does not ratify his acts.[593] Also, such agent has no authority to require the performance of the contract.[594] The (alleged) principal of an unauthorized agent is generally not bound by his performed acts and incurred obligations. However, he might be bound by such, if he has by his words or conduct induced said third persons to believe that such acts and obligations were within the scope of the agent's authority.[595] Lastly, misrepresentations and frauds committed by agents have the same effect in agreements as if such actions had been committed by the principals, as long as they were committed in matters falling within the agents' authority.[596]

§6. Termination of Agency

202. An agency can be terminated in the following ways: when the principal revokes his authority; when the agent renounces the business of the agency; when the business of the agency has been completed; when the principal or the agent dies or becomes of unsound mind; and when the principal is being adjudicated a bankrupt or insolvent under applicable provisions.[597] Termination takes effect as soon as it becomes known to the agent, as regards to him, or third persons, as regards to them.[598] Especially in cases of the agent having an interest in the property forming the subject matter of the agency, where an express contract is absent, the agency

590. Section 193 *ibid. See* in this respect *Prokopiou v. Adelfoi Tymvioi Ltd* 1 CLR 903 (2007).
591. Section 194 Cap. 149.
592. *Markides v. Ellinas Finance Public Company Ltd*, Supreme Court of Cyprus, Civil Appeal No. 97/2011, Judgment of 5 May 2017, not published in CLR.
593. Section 195 Cap. 149.
594. Section 196 *ibid.*
595. Section 197 *ibid. See* in this respect *Filiki Asfalistiki Etaireia Ltd v. Demetri* 1 CLR 551 (1999).
596. Section 198 Cap. 149.
597. Section 161 *ibid.*
598. Section 168 *ibid.*

cannot be terminated to the prejudice of such interest.[599] Termination of an agent's authority causes the termination of the authority of all subagents appointed by him.[600]

203. Revocation underlies specific statutory provisions. First, it may be exercised through giving reasonable notice,[601] expressed or implied,[602] by the principal at any time before the authority has been exercised so as to bind the principal.[603] If the authority has been exercised only partly, it may not be revoked so far as regards such acts and obligation as arise from acts already done in the agency.[604] When it was agreed that the agency should be continued for any period of time, the principal must make compensation to the agent for any previous revocation of the agency without sufficient cause.[605] Also, if no reasonable notice of revocation is given and damage thereby resulted to the agent, the damage must be made good.[606]

204. Similarly, renunciation underlies specific statutory provisions. In particular, it prerequisites reasonable notice, which may be expressed or implied in the conduct of the agent.[607] Whether a notice is reasonable or not, it is a matter to be decided upon the specific circumstances of each case. Decisive factors may be the expenses incurred for establishing and maintaining the agency or the work imposed by the principal.[608] If no notice or no such notice is given, the damage resulting to the principal, if any, must be made good by the agent.[609] Further, in cases, where the agency was agreed to be continued for any period of time, the agent must make compensation to the principal for any previous revocation of the agency without sufficient cause.[610]

205. Lastly, in the events that the principal's death or unsound mind causes the agency to be terminated, the agent bears the statutory duty to take, on behalf of the representatives of his late principal, all reasonable steps for the protection and preservation of the interests entrusted to him.[611]

---

599. Section 162 *ibid.*
600. Section 170 *ibid.*
601. Section 166 *ibid.*
602. Section 167 *ibid.*
603. Section 163 *ibid.*
604. Section 164 *ibid.*
605. Section 165 *ibid.*
606. Section 166 *ibid.*
607. Sections 166 and 167 *ibid.*
608. *Costas Chr. Karacis Ltd v. Doritis Makaroni Factory Ltd* 1 CLR 251 (2001), citing *Martin-Baker Aircraft Co Ltd v. Canadian Flight Equipment* 2 All ER 722 (1955) and *Decro Wall International S.A. v. Practitioners in Marketing* 2 All ER 216 (1971).
609. Section 166 Cap. 149.
610. Section 165 *ibid.*
611. Section 169 *ibid.*

Chapter 2. Bailment

206. Bailment ('παρακαταθήκη με ευρεία έννοια' in Greek, 'saklatım' in Turkish) is statutory defined as the delivery of goods by one person to another for some purpose, upon a contract that they shall, when the purpose is accomplished, be returned or otherwise disposed of according to the directions of the person delivering them.[612] Joint ownership of a good does not prevent it from being the object of a bailment.[613] Goods ('αγαθά' in Greek, 'eşya' in Turkish) in this respect means every kind of movable property and includes bills of exchange, promissory notes, bonds whether in customary form or not other than those secured by mortgage of immovable property, share certificates[614] or share warrants for shares in a company.[615] Immovable property may not be the object of a bailment.[616]

207. Alongside the aforementioned statutory definition of bailment, this is also established in common law. Bailment under common law derives from Roman law ('depositum') and indicates a legal relationship between the bailor and the bailee, whereby a movable thing is delivered for safekeeping with or without consideration.[617] It has been further ruled that unless it is sought to increase or diminish the burden imposed upon a bailee by the very fact of bailment, it is not necessary to incorporate it into the Law of Contract and to prove a consideration.[618] Common law also recognizes the institution of sub-bailment.[619] This involves a third party who, with the bailor's consent, accepts the custody of chattels from a bailee and thereby assumes the obligations of a bailee towards the bailor. The nature of these obligations will, as in the case of an ordinary bailment, vary according to the circumstances in which and the purposes for which the goods are delivered. The sub-bailee also owes, concurrently, the same duties to the original bailee, whose obligations to the bailor are not extinguished by the sub-bailment.[620]

§1. Parties to Bailment

208. Bailee ('θεματοφύλακας' in Greek, 'saklayıcı (müstevdi)' in Turkish) is called the person to whom they are delivered.[621] The delivery to the bailee may be made by doing anything which has the effect of putting the goods in the possession

612. Section 106(1)(b) *ibid.*
613. Section 123 *ibid.*
614. *Markides v. Ellinas Finance Public Company Ltd*, Supreme Court of Cyprus, Civil Appeal No. 97/2011, Judgment of 5 May 2017, not published in CLR.
615. Section 106(1)(a) Cap. 149.
616. *Christoforou v. Christoforou* 1 CLR 1551 (1998).
617. *Ioannou v. Kounnides* 1C CLR 1215 (1998).
618. *Kourris v. Alpo Ltd a.o.* 1 CLR 217 (1981), citing *State of Gujarat v. Memon Mohammad* 3 SCR 938 (1967).
619. *Ioannou v. Kounnides* 1C CLR 1215 (1998).
620. *Kourris v. Alpo Ltd a.o.* 1 CLR 217 (1981), citing *Gilchrist Watt and Sanderson Pty Ltd v. York Products Pty Ltd* 3 All ER 825 (1970).
621. Section 106(1)(b) Cap. 149.

of the intended bailee or of any person authorized to hold them on his behalf.[622] Notwithstanding this, a person already in possession of the goods of another may make a contract to hold them as a bailee. He shall then become the bailee, despite him being already in possession of the goods.[623]

209. Bailor ('παρακαταθέτης' in Greek, 'saklatan (mudi)' in Turkish) is called the person delivering the goods, as well as the owner of such goods, in the aforementioned event of a bailee already being in possession of the goods, where delivery by way of bailment is absent.[624]

§2. Formation of Bailment

210. Bailment is a contract and therefore all aforementioned essential conditions for the formation of a contract, such as an agreement,[625] (*see* in this respect paragraphs 20 et seq. above), equally apply here. However, consideration is merely an optional condition for the formation of a bailment.[626] To the contrary, a contract gratuitous or not, in order to be construed as a statutory bailment, it needs to provide for return of the delivered (or already possessed) goods, or delivery of same, upon the lapse of a time period or the accomplishment of a purpose.[627]

§3. Content of Bailment

211. Bailment may have such terms and conditions, as the parties may agree. In particular, it may set out the bailee's right to use the bailed goods,[628] instructions to the bailee regarding returning of the bailed goods, in case of joint ownership,[629] or instructions to the bailee not to deliver to the bailor or deliver to third parties any increase or profit accrued from the bailed goods.[630]

212. The effect of mixing bailor's goods with the bailee's goods is statutory specified and depends upon, whether this occurred with bailor's consent or not, as well as, whether mixed goods can be separated or not. If the bailor consented to such action of the bailee, they shall have an interest, in proportion to their respective shares, in the mixture such produced.[631] If the bailor did not consent and the goods can be separated or divided, the property in the goods remains in the parties

622. Section 107 *ibid.*
623. Section 106(2) *ibid.*
624. Section 106(1)(a) and 106(2) *ibid.*
625. *Hamade v. Anthimos Demetriou Ltd a.o.* 1 CLR 443 (1994); *St. George (G.N.W.) Ltd v. National Bank of Greece (Cyprus) Ltd* 1 CLR 337 (2010).
626. Sections 117 and 120 Cap. 149.
627. Section 118 *ibid.*
628. Section 112 *ibid.*
629. Section 123 *ibid.*
630. Section 121 *ibid.*
631. Section 113 *ibid.*

respectively. However, the bailee is bound to bear the expense of separation or division, as well as any damage arising from the mixture.[632] Lastly, in the case of lack of consent and impossibility of separation or division, the bailor is entitled to be compensated by the bailee for the loss of the goods.[633]

§4. The Parties' Duties and Responsibilities

I. Duties and Responsibilities of a Bailee

213. In all cases of bailment, the bailee is bound to take as much case of the goods bailed to him as a man of ordinary prudence would, under similar circumstances, take of his own goods of the same bulk, quality and value as the goods bailed.[634] In the absence of any special contract, he is not responsible for the loss, destruction or deterioration of the thing bailed, if he has taken the amount of care of it described above.[635] These provisions are similar to Articles 18(1) and (2) and 20(1)[636] of the Warsaw Convention of 1929.[637,638]

214. The bailment may foresee the bailee's right to use the bailed goods in a specific manner or under specific conditions. If said goods are not used in the agreed manner or under such conditions and damage arose from or during this use, the bailee is liable to make compensation to the bailor therefor.[639]

215. Most importantly the bailee has the duty to return the bailed goods. This duty may be triggered by time, a quantity factor, or accomplishment of purpose, a quality factor. More specifically, the statute sets out that it is the duty of the bailee

632. Section 114 *ibid.*
633. Section 115 *ibid.*
634. Section 109 *ibid.*
635. Section 110 *ibid.*
636. These provisions read: 'Article 18(1): The carrier is liable for damage sustained in the event of the destruction or loss of, or of damage to, any registered luggage or any goods, if the occurrence which caused the damage so sustained took place during the carriage by air; (2) The carriage by air within the meaning of the preceding paragraph comprises the period during which the luggage or goods are in charge of the carrier, whether in an aerodrome or on board an aircraft, or, in the case of a landing outside an aerodrome, in any place whatsoever.

Article 20(1): The carrier is not liable if he proves that he and his agents have taken all necessary measures to avoid the damage or that it was impossible for him or them to take such measures.'
637. Convention for the Unification of Certain Rules Relating to International Carriage by Air, signed at Warsaw on 12 Oct. 1929 (the 'Warsaw Convention'). This convention, drafted at a time when aviation was a fledgling industry with a dubious safety record and in need of protection from excessive claims for compensation, it imposed a series of limits on the liability of air carriers for damages. In the 1990s the inadequacy of the Warsaw Convention was recognized (*see Proposal for a Council Decision on the approval by the European Communities of the Montreal Convention*, COM(2000)0446 final, OJ C 337 E of 28 Nov. 2000, p. 225) and it was replaced in 1999 by the Convention for the Unification of Certain Rules for International Carriage by Air (the 'Montreal Convention').
638. *Austrian Airlines v. Genikes Asfaleies Kyprou Ltd* 1 CLR 764 (1991).
639. Section 112 Cap. 149.

to return, or deliver according to the bailor's directions, the goods bailed, without demand, as soon as the time for which they were bailed has expired, or the purpose for which were bailed has been accomplished.[640] If the bailee fails to do so, he shall have to compensate the bailor for the market value of the goods in dispute during the time that their delivery was denied.[641] In the event that the bailor is not the owner of the bailed goods, and the bailee in good faith, delivers them back to the bailor, or according to the latter's instructions, the bailee has no responsibility to the owner for such delivery.[642] Also, if the bailors are several, but not all owners of the bailed goods, in a case of joint ownership, the bailee may deliver them back to, or according to the instructions of one joint owner without the consent of all, save for any agreement to the contrary.[643] Further, the bailee bears the duty to deliver to the bailor, or according to his instructions, any increase or profit, which may have accrued from the goods bailed, save for a contract to the contrary.[644]

216. The bailee may request from the bailee to repay the necessary expenses incurred by him for the purpose of the bailment, where by the conditions thereof, the goods were to be kept, carried or have work done upon them by the bailee for the bailor and no remuneration was foreseen for the bailee.[645] The bailee has further the right to treat bailed goods as lien, under specific statutory conditions. Generally, where the bailee has, in accordance with the purpose of the bailment, rendered any service involving the exercise of labour or skill of labour or skill in respect of the bailed goods, he has, save for an agreement to the contrary, a right to retain such goods until he receives due remuneration for the services he has rendered in respect of them.[646] Especially, when bankers, factors and wharfingers act as bailees, they may, in the absence of an agreement to the contrary, retain as a security for a general balance of account any goods bailed to them. Other persons may do so only if an express contract to that effect was made.[647]

II. Duties and Responsibilities of a Bailor

217. The bailor has the statutory duty to disclose to the bailee faults in the goods bailed, as long as he is aware of them and they materially interfere with the use of them or expose the bailee to extraordinary risks. If he fails to do so, he is responsible for damage arising to the bailee directly from such faults.[648] In the specific

640. Section 118 *ibid.*
641. *Merkis v. Intertobacco (Cyprus) Ltd* 1 CLR 1091 (2003), citing *Henderson & Co v. Williams* 1 QB 521 (1895).
642. Section 124 Cap. 149.
643. Section 123 *ibid.*
644. Section 121 *ibid.*
645. Section 116 *ibid.*
646. Section 128 *ibid.*
647. Section 129 *ibid.*
648. Section 108(1) *ibid.*

event that the goods are bailed for hire, the bailor bears said responsibility for damage, regardless of his knowledge of faults.[649] The bailor has further the statutory duty to repay to the bailee the necessary expenses incurred for the goods being kept or carried, or having work done upon them by the bailee, only if it agreed that the bailee receives no remuneration.[650] Lastly, if the bailor had no right to make the bailment or to receive back the goods or to give instructions in respect of same goods, he is responsible to the bailee for any loss, which he might suffer.[651]

218. Especially for goods lent gratuitously ('για χαριστική αιτία' in Greek, 'bedava' in Turkish), it is set out that the lender may require their return at any time. However, if, on the faith of such a loan, the borrower has acted in such a manner that the extraordinary return of the thing lent would cause him loss exceeding the benefit actually derived by him from the loans, the lender must, if he compels the return, indemnify the borrower. Indemnification has to cover the amount in which the loss so occasioned exceeds the benefit so derived.[652]

§5. Bailment and Third Persons

219. Persons being third parties to bailment have the following statutory rights. Third persons claiming goods bailed may take legal proceedings to stop the delivery of the goods to the bailor, along with deciding the title to the same goods.[653] Third persons, being finders of goods may retain these against the owner until they receive compensation for trouble and expense voluntarily incurred by him to preserve the goods and to find the owner, but may not sue the owner for such compensation.[654] If the owner refuses to pay the lawful charges of the finder, or if he cannot with reasonable diligence be found, the finder may sell the found thing, when it is commonly the subject of sale, as long as one of the following condition is fulfilled: the thing is in danger of perishing or of losing the greater part of its value;[655] or the lawful charges of the finder, in respect of the thing found, amount to two-thirds of its value.[656]

220. In the event that a third party wrongly deprives the bailee of the use or possession of the goods bailed, or injures them in any manner, the bailee is entitled to use such remedies as the owner might have used in the like case, of no bailment had been made. However, such deprivation or injury gives the right to either the bailor or the bailee to bring legal proceedings against this third person.[657] The relief

649. Section 108(2) *ibid.*
650. Section 116 *ibid.*
651. Section 122 *ibid.*
652. Section 117 *ibid.*
653. Section 125 *ibid.*
654. Section 126 *ibid.*
655. Section 127(a) *ibid.*
656. Section 127(b) *ibid.*
657. Section 140 *ibid.*

or compensation obtained in such legal proceedings is dealt with, between the bailor and the bailee, according to their respective interests.[658]

§6. Termination of Bailment

221. Bailment is ordinarily terminated upon lapse of agreed time or achievement of agreed purpose. Alternatively, it is terminated, in the form of being a voidable contract at the option of the bailor, if the bailee does any act with regard to the goods bailed, which is inconsistent with the conditions of the bailment.[659] Also, death of either party terminates bailments, as long as they are gratuitous.[660]

658. Section 141 *ibid.*
659. Section 111 *ibid.*
660. Section 120 *ibid.*

Chapter 3. Gaming and Wagering

222. Generally, gaming is prohibited under section 30 Cap. 149 (*see* in this respect at paragraph 103 above). However, this provision coexists with the Law on Betting[661] (hereinafter 'Law No. 37(I)/2019') and the Law on Operation and Control of Casinos[662] (hereinafter 'Law No. 124(I)/2015'). Hence, it is safe to conclude that gaming is not allowed in Cyprus, but for gaming services, casino games and slots machines offered through the authorized persons at authorized premises under either Law No. 37(I)/2019 or Law No. 124(I)/2015.

§1. Law on Betting

223. This law is part of the Cypriot legislation, which implements Directive 98/34/EC.[663] It defines betting ('στοίχημα' in Greek, 'bahse' in Turkish) as any kind of betting conducted with reference to sports, the contestants of which are natural persons, and/or other events, where natural persons participate therein and that actually takes place, under the conditions that: the profits of every player are defined by the person organizing the bet, before or during its conduction, with reference to both the amount that every player has paid in order to participate in the bet and the specified performance value of the specific bet; and that it is conducted under a Class A or Class B permit.[664] Slots machines, online casinos, betting exchanges, spread bets and dog racing betting are strictly prohibited.[665] Operation of such activity may lead to monetary fine of up to EUR 300,000 and/or imprisonment of up to five years.[666]

224. Nothing in this law regulates anything related to formation, conditions, content or privity of contracts made for betting. However, the following statutory prohibitions deserve mention, as an agreement made without taking regard to these, is void under section 23 Cap. 149 (*see* in this regard paragraphs 81 et seq. above). In essence, betting services without obtaining the necessary permits, those being Class A permit,[667] Class B permit[668] and authorized representative permit[669] along

661. Law on Regulating Betting ('ο περί Στοιχημάτων Νόμος') No. 37 of 2019, OG I(I) No. 4692 of 21 Mar. 2019, p. 151.
662. Law on Operation and Control of Casinos ('ο περί της Λειτουργίας και του Ελέγχου Καζίνου Νόμος') No. 124 of 2015, OG I(I) No. 4524 of 17 Jul. 2015, p. 1039.
663. Directive 98/34/EC of the European Parliament and of the Council of 22 Jun. 1998 laying down a procedure for the provision of information in the field of technical standards and regulations, OJ L 204 of 21 Jul. 1998, p. 37. Yet, this has been repealed and replaced by Directive (EU) 2015/1535 of the European Parliament and of the Council of 9 Sep. 2015 laying down a procedure for the provision of information in the field of technical regulations and of rules on Information Society services, OJ L 241 of 17 Sep. 2015, p. 1.
664. Section 2 Law No. 37(I)/2019.
665. Sections 83, 84, 85(1), 86(2) and 87(2) *ibid.*
666. Sections 83, 84, 85(5), 86(2) and 87(2) *ibid.*
667. Sections 16–31 and 51–57 *ibid.*
668. Sections 16–31 and 58–70 *ibid.*
669. Sections 16–31 and 36–38 *ibid.*

with authorized premises permit[670] is prohibited. Such actions constitute criminal offences leading to imprisonment of up to five years and/or monetary fine of up to EUR 300,000 (section 79 Law No. 37(I)/2019).[671] Similarly, liable to a monetary fine of up to EUR 170,000 and/or imprisonment of up to three years is any person performing betting services in violation of the permit's terms and conditions (section 80 Law No. 37(I)/2019).[672] Further, anyone participating in any betting conducted in violation of any of the provisions of this law is liable to a monetary fine of up to EUR 50,000 and/or imprisonment of up to one year.[673] Also, when betting services are on unauthorized premises or are taking place in violation of the premises' authorization, a monetary fine of up to EUR 100,000 and/or imprisonment of up to two years may be imposed on the operator of the premises,[674] whereas an abatement order for such premises is within the court's discretionary power, depending on the case.[675]

225. In addition to the above prohibitions, statutory restrictions are applied to advertising betting, although the activity as such is not prohibited. In particular, any person advertising betting in a manner:

- suggesting that this relates to or promotes social acceptance, personal or financial success or solving any personal, financial or social problem; or
- including the support of famous personalities in a manner suggesting that their success relates to betting; or
- that may influence in any way underaged persons into participating therein; or
- promoting usage of betting services offered by persons not having the statutory permits; or
- that is neither honest ('τιμιότητα' in Greek, 'samimiyet' in Turkish) nor decent ('ευπρέπεια' in Greek, 'nezaket' in Turkish)

is committing a crime and, in the event of him being convicted, he is liable to a monetary fine of up to EUR 30,000 and/or imprisonment of up to six months.[676]

226. Special provisions ensure and facilitate the protection of minors. Generally, minors may not participate in betting, although no explicit provision stating such prohibition is to be found in the wording of the law. However, it is clear that they are not allowed to enter premises authorized for betting. To this effect, every occupier of such premises is obliged to post a relevant notice in Greek, Turkish and English.[677] The same warning must be stated in a webpage when electronic betting is conducted through such.[678] Further, when any person invites, motivates or allows

670. Sections 39–50 *ibid.*
671. Section 79 *ibid.*
672. Section 80 *ibid.*
673. Section 81 *ibid.*
674. Section 82(1) *ibid.*
675. Section 82(4) *ibid.*
676. Section 89(1)(a), (b), (c), (d) and (e) *ibid.*
677. Section 45(1)(b) *ibid.*
678. Section 67(g) *ibid.*

an underaged person to participate in betting or enter to authorized premises, such a person is liable to monetary fine of up to EUR 50,000 and/or imprisonment of up to one year, if found guilty by the court.[679]

§2. Law on Operation and Control of Casinos

227. This law regulates the operation of casinos ('καζίνο' in Greek, 'casino' in Turkish), those being the premises approved by the competent authority, on which it is allowed to play casino games and to have slot machines available for use, including at the main area of the casino, in any corridors within this area that lead to other areas of a casino resort and any areas or other facilities accommodated therein. The term establishment of casino is a synonym.[680] Casino game ('παίγνιο καζίνου' or 'παιχνίδι καζίνου' in Greek, 'şans oyunu' in Turkish) means a game of luck or a game that is partly of luck and partly of dexterity, which is playing in a casino with cards, dices, equipment or any mechanical, electromechanical or electrical apparatus or machine for money, checks, credit cards or other means of value. Slot machine ('παιγνιομηχάνημα' in Greek, 'slot makineleri' in Turkish) means an apparatus or object that fully or partly operates mechanically or electronically and which: is designed to the purpose of being used to the aim of conducting games of luck or games combining luck and dexterity; is designed to the purpose of gaining profit upon installing betting in the apparatus; and is approved by the competent authority as such.[681]

228. This law regulates the operation of casino resorts and provides detailed provisions for authorizations for casino resorts[682] and their employees,[683] the operation of casinos,[684] the general prohibition of complementary services, gifts, cash or other objects of value,[685] internal controls of casinos,[686] supervision and controls of the operator,[687] fraud,[688] taxation[689] and the casino supervising authority.[690] Central provision is the one prohibiting any person from conducting or offering any facilitation for casino games or slot machines without having obtained a valid authorization by the competent authorities. Any person acting in violation of this prohibition is guilty of a crime and in case of conviction, he is liable to a monetary fine of up to EUR 1 million and/or imprisonment of up to five years.[691]

679. Section 91(a) and (b) *ibid.*
680. Section 2 Law No. 124(I)/2015.
681. Section 2 *ibid.*
682. Sections 14–32 *ibid.*
683. Sections 51–53 *ibid.*
684. Sections 33–44 *ibid.*
685. Section 42 *ibid.*
686. Sections 54–59 *ibid.*
687. Sections 60–66 *ibid.*
688. Sections 67–73 *ibid.*
689. Sections 79–88 *ibid.*
690. Sections 5–13 *ibid.*
691. Sections 18 and 89 *ibid.*

229. This law states explicitly that any contract made between the administrator of a casino resort and clients of such regarding casino games conducted pursuant to the provisions of this law and any relevant Regulations are valid.[692] Equally, such contracts are valid when they relate to slot machines authorized and operating according to the same provisions.[693]

230. Advertisement of casino resorts is restricted, as it underlies strict statutory conditions, both positive and negative. Such advertisement must be true, of good taste, informative and not insulting in any manner.[694] In addition, it shall not advance casino games as an alternative financial solution, and it shall promote a casino resort as a whole and not just the facility of games.[695] Further, it shall take into consideration the need to protect minors and other vulnerable persons from any negative effects that may be caused by casino games.[696] Finally, an advertisement has to guide persons that wish to engage in casino games towards a strictly controlled and safe casino resort, so that they refrain from visiting illegal casinos or casinos operating in a not-adequately controlled environment.[697] Non-compliance with these conditions by any person is a crime and, upon conviction, it may lead to monetary fine of up to EUR 600,000 and/or imprisonment for a maximum of three years.[698] If the person violating these conditions is the operator of the casino resort, he is liable solely to a monetary fine of up to EUR 1 million.[699] Oddly, the law states, in addition and parallel to the aforementioned penalties, that violation of section 65 of this law, that being the conditions of advertisement, may lead to imprisonment of up to six months and/or a monetary fine of up to EUR 100,000.[700]

231. Turning to minors, as already seen above under the Law on Betting, special provisions ensure and facilitate the protection of minors. Vital statutory provision is the one specifying minors, according to which minors for the purpose of this law are any persons younger than twenty-one years.[701] Minors are not allowed to play any casino games or slot machines, or be next to or coming close to any equipment of game or table of game in the main area of casino resorts.[702] However, they enjoy a restricted permission to transit through the facilities of a casino resort, which does not extend to staying in them, using specific corridors towards other facilities not related to casino games, as long as they are accompanied by their parents or other adult persons.[703] Any violation of these restrictions may lead to opening a disciplinary procedure against any operator or employee of the casino, who allows a

692. Section 14(a) *ibid.*
693. Section 14(b) *ibid.*
694. Section 65(3)(a) *ibid.*
695. Section 65(3)(b) and (c) *ibid.*
696. Section 65(3)(d) *ibid.*
697. Section 65(3)(e) *ibid.*
698. Sections 65(5) and 96(2) *ibid.*
699. Sections 65(5) and 96(1) *ibid.*
700. Section 93 *ibid.*
701. Section 2 *ibid.*
702. Section 39(1) *ibid.*
703. Section 39(2) *ibid.*

minor to violate them.[704] Finally, any person encouraging or allowing a minor to participate to casino games or to use slot machines or to enter premises of casino games is guilty of a crime and if convicted may be imprisoned for up to one year and/or ordered to pay a monetary fine of up to EUR 200,000. For a conviction, it is necessary that actions to said aim were knowingly performed. Omission does not suffice.[705]

704. Section 39(6) and (7) *ibid.*
705. Section 95 *ibid.*

Chapter 4. Sale of Goods

232. Sale of goods is regulated by Law on Sale of Goods of 1994.[706] The provisions of Cap. 149 also apply to such contracts, save in so far as they are inconsistent with the express provisions of Law No. 10(I)/94.[707]

233. A contract of sale of goods is a contract whereby the seller transfers or agrees to transfer the property in goods to the buyer for a price.[708] Yet, when such contract is made between parties, whose places of business are in different states, the Law on Contracts for the International Sale of Goods[709] (hereinafter 'Law No. 55(III)/2004') is applied.[710] This law ratifies the United Nations Convention on Contracts for the International Sale of Goods.[711] The fact that the parties have their places of business in different states has to appear either from the contract or from any dealings between, or from information disclosed by, the parties at any time before or at the conclusion of the contract. If such disclosure does not take place, this fact shall be disregarded.[712] The nationality of the parties or the civil or commercial character of the same or of the contract is not a factor relevant to the application of this law.[713] Finally, the parties to a contract have the power to exclude the application of this law, to derogate therefrom or to vary the effect of any of its provisions.[714] This law has been neither discussed nor analysed in any court judgments in Cyprus.

§1. Parties to a Contract of Sale

234. Seller ('πωλητής' in Greek, 'satıcı (satan)' in Turkish) means a person who sells or agrees to sell goods. Goods ('αγαθά' in Greek, 'emtia' in Turkish) means every kind of movable property other than actionable claims and money and includes stock and shares, growing crops, grass, and things attached to or forming part of the land which are agreed to be severed before sale or under the contract of sale. Buyer ('αγοραστής' in Greek, 'satın alıcı (alıcı) (satın alan)' in Turkish) means a person who buys or agrees to buy goods.[715] It was held that the word 'sold' in its

706. Law on Sale of Goods ('ο περί Πώλησης Αγαθών Νόμος') No. 10 of 1994, OG I(I) No. 2863 of 4 Mar. 1994, p. 17. As last amended by amending Law No. 101 of 1999, OG I(I) No. 3339 of 23 Jul. 1999, p. 321.
707. Section 3 Law No. 10(I)/1994.
708. Section 4(1) *ibid.*
709. Law on the United Nations Convention for the International Sale of Goods ('ο περί της Σύμβασης των Ηνωμένων Εθνών για τις Διεθνείς Πωλήσεις Κινητών Πραγμάτων (Κυρωτικός) Νόμος') No. 55 of 2004, OG I(III) No. 3927 of 26 Nov. 2004, p. 4285.
710. Section 2 and Table Part I, Art. 1(1) Law No. 55(III)/2004.
711. Section 3 *ibid.*
712. Section 2 and Table Part I, Art. 1(2) *ibid.*
713. Section 2 and Table Part I, Art. 1(3) *ibid.*
714. Section 2 and Table Part I, Art. 6 *ibid.*
715. Section 2 Law No. 10(I)/1994.

ordinary meaning connoted mutual assent and things compulsorily acquired were not 'sold' within the ordinary meaning of that word.[716]

§2. Formation of a Contract of Sale

235. A contract of sale is made by an offer to buy or sell goods for a price and the acceptance of such offer.[717] It may be made in writing or by word of mouth, or partly in writing and partly by word of mouth or may be implied from the conduct of the parties.[718] Also, necessary condition for a contract of sale is to transfer property in the goods from the seller to the buyer at the time of making this contract. If this is agreed to take place in the future, it is an agreement to sell.[719]

236. The price in a contract of sale may be fixed by the contract or may be left to be fixed in manner thereby agreed or may be determined by the course of dealing between the parties.[720] Where the price is not determined in such manner, the buyer pays the seller a reasonable price, which is a question of fact dependent on the circumstances of each particular case.[721] In the event that it was agreed for the price to be fixed by the valuation of a third party and such third party cannot or does not make such valuation, the agreement is avoided. If in such a case the goods, in full or in part, have been delivered to and appropriated by the buyer, he pays a reasonable price therefor.[722] If the valuation is hindered by the fault of the seller or the buyer, the party not in default may maintain a suit for damages against the party in fault.[723]

§3. Content of a Contract of Sale

237. A contract of sale may provide for the immediate delivery of the goods or immediate payment of the price or both, or for the delivery or payment by instalments, or that the delivery or payment or both shall be postponed.[724] It may further be absolute or conditional.[725] Especially, where the transfer of the property in the goods is to take place at a future time or subject to some condition thereafter to be

716. *Pantzaris v. Cyprus* 3A CLR 861 (1989), citing *Kirkness v. Lord Hudson & So Ltd* 2 All ER 345 (1955).
717. Section 5(1) Law No. 10(I)/1994.
718. Section 5(2) *ibid.*
719. Sections 4(3) and 6(3) *ibid.*
720. Section 9(1) *ibid.*
721. Section 9(2) *ibid.*
722. Section 10(1) *ibid.*
723. Section 10(2) *ibid.*
724. Section 5(1) *ibid.*
725. Section 4(2) *ibid.*

fulfilled, the contract is called an agreement to sell.[726] An agreement to sell becomes a sale when the time elapses or the conditions are fulfilled subject to which the property in the goods is to be transferred.[727]

238. Regarding the subject matter of contract, which is the goods in the aforementioned meaning, they may be either existing goods, owned or possessed by the seller or future goods.[728] It may be agreed that the acquisition of goods by the seller depends upon a contingency, which may or may not happen.[729]

239. In particular, a stipulation in a contract of sale with reference to goods, which are the subject thereof, may be a condition or a warranty.[730] A condition ('ουσιώδης όρος' in Greek, 'şart' in Turkish) is a stipulation essential to the main purpose of the contract, the breach of which gives right to a right to treat the contract as repudiated.[731] A warranty ('εγγυητική διαβεβαίωση' in Greek, 'taahhüt' in Turkish) is a stipulation collateral to the main purpose of the contract, the breach of which gives rise to a claim for damages but not a right to reject the goods and treat the contract as repudiated.[732] Whether a stipulation in a contract of sale is a condition or a warranty depends in each case on the construction of a contract.[733] However, a condition may be treated as warranty. This is possible when the buyer waives the condition, which was agreed to be fulfilled by the seller, or elect to treat the breach of the condition as a breach of warranty and not as a ground for treating the contract as repudiated.[734] This is equally possible, in the event that a contract of sale is not severable and the buyer has accepted the goods or part thereof, or where the contract is for specific goods the property of which has passed to the buyer, unless there is a term of the contract, express or implied to the contrary (section 13(2) Law No. 10(I)/1994).[735]

240. Stipulations as to time of payment are not deemed to be of the essence of a contract of sale, unless a different intention appears from the terms of the contract. Whether any other stipulation as to time is of the essence of the contract or not depends on the terms of the contract.[736]

---

726. Section 4(3) *ibid.*
727. Section 4(4) *ibid.*
728. Section 6(1) *ibid.*
729. Section 6(2) *ibid.*
730. Section 12(1) *ibid.*
731. Section 12(2) *ibid.*
732. Section 12(3) *ibid.*
733. Section 12(4) *ibid.*
734. Section 13(1) *ibid. See* in this regard *Shacolas v. Michaelides* a.a. 1 CLR 290 (1967), citing *Alexander v. Gardner* 4 LJ CP 223 (1835); *Bentsen v. Taylor Sons & Co* 2 QB 274 (1893); *Panoutsos v. Raymond Hadley Corporation of New York* 2 K.B. 473 (1917); *Hartley v. Hymans* 3 K.B. 475 (1920); *Charles Rickards Ltd v. Oppenhaim* 1 K.B. 616 (1950); *Central London Property Trust Ltd v. High Trees House Ltd* 1 K.B. 130 (1947). This also ruled that s. 13(1) Law No. 10(I)/1994, which is identical to s. 13(1) of the upheld Cap. 267, is identical to s. 11(1)(a) of the English Sale of Goods Act 1893.
735. Section 13(2) Law No. 10(I)/1994.
736. Section 11 *ibid. See* in this respect *Photiou Bros. Co. Ltd a.a. v. Autolifts and Engineering Co Ltd* 1 CLR 422 (1984), citing *Decro Well international SA v. Practitioners in Marketing Ltd* 2 All ER 216 (1971).

241. Further, a contract of sale has certain implied conditions, unless the circumstances of the contract are such as to show a different intention. First, there is an implied condition on the part of the seller that, in the case of a sale, he has the right to sell the goods and that, in the case of an agreement to sell, he will have the right to sell the goods at the time when the property is to pass.[737] Second, there is an implied warranty that the buyer shall have and enjoy quiet possession of the goods.[738] Lastly, said contract entails an implied warranty that the goods shall be free from any change or encumbrance in favour of any third party not declared or known to the buyer before or at any time when the contract is made.[739] Especially in sale of goods by description, there is a further implied condition that the goods shall correspond with the description.[740] A sale of goods by description may provide for the goods to be selected by the buyer, after being displayed for sale or rent.[741] If the sale is by sample along with by description, it is not sufficient that the bulk of the goods corresponds with the sample, if the goods do not also correspond with the description.[742]

242. More implied conditions relate to the quality or suitability of the goods. When the seller is in the business of selling goods, the implied condition is that the supplied goods are of acceptable quality.[743] This is the case, when they respond to the level that every reasonable person would consider acceptable, unless the specific purpose for which the goods are being purchased is communicated prior to sale,[744] taking into consideration any description of the goods, the price, under the condition that this is relevant and every other related factor.[745] Especially for the quality of goods, the following factors need to be considered: (a) the suitability of these goods for all purposes, for which they are supplied;[746] (b) appearance and final process; (c) non-existence of minor defects; (d) safety; and (e) resilience, meaning reasonable strength through time and includes, where needed, availability of spare parts and specialized techniques for ensuring it.[747] Said implied condition does not extend to any matter which was brought to the attention of the buyer before making the contract, any matter, which was had to be exposed during an examination of the

---

737. Section 14(a) Law No. 10(I)/1994.
738. Section 14(b) *ibid.*
739. Section 14(c) *ibid.*
740. Section 15(1) *ibid.*
741. Section 15(3) *ibid.*
742. Section 15(2) *ibid. See* in this respect *Demetriades v. Caxton Publishing Co Ltd* 1 CLR 35 (1973).
743. Section 16(2) Law No. 10(I)/1994. *See* in this respect *Attorney-General v. Pentaliotis Papapetrou Estates Limited a.o.* 1 CLR 1931 (1988).
744. Section 16(6) Law No. 10(I)/1994. *See* in this respect *Magistrato Gardens Limited v. Attorney-General* 1 CLR 220 (2012).
745. Section 16(3) Law No. 10(I)/1994.
746. *Papavasiliou v. Kleanthous a.a.* 1 CLR 200 (1984).
747. Section 16(4) Law No. 10(I)/1994.

goods performed by the buyer prior to selling, and any matter, which should be evident following a reasonable examination of the sample, in case of sale by sample.[748] An implied condition or warranty may further be deduced from the usual commercial practice.[749]

243. Especially sale by sample is a contract of sale, which entails as an explicit or implied condition of the sample being the base of this contract.[750] Such contracts also have the implied condition of the quality of the goods corresponding to the quality of the sample,[751] and of the goods being free of any defect that renders their quality unacceptable and that would not be obvious following a reasonable examination of the sample.[752]

§4. The Parties' Duties and Responsibilities

244. It is the duty of the seller to deliver the goods and of the buyer to accept and pay for them, in accordance with the terms of the contract of sale.[753] Unless otherwise agreed, delivery of goods and payment of the price are concurrent conditions, that is to say, the seller shall be ready and willing to give possession of the goods to the buyer in exchange for the price, and the buyer shall be ready and willing to pay the price in exchange for the possession of the goods.[754]

245. Delivery of goods sold may be made by doing anything, which the parties agree shall be treated as delivery or which has the effect of putting the goods in the possession of the buyer or of any person authorized to hold them on his behalf.[755] For the delivery to be affected, the buyer has to apply for it, apart from any express contract.[756] Delivery may consist of the buyer taking possession of the goods or the seller sending them to the buyer, depending in each case on the contract, express or implied, between the parties. Apart from any such contract, goods sold are to be delivered at the place at which they are at the time of the sale, and goods agreed to be sold are to be delivered at the place at which they are at the time of the agreement to sell, or, if not then in existence, at the place at which they are manufactured or produced.[757] If no time is fixed for sending the goods to the buyer, the seller is bound to send them within a reasonable time[758] and at a reasonable hour.[759] Expenses of and incidental to putting the goods into a deliverable state are borne by

748. Section 16(5)(a), (b) and (c) *ibid.*
749. Section 16(7) *ibid.*
750. Section 17(1) *ibid.*
751. Section 17(2)(a) *ibid.*
752. Section 17(2)(b) *ibid.*
753. Section 31 *ibid.*
754. Section 32 *ibid.*
755. Section 33 *ibid.*
756. Section 35 *ibid.*
757. Section 36(1) *ibid.*
758. Section 36(2) *ibid.*
759. Section 36(4) *ibid.*

the seller, unless otherwise agreed.[760] Delivery of wrong quantity, that being less, more or mixed with goods of a different description, gives the option to the buyer to reject them or accept the goods so delivered and pay for them at the contract rate, in the first two cases.[761] This is subject to any usage of trade, special agreement or course of dealing between the parties.[762] Instalment deliveries may not be accepted by the buyer, unless otherwise agreed.[763] In the latter case, failure to deliver or defect delivery may under circumstances constitute breach of contract repudiating the whole contract or giving rise to a claim for compensation. This applies also for failure to take delivery or to pay instalments.[764] When the seller tenders delivery of goods to the buyer, he is bound, on request, to afford the buyer a reasonable opportunity of examining the goods for the purpose of ascertaining whether they are in conformity with the contract, unless otherwise agreed.[765] When the seller is ready and willing to deliver the goods and requests the buyer to take delivery, and the buyer does not within reasonable time after such request take delivery of the goods, he is liable to the seller for any loss occasioned by his neglect or refusal to take delivery. He is also liable for a reasonable charge for the care and custody of the goods. The rights of the seller are not hereby affected, where the neglect or refusal of the buyer to take delivery amounts to a repudiation of the contract.[766]

246. Specifically with regard to delivery to carrier or wharfinger, the following is set out. Where, according to a contract of sale, the seller is authorized or required to send the goods to the buyer, delivery of the goods to a carrier, whether named by the buyer or not, for the purpose of transmission to the buyer is prima facie deemed to be a delivery of the goods to the buyer. The same applies to delivery of the goods to a wharfinger for safe custody.[767] The seller makes such contract with the carrier or wharfinger on behalf of the buyer as may be reasonable having regard to the nature of goods and the other circumstances of the case, unless otherwise authorized by the buyer. Should the seller omit to do so, and the goods are lost or damaged in course of transit or while in the custody of the wharfinger, the buyer may decline to treat the delivery to the carrier or wharfinger as a delivery to himself, or may hold the seller responsible in damages.[768]

247. The buyer is deemed to have accepted the goods, if he declares this to the seller, if he does anything contrary to the ownership right of the seller, following delivery of the goods, or if, after reasonable time, he keeps the goods without

---

760. Section 36(5) *ibid.*
761. Section 37(1), (2) and (3) *ibid. See* in this regard *Demetriades v. Caxton Publishing Co Ltd* 1 CLR 35 (1973). Section 37(3) Law No. 10(I)/1994, which is identical to s. 37(3) Cap. 267, corresponds to s. 30(3) of the English Sale of Goods Act 1893.
762. Section 37(4) Law No. 10(I)/1994.
763. Section 38(1) *ibid.*
764. Section 38(2) *ibid.*
765. Section 41 *ibid.*
766. Section 44 *ibid.*
767. Section 39(1) *ibid.*
768. Section 39(2) *ibid.*

declaring to the buyer that he declined them.[769] Goods are not deemed to have been accepted solely when the buyer asks or agrees them to be repaired by the seller or following agreement with the latter, as well as, when the goods are delivered to another due to resale or other disposal.[770]

248. In the event that only some of the goods are accepted and the rest of the goods are affected by any violation of the seller, such acceptance does not interfere with the buyer's right to declining the rest. This also applies to instalment deliveries.[771] However, it is possible for the parties to make a contract to the contrary.[772] Delivery of the declined goods is not necessary. Sole declaration of denial of acceptance to the seller by the buyer suffices.[773]

249. Where the buyer is ready and willing to deliver the goods and notifies the buyer to receive them and the buyer does not receive them within reasonable time following such notice, the buyer is liable towards the seller for any loss caused due to the buyer's negligence or denial to receive them. He is further liable for reasonable costs relating to the maintenance and safekeeping of the goods. Naturally, the rights of the seller, when negligence or denial of the buyer to receive the goods equals to termination of the contract, are not affected.[774]

250. Transfer of property is affected in the following manners, depending on whether the goods are ascertained ('εξακριβωμένα αγαθά' in Greek, 'tesbiti yapılmış' in Turkish) or not ('μη εξακριβωμένα αγαθά' in Greek, 'tesbit edilmemiş' in Turkish). Property in unascertained goods is transferred to the buyer when the goods are ascertained.[775] Property in specific ('συγκεκριμένα' in Greek, 'belirlenmiş' in Turkish) or ascertained goods is transferred to the buyer at such time as the parties to the contract intend it to be transferred.[776] For the purpose of interpreting the intention of the parties, the terms of the contract, the conduct of the parties and the circumstances of the case are taken into consideration.[777] Furthermore, the following statutory rules that are set out in sections 20–24 of this law are rules for crystalizing the intention of the parties as to the time at which the property in said goods is to pass to the buyer.[778] With regard to specific goods in a deliverable state, the property in the goods passes to the buyer when the contract is made, and it is immaterial whether the time of payment of the price or the time of delivery of the goods, or both, is postponed, as long as nothing else is provided in the contract.[779] In such cases, if the seller is bound to weigh, measure, test or do some other act or thing

769. Section 42(1) and (6) *ibid.*
770. Section 42(7) *ibid.*
771. Section 43(1) and (2) *ibid.*
772. Section 43(2) *ibid.*
773. Section 44 *ibid.*
774. Section 45 *ibid.*
775. Section 18 *ibid.*
776. Section 19(1) *ibid.*
777. Section 19(2) *ibid.*
778. Section 19(3) *ibid.*
779. Section 20 *ibid.*

with reference to the goods for the purpose of ascertaining the price, the property does not pass until such act or thing is done and the buyer has notice thereof.[780] When specific goods are not in a deliverable state, and the seller is bound to do something to the goods for the purpose of putting them into a deliverable state, the property does not pass until such thing is done and the buyer has notice thereof.[781] With reference to contracts for the sale of unascertained or future goods by description, which are in a deliverable state, ownership in these goods passes to the buyer, when they are unconditionally appropriated to the contract, either by the seller with the assent of the buyer or by the buyer with the assent of the seller; such assent, which may be express or implied, may be given either before or after the appropriation.[782] Unconditional appropriation of the goods to the contract takes place, when the seller delivers the goods to the buyer in pursuance of the contract. It equally takes place when the seller delivers the goods to a carrier or other bailee for the purpose of transmission to the buyer.[783] Turning to goods that are delivered to the buyer on approval or 'on sale or return' or other similar terms, the property therein passes to the buyer in the following manner. First, this happens, when the buyer signifies his approval or acceptance to the seller or does any other act adopting the transaction.[784] This equally happens when the seller does not signify his approval or acceptance to the seller, but retains the goods without giving notice of rejection, on the expiration of a reasonable time, when no time for the return of goods has been fixed. In the event that time has been fixed, the property passes to the buyer on the expiration of such time.[785] Special mention deserves the reservation of the right of disposal of the goods until certain conditions are fulfilled, which the seller may impose by the terms of the contract, where there is a contract for the sale of specific goods. In such a case, notwithstanding the delivery of the goods to a buyer, or to a carrier or other bailee for the purpose of transmission to the buyer, the property in the goods does not pass to the buyer until the conditions imposed by the seller are fulfilled. This may equally take place where goods are subsequently appropriated to the contract.[786] In particular, where goods are shipped and by the bill of lading the goods are deliverable to the order of the seller or his agent, the seller is prima facie deemed to reserve the right of disposal.[787] The property in the goods does not pass to the buyer, if he does not honour the bill of exchange and if he wrongfully retains the bill of lading, where the seller of goods draws on the buyer for the price and transmits the bill of exchange and bill of lading to the buyer together, to secure acceptance or payment of the bill of exchange. Then the buyer is bound to return the bill of lading.[788]

---

780. Section 22 *ibid.*
781. Section 21 *ibid.*
782. Section 23(1) *ibid.*
783. Section 23(2) *ibid.*
784. Section 24(a) *ibid.*
785. Section 24(b) *ibid.*
786. Section 25(1) *ibid.*
787. Section 25(2) *ibid.*
788. Section 25(3) *ibid.*

251. In regard to lien or other right of the original seller, the following is provided. Where a person having bought or agreed to buy goods obtains with the consent of the seller possession of the goods or the documents of title to the goods, the delivery or transfer by that person or by a mercantile agent acting for him of those under any sale, pledge or other disposition thereof to a person, the lien or other right to the goods shall have no effect. For this effect to unfold, two conditions are pertinent. First, the person receiving said goods or documents of title must do so in good faith. Second, the same person must have no notice of any lien or other right of the original seller.[789]

252. With reference to risk ('κίνδυνος' in Greek, 'riziko' in Turkish) precedence takes the agreement among the parties. Under this reservation, the statute provides that the goods remain at the seller's risk until the property therein is transferred to the buyer. However, when the property in the goods is transferred to the buyer, the goods are at the buyer's risk whether delivery has been made or not: provided that, where delivery has been delayed through the fault of either buyer or seller, the goods are at the risk of the party in fault as regards any loss which might not have occurred but for such fault; provided also that nothing in this regard affects the duties or liabilities of either seller or buyer as a bailee of the goods of the other party.[790] In particular where goods are sent by the seller to the buyer by a route involving sea transit, in circumstances, on which it is usual to insure, the seller gives such notice to the buyer as may enable him to insure them during their sea transit. If the seller fails to do so, the goods shall be deemed to be at his risk during such sea transit.[791] Further, where the seller of goods agrees to deliver them at his own risk at a place other than that where they are when sold, the buyer shall take any risk of deterioration in the goods necessarily incident to the course of transit, unless otherwise agreed.[792]

253. Unpaid sellers have special statutory rights. The seller of goods is deemed to be an unpaid seller ('απλήρωτος πωλητής' in Greek, 'ödenmemiş satıcı' in Turkish), when the whole of the price has not been paid or tendered, or when a bill of exchange or other negotiable instrument has been received as conditional payment, and the condition on which it was received has not been fulfilled by reason of the dishonour of the instrument or otherwise.[793] Seller here includes any person who is in the position of a seller, as for instance, an agent of the seller to whom the bill of lading has been indorsed or a consignor or agent who has himself paid, or is directly responsible for, the price.[794] First, the unpaid seller of goods has by implication of law a lien on the goods for the price while he is in possession of them, a right of stopping the goods, in case of bankruptcy of the buyer, and a right of resale limited by law.[795] If the property in goods has not passed to the buyer, the unpaid seller has

789. Section 30(2) *ibid.*
790. Section 26 *ibid.*
791. Section 39(3) *ibid.*
792. Section 40 *ibid.*
793. Section 46(1) *ibid.*
794. Section 46(2) *ibid.*
795. Section 47(1)(a), (b) and (c) *ibid.*

in addition to the aforementioned, a right of withholding delivery similar to and coextensive with his rights of lien and stoppage in transit, where the property has passed to the buyer.[796] Further, the unpaid seller has a lien. In particular, when he is in possession of the goods, he is entitled to retain possession of them until payment or tender of the price in the following cases: (a) where the goods had been sold without any stipulation as to credit; (b) where the goods have been sold on credit, but the term of the credit has expired; and (c) where the buyer becomes bankrupt.[797] This right may be exercised notwithstanding the possession of goods due to agency or bailment.[798] In case of part delivery, his right may be exercised on the remainder, unless such part delivery has been made under such circumstances as to show an agreement to waive the lien.[799] Said right is lost: (a) when the unpaid seller delivers the goods to a carrier or other bailee for the purpose of transmission to the buyer without reserving the right of disposal of the goods; (b) when the buyer or his agent lawfully obtains possession of the goods; and (c) by waiver thereof.[800] Obtaining a judgment for the price of the goods does not have the effect of losing the lien.[801] In addition to the aforementioned, when the unpaid seller has parted with the possession of the goods and the buyer of goods becomes bankrupt, the unpaid seller has the right of stopping the goods in transit,[802] which takes place either by taking actual possession of the goods or by giving notice of his claim to the carrier or other bailee.[803] Goods are deemed to be in course of transit from the time when they are delivered to a carrier or other bailee for the purpose of transmission to the buyer, until the buyer or his agent in that behalf takes delivery of them from such carrier or other bailee.[804]

§5. Contract of Sale and Third Persons

254. In the event of sale by a person not being the owner of the sold goods and not having the authority of the owner to sell them, or his consent to do so, the buyer acquires no better title to the goods than the seller had. However, this does not apply, if the owner of the goods is by his conduct precluded from denying the seller's authority to sell. In the case of a mercantile agent possessing, with the consent of the owner, the goods or titles thereof, any sale made by such agent in his ordinary course of business, is as valid as if he were expressly authorized by the owner of the goods to make the same, under the condition that the buyer acts in good faith and has nor at the time of the contract of sale notice that the seller has not authority to sell.[805]

796. Section 47(2) *ibid.*
797. Section 48(1) *ibid.*
798. Section 48(2) *ibid.*
799. Section 49 *ibid.*
800. Section 50(1) *ibid.*
801. Section 50(2) *ibid.*
802. Section 51 *ibid.*
803. Section 53(1) *ibid.*
804. Section 52(1) *ibid.*
805. Section 27 *ibid.*

255. Where a person having sold goods continues to be in possession of the goods or of the documents of title to the goods, the delivery or transfer by that person or by a mercantile agent acting for him, of the goods or documents of title under any sale, pledge or other disposition thereof to a person receiving those in good faith and without notice of the previous sale, has the same effect as if the person making the delivery or transfer were expressly authorized by the owner of the goods to make the same.[806]

256. Turning to goods being owned by several joint owners, but being in possession of one of them with the consent of the rest of the owners, the following applies. The property in the goods is transferred, as long as the buyer acts in good faith and has not at the time of the contract of sale notice that the seller has not authority to sell.[807]

257. If a third person is in possession of the sold goods, delivery by seller to buyer is affected when such third person acknowledges to the buyer that he holds the goods on his behalf.[808]

§6. Hire Purchase Agreements

258. The hire purchase agreement is considered to be an amalgam of a contract of bailment and a contract of sale though distinguished from the parent concepts in that the offspring of this fusion has some feature peculiar to itself.[809] The Courts have stated that at common law the term hire purchase properly applies only to contracts of hire conferring an option to purchase, but it is often used to describe contracts which are in reality agreements to purchase chattels by instalments subject to a condition that the property in them is not to pass until all instalments have been paid. Thus, they noted that it is of the essence of the contract that until the conditions have been fulfilled by the hirer, the property in the chattel will remain with the owner, and in such a way the hirer will normally be unable to pass a good title to a third party during the continuance of the bailment.[810]

259. It is regulated in the Hire Purchase Law[811] (hereinafter 'Law No. 32/1966'). In this law, unless the context otherwise requires *hire purchase agreement* ('σύμβαση ενοικιαγοράς' in Greek, 'icar-satış mukavelesi' in Turkish) is defined as an agreement in any form under any name or description, by virtue of which a person receives from another person a specific item of property on hire in return for

---

806. Section 30(1) *ibid.*
807. Section 28 *ibid.*
808. Section 36(3) *ibid.*
809. *Costas Panayi and Eleftherios Costa Artemiou and Others*, District Court of Famagusta, Civil Action No. 3299/73, Judgment of 30 Mar. 1974, not published in CLR.
810. *Constantinou v. Firm S. Mamas & Co* 9 JSC 1098 (1973).
811. Hire Purchase, Credit Sale and Hiring of Property (Control) Law ('Νόμος Προνοών Περί Ελέγχου Ενοικιαγοράς, Πωλήσεως επί Πιστώσει και Μισθώσεως Ιδιοκτησίας') No. 32 of 1966, OG I 508 of 7 Jul. 1966, p. 389.

periodic payments, and with the option to purchase or acquire the ownership thereof, and includes two or more agreements in any form having collectively the same effect.[812]

260. Nonetheless, possession of property on the ground of a hire purchase agreement faces statutory limitations. More specifically, the following conditions have to be fulfilled for the possession to be lawful. First, the hire purchase agreement has to be in writing and provide for the cash price, that being the price at which the prospective hirer or buyer may, at the date of the agreement, purchase or agree to purchase the property for cash, as well as for price that shall be paid in instalments on the base of the agreement for the instalment or the preservation of property. Especially for motor vehicles, it must further set out for the duties due for registration, licence and insurance, in the event that these are paid to the owner.[813] Further, the agreement must provide for the payment of the amount either in instalments, which must be approximately equal and due in equal terms, or in block within three months since the date of the first agreement, under which property was disposed. In the event that the agreed duration of the agreement, and therefore the time that the unpaid amount becomes due, is amended, it is deemed that compliance with the aforementioned has been achieved regarding the period that has not yet lapsed, when the amount due at the time of the amendment becomes due in almost equal instalments in equal terms during same period.[814]

261. No further statutory provisions regarding the terms and conditions of a hire purchase agreement are set out. Thus, such an agreement may freely provide for guarantee[815] or be tainted by fraud or fraudulent misrepresentation.[816] Nonetheless, the Courts have found that they examine the essence of the agreement and not just its wording, whereas further it is possible to surpass the terms or words or the documents that the parties used for the agreement. They consider their duty to reveal the true nature of the transaction, letting aside anything that is established to function as a cloak or a mask.[817] Moreover, they have endorsed the view that 'hire-purchase, as unhappily so often happens with hire-purchase transactions, creates complicated, artificial and obscure legal relationships between the parties'.[818,819]

---

812. Section 2 Law No. 32/1966.
813. Section 5(a) and Annex Part I (1) and (2) *ibid.*
814. Section 5(c)(i) and (ii) *ibid.*
815. *Savvides v. Christofides* 1 CLR 303 (1978).
816. *Charalambous and another v. Stefanou* JSC 223 (1987).
817. *Laiki Kypriaki Trapeza (Chrimatodotises) Ltd v. Konstantinou and another* 1 CLR 1432 (2001); *Laiki Kypriaki Trapeza (Chrimatodotiseis) Ltd v. Christou Iordanous and another*, District Court of Nicosia Action No. 13803/03, Judgment of 20 May 2008, not reported in CLR.
818. *Financings Ltd v. Stimson* 3 All ER 386, 391 (1962).
819. *Laiki Kypriaki Trapeza (Chrimatodotises) Ltd v. Konstantinou and another* 1 CLR 1432 (2001); *Laiki Kypriaki Trapeza (Chrimatodotiseis) Ltd v. Christou Iordanous and another,* District Court of Nicosia Action No. 13803/03, Judgment of 20 May 2008, not reported in CLR.

262. Case law, on the basis of *Brooks v. Beirnstein*,[820] has further established that during the continuance of the hiring, the hirer must pay the instalments of hire-rent stipulated for in the agreement. When these become due, they represent an accrued debt to the owner, even so that the subsequent repossession of the goods by the owner in no way relieves the hirer from his obligation to pay his debts.[821] Moreover, on the basis of *Modern Light Cars v. Seals*,[822] it has been noted on the question of collateral security that the execution by the hirer of bills of exchange or promissory notes for the instalments falling due under the hire purchase agreement does not constitute payment of these instalments (even if the notes are subsequently discounted to a third party) so as to convert the agreement into a sale or an agreement of sale. It is presumed that the notes are given merely as collateral security for the payment of the instalments and not as payment whether absolute or conditional, of the hire purchase price.[823]

263. In addition, according to case law, it is settled that the hirer is under an implied obligation to take reasonable care of the goods let on hire. The hirer is required to use ordinary diligence. He is not liable for fair wear and tear; nonetheless he does assume responsibility for loss of or damage to the goods caused by the negligent, as well as fraudulent or dishonest, act of his servants whom he has permitted to use the goods. The liability of the hirer for breach of his implied obligation to take reasonable care of the goods does not normally extend to consequential loss which may be suffered by the owner as a result of the breach. However, the liability of the hirer may be increased by the express terms of the hire purchase agreement.[824]

264. Moreover, it has been held that hire purchase agreements constitute an exception from the rule *nemo dat non quod habet*, enshrined in section 27 Law No. 10(I)/1994, stipulating that where goods are sold by a person who is not the owner thereof, and who does not sell them under the authority or with the consent of the owner, the buyer acquires no better title to the goods than the seller had, unless the owner of the goods is by his conduct precluded from denying the seller's authority to sell.[825]

265. The Council of Ministers has the power to declare certain property as controlled property under the following statutory grounds. These include taking measures against inflation or for the purpose of improving the foreign exchange position and the balance of payments or to ensure the optimal use of the sources of revenue for the purpose of economic development or to the purpose of facilitating fair trade competition.[826] Still, the majority of these grounds has become obsolete since

820. *Brooks v. Beirnstein* 1 KB 98 (1909).
821. *Constantinou v. Firm S. Mamas & Co* 9 JSC 1098 (1973).
822. *Modern Light Cars Ltd v. Seals* 1 KB 32 (1934).
823. *Constantinou v. Firm S. Mamas & Co* 9 JSC 1098 (1973).
824. *Alpha Bank Cyprus Ltd v. A.G. Demetriou Metafores Ltd and another*, District Court of Limassol, Action No. 1048/2007, Judgment of 16 Apr. 2013, not reported in CLR.
825. *A.A. Pilottos Ltd and another v. George Houghton and another* 1 CLR 783 (2007).
826. Section 3(1) Law No. 32/1966.

Cyprus joined the Eurozone in 2008. Importantly, in declaring property as controlled property minimum cash deposit shall be set out.[827] By virtue of the First Schedule of the relevant Order ('Διάταγμα Ελέγχου δυνάμει του Άρθρου 3'), published in the Official Gazette No. 533, dated 3 November 1966, the minimum cash deposit has to be 33⅓% of the agreed price and the maximum period of time for the balance to be paid off is twenty-four months.[828] Non-compliance renders the hire purchase agreement illegal and void depriving the parties from the power to enforce it.[829]

266. Where the hirer omits to return the goods the measure of damages is the total amount payable under the hire purchase agreement, less the amount of hire instalments already paid.[830]

267. Any violation of the statutory restrictions on the possession of property, that being possession of property, while the aforementioned conditions are not fulfilled, is guilty of a crime and may face imprisonment of up to twelve months and/ or fine of up to EUR 854.3 (CYP 500). Moreover, the Court has the power to transform the hire purchase agreement into an agreement in cash allowing for the buyer to become owner of the property in question upon payment of the amount due.[831] In this respect, the accused person may put forward and establish the defence that he undertook all necessary research and satisfied himself that the property in question was about to be exported and remain abroad for a period not less than twenty-four months from the date of its disposal.[832]

268. On the difference between a loan and a hire purchase agreement, the case law has aligned with the view adopted *in Olds Discount v. John Playfair.*[833] According to this, almost all bodies which finance hire purchase agreements have as a real function the lending of money. Still, the question is the method that they have of employing it. Should the method employed constitute a sale, then the transaction is not only the lending of money but also a purchase of the goods, even although it is only for the purpose of lending money that it is being done in that way. Therefore, the question to be decided is whether the plaintiffs have succeeded, by means of the form they adopted, in making a real, though technical, purchase of the goods, or whether they have merely had a security on the goods.[834]

---

827. Section 4(1) and Annex Part I *ibid.*
828. *D. I. Demades & Sons Ltd v. Georghios Adamou Kaoullas and another* JSC 270 (1972).
829. *Chr. Tornari & Co & F. Vassiliades and Panayiotis Savva*, District Court of Famagusta Action No. 1241/72, Judgment of 6 Mar. 1973, not reported in CLR.
830. *Alpha Bank Cyprus Ltd v. A.G. Demetriou Metafores Ltd a.a.*, District Court of Limassol Action No. 1048/2007, Judgment of 16 Apr. 2013, not reported in CLR; *Elliniki Trapeza Ltd and another v. Nikos Tsartellis* 1 CLR 246 (2003).
831. Section 10(1) Law No. 32/1966.
832. Section 10(3)(b) *ibid.*
833. *Olds Discount Co. Ltd v. John Playfair Ltd* 3 All ER 275 (1938).
834. *Marfin Popular Bank Public Co Ltd v. Demos Hadjineocleous and others* 1 CLR 595 (2013); *Laiki Kypriaki Trapeza (Chrimatodotiseis) Ltd v. Thomas Liobay Developments Ltd and others*, District Court of Nicosia Action No. 369/01, Judgment of 31 May 2007, not published in CLR.

§7. FINANCIAL LEASING

269. Financial leasing is regulated by Law on Financial Leasing[835] (hereinafter 'Law No. 72(I)/2016'). The scope of this law is to regulate the provision of services of financial leasing to the public, as well as the regulation and supervision of the activities of the providers of services of financial leasing, aiming to the smooth operation of the institute of financial leasing.[836] Outside the scope of this law is the provision of services of financial leasing that is not addressed to the public, including the provision of services of financial leasing from legal persons exclusively to their mother or daughter company or to a daughter company of their mother company, among others.[837] Equally excluded is financial leasing provided by natural or legal persons having as principal professional activity the selling of immovable property and that provide services of financial leasing for the sale of movable property of no more than EUR 5,000 per object of sale and only to the degree necessary for the purpose of pursuing their main activity.[838] Finally, services of financial leasing providing for credit for a period of less than three months fall outside the scope of this law.[839]

270. To the end of optimal application of the provisions of this law, the Central Bank of Cyprus has the power to issue general or specific directives or guidelines, which are to be published in the Official Gazette.[840] During the exercise of its discretionary powers, as these are set out in this law, the Central Bank of Cyprus acts, following consideration of international practice, the Directives of the EU, the protection of the interests of lessors and the clients of companies of financial leasing in general, as well as the smooth operation of the system of financial leasing.[841] Interestingly, it seems that the market and not the law marks the borders of the discretion of the Central Bank of Cyprus on the matters analysed in these paragraphs.

271. Financial leasing ('χρηματοδοτική μίσθωση' in Greek, 'vadeli kira' in Turkish) is defined as a special contract of leasing that constitutes a manner of financing, different from a loan, and is made in writing, under which the lessee takes exclusive possession of a particular property from the lessor towards payment of the agreed rent and which provides explicitly to the lessee the right to buy the property during the period of the contract or any renewal.[842] In particular for immovable property, financial leasing concerns the whole share of immovable property and is possible only if the immovable property is registered under the name of the lessor,

835. Law Regulating Financial Leasing and the Activities of the Financial Leasing Companies ('Νόμος που Ρυθμίζει τις Χρηματοδοτικές Μισθώσεις και τις Δραστηριότητες των Εταιρειών Χρηματοδοτικής Μίσθωσης') No. 72 of 2016, OG I(I) No. 4565 of 28 Apr. 2017, p. 805.
836. Section 3(1) Law No. 72(I)/2016.
837. Section 3(2)(a) *ibid.*
838. Section 3(2)(b) *ibid.*
839. Section 3(2)(c) *ibid.*
840. Section 12(1) *ibid.*
841. Section 12(3) *ibid.*
842. Section 2 *ibid.*

free of any onus in rem.[843] Every company of financial leasing may design various categories of financial leasing for all kinds of property, which can be: (a) simple financial leasing ('απλή χρηματοδοτική μίσθωση' in Greek, 'basit vadeli kirası' in Turkish); (b) hire purchase ('ενοικιαγορά' in Greek, 'icar-satış mukavelesi' in Turkish); (c) equity financial leasing ('συμμετοχική χρηματοδοτική μίσθωση' in Greek, 'hakkaniyet vadeli kirası' in Turkish); (d) reverse financial leasing ('αντίστροφη χρηματοδοτική μίσθωση' in Greek, 'vadeli kirasın bozulması' in Turkish); (e) syndicated financial leasing ('κοινοπρακτική χρηματοδοτική μίσθωση' in Greek, 'sendikasyon vadeli kirası' in Turkish); (f) financial leasing with subleasing ('κρίση' in Greek, 'devren vadeli kirası' in Turkish). Law No. 72(I)/2016 further explicitly provides that these categories are simply demonstrative and may include a combination of those or other categories of financial leasing.[844] It is here noted that, although it is provided that Law No. 32/1966 does not apply to financial leasing agreed under Law No. 72(I)/2016,[845] the latter does not repeal the first one, which as already described above regulates hire purchase agreements. It could be argued that Law No. 72(I)/2016 silently annuls and repeals Law No. 72(I)/1966 under application of the traditional conflict-of-norms rule *lex posterior generalis non derogat priori speciali* that has been found applicable in Cyprus.[846] At the same time, it may be purported that this is not the case as Law No. 32/1966 has a specific nature contrary to Law No. 72(I)/1966, whose scope is broader and more general, under the rule *lex specialis derogat legi generali.*[847] In any event, the final answer to this issue shall be given by the Courts, which are yet to decide thereon.

272. The contract of financial leasing has a statutory defined content, which includes the following: (a) description of the rental property and its value that must be free of any *onus* in rem upon making of the contract; (b) the total amount of the lease; (c) the amount of the regular instalments; (d) the nominal and actual interest that is calculated on the regular instalments and their amendment; (e) the contracting party, which has the responsibility and bears the costs of installation, maintenance or insurance of the rental property or the dangers associated with it, under the provisions of any relevant legislation, save for duties, taxes, fees for licences and rights, which are imposed on the basis of the applicable legislation; (f) the forbearance period, if any; (g) the date of initiation and expiration of the financial leasing; (h) description of the option right, that being the time and purchase price of the rental property by the lessee, as well as the right to renewal of the financial leasing; (i) the terms and conditions for the termination of the financial leasing before its expiration by the lessor or the lessee, as well as the methodology for the calculation of the consideration of the lessor and the lessee; (j) full description and the methodology for calculating any expenses of the financial leasing; (k) provision for the option of amending the terms of the financial leasing in case of restructuring, that

843. Section 42(1) *ibid.*
844. Section 28(1) *ibid.*
845. Section 41(2) *ibid.*
846. *Ajero J Kristoffer Castardo* 1 CLR 1165 (2006); *Philippou v. Philippou* 1 CLR 689 (1986); *Elliniki Trapeza Ltd v. Lextalionis Investments Ltd and others*, District Court of Larnaca, Action No. 3172/99, Judgment of 25 Jan. 2007, not reported in CLR.
847. *See* in this regard *Antenna Ltd v. Arhis Radiotileorasis Kyprou* 3 CLR 29 (2010).

being the possibility of amending the amount of the regular instalments, the date of expiration of the leasing and the new total amount of the financial leasing; and (l) the names of the guarantors, if applicable.[848] In particular for financial leasing of immovable property, the contract must include a full description of the leasing object with reference to the specifics of the plot and the title of ownership along with architectural or other plans, terms and standards.[849] The duration of said contract is freely agreed among the parties. However, specifically for immovable property, that is at least ten years, regardless of any option for its renewal.[850] Furthermore, the content of financial leasing is negatively defined. It is prohibited to agree instalments with compound interest calculated more frequently than twice per year. In the event of such an agreement, a penal fine of imprisonment of up to two years and/or monetary fine of up to EUR 250,000 may be imposed.[851]

273. Prior to the making of a financial leasing, the providers of services of financial leasing bear the statutory obligation to provide to the lessees all necessary pre-contractual information and data, as it may be specified by regulation of the Central Bank.[852] Upon making of the financial leasing, the property is registered under the name of the lessor, free of any *onus* in rem.[853] Within one month since its making a financial leasing is registered with the registries kept by the competent authorities in Cyprus, under the applicable laws: in cases of aircraft, that is the registry of the Civil Aviation Department kept under the provisions of the Law on Civil Aviation;[854] in cases of motor vehicles, that is the registry of the Road Transport Department kept under the provisions of the Law on Motor Vehicles;[855] in cases of immovable property, that is the registry kept by the Department of Lands and Surveys kept under the provisions of the Law on Immovable Property.[856] Upon registration, a burden in rem is created on the leasing object, whereas in particular regarding immovable property, this takes effect upon application for registration.[857] Further, the leasing object is required to be insured during the duration of the contract with an insurance company possessing a licence of insurance activities in Cyprus under the applicable laws for an amount not less than that of its purchasing value.[858]

---

848. Section 27(1) Law No. 72(I)/2016.
849. Section 42(2) *ibid.*
850. Section 29(1) *ibid.*
851. Section 39(1) and (2) *ibid.*
852. Section 27(4) *ibid.*
853. Section 36(1) *ibid.*
854. Law on Civil Aviation ('ο Περί Πολιτικής Αεροπορίας Νόμος') No. 213 of 2002, OG I(I) No. 3662 of 13 Dec. 2002, as amended.
855. Law on Motor Vehicles and Traffic ('ο περί Μηχανοκίνητων Οχημάτων και Τροχαίας Κινήσεως Νόμος') No. 86 of 1972, OG I No. 976 of 1 Dec. 1972, p. 901, as amended.
856. Immovable Property (Tenure, Registration and Valuation) of 1 Sep. 1946, Ch. 224 of the Laws, London, 1959 edition, as amended.
857. Section 37(a), (b) and (c) Law No. 72(I)/2016.
858. Section 38 *ibid.*

274. The object of financial leasing is possessed exclusively by the lessee, his or her heirs, in case of natural persons, or the tenant in case of financial leasing with sublease,[859] whereas the ownership of the leasing object remains to the lessor.[860]

275. During the duration of the contract of financial lease, both the lessor and the lessee have certain rights, save for a clause to the contrary agreed under said contract. The lessor, as long as he gives a prior notice to the lessee, may transfer the leasing object to another provider of services of financial lease that becomes the new lessor in the financial leasing, which remains in force.[861] He may further register a hypothec ('υποθήκη' in Greek, 'ipotek' in Turkish), a pledge ('ενέχυρο' in Greek, 'menkul rehni' in Turkish) or any other *onus* in rem or impose any other charge on the leasing object. Said rights in rem and charges have no effect on the validity and the provisions of the financial leasing and do not affect the rights of the lessee deriving from same. It is explicitly provided that the rights of the lessee take lead towards third parties registering rights in rem or imposing charges. Moreover, when the option of acquiring ownership is exercised and the object of leasing is transferred to the lessee, all rights in rem and charges are annulled and deleted from the relevant registries.[862] The lessee, as long as the lessor consents in writing, may rent the leasing object to a third person, or impose a hypothec, or transfer or assign his rights and obligations under the financial leasing, including the option of acquisition, to a third person.[863] The creation of such rights has no effect on the financial leasing, as already explained *mutatis mutandis*.[864]

276. Financial leasing is terminated on the following grounds. The first one is when the time period of the financial leasing has lapsed and the lessee has not affected his renewal right or the option for acquiring the leasing object, as long as he has fulfilled all his contractual obligations.[865] Financial leasing is equally terminated when the lessee acquires the leasing object according to the relevant option set out in the contract.[866] Moreover, financial leasing is terminated when a court order for receiving, unwinding, dissolution or bankruptcy of the lessee is issued.[867] The destruction of the leasing object does not cause the termination of the financial leasing, unless otherwise provided therein.[868]

277. Financial leasing may be terminated on the grounds explained below. The lessor has the right to terminate it when the lessee delays the instalments for a period longer than the one prescribed in the contract that however may not be shorter than

859. Section 31(a), (b) and (c) *ibid.*
860. Section 32(1) *ibid.*
861. Section 36(2)(a) *ibid.*
862. Section 36(2)(b) and 36(3)(a), (b) and (c) *ibid.*
863. Section 36(4) *ibid.*
864. Section 36(3)(a), (b) and (c) *ibid.*
865. Section 33(1)(a) *ibid.*
866. Section 33(1)(b) *ibid.*
867. Section 33(7) *ibid.*
868. Section 35 *ibid.*

four months in the case of immovable property or two months in the case of movable property. Nonetheless, the contract must clearly and explicitly provide that such delay constitutes a ground for termination. Moreover, the lessor may only perform this right via registered mail to the lessee,[869] and under the condition that he has prior called the lessee to restructure the financial leasing to no avail.[870] The lessor is further obliged to set a time period of no less than two months in cases involving immovable property and one month in instances of movable property, during which the lessee may find another lessor or buyer for the leasing object.[871] Thereafter, the lessor may acquire the possession of the leasing movable object in order to sell it or lease it to another lessee.[872] Should the leasing object be immovable property, acquisition of possession may take place six months after said two-month period, or earlier as long as the lessee agrees thereto.[873] Finally financial leasing may be terminated in case of breach of a condition ('ουσιώδης όρος' in Greek, 'esas' in Turkish) of the contract, or under any term ('όρος' in Greek, 'koşul' in Turkish) of the contact or under Cap. 149 that is made known to the lessor when the financial leasing is made, under the condition that such a right is exercised via registered mail.[874] Thereafter, the lessor may acquire possession of the object of leasing in order to sell it or lease it to another lessee.[875] Should the lessee refuse to deliver possession of movable property, the lessor has the power to submit an ex parte application to the competent court requesting acquisition of said property. Such an application needs to be accompanied by (i) the financial leasing agreement, (ii) the letter terminating this financial leasing agreement, (iii) the rents due and (iv) any other document that the court may deem relevant. If the court grants the request, the lessor may execute this judgment thirty days after its service to the lessee.[876] If the lessee does not have the leased movable property in his possession and/ or under his control, he is obliged to inform the lessor in writing about the location of same property; if the leased object is untraceable or has been destroyed, the lessee is responsible for damages towards the lessor.[877] If the lessee violates these statutory obligations, he commits a crime and may be imprisoned for up to three months and/ or fined for up to EUR 855, unless he proves that such lack of knowledge or control is due to reasons and/ or representations, for which he bears no responsibility.[878]

278. When the lessor terminates the financial leasing on the grounds of payment delay or breach of condition or any term[879] he pays to the lessee any amount that may be attributed to him as calculated under the methodology described in the financial leasing and on the basis of directives issued by the Central Bank of

869. Section 33(2)(a)(i) and (ii) *ibid.*
870. Section 33(3)(a) and (b) *ibid.*
871. Section 33(4) *ibid.*
872. Section 33(5)(b) *ibid.*
873. Section 33(5)(a) *ibid.*
874. Section 33(2)(b) *ibid.*
875. Section 33(5)(c) *ibid.*
876. Section 33(5)(d) *ibid.*
877. Section 33(5)(e) *ibid.*
878. Section 33(5)(f) *ibid.*
879. Section 33(2) *ibid.*

Cyprus.[880] Similarly, when the financial leasing is terminated due to receiving, unwinding, dissolution or bankruptcy of the lessee, the amount that may be attributed to the lessee is calculated under the methodology described in the financial leasing or on the basis of directives issued by the Central Bank of Cyprus.[881] However, in the event of death of the lessee his heirs or his receiver, as the case may be, enjoy the rights and the obligations of the lessee under the financial leasing. They do have the statutory right to terminate the financial leasing, unless otherwise provided therein.[882]

279. Violation of the aforementioned statutory provisions or of the directives issued by the Central Bank of Cyprus by a company of financial leasing may lead to monetary fine of up to EUR 250,000 and revocation of the operating licence of said company, as long as same company and its members of Board of Directors have knowledge thereof.[883] In addition to said fines, the Court has the power to order that the terminated financial leasing is considered to be a cash contract and therefore give the right to the lessee to obtain ownership of the property upon payment of the amount due.[884] The same applies in the event of provision of false or incomplete information or reports.[885]

§8. Termination of a Contract of Sale

280. The aforementioned on voidable contracts (*see* in this respect above at paragraphs 50 et seq.) equally apply here. However, when the seller of goods has obtained possession thereof under a contract voidable under section 18 or section 19 Cap. 149, but the contract has not been rescinded at the time of sale, the buyer acquires a good title to the goods, provided he buys them in good faith and without notice of the seller's defect of title.[886]

281. Further, a contract of goods is void, if the goods without the knowledge of the seller have, at the time when the contract was made, perished or become so damaged as no longer to answer to their description in the contract.[887] The agreement is further avoided, where there is an agreement to sell specific goods, and subsequently the goods without any fault on the part of the seller or buyer perish or become so damaged as no longer to answer to their description in the agreement before the risk passes to the buyer.[888]

---

880. Section 33(6) *ibid.*
881. Section 33(7) *ibid.*
882. Section 34 *ibid.*
883. Section 45(1)(c) *ibid.*
884. Section 45(2) *ibid.*
885. Section 45(1)(b) *ibid.*
886. Section 29 Law No. 10(I)/1994.
887. Section 7 *ibid.*
888. Section 8 *ibid.*

§9. Actions for Breach of Contract of Sale

282. The specific actions for breach of contract of sale are action for price, damages for non-acceptance and non-delivery, specific performance, breach of warranty, special damages and repudiation of contract before due date. Where under a contract of sale the property in the goods has passed to the buyer and the buyer wrongfully neglects or refuses to pay for the goods according to the terms of the contract, the seller may sue him for the price of the goods.[889] Should the price be payable on a day certain irrespective of delivery, the seller may exercise said right although the property in the goods has not passed and the goods have not been appropriated to the contract.[890] Wrongful neglect or refusal to accept and pay for the goods gives the right to the seller to sue him for damages for non-acceptance.[891] The measure of damages for non-acceptance of goods sold was held to be the estimated loss directly and naturally resulting in the ordinary course of events from the buyer's breach of contract.[892] It has been further held that the compensation which must be paid to him should be measured by ascertaining the difference between the contract and the market price on the date when payment was made, subject to the limitation that the Law imposes a duty upon the plaintiff to take all reasonable steps to mitigate his loss caused by the breach of contract and debars him from claiming compensation for any part of the damages which is due to his neglect to do so.[893] Loss of profit is not recoverable as a rule.[894] Damages for non-delivery may be claimed, where the seller wrongfully neglects or refuses to deliver the goods to the buyer.[895] Breach of warranty by the seller does not provide the legal right to reject the goods. However, the buyer may set up against the seller the breach of warranty in diminution or extinction of the price, or sue the seller for damages for breach of warranty.[896] Exercising these rights does not prevent the buyer from suing for the same breach of warranty if he has suffered further damage.[897] Nothing in this law affects the right of the seller or the buyer to recover special damages in any case where by law this may be recoverable, or to recover the money paid where the consideration for the payment of it has failed.[898]

283. In any action for breach of contract to deliver specific or ascertained goods, the Court may, if it thinks fit, on the application of the plaintiff, by its judgment direct that the contract shall be performed specifically, without giving the defendant the option of retaining the goods on payment of damages. The judgment may be

889. Section 56(1) *ibid.*
890. Section 56(2) *ibid.*
891. Section 57 *ibid. See* in this regard *Christodoulou v. Kazafaniotis* 1 CLR 325 (1988). This corresponds to s. 50(1) of the English Sale of Goods Act 1893.
892. *Shacolas v. Michaelides a.a.* 1 CLR 290 (1967).
893. *Anastasiou v. Stylianou* 1 CLR 62 (1974).
894. *Philippou Ltd v. Josephy Hoyle & Son Ltd* 1 CLR 625 (1982).
895. Section 58 Law No. 10(I)/1994.
896. Section 60(1)(a) and (b) *ibid. See* in this regard *Stylianou v. Lalakis* 1 CLR 287 (1982).
897. Section 60(2) Law No. 10(I)/1994.
898. Section 62(1) *ibid.*

conditional or unconditional, as the Court may deem just. The application of the plaintiff may be made at any time before the judgment.[899]

284. In the event that either party to a contract of sale repudiates the contract before the date of delivery, the other party may either treat the contract as subsisting and wait until the date of delivery or he may treat the contract as rescinded and sue for damages for the breach.[900]

899. Section 59 *ibid.*
900. Section 61 *ibid.*

Chapter 5. Building Contracts, Hire of Work and Skills

§1. Building Contracts

285. It has been ruled that building contracts are conceived to be ordinary contracts and thus regulated by Cap. 149, rather than by a specific statute.[901] In addition and further to this settled case law, some cases involving such contracts have been raised, argued and ruled by courts in Cyprus. As they shed light on specific aspects of building contracts, they are discussed below.

286. A case involving a building owner ordering by word of mouth works which from their very nature he must know or be taken to know will entail extra cost to carry out, is *Konteades v. Yusukjian.*[902] The court adopted the ruling that it would be a fraud on the part of the employer to have desired these alterations and additions to be made, to have stood and seen the expenditure going on upon them, to have taken the benefit of that expenditure, and to refuse payment on the ground that the expenditure was incurred without proper orders having been given for the purpose.[903] It further affirmed that it is within the power of a building owner to dismiss the architect or engineer for any fraudulent or dishonest act, and such conduct besides dismissal renders him liable to an action on the part of the employer. However, in the given case the court noted that the appellant neither alleged nor dismissed the engineer on these grounds. It further stated that the disputed contract left to the sole discretion of the architect he approval or condemnation of works and materials. Hence, the architect is placed in a position in which he is bound to exercise his judgment impartially as between the two parties to the building contract.[904] In such a case, the building owner may not invoke his authority nor dispute his judgment and thus he is bound by his certificate both as to the extras and the execution of the works under the contract.[905]

287. Extra works is one more specific aspect of building contracts. It has been ruled that the purpose of provisions ordering extras usually is to prevent unauthorized or extravagant claims for extras. Should a written order signed by the architect, be required for payment of such, a proper written order is a condition precedent to said payment. Lastly, if the court is called to interpret such a contract, it is restricted to the written terms and conditions of the contract.[906]

288. Qualifications of a promisor of constructing the agreed building is a further aspect and in particular, whether he is properly authorized for conducting such

901. *A. Panayides Contracting Ltd v. M & M Frangos Engineering & Contracting Ltd,* Supreme Court of Cyprus, Civil Appeal No. 301/2008, Judgment of 31 May 2012, not published in CLR.
902. *Konteades v. Yusukjian* 15 (1) CLR 83.
903. *Ibid.*, citing *Hill v. South Staffordshire Railway* 12 L.T. 63 (1865).
904. *Konteades v. Yusukjian* 15 (1) CLR 83, citing *Chambers v. Goldthorpe* 1 K.B. 638 (1901).
905. *Konteades v. Yusukjian* 15 (1) CLR 83, citing *Mills v. Bayley* 133 R.R. 579 (1863); *Murray v. Cohen* 9 LR (NSW) Eq 124 (1888).
906. *Ch. P. Th. Alexandrou Ltd v. Symvouliou Apoheteuseon Leukosias* 1 CLR 630 (1999).

works. In *Christophi v. Phetokaki*,[907] the case discussing this, the contractor not having the necessary qualifications due to him not being member of the relevant association, was not a disputed fact. The discussion was rather shifted on the question, whether the contract in question was a management or a building one. The appellant purported that it was a management contract, in an effort to avoid rescission of contract due to illegality caused by the contractor's lack of qualifications. The court underlined the established principle, according to which the words used in a contract do not bound the court's assessment regarding the true nature thereof.[908] The assertion put forward by the appellant that the title of a contract is not an irrelevant factor,[909] did not convince the court. It rather noted that in the case law quoted it was ruled that despite its relevance, said factor was not decisive and repeated the principle that a court, when estimating the nature of a contract, is not bound by its original wording and takes regard of all relevant circumstances.[910] The court further agreed with the finding of the ruling court, according to which a management contract does not underlie a specific form or stereotype. It was equally convinced after taking into consideration the factual surrounding that the performance of the specific work was awarded to the appellant. Thereafter the court disregarded the allegation of the appellant that he had appointed a representative of him to conduct the agreed work, as this was neither substantiated by the appellant's arguments nor proved by furnished evidence. Hence, it reaffirmed the ruling court's finding that the contract was void due to lack of necessary qualifications.

§2. Hire of Work and Skills

289. Hire of work and skills is equally an ordinary contract ruled by Cap. 149. Nevertheless, specific statutory provisions, the majority of which consists of national law implementing European legislation, provide for regulating specific aspects of such contracts and protection of employees.

I. Statutory Provisions Applicable to All Contracts of Employment

290. Provisions that apply to all contracts of employment in addition to Cap. 149 refer to informing the employee on his employment, and thus the content of the contract, to prohibition of discrimination and to termination of employment. These are foreseen in separate laws, as elaborated below.

---

907. *Christophe a.a. v. Phetokaki* 1 CLR 1208 (2009).
908. *Ibid.*, citing *Georgiades v. Georgiades* 1 CLR 428 (1988).
909. *Christophe a.a. v. Phetokaki* 1 CLR 1208 (2009), citing *Alexandrou v. Komodromou a.o.* 1 CLR 576 (1997) and *Theodoulou v. Aspis Pronia Asphalistiki Etairia Zois* 1 CLR 1551 (1997).
910. *Anorthosis v. Apollon* 1 CLR 518 (2002).

291. Law on Informing on the Terms of Employment Contract[911] enacts an obligation of the employer to inform the employee on the material terms of the employment contract or relationship.[912] More specifically, the statutory information obligation extends to: the identity of the parties; the place, where work is to be provided, and the seat of the employer's company; the position or speciality of the employee, his rank, his work's category and his work's object; the date on which the employment contract or relationship starts and its validity period, if it is made for a specific time; the duration of the annual leave,[913] as well as the manner and time of it being granted; the length of the required notice in case of its termination; all remuneration and the manner that it shall be provided; the length of his regular daily or weekly employment; and stating any collective agreements that additionally specify the terms and conditions of the employee's employment.[914] Finally, it is specified that no agreed term and condition in a contract of employment may be less favourable for an employee than the statutory provisions.[915] Any employer violating said obligations without reasonable cause is guilty of a crime and is liable to a monetary fine of up to CYP 500 (EUR 855).[916]

292. Law on Equal Payment[917] provides that for the same work or for work to which equal value is attributed, any discrimination on grounds of sex with regard to all aspects and conditions of remuneration shall be eliminated.[918] It is further set out

---

911. Law on Informing the Employee on the Terms of Employment Relationship or Contract or of Employment by the Employer ('ο περί Ενημέρωσης του Εργοδοτουμένου από τον Εργοδότη για τους Όρους που διέπουν τη Σύμβαση ή τη Σχέση Εργασίας Νόμος') No. 100 of 2000, OG I(I) No. 3417 of 7 Jul. 2000, as last amended by amending Law No. 12 of 2007, OG I(I) No. 4112 of 16 Feb. 2007. This law implements Council Directive 91/533/EEC of 14 Oct. 1991 on an employer's obligation to inform employees of the conditions applicable to the contract or employment relationship, OJ L 288 of 18 Oct. 1991, p. 32. Amendments to this directive have been proposed through Proposal for a directive of the European Parliament and of the Council on transparent and predictable working conditions in the European Union, COM(2017) 797 final of 21 Dec. 2017: https://eur-lex.europa.eu.
912. Section 4(1) Law No. 100(I)/2000.
913. Annual leave is regulated in Law on Annual Leave ('ο περί Ετήσιων Αδειών μετ' Απολαβών Νόμος') No. 8 of 1967, OG I No. 562 of 3 Mar. 1967, p. 383, as last amended by amending Law No. 42 of 2011, OG I(I) No. 4277 of 31 Mar. 2011.
914. Section 4(2) *ibid.*
915. Section 4(3) *ibid.*
916. Section 12(1) *ibid.*
917. Law on Equal Payment between Men and Women for the Same Employment or Employment of Same Value ('ο περί Ίσης Αμοιβής μεταξύ Ανδρών και Γυναικών για την Ίδια Εργασία ή για Εργασία Ίσης Αξίας Νόμος') No. 177 of 2002, OG I(I) No. 3638 of 27 Sep. 2002, as last amended by amending Law No. 151 of 2014, OG I(I) No. 4466 of 24 Oct. 2014. According to its preamble this law has implemented Council Directive 97/80/EC of 15 Dec. 1997 on the burden of proof in cases of discrimination based on sex, OJ L 14 of 20 Jan. 1998, p. 6 and Council Directive 75/117/EEC of 10 Feb. 1975 on the approximation of the laws of the Member States relating to the application of the principle of equal pay for men and women, OJ L 45 of 19 Feb. 1975, p. 19, while 'better implementing' Article 19 of Directive 2006/54/EC of the European Parliament and of the Council of 5 Jul. 2006 on the implementation of the principle of equal opportunities and equal treatment of men and women in matters of employment and occupation, OJ L 204 of 26 Jul. 2006, p. 23. Still, Directives 97/80/EC and 75/117/EEC have been repealed and replaced on 14 Aug. 2009 by Directive 2006/54/EC.
918. Section 5(1) Law No. 177(I)/2002, which corresponds to Art. 4 Directive 2006/54/EC.

that in particular, where a job classification system is used for determining pay, it shall be based on the same criteria for both men and women and so drawn up as to exclude any discrimination on grounds of sex.[919] Violation of these prohibitions, if made knowingly, may lead to a fine of up to CYP 4,000 (EUR 6,840) and/or imprisonment of up to six months.[920] Additionally, it is here stated that Cyprus has signed and ratified the Optional Protocol to the Convention on the Elimination of All Forms of Discrimination against Women of 2000.[921]

293. Law on Termination of Employment[922] sets out the grounds, on which an employment contract may be terminated and provides for remuneration. Generally, an employer may terminate on any ground an employment contract, whereby he is under obligation to remunerate the employee for such termination, as long as employment lasted for at least twenty-six weeks.[923] Precise remuneration is calculated in a statutory prescribed manner. The exact amount depends on the length of employment time and extends from the minimum amount of two-week wages up to the maximum amount of two-year wages.[924] An employee equally has the right to terminate employment on the ground of his employer's conduct, along with the burden of proof of the purported allegations.[925] Furthermore, employment may be terminated due to specific grounds that deprive the employee of receiving remuneration. Said grounds are the following:

- when work is not conducted in a reasonable satisfactory manner;[926]
- when the employer stops or intends to stop his business, including for reasons related to business' operation such as credit difficulties, lack of orders or raw materials, change in the manner of production or organization leading to minimizing the number of necessary employees, or limiting work bulk;[927] yet, in such a dismissal, an employee generally has the right to receive payment determined in a specific statutory manner;[928]
- when termination is due to force majeure, war, civil uprising, natural disaster or destruction of the facilities due to fire not caused knowingly or negligent by the employer;[929]

---

919. Section 5(2) Law No. 177(I)/2002, which corresponds to Art. 4 Directive 2006/54/EC.
920. Section 24(1) Law No. 177(I)/2002.
921. Law Ratifying the Optional Protocol to the Convention on the Elimination of All Forms of Discrimination against Women ('ο περί του Προαιρετικού Πρωτοκόλλου στη Σύμβαση των Ηνωμένων Εθνών για την Εξάλειψη κάθε Μορφής Διάκρισης σε βάρος της Γυναίκας (Κυρωτικός) Νόμος') No. 1 of 2002, OG I(III) No. 3580 of 1 Mar. 2002.
922. Law on Termination of Employment ('ο περί Τερματισμού Απασχολήσεως Νόμος') No. 24 of 1967, OG I(I) No. 577 of 27 May 1967, p. 485, as last amended by amending Law No. 89 of 2016, OG I(I) No. 4572 of 25 Jul. 2016, p. 1041.
923. Section 3(1) *ibid.*
924. Table 1(1), (2), and (3) and Table 4(1)(a) *ibid.*
925. Section 7(1) and (2) *ibid.*
926. Section 5(a) *ibid.*
927. Sections 5(b) and 18 *ibid.*
928. Section 16(1) and Table 4 *ibid.*
929. Section 5(c) *ibid.*

- when employment is terminated after expiration of its validity period or due to employee having satisfied all prerequisites set out for pension;[930]
- when employee demonstrates such behaviour that makes him eligible to dismissal without notice, as long as employer acts within reasonable time;[931] and
- without prejudice to the immediate aforementioned general reason, the following constitute grounds for dismissal without notice: employee's conduct illuminating that the relationship between employer and employee shall reasonably not continue as expected; the employee committing a serious misconduct during performance of his duties; the employee committing a criminal offence during performance of his duties without the explicit or implied consensus of his employer; inappropriate conduct of the employee during performance of his duties; serious or repeated violation or disregarding employment rules or other rules related to his employment.[932]

294. Termination of employment prerequisites serving a notice prior to it taking effect. The precise time that such notice needs to be served depends on the duration of the employment and differentiates from one to eight weeks.[933] Should the employee be the one terminating the employment said time differentiates from one to three weeks.[934] Upon termination of employment the employee has the right to request from the employer an employment's certificate, which by law may not contain anything negative for the employee.[935] Finally, criminal provisions ensuring proper compliance with the provisions of this law are set out. However, these provisions criminalize illegal conduct towards the state authorities regarding remuneration and payment, employer's refusal to issue an employment certificate and employer's failure to properly proceed with notifications, when dismissing employers due to stopping or intending to stop his business.[936] No criminal provision penalizes any violation of the law relating to dismissal, grounds thereof and related remuneration. Further, the monetary fines set out for said offences are quite modest, that being of up to CYP 450 (EUR 770) and/or imprisonment of up to six months for illegal conduct towards state authorities and penalty of up to CYP 250 (EUR 428) for the rest. These monetary fines along with the wide exceptions on prohibiting employment termination without remuneration appear weak in giving proper effect to the scope of the law.

295. Collective redundancies are regulated in a separate law.[937] The term collective redundancies means dismissals effected by an employer for one or more reasons not related to the individual workers concerned where the number of

930. Section 5(d) *ibid.*
931. Section 5(e) *ibid.*
932. Section 5(f)(i), (ii), (iii), (iv) and (v) *ibid.*
933. Section 9(1) *ibid.*
934. Section 10 *ibid.*
935. Section 8 *ibid.*
936. Sections 27, 28 and 29 *ibid.*
937. Law on Collective Redundancies ('ο περί Ομαδικών Απολύσεων Νόμος') No. 28 of 2001, OG I(I) No. 3480 of 9 Mar. 2001, as last amended by amending Law No. 161 of 2018, OG I(I) No. 4679

redundancies is over a period of thirty days: at least ten in establishments normally employing more than twenty and less than 100 workers; at least 10% of the number of workers in establishments normally employing at least 100 but less than 300 workers; at least thirty in establishments normally employing 300 workers or more.[938] In such cases, employers are under a statutory duty to inform and negotiate with employees' representatives[939] and provide them with specific pieces of information,[940] along with sending notifications to the competent authorities.[941] Where the projected collective redundancy concerns members of the crew of a sea-going vessel, the employer shall notify the competent authority of the state of the flag which the vessel flies.[942] An employer violating said statutory duties is liable to a monetary fine of no more than CYP 1,000 (EUR 1,710).[943] Once again, as seen above in the Law on Termination of Employment, these modest monetary fines, in all probability, fail to ensure and promote the scope of the law.

II. Statutory Provisions on Protection of Specific Categories of Employees

296. Specific employees are granted statutory protection, as this is considered necessary due to certain qualities they possess. Alternatively, statutory protection is given to employees due to their working environment conditions. Hence, in the latter case solely specific sectors are protected, whereas in the first one applicability across all sectors is ensured.

297. Protection across all sectors first relate to protection of pregnant workers and workers who have recently given birth to or are breastfeeding.[944] Such workers

---

of 19 Dec. 2018. This law implements Council Directive 98/59/EC of 20 Jul. 1998 on the approximation of the laws of the Member States relating to collective redundancies, OJ L 225 of 12 Aug. 1998, p. 16, as last amended by Directive (EU) 2015/1794 of the European Parliament and of the Council of 6 Oct. 2015 amending Directives 2008/94/EC, 2009/38/EC and 2002/14/EC of the European Parliament and of the Council, and Council Directives 98/59/EC and 2001/23/EC, as regards seafarers, OJ L 263 of 8 Oct. 2015, p. 1.

938. Section 2 Law No. 28(I)/2001, which corresponds to Art. 1(1)(a)(i) Directive 98/59/EC.
939. Section 4(1) and (2) Law No. 28(I)/2001, which corresponds to Art. 2(1) and (2) Directive 98/59/EC.
940. Section 5(1) and (2) Law No. 28(I)/2001, which corresponds to Art. 2(3) Directive 98/59/EC.
941. Section 6(1), (2) and (3) Law No. 28(I)/2001, which corresponds to Art. 3(1) and (2) Directive 98/59/EC.
942. Section 6(1A) Law No. 28(I)/2001, which corresponds to Art. 1 of the Directive (EU) 2015/1794 (*see* in this regard n 925 above).
943. Section 13(1) Law No. 28(I)/2001.
944. Law on Protection of Motherhood ('ο περί Προστασίας της Μητρότητας Νόμος') No. 100 of 1997, OG I(I) No. 3207 of 19 Dec. 1997, p. 1408, as last amended by amending Law No. 11 of 2019, OG I(I) No. 4686 of 1 Mar. 2019, p. 46. This law implements Council Directive 92/85/EEC of 19 Oct. 1992 on the introduction of measures to encourage improvements in the safety and health at work of pregnant workers and workers who have recently given birth or are breastfeeding, OJ L 348 of 28 Nov. 1992, p. 1. It further ensures that the national legislation is in alignment with the following judgments of the Court of Justice of the European Union: *Nadine Paquay v. Société d'architectes Hoet + Minne SPRL*, CJEU Case C-460/06, Judgment of 11 Oct. 2007, ECR I-08511 (2007); *Dita Danosa v. LKB Līzings SIA*, CJEU Case C-232/09, Judgment of 11 Nov. 2010, ECR I-11405

are entitled to a continuous period of maternity leave of at least eighteen weeks,[945] while not being liable to dismissal from the begin of the pregnancy until five months after maternity leave is over.[946] The latter prohibition equally applies to female workers having adopted a child.[947] Any person acting in violation thereof is liable to a monetary fine of up to EUR 7,000.[948] Twenty years after this law, legislation for the protection of fatherhood[949] was enacted. According to this, fathers are eligible to a two-consecutive week leave.[950] During this period, he generally may not be dismissed.[951] Violation of these statutory provisions leads to a monetary fine of up to EUR 7,000.[952] Second, protection across all sectors is offered to persons with disabilities.[953] This national law was enacted to the purpose of responding to the call of the United Nations to support the implementation of the Standard Rules on the Equalization of Opportunities for Persons with Disabilities.[954] In particular with reference to employment, it has been decreed that the principle of equal treatment in relation to persons with disabilities has to be implemented with reference to: the terms of entering into and being in the labour market on all levels of professional hierarchy, including promotions; access to all kinds of professional education, including acquiring professional experience; employment conditions and terms, including dismissals and remuneration; and membership and participation to the organization of employees or employers or any association, including advantages given by such associations. Employers have a positive statutory duty to implement these in their workplace, even if this means that they have to provide reasonable access points and other facilitations.[955] Violation of said obligations may lead to a monetary fine of up to CYP 4,000 (EUR 6,840) and/or imprisonment of up to six months.[956]

(2010). Directive 92/85/EEC has last been amended by Directive 2014/27/EU of the European Parliament and of the Council of 26 Feb. 2014 amending Council Directives 92/58/EEC, 92/85/EEC, 94/33/EC, 98/24/EC and Directive 2004/37/EC of the European Parliament and of the Council, in order to align them to Regulation (EC) No. 1272/2008 on classification, labelling and packaging of substances and mixtures, OJ L 65 of 5 Mar. 2014, p. 1.

945. Section 3(1) Law No. 100(I)/1997, which corresponds to Art. 8 Directive 92/85/EEC.
946. Section 4(1) Law No. 100(I)/1997, which corresponds to Art. 10 Directive 92/85/EEC.
947. Section 4A Law No. 100(I)/1997.
948. Section 9 *ibid.*
949. Law on Protection of Fatherhood ('ο περί Προστασίας της Πατρότητας Νόμος') No. 117 of 2017, OG I(I) No. 4615 of 24 Jul. 2017, p. 974.
950. Section 3(1) *ibid.*
951. Section 5(1)(a) *ibid.*
952. Section 15 *ibid.*
953. Law on Persons with Disabilities ('ο περί Ατόμων με Αναπηρίες Νόμος') No. 127 of 2000, OG I(I) No. 3420 of 21 Jul. 2000, p. 1386, as last amended by amending Law No. 182 of 2017, OG I(I) No. 4633 of 22 Dec. 2017, p. 1197. This law implements Council Directive 2000/78/EC of 27 Nov. 2000 establishing a general framework for equal treatment in employment and occupation, OJ L 303 of 2 Dec. 2000, p. 16.
954. UN, General Assembly, 85th plenary meeting, *Standard Rules on the Equalization of Opportunities for Persons with Disabilities*, A/RES/48/96 of 20 Dec. 1993. Available: http://www.un.org/documents.
955. Section 5(1) and (2) Law No. 127(I)/2000.
956. Section 5(4) *ibid.*

298. Specific protective measures are further attributed to employees working under certain environmental conditions. These conditions are first the recreational centres,[957] that being any shop where beverages, food or sweets are sold, regardless of whether music or artistic programme is offered. Employees in such centres are required to have a health certificate.[958] Another environment condition is carriage by road,[959] that being any journey made entirely or in part on roads open to the public by a vehicle, whether laden or not, used for the carriage of passengers or goods.[960] In these conditions driving times, breaks and rest periods for drivers are statutorily regulated throughout the internal market, in order to harmonize the conditions of competition between modes of inland transport, especially with regard to the road sector, and to improve working conditions and road safety, as well as improved working practices in the road transport industry.[961] Similarly, the minimum standards of health and safety regarding organizing working time of mobile staff in civil aviation[962] and of seafarers[963] are regulated in specific laws.

957. Law on Recreational Centres ('ο περί Κέντρων Αναψυχής Νόμος') No. 29 of 1985, OG I No. 2045 of 6 Apr. 1985, p. 875, as last amended by amending Law No. 65 of 2007, OG I(I) No. 4127 of 6 Jun. 2007.
958. Sections 2 and 17 *ibid.*
959. Regulation (EC) No. 561/2006 of the European Parliament and of the Council of 15 Mar. 2006 on the harmonisation of certain social legislation relating to road transport, OJ L 102 of 11 Apr. 2006, p. 1, as last amended by Regulation (EU) No. 165/2014 of the European Parliament and of the Council of 4 Feb. 2014 on tachographs in road transport, repealing Council Regulation (EEC) No. 3821/85 on recording equipment in road transport and amending Regulation (EC) No. 561/2006 of the European Parliament and of the Council on the harmonisation of certain social legislation relating to road transport, OJ L 60 of 28 Feb. 2014, p. 1. On the currently discussed amendments *see* Proposal for a Regulation of the European Parliament and of the Council amending Regulation (EC) No. 561/2006 as regards on minimum requirements on maximum daily and weekly driving times, minimum breaks and daily and weekly rest periods and Regulation (EU) 165/2014 as regards positioning by means of tachographs, COM(2017) 277 final of 31 May 2017: https://eur-lex.europa.eu.
960. Article 4(a) *ibid.*
961. Article 1 *ibid.*
962. Law on the Organisation of Working Time of Mobile Staff in Civil Aviation ('ο περί Οργάνωσης του Χρόνου Εργασίας του Ιπτάμενου Προσωπικού της Πολιτικής Αεροπορίας Νόμος') No. 12 of 2004, OG I(I) No. 3810 of 13 Feb. 2004, as last amended by amending Law No. 16 of 2007, OG I(I) No. 4112 of 16 Feb. 2007. This law implements Council Directive 2000/79/EC of 27 Nov. 2000 concerning the European Agreement on the Organisation of Working Time of Mobile Workers in Civil Aviation concluded by the Association of European Airlines (AEA), the European Transport Workers' Federation (ETF), the European Cockpit Association (ECA), the European Regions Airline Association (ERA) and the International Air Carrier Association (IACA), OJ L 302 of 1 Dec. 2000, p. 57.
963. Law on Merchant Shipping ('ο περί Εμπορικής Ναυτιλίας Νόμος') No. 79 of 2003, OG I(I) No. 3738 of 18 Jul. 2003. This law implements Council Directive 1999/63/EC of 21 Jun. 1999 concerning the Agreement on the organization of working time of seafarers concluded by the European Community Shipowners' Association (ECSA) and the Federation of Transport Workers' Unions in the European Union (FST), OJ L 167 of 2 Jul. 1999, p. 33. This directive has been last amended by Council Directive 2009/13/EC of 16 Feb. 2009 implementing the Agreement concluded by the European Community Shipowners' Associations (ECSA) and the European Transport Workers' Federation (ETF) on the Maritime Labour Convention, 2006, and amending Directive 1999/63/EC, OJ L 124 of 20 May 2009, p. 30.

III. Statutory Provisions on Protection from the Working Environment

299. Trigger of the statutory provisions set out here is a danger arising out of the working environment itself, while they aim to preventing any damage caused by such dangers. The basic set of provisions is enacted in the Law on Safety and Health at Work.[964] This law contains general principles concerning the prevention of occupational risks, the protection of safety and health, the elimination of risk and accident factors, the informing, consultation, balanced participation and training of workers and their representatives, as well as general guidelines for the implementation of the said principles.[965] Hence, employers have duties towards employees that derive from these statutory provisions, in addition to the terms and conditions agreed in the employment contract. Especially for the control of major-accident hazards involving dangerous substances, a special legislation has been decreed,[966] which applies to establishments, those being the whole location under the control of an operator where dangerous substances are present in one or more installations, including common or related infrastructures or activities; establishments are either lower-tier establishments or upper-tier establishments.[967] Along with the general obligations of the operator that include him taking all necessary measures to prevent major accidents and limiting their consequences for human health and the environment,[968] he is obliged to draw up a document in writing setting out the major-accident prevention policy and to ensure that it is properly implemented. Said document must: be designed to ensure a high level of protection of human health and the environment; be proportionate to the major-accident hazards; include the operator's overall aims and principles of action; describe the role and responsibility

964. Law on Safety and Health at Work ('ο περί Ασφάλειας και Υγείας στην Εργασία Νόμος') No. 89 of 1996, OG I(I) No. 3096 of 1 Nov. 1996, p. 382, as last amended by amending Law No. 178 of 2015, OG I(I) No. 4543 of 9 Dec. 2015, which implements Council Directive 89/391/EEC of 12 Jun. 1989 on the introduction of measures to encourage improvements in the safety and health of workers at work, OJ L 183 of 29 Jun. 1989, p. 1. It further implements Council Directive 1999/70/EC of 28 Jun. 1999 concerning the framework agreement on fixed-term work concluded by ETUC, UNICE and CEEP, OJ L 175 of 10 Jul. 1999, p. 43; and Directive 2013/30/EU of the European Parliament and of the Council of 12 Jun. 2013 on safety of offshore oil and gas operations, OJ L 178 of 28 Jun. 2013, p. 66. Directive 89/391/EEC has been last amended by Regulation (EC) No. 1137/2008 of the European Parliament and of the Council of 22 Oct. 2008 adapting a number of instruments subject to the procedure laid down in Article 251 of the Treaty to Council Decision 1999/468/EC, with regard to the regulatory procedure with scrutiny – Adaptation to the regulatory procedure with scrutiny – Part One, OJ L 311 of 21 Nov. 2008, p. 1. Directive 2013/30/EU has been last amended by Regulation (EU) 2018/1999 of the European Parliament and of the Council of 11 Dec. 2018 on the Governance of the Energy Union and Climate Action, OJ L 328 of 21 Dec. 2018, p. 1.

965. Section 2A(2) Law No. 89(I)/1996, which corresponds to Art. 1(2) Directive 89/391/EEC.

966. Regulations on Safety and Health at Work (Control of Major-Accident Hazards Involving Dangerous Substances) ('οι περί Ασφάλειας και Υγείας στην Εργασία (Αντιμετώπιση Κινδύνων Ατυχημάτων Μεγάλης Κλίμακας Σχετιζόμενων με Επικίνδυνες Ουσίες) Κανονισμοί') No. 347 of 2015, OG III(I) No. 4900 of 23 Oct. 2015, p. 2109. These implement Directive 2012/18/EU of the European Parliament and of the Council of 4 Jul. 2012 on the control of major-accident hazards involving dangerous substances, OJ L 197 of 24 Jul. 2012, p. 1.

967. Regulations 4(1) and 2 Regulations 347/2015, which correspond to Arts 2(1) and 3(1) Directive 2012/18/EU.

968. Regulation 6(1) Regulations 347/2015, which corresponds to Art. 5(1) Directive 2012/18/EU.

of management; set out the commitment towards continuously improving the control of major-accident hazards; and ensure a high level of protection.[969]

969. Regulation 8(1) Regulations 347/2015, which corresponds to Art. 8(1) Directive 2012/18/EU.

Chapter 6. Lease, Commercial and Agricultural Leases

300. Lease, including ordinary, commercial and agricultural, is a plain contract. Hence, the aforementioned provisions and principles are applied thereto. Nevertheless, additional provisions are set out in Law on Rent Control[970] (hereinafter 'Law No. 23/1983').

301. The scope of this law extends to statutory tenant. The meaning of said tenant, along with the further components of this legal notion is thoroughly defined in this law. In particular, tenant ('ενοικιαστής' in Greek, 'kiracı' in Turkish) means any natural or legal person that usually resides or has its seat in Cyprus, but for aliens or legal persons controlled by foreigners, with the exception of spouses of Cypriot nationals, and includes: a statutory tenant; any subtenant and any other person deriving a right from the original tenant or subtenant to possess the premises; the surviving husband or child of a tenant who was residing with him, or who had his main occupation therein, at the time of his death, or was regularly studying abroad or was working temporarily abroad at the time of his death, or, in the case of rending a dwelling house, where a tenant does not desert his wife, or the tenant is a woman, such member of the tenant's family as was residing with same for not less than six months immediately before the death of the tenant; the wife living in separation due to her husband having deserted the marital house, when he is the tenant, as well as their children; and the Government of the Republic of Cyprus and any legal person governed by public law.[971] Obviously, the provisions referring to husbands and wives and providing rights and duties on the basis of gender are obsolete. Despite the plain language of the statute, which prohibits any further interpretation, both terms must be construed as spouse in order to avoid violation of the fundamental principle of equality and prohibition of discrimination, enshrined in Article 28 of the Constitution, Articles 21(1) and 23 of the Charter of Fundamental Rights of the EU and Article 14 of the European Convention on Human Rights. Same observations apply to the statutory restrictions solely for Cypriot nationals or legal persons controlled by same nationals due to discrimination on the ground of nationality, which violates all aforementioned provisions along with Article 18 of the Treaty for the Functioning of the European Union (TFEU).

302. Further to the statutory defined legal notions, statutory tenant ('θέσμιος ενοικιαστής' in Greek, 'yasal kiracı' in Turkish) is a tenant who, at the expiration or determination of his tenancy continues to be in possession of the premises. Premises ('ακίνητο' in Greek, 'taşınınaz mal' in Turkish) means building for rent as a dwelling house or shop. Dwelling house ('κατοικία' in Greek, 'ikametgâh' in Turkish) on its part stands for building or construction or part of such, let as a dwelling of a person or for the housing of unions, foundations and non-professional organizations, even if part thereof is used for professional purposes. Business premises

970. Law on Rent Control ('ο περί Ενοικιοστασίου Νόμος') No. 23 of 1983, OG I No. 1859 of 22 Apr. 1983, p. 719, as last amended by amending Law No. 173 of 2013, OG I(I) No. 4422 of 27 Dec. 2013, p. 1494.

971. Section 2 Law No. 23/1983.

('κατάστημα' in Greek, 'işyeri' in Turkish) means any premises let for any business, trade or professional purposes and used as such. Finally, owner ('ιδιοκτήτης' in Greek, 'kiralayan' or 'mal sahibi' in Turkish) is, in relation to any premises, any natural or legal person,[972] other than the tenant, who is or should be, but for the provisions of this law, entitled to possession of the premises, and in the case of subtenancy a tenant, who sublets the premises or any part thereof.[973]

303. In addition to statutory tenants, this law is applicable to all or some of the dwelling houses and business premises situated within any part of Cyprus, should the Council of Ministers decide so and the relevant regulation is published in the Official Gazette. The Council of Ministers has wide discretionary powers, as the statutory requirements for such a decision comprise of abstract legal notions. In particular, these are necessity or advisability to the purpose of availability of premises with reasonable rents and the security of their possession, or whenever public interest ('δημόσιο συμφέρον' in Greek, 'kamu yararı' in Turkish) demands such action.[974] Issued regulations need to be re-examined every five years by the same public body while taking into consideration the commercial and touristic development of the relevant area.[975] The Council of Ministers equally has the power to annul the regulation in whole or in part, when the circumstances that led to issuing such a legislative action have lapsed or alternatively when public interest demands such action.[976]

304. The core of this law consists of it prescribing the only manner of increasing the rent of statutory tenants.[977] Whenever a statutory tenant of a house dwelling or business premise feels to have suffered injustice, he may file a petition to the Court to define the just ('δίκαιο' in Greek, 'doğru' in Turkish) rent that he must pay for such a premise. The owner of the premises bears the same right equally. Alternatively, they have the right to negotiate and agree in writing an increase of rent of no more than the increase decided by the Council of Ministers in Regulations. For such a negotiation to be effective, no more than two years since the date that the statutory tenant took possession of the premises or since the last rent increase, may have passed. To the contrary, for said court petition to be accepted by the competent court, the time frame is at least two years since premises' occupation by the tenant or since the last increase or decrease of rent.[978] In any event, when the tenant becomes statutory tenant, the terms and conditions set out in the rent contract do not apply.[979]

---

972. The notion 'natural or legal person' does not include the state. *Larcos v. Attorney-General* 1 CLR 510 (1995); *Constantinou v. Attorney-General* 1 CLR 741 (1997).
973. Section 2 Law No. 23/1983.
974. Section 3(1) *ibid.*
975. Section 3(3) *ibid.*
976. Section 3(2) *ibid.*
977. Section 8(1) *ibid.*
978. Section 8(2) *ibid.*
979. *Katsikides v. Constantinides* 1 CLR 31 (1969); *Katsikides v. Constantinides* 1 CLR 147 (1970); *Level Tachexcars Ltd v. Kargotis* 1 CLR 163 (1970); *Elli Meitz a.a. v. Andreas Pelengaris* 1 CLR 226 (1977); *Chrystalla Demetriou a.a. v. Savvas Ioannides* 1 CLR 16 (1982).

305. This law also prescribes the cases, when statutory tenants may be evicted from occupied premises and such premises may be reclaimed by their owners.[980] These are the following:

- when any rent lawfully due was in arrear for twenty-one days or upwards after notice of demand in writing has been given to the tenant and there was no tender thereof before the institution of the action;[981] or
- when the statutory tenant or any other person occupying the premises under him has been guilty of conduct constituting a nuisance or persistent annoyance to persons in the same or neighbouring premises or of causing or permitting the use of the premises for illegal[982] or immoral ('ανήθικους' in Greek, 'ahlâka aykırı' in Turkish) purposes;[983] or
- where the condition of the premises has, in the opinion of the court, deteriorated owing to acts of waste by, or the neglect or default of, the tenant or where the tenant has wrongfully caused or suffered to be caused substantial damage to the premises; however, the court may not issue an eviction order, when the statutory tenant has repaired the damage in full within two months since the service of the petition;[984] or
- where the statutory tenant despite the explicit prohibition of subletting has violated said prohibition and the court considers reasonable ('λογική' in Greek, 'mâkul' in Turkish) to give such judgment or make such order;[985] or
- where the tenant, by taking in lodgers or by subletting or otherwise parting with the possession of the whole or any part of the premises, is making a profit, whether directly or indirectly, which, having regard to the rent paid by the tenant is unreasonable to give such judgment or make such order and the court considers reasonable ('λογική' in Greek, 'mâkul' in Turkish) to give such judgment or make such order;[986] or
- where the premises, being a dwelling house, are reasonably required by the owner for occupation as a residence for himself or spouse, child or dependent parents,[987] or spouse of the latter, or when the owner is a family company, where the premises are required for the occupation of a member of this family and the court considers it reasonable ('λογική' in Greek, 'mâkul' in Turkish) to give such judgment or make such order. Provided that no judgment or order shall be made or given under this paragraph if the court is satisfied that, having regard to all the circumstances of the case, greater hardship would be caused by granting the order

---

980. Section 11(1) Law No. 23/1983.
981. Section 11(1)(a) *ibid.*
982. Use of the premises that does not comply with the use authorized by the competent authorities does not constitute use for illegal purposes, when the authorization was altered after the rent contract was made, by application of the owner to the authorities. *Pelidou-Kalli a.a. v. Golden Star Supermarket Ltd* 1 CLR 1624 (2010).
983. Section 11(1)(b) Law No. 23/1983.
984. Section 11(1)(c) *ibid.*
985. Section 11(1)(d) *ibid.*
986. Section 11(1)(e) *ibid.*
987. It has been ruled that this notion includes solely natural parents and not parents-in-law. *Pierides v. Youlielmou* 1 CLR 470 (1985).

or judgment than by refusing to grant it. For these purposes the expression *circumstances of the case* shall include the question whether other accommodation is available for the owner or the tenant;[988] or

- where business premise is reasonably being required by the owner, his wife or his children, under the condition that none of them was able to require other adequate and with reasonable rent premise for or to the purpose of business and the court considers it reasonable ('λογική'-1 in Greek, 'mâkul' in Turkish) to give such judgment or make such order. Provided that no judgment or order shall be made or given under this paragraph if the court is satisfied that, having regard to all the circumstances of the case, greater hardship would be caused by granting the order or judgment than by refusing to grant it;[989] or
- where the premises are reasonably required by the owner for the demolition of the premises, as long as this does not constitute abuse of right, for the demolition thereof and the construction of new premises, for substantial alteration that cause substantial and important changes that cause substantial and important alteration to its reclamation purpose, or for the construction of works in the listed site. The court has to be convinced on the one hand that the owner has obtained all necessary permits and authorizations for such works, and on the other hand that the owner may not reasonably[990] proceed with such works without recovery of possession. Finally, the owner has to give to statutory tenant a four-month notice in writing to vacate the premises;[991] or
- where vacant possession of the premises is required for the purpose of carrying out a scheme of development or redevelopment under the laws regulating town planning;[992] or
- where the premises or any part thereof have been compulsory acquired under any law empowering compulsory acquisition of property;[993] or
- where the premises are reasonably required for the purpose of the exercise of the statutory duties or powers of a local authority or for any purpose which in the opinion of the court is in the public interest;[994] or
- where the tenancy has been determined by notice to quit given by the statutory tenant and following this notice, the owner has made a sale or rent contract or has taken any other measures, as a result of which the owner in the opinion of the court shall be seriously damaged, if he does not recover possession of the premises;[995] or
- where any dwelling house, which is under state ownership, has been lawfully granted to the purpose of serving the public interest that is connected to the status

988. Section 11(1)(f) Law No. 23/1983.
989. Section 11(1)(g) *ibid.*
990. Reasonableness is here linked only to whether or not it is reasonable for the owner to obtain possession for the purpose of the alterations and it is unrelated to any other factor. *Poyiatzis v. Pilavakis* a.a. 1 CLR 411 (1988).
991. Section 11(1)(h) Law No. 23/1983.
992. Section 11(1)(i) *ibid.*
993. Section 11(1)(j) *ibid.*
994. Section 11(1)(k) *ibid.*
995. Section 11(1)(l) *ibid.*

of the tenant, being a servant or officer of the state or fulfilling statutory requirements, and the same tenant has lost such status or does not fulfil anymore same requirements.[996]

306. Unless a specific period for serving a notice has been set out above, the owner is statutorily obliged to serve a written notice at least one month in advance.[997]

307. In the aforementioned cases, where a premise is claimed by the owner for occupation by himself and his family under section 11(1)(f) and (g) Law No. 23/1983, the court has the discretionary power to order the claimant to pay to the statutory tenant compensation of no more than the rent of eighteen months, should the order or judgment relate to business premise.[998] Furthermore, when trade or business has been so attached to the premises that he shall suffer a loss if he removes and carries on his trade or business in other premises, and the aforementioned compensation is deemed by the court not to suffice, further compensation may be ordered up to the value of trade or business being attached to such premises, taking into account all conditions of the tenant, as well as the possibility of the premises gaining more value after reclaiming occupation by the owner.[999] In addition to the above, in the latter case,[1000] if the new premises shall be including business premises, the statutory tenant may claim a rent offer for reasonable rent within three months after the eviction order or judgment.[1001] Should the owner reject the claim or even not react to such actions of the statutory tenant, the latter may apply to the court for being granted such a rent. If the court finds this claim to be reasonable ('λογική' in Greek, 'mâkul' in Turkish), it shall accept the claim and order the rent under the terms and conditions it deems fit, should the parties fail to agree. In such a case, the statutory tenant is statutory obliged to return the compensation paid to him under sections 12 and 13 of this law.[1002]

---

996. Section 11(1)(m) *ibid.*
997. Section 11(2) *ibid.*
998. Section 12 *ibid.*
999. Section 13 *ibid.*
1000. Section 11(1)(g) *ibid.*
1001. Section 14(1)(a) and (b) *ibid.*
1002. Section 14(2)(a) and (b) *ibid.*

Chapter 7. Compromise Settlement

308. Compromise settlement is a manner of bringing court proceedings to an end. Settlement can either be general or have the form of mediation settlement.

§1. Settlement

309. Settlement ('συμβιβασμός' in Greek, 'uzlaşma' in Turkish) is not regulated in a specific statute. However, case law sheds some light thereon, especially regarding settling disputes during litigation.

310. Settlement is a matter within the apparent general authority of an advocate.[1003] In the context of an effort to ascertain whether there is room for settlement of an action, communication between the parties is expected to take place. Such correspondence addressed to adversaries 'without prejudice' is inadmissible in evidence on grounds of privilege.[1004] The reason behind this rule is that disclosure would inhibit frank communications for a settlement.[1005] Similarly, an appeal against a judgment on the ground of violation of natural justice due to the judge having expressed himself regarding the credibility of a party during discussion in the judge's chambers with a view to settlement was rejected. The Supreme Court found nothing in the judgment to lend any support to the contention for irregularity as suggested by the appellant. To the contrary, careful consideration of claim and counterclaim along with analysing and assessing evidence adduced on both sides supported that natural justice was well served.[1006] Finalizing a settlement between disputing parties is further a valid reason for adjourning an action following proper application by the parties.[1007] A settlement agreed among the parties, declared in court and made rule of court is a contract.[1008] Settlements are not restricted in matters of civil law, but may equally be reached on issues of public law between the administration and citizens.[1009] Especially regarding infants, who do not possess full legal competence due to them being regarded as of immature intellect and imperfect discretion, the law endorses their protection by disabling them to binding themselves, except where it is for their own benefit.[1010] Hence, courts have the power to

1003. *In re Charalambous* 1 CLR 736 (1985), citing *Matthews v. Munster* 20 QBD 141 (1887); *Waugh a.o. v. H.B. Clifford & Sons* 1 All ER 1095 (1982).
1004. *Skattou v. M/V 'KOREIZ' a.a.* 1 CLR 804 (1982), citing *Rabin v. Mendoza* 1 WLR 271 (1954).
1005. *Skattou v. M/V 'KOREIZ' a.a.* 1 CLR 804 (1982).
1006. *Ahapittas v. Poc-chik Ltd* 1 CLR 1 (1968).
1007. *In re Charalambous* 1 CLR 736 (1985).
1008. *Georgiades v. Georgiades* 1 CLR 428 (1988).
1009. *Gregoriades v. Cyprus* 3 CLR 2178 (1986).
1010. *Georgiou v. Constantinides* 1 CLR 62 (1976), citing *Duncan v. Dixon* 44 Ch. D. 211 (1890); *Nash v. Inman* 2 K.B. 1 (1908); *Papadopoulou v. Polycarpou* 1 CLR 352 (1968).

approve settlements on behalf of infants, as long as they are beneficial.[1011] In fact, settlements involving infants cannot be effected without the sanction of the Court, in which an action is pending.[1012]

311. In view of the contractual nature of settlements, it comes as no surprise that interpretation of such underlies the same rules and principles as the ones already discussed on contracts[1013] (*see* in this regard paragraphs 120 et seq. above). Nevertheless, it has been ruled that where the content of an agreed settlement is ambiguous, the judge, who has been called to decide on purported claims on the basis of such settlement, resorts to evidence of surrounding circumstances in order to be enabled to proceed with defining and clarifying its terms and conditions.[1014]

312. With reference to the effect of agreeing a settlement, it has been well established that where the parties are agreed that litigation should come to an end because of an out of court settlement, any attempt on the part of the court to keep the proceedings in being and, further, initiate enquiries about the fate of the proceedings, is a serious diversion from the adversary system of trial and as such cannot be countenanced.[1015] Similarly, settlements may form the basis for court orders, such as a stay of execution.[1016] Further, it has been ruled that settlement declared in court leads to the court dismissing the resource, but not to establishing res judicata. In any event, it does create estoppel arising from contract, which is a species of estoppel by representation, entitling the one party to the contract to insist in a proper case, i.e., where his promise is dependent on the performance of another mutual promise by the other party to the contract, that before he be held bound and stopped by his promise, the other party must also perform his own corresponding obligation.[1017]

§2. Mediation Settlement

313. Mediation settlement ('συμφωνία συμβιβασμού' in Greek, 'arabuluculuk sözleşmesi' in Turkish) is today being statutory regulated in Law on Certain Aspects of Mediation in Civil Matters[1018] (hereinafter 'Law No. 159(I)/2012'), which implements Directive 2008/52/EC.[1019] However, even before the enactment thereof, efforts to settle a dispute through a retired judge and most importantly a person of common trust has been documented in the case law. This settlement agreement was

1011. *Georgiou v. Constantinides* 1 CLR 62 (1972), citing *Re Wells Boyer v. MacLean* 1 Ch. D. 848 (1903).
1012. *Georgiou v. Constantinides* 1 CLR 62 (1972).
1013. *Georghiades v. Georghiades* 1 CLR 623 (1985).
1014. *Touloumi a.a. v. Militadou* 1 CLR 129 (1982).
1015. *Eleftheriades v. Cyprus Hotels Ltd* 1 CLR 677 (1985).
1016. *Pamborides v. Michaelides* 1 CLR 685 (1984).
1017. *Georghiades v. Cyprus* 1 CLR 239 (1989).
1018. Law on Certain Aspects of Mediation in Civil Matters ('ο περί Ορισμένων Θεμάτων Διαμεσολάβησης σε Αστικές Διαφορές Νόμος') No. 159 of 2012, OG I(I) No. 4365 of 16 Nov. 2012, p. 1719.
1019. Directive 2008/52/EC of the European Parliament and of the Council of 21 May 2008 on certain aspects of mediation in civil and commercial matters, OJ L 136 of 24 May 2008, p. 3.

considered to be a contract under Cyprus law and the allegation of avoiding the contract on the ground of undue influence brought later before the courts failed, as influence, if any, was exercised by a third party and not by or on behalf of a party (*see* in this regard paragraphs 61 et seq. above).[1020]

314. This law applies to both domestic and cross-border civil matters,[1021] but for those concerning rights and obligations which are not at the parties' disposal under the relevant applicable law.[1022] Equally, it does not extend to revenue, customs or administrative matters or to the liability of the state for acts and omissions in the exercise of state authority (*acta iure imperii*).[1023] Employment and labour law issues do not fall within the scope of this law.[1024]

315. A mediation settlement is merely one of the ways of ending a mediation procedure,[1025] but it is always the result of a mediation procedure. Said procedure is quite flexible, as regards to venue, language, representation of the parties and experts' reports.[1026] Yet, it has confidential character, contrary to the public character of court proceedings, and the statutory confidentiality requirements are both strict and absolute. In particular, it is set out that any person participating in such procedure is bound by confidentiality.[1027] Further, neither mediators nor those involved in the administration of the mediation process shall be compelled to give evidence in civil and commercial judicial proceedings or arbitration regarding information arising out of or in connection with a mediation process, unless the parties agree otherwise. Exception thereto poses situations, where this is necessary for overriding considerations of public policy, in particular when required to ensure the protection of the best interests of children or to prevent harm to the physical or psychological integrity of a person.[1028] Equally, the aforementioned rule does not apply, where disclosure of the content of the agreement resulting from mediation is necessary in order to implement or enforce that agreement.[1029] Mediation settlement's content is flexible, as it may concern all or some of the disputed matters,[1030] but it underlies specific typical formal requirements. In particular, the agreed mediation settlement is conducted in writing by the mediator and includes the particulars of the mediator, the place and time of mediation, the particulars of the parties, the particulars of the persons participating in mediation procedure, the agreement of the parties to bring the dispute to mediation, the terms of the settlement reached by the

1020. *Coudounaris v. Coudounaris* 1 CLR 581 (1980).
1021. Section 3(1) Law No. 159(I)/2012, which is broader than Art. 1(1) Directive 2008/52/EC, as the latter restricts its application to cross-border mediation.
1022. Section 3(2)(a) Law No. 159(I)/2012, which corresponds to Art. 1(2) Directive 2008/52/EC.
1023. Section 3(2)(c) Law No. 159(I)/2012, which corresponds to Art. 1(2) Directive 2008/52/EC.
1024. Section 3(2)(b) Law No. 159(I)/2012.
1025. Section 28(1)(a) *ibid.*
1026. Sections 19, 20 and 21 *ibid.*
1027. Section 18(1) *ibid.*
1028. Section 23(1)(a) *ibid.*, which corresponds to Art. 7(1)(a) Directive 2008/52/EC.
1029. Section 23(1)(b) Law No. 159(I)/2012, which corresponds to Art. 7(1)(b) Directive 2008/52/EC.
1030. Section 30(1) Law No. 159(I)/2012.

parties during mediation and the date of its making.[1031] In addition, mediation settlement needs to bear the signature of the mediator and the parties.[1032] Finally, said settlement may be made enforceable upon explicit consent of the parties and a relevant provision shall be included therein.[1033]

1031. Section 30(1)(a)–(g) *ibid.*
1032. Section 30(2) *ibid.*
1033. Section 30(2) *ibid.*, which corresponds to Art. 6(1) Directive 2008/52/EC.

Chapter 8. Suretyship

316. A contract of guarantee ('σύμβαση εγγύησης' in Greek, 'kefillik sözleşmesi' in Turkish), which is the term used for suretyship in Cyprus, is a contract to perform the promise, or discharge the liability of a third person in case of his default.[1034] Guarantee is only one manner to secure a claim, alongside bond, indemnity and pledge.

§1. Parties to a Contract of Guarantee

317. The person who gives the guarantee is called the surety ('εγγυητής' in Greek, 'kefil' in Turkish) (section 84 Cap. 149). The person in respect of whose default the guarantee is given is called the principal debtor ('πρωτοφειλέτης' in Greek, 'temel borçlu' in Turkish). The person to whom the guarantee is given is called the creditor ('πιστωτής' in Greek, 'alacaklı' in Turkish).[1035]

§2. Formation of a Contract of Guarantee

318. A contract of guarantee is a contract and therefore the aforementioned on formation of a contract equally apply here. Thus, a guarantee agreement in violation of a statutory provision is void.[1036] In addition to those, it is set out that anything done, or any promise made, for the benefit of the principal debtor may be a sufficient consideration to the surety for giving a guarantee.[1037] Accepting a claim put forward in a statement of claim and not persisting on the counterclaim was decided to be sufficient consideration.[1038] It has been further ruled, that the exact amount guaranteed through the contract of guarantee needs not to be explicitly stated in this contract. It suffices when it can be deduced with certainty.[1039] Equally, important, a contract of guarantee functions parallel and auxiliary to the principal contract, which usually provides for a loan or a purchase. Should this principal agreement be void or legally non-existent, due to lack of a formation condition or formal requirement, the guarantee is of no legal importance.[1040]

319. Especially regarding contracts of guarantee, where a husband is the principal debtor, who has taken up a loan from a bank, the creditor, and his wife is the surety to this loan, an effort took place[1041] to establish that such contracts were made

1034. Section 84 Cap. 149.
1035. Section 84 *ibid.*
1036. *Harrow Trading Ltd a.a. v. ADM Investor Services International Ltd* 1 CLR 161 (2004).
1037. Section 85 Cap. 149. *Etaireia Diatheseos Tsimenton Basilikou Apollon Ltd v. Akthitzioti* 1 CLR 687 (1998).
1038. *Ioannou v. Karageorgiades* 1 CLR 2240 (1998).
1039. *Karatsiolis v. Royal Sports Betting Ltd* 1 CLR 669 (2008).
1040. *Poly G. Knitwear Ltd v. Loukos Trading Co. Ltd a.a.* 1 CLR 96 (2007).
1041. *Mavroskoufi v. Piraeus Bank (Cyprus) Ltd*, Supreme Court of Cyprus, Civil Appeal No. 352/2008, Judgment of 16 Apr. 2014, not published in CLR.

under undue influence and were thus voidable. It was purported that the relevant English case law[1042] was applicable. According to this, if the conditions surrounding signing the suretyship are such that lead to the presumption of the creditor being aware of the wrongful conditions, under which the wife signed the guarantee, then the wife has the right to set aside the contract, unless the creditor sufficiently notified her about the obligations to which she enters by signing the guarantee. The Court[1043] declined to accept the purported case law. It rather ruled that for accepting undue influence, it was necessary to prove that the bank was acting as a representative of the husband since no special relationship existed between the wife and the bank. As this was not the case, it went on deciding that independent legal advice was not necessary, in view of the fact that the bank gave copies of the contract of guarantee to the wife prior to signing. This was deemed to suffice.[1044] In an earlier case involving similar factual background,[1045] the Court reached a different conclusion. It took into consideration the facts that the disputed supplementary agreements of guarantee, although drafted by the bank, were not signed in the presence of any bank's representative by the surety, whereas the responsible bank manager did not interview or meet the surety. It further held as material fact that the overdraft account had been already overdrawn when the supplementary agreements of guarantee were signed. In addition, the amounts overdrawn were well beyond the agreed credit limit, a fact that the Court decided to amount to misrepresentation. The Court also considered the fact that the periodical statements of account were only sent to the debtor and therefore it could not infer that the surety was aware of her husband's debit balances with the hank at the material dates. The Court further held that the fact that the guarantor was the wife of the principal debtor did not detract anything from the duty of a creditor not to mislead the guarantor on any material circumstance touching the solvency or financial standing of her husband, the debtor. It further decided that owing to the fiduciary relations existing between a husband and wife it behoves a creditor or banker to be more strict and careful when accepting as guarantor a wife for a husband's debt.[1046] It is not clear, why this case law was not followed in later cases.

320. Further to formation of contract, the statute sets out that any guarantee, which has been obtained by means of misrepresentation made by the creditor, or with his knowledge and assent, concerning a material part of the transaction, is invalid.[1047] With reference to the extent of information disclosure by the creditor to the surety, Courts in Cyprus accept that, unless the surety submits questions to the

1042. *Bank of Montreal v. Stuart* AC 120 (1911); *C.I.B.C. Mortgages Plc v. Pitt a.a.* 1 AC 200 (1994); *Barclay's Bank plc v. O'Brien* 4 All ER 417 (1993); *Royal Bank of Scotland v. Etridge (No. 2)* 4 All ER 705 (1998); *Bank of Cyprus (London) Ltd v. Markou a.a.* 2 All ER 707 (1999).

1043. *Mavroskoufi v. Piraeus Bank (Cyprus) Ltd*, Supreme Court of Cyprus, Civil Appeal No. 352/2008, Judgment of 16 Apr. 2014, not published in CLR.

1044. Citing *Kountourou v. Cyprus Bank of Development Ltd* 1A CLR 322 (2008) and, *Synergatiki Pistotiki Etaireia Agias Fylaxeos v. Poulla a.a.* 1 CLR 961 (2004), which declined the application of *Lloyd's Bank Ltd v. Bundy* 3 All ER 757 (1974).

1045. *Nicolaides v. The Chartered Bank of Famagusta* 1 CLR 56 (1966).

1046. *Ibid.*, citing *Chaplin & Co Ltd v. Brammail* 1 K.B. 233 (1908); *London General Omnibus Company Ltd v. Holloway* 2 K.B. 72 (1912); *Jean Mackenzie v. Royal Bank of Canada* AC 468 (1934).

1047. Section 100 *ibid.*

creditor, the creditor has no general obligation of disclosing information about the principal debtor.[1048] This applies also to any guarantee, which the creditor has obtained by means of keeping silence as to material circumstance.[1049] Should the contract of guarantee entail a specific condition, according to which the creditor shall not act upon it until another person has joined in it as co-surety, this contract is not valid, if that other person does not join.[1050]

§3. CONTENT OF A CONTRACT OF GUARANTEE

321. A contract of guarantee provides for performing a promise, as already noted above. In addition to that it may provide for continuing guarantee ('συνεχής εγγύηση' in Greek, 'sürekli kefillik' in Turkish), that being a guarantee, which extends to a series of transactions.[1051] Whether a guarantee is a continuing guarantee, is a matter to be decided according to the construction of the specific contract taking into consideration its wording and the surrounding circumstances. References to 'any debt' and 'any sums of money' could well indicate a continuing guarantee.[1052] Also, the same or different contracts may be made with two or more persons as co-sureties ('συνεγγυητές' in Greek, 'birlikte kefil' in Turkish) for the same debt or duty, either jointly or severally, with or without the knowledge of each other.[1053] Co-suretyship has its roots in equity.[1054]

322. Further, a particular implied promise is entailed in every contract of guarantee. More specifically, the principal debtor promises to indemnify the surety and the surety is entitled to recover from the principal debtor whatever sum he has rightfully paid under the guarantee, but no sums which he has paid wrongfully ('κακώς' in Greek, 'haksız' in Turkish).[1055] This statutory right was initially established as a principle by the courts of equity.[1056]

1048. *Panayiotou v. Bank of Cyprus Ltd*, Supreme Court of Cyprus, Civil Appeal No. 276/2009, Judgment of 9 Jul. 2014, not published in CLR, citing *Hamilton v. Watson* 12 Cl. & F. 109 (1845).
1049. Section 101 Cap. 149. *Konstantinou a.o. v. National Bank of Greece (Cyprus) Ltd* 1 CLR 1327 (2007).
1050. Section 102 Cap. 149.
1051. Section 87 *ibid.*
1052. *Cyprus Popular Bank Ltd v. T.G. & Sons Importing Ltd a.o.* 1 CLR 180 (2004), citing *Governor of the Bank of Ireland v. McCabe* 4 J.I. B.L. 9 (1995).
1053. Section 104 Cap. 149.
1054. *Hellenic Bank Ltd v. Polydorides a.o.* 1 CLR 68 (1993), citing *Scholefield Goodman & Sons v. Zyngier* 3 All ER 105 (1985).
1055. Section 103 Cap. 149.
1056. *Nicolas Droushiotis (Import-Export) Ltd v. L'Union Des Assurances De Paris a.o.* 1 CLR 19 (1983) citing *Craythorne v. Swinburne* 14 Ves. Jun. 160 (1807) and *Duncan, Fox & Co. v. North and South Wales Bank* 6 App. Cas. 1 (1880).

§4. The Parties' Duties and Responsibilities

323. Surety's liability is coextensive with that of the principal debtor, unless it is otherwise provided by the contract.[1057] On this provision, case law has been established, allowing for creditors to bring actions solely against the surety and not against the principal debtor.[1058] Changes to the principal contract do not affect surety's liability when made without his consent. In particular, any variance, made without the surety's consent, in the terms of the contract between the principal and the creditor, discharges the surety as to transactions subsequent to the variance.[1059]

324. Parallel to said duties, surety enjoys the following rights. Where a guaranteed debt has become due, or default of the principal debtor to perform a guaranteed duty has taken place, the surety, upon payment or performance of all that he is liable for, is vested with all the rights which the creditor had against the principal debtor.[1060] Further, a surety is entitled to the benefit of every security, which the creditor has against the principal debtor at the time, when the contract of guarantee is entered into, whether the surety knows of the existence of such security or not. If the creditor loses, or, without the consent of the surety, parts with such security, the surety is discharged to the extent of the value of the security.[1061]

325. Co-sureties, in the absence of any contract to the contrary, are liable, as between themselves, to pay each an equal share of the whole debt, or of that part of it which remains unpaid by the principal debtor.[1062] Co-sureties, who are bound in different sums, are liable to pay equally as far as the limits of their respective obligations permit.[1063] These statutory rights were initially established as principles of the courts of equity.[1064]

326. Lastly, the law regulates the liability of two persons, primarily liable and agreeing between them that one shall be surety on other's default. In particular, where such persons contract with a third person to undertake a certain liability, this second contract does not affect the liability of each of such two persons to the third one under the first agreement, although the third person may have been aware of its existence.[1065]

1057. Section 86 Cap. 149.
1058. *Argyri v. Chrysostomou* 1 CLR 1362 (2006); *Demetriou v. Bank of Cyprus Public Company Ltd*, Supreme Court of Cyprus, Civil Appeal No. 167/2010, Judgment of 21 Oct. 2015, not published in CLR.
1059. Section 91 Cap. 149. *Panpa Estates & Investments Ltd a.o. v. Rodou Charalambous & Son Ltd* 1 CLR 1897 (2013); *Synergatiki Pistotiki Etaireia Makrasykas v. Kapetaniou*, Supreme Court of Cyprus, Civil Appeal No. 200/2009, Judgment of 9 Jan. 2014, not published in CLR.
1060. Section 98 Cap. 149.
1061. Section 99(1) *ibid.*
1062. Section 104 *ibid.*
1063. Section 105 *ibid.*
1064. *Nicolas Droushiotis (Import-Export) Ltd v. L'Union Des Assurances De Paris a.o.* 1 CLR 19 (1983) citing *Craythorne v. Swinburne* 14 Ves. Jun. 160 (1807) and *Duncan, Fox & Co. v. North and South Wales Bank* 6 App. Cas. 1 (1880).
1065. Section 90 Cap. 149.

§5. Contract of Guarantee and Third Persons

327. No specific provision provides for the effect of contract of guarantee to third persons, but for the ones already mentioned on the principal debtor, who is a third party in a contract of guarantee.

§6. Termination of a Contract of Guarantee

328. The surety is discharged by any contract between the creditor and the principal debtor, by which the principal debtor is released, or by any act or omission of the creditor, the legal consequence of which is the discharge of the debtor.[1066] This effect equally has any contract between the creditor and the principal debtor, by which the creditor makes a composition with, or promises to give time to, or not to sue, the principal debtor, unless the surety assents to such contract.[1067] The aforementioned effect is equally caused by mere forbearance on the part of the creditor to sue the principal debtor or to enforce any other remedy against him, in the absence of any provision in the guarantee to the contrary.[1068] Surety is also discharged, if the creditor does any act which is inconsistent with the rights of the surety, or omits to do any act, which his duty to the surety requires him to do, and the eventual remedy of the surety himself against the principal debtor is thereby impaired.[1069] However, a contract to give time to the principal debtor made between the creditor and a third person, other than the principal debtor, does not result in discharging the surety.[1070]

329. If a surety discharged in any aforementioned manner, is co-surety, the following are foreseen with regard to co-suretyship. Such a release of one of them by the creditor does not discharge the others. Further, neither does it free the surety so released from his responsibility to the other sureties.[1071]

330. Especially continuing guarantee may at any time be revoked by the surety, as to future transactions, by notice to the creditor (section 88 Cap. 149).[1072] The same effect has the death of the surety, so far as regards future transactions, in the absence of any contract to the contrary (section 89 Cap. 149).[1073]

1066. Section 92 *ibid.*
1067. Section 93 *ibid.*
1068. Section 95 *ibid.*
1069. Section 97 *ibid. Cyprus Popular Bank Ltd v. General District Attorney* 1 CLR 83 (2004).
1070. Section 94 Cap. 149.
1071. Section 96 *ibid. Miaris v. Cyprus Popular Bank Ltd* 1 CLR 1625 (2011).
1072. Section 88 Cap. 149.
1073. Section 89 *ibid.*

Chapter 9. Pledge

331. Pledge ('ενέχυρο' in Greek, 'sağlancalama' in Turkish) is bailment of goods as security for payment of a debt or performance of a promise.[1074] Hence the aforementioned on bailment (*see* in this respect paragraphs 206 et seq. above) equally apply here. Pledge, alongside guarantee, is only one manner to secure a claim.

§1. Parties to Pledge

332. The bailor, that being the person to whom they are delivered (*see also* paragraph 207 above) is called the pawnor ('ενεχυριαστής' in Greek, 'sağlanca veren (rehin)' in Turkish).[1075]

333. The bailee, that being the person delivering the goods, as well as the owner of such goods, in the event of a bailee already being in possession of the goods (*see also* paragraph 206 above) is called the pawnee ('ενεχυροδανειστής' in Greek, 'sağlanca alan (mürtehin)' in Turkish).[1076] In this regard, it has been ruled that, in general, no man can pledge goods so as to convey any valid interest in them, unless he be the owner.[1077]

§2. Formation of Pledge

334. Both goods and documents may be pledged in good faith. In particular, it is set out that a person, who is in possession of any goods, or of any bill of lading, dock-warrant, warehouse-keeper's certificate, or warrant or order of delivery, or any other document of title to goods, may make a valid pledge of such goods or documents, provided that the pawnee acts in good faith, and under circumstances which are not such as to raise a reasonable presumption that the pawnor is acting improperly; equally provided that such goods or documents have not been obtained from their lawful owner or from any person in lawful custody of them, by means of an offence or fraud.[1078]

335. Specific formation conditions are foreseen for pledge of documents incorporating rights. In particular these are bills of exchange, promissory notes, bonds, whether in customary form or not, other than those secured by mortgage of immovable property, share certificates and share warrants for shares in a company, as security for payment of a debt or performance of a promise.[1079] In this context, company

1074. Section 130 *ibid.*
1075. *Ibid.*
1076. *Ibid.*
1077. *Thomas and James Bernard Ltd v. Lanitis* 13 (1) CLR 43.
1078. Section 136 Cap. 149.
1079. Section 138(1) (a), (b), (c) and (d) *ibid.*

('εταιρεία' in Greek, 'şirket' in Turkish) is a limited liability company formed under the provisions of the Companies Law, or any amendment thereof, or an anonyme company originally formed under the provisions of the Ottoman Commercial Code.[1080] Such a pledge is valid and enforceable if it is expressed in writing in the presence of at least two witnesses themselves competent to contract and bears at the end thereof the signature of the pawnor as well as being subscribed by them with their names as witnesses.[1081]

§3. Content of Pledge

336. Pledge secures a claim, that being payment of debt or performance of promise, and it therefore functions auxiliary to another contract that has given rise to the secured claim. In the event that the pawnee only has a limited interest in the pledged goods, the pledge is valid only to the extent of that interest.[1082]

§4. The Parties' Duties and Responsibilities

337. In effect, a pledge creates solely rights to the benefit of the pawnee. He may retain the goods pledged, not only for the secured claim but also for the interest of the debt and all necessary expenses incurred by him in respect of the possession or for the preservation of the pledged goods.[1083] He may further do that for any debt or promise other than the debt or promise for which they are pledged, as long as a contract to this effect was made. Such contract is however presumed in regard to subsequent advances made by the pawnee.[1084] In addition, the pawnee has a statutory right to receive from the pawnor any extraordinary expenses incurred by him for the preservation of the goods pledged.[1085]

338. Specific in the event of the pawnor being in default, the pawnee may bring legal proceedings against the pawnor upon the debt or promise, and retain the goods pledged as a collateral security. Alternatively, he has the right to sell the pledged goods, under the condition that he provides the pawnor with reasonable notice of the sale.[1086] If the second option is followed and the proceeds are less than the amount due, the pawnor is still liable to pay the balance. If, to the contrary, the proceeds are greater than the amount due, the pawnee is obliged to pay over the surplus to the pawnor.[1087] Equally, in such cases, under the condition that the object of pledge had the form of documents incorporating rights, the pawnee has the same rights and remedies on the pledge against third parties as the pawnor himself would

1080. Section 106(1)(a) *ibid.*
1081. Section 138(i), (ii) and (iii) *ibid.*
1082. Section 137 *ibid.*
1083. Section 131 *ibid.*
1084. Section 132 *ibid.*
1085. Section 133 *ibid.*
1086. Section 134(1) *ibid.*
1087. Section 134(2) *ibid.*

have had but for the contract of pledge. In addition, all payments made to the pawnee by third parties on such pledge are as valid and effective as if made to the pawnor himself.[1088]

339. The issue of pledge of shares has been discussed in a court procedure[1089] aiming to assist an international commercial arbitration launched in Germany. The factual surrounding involved the Commerzbank Group of Germany entering into a share-purchase agreement and a deferred purchase price agreement, which were governed by German law, with two Cypriot legal entities, Yernamio Consulting Ltd and Elianta Trading Ltd of the Smart Group of Ukraine in summer 2012. Object of these agreements was the sale of the public joint-stock company Bank Forum and eight companies of Ukraine for USD 130 million that was agreed to be paid in instalments. The collaterals for these agreements were twofold. First, Adeona Holdings Ltd, which was a Cypriot limited liability company having as major asset shares in the Dutch company Metinvest B.V. that owned steel production companies in Ukraine, was the surety to both agreements for the amount of USD 80 million. At the same time, the shares of the purchased bank and companies were pledged. Yernamio Consulting Ltd and Elianta Trading Ltd received the shares of the bank and the companies and paid the first instalments. However, in late spring 2013, the Cypriot buyers complained to Commerzbank that the financial data of the purchased companies had been tampered and/or were inaccurate. Commerzbank initiated an internal investigation on this complaint, which did not reveal anything to support any such allegation. When Commerzbank persisted on requesting additional information from the Cypriot companies, they replied that Ukrainian law prohibited any such disclosure due to obligations related to bank secrecy. They further declined Commerzbank's proposal to appoint an independent controller. It rather proceeded with appointing KPMG of Ukraine to investigate. Commerzbank disagreed with the findings of the auditor's investigation purporting that it focused on a small number of bad loans, which were indicated by the Cypriot companies. The Cypriot companies did not pay the third instalment and served an avoidance notice due to fraud ('arglistige Täuschung' in German) under section 123 of the German Civil Code[1090] to Commerzbank. Efforts for reconciliation took place between the parties, but no amicable solution was found and Commerzbank proceeded with filing a request for arbitration under the agreed arbitration clause along with requesting interim measures against and disclosure from Adeona Holdings Ltd, the surety to both agreements, before the courts in Cyprus.

1088. Section 139 *ibid.*

1089. *Commerzbank Auslandsbanken Holding AG a.a. v. Adeona Holdings Ltd*, Supreme Court of Cyprus, Civil Appeal No. E6/2014, Judgment of 27 Feb. 2015, not published in CLR.

1090. Section 123 of the German Civil Code reads '(1) A person who has been induced to make a declaration of intent by fraud or unlawfully by duress may avoid his declaration.

(2) If a third party committed this fraud, a declaration that had to be made to another may be avoided only if the latter knew of the deceit or ought to have known it. If a person other than the person to whom the declaration was to be made acquired a right as a direct result of the declaration, the declaration made to him may be avoided if he knew or ought to have known of the deceit.' Translation provided by the Langenscheidt Translation Service. Original text and the translation thereof is available: https://www.gesetze-im-internet.de.

340. The case was brought before the Supreme Court of Cyprus, as the ex parte request for an interlocutory injunction against Adeona Holdings Ltd was granted by the Court of First Instance but, on the day that it was made returnable, this was discharged in view of the pledged shares, whereas the disclosure request was overall dismissed. Said request was based on section 9[1091] Law No. 101/87,[1092] which is made after Article 9 of the UNCITRAL Model Law on International Commercial Arbitration.[1093] The Supreme Court of Cyprus affirmed that the principles applicable to section 9 Law No. 101/87 are the ones also applicable to section 32[1094] Law No. 14/60.[1095] Hence, the elements envisaged in the law as prerequisites for the making of such an injunction are:

(a) a serious question to be tried at the hearing,[1096] meaning nothing beyond the disclosure of an arguable case on the strength of the pleadings;[1097]
(b) probability that plaintiff is entitled to relief,[1098] which requires the applicant to demonstrate that he has a visible chance of success;[1099] and
(c) unless an interlocutory injunction is granted it shall be difficult or impossible to do complete justice at a later stage.[1100] If harm has already been caused to plaintiff and for suffered damage pecuniary compensation is adequate compensation, injunction shall be dismissed.[1101]

1091. Section 9 reads '[t]he Court has the power, following a request of a party, to order an interim measure of protection, at any time before or during arbitral proceedings'.
1092. Law on International Commercial Arbitration('ο περί Διεθνούς Εμπορικής Διαιτησίας Νόμος') No. 101 of 1987, OGI(I) No. 2231 of 29 May 1987, p. 933.
1093. Article 9 reads '[i]t is not incompatible with an arbitration agreement for a party to request, before or during arbitral proceedings, from a court an interim measure of protection and for a court to grant such a measure'.
1094. Section 32 reads '(1) Subject to any Rules of Court every Court, in the exercise of its civil jurisdiction, may, by order, grant an injunction (interlocutory, perpetual or mandatory) or appoint a receiver in all cases is which it appears to the Court just or convenient so to do, notwithstanding that no compensation or other relief is claimed or granted together therewith: Provided that an interlocutory injunction shall not be granted unless the Court is satisfied that there is a serious question to be tried at the hearing, that there is a probability that the plaintiff is entitled to relief and that unless an interlocutory injunction is granted it shall be difficult or impossible to do complete justice at a later stage. (2) Any interlocutory order made under subsection (1) may be made under such terms and conditions as the Court thinks just, and the Court may at any time, on reasonable cause shown discharge or vary any such order.'
1095. Law on Courts ('ο περί Δικαστηρίων Νόμος') No. 14 of 1960, OGI(I) No. 24 of 17 Dec. 1960, p. 83.
1096. *The Jonitexo Ltd v. Adidas Sportschufabrieken Adi Dassler KG* 1 CLR 263 (1984); *Inter Depol Ltd v. Kyriacos Papavassiliou Ltd* 1 CLR 769 (1984).
1097. *Resola (Cyprus) Ltd v. Christou* 1 CLR 598 (1998), citing *Odysseos v. Pieris Estates a.o.* 1 CLR 557 (1982).
1098. *Acropol Shipping Company Ltd a.o. v. Rossis* 1 CLR 38 (1976), citing *Preston v. Luck* 27 Ch. D. 497 (1884); *J T Stratford & Son Ltd v. Lindley* 3 All ER 102 (1964); *Nippon Yusen Kaisha v. Karageorgis* a.a. 3 All ER 282 (1975). *See also Karydas Taxi Co Ltd v. Komodikis* 7 JSC 1101 (1976); *Nemitsas Industries Ltd v. S & S Maritime Ltd a.o.* 10 JSC 1542 (1976).
1099. *Odysseos v. Pieris Estates a.o.* (1982) 1 CLR 557, citing *J.S. (a minor)* 1 All ER 1061 (1980).
1100. *Geo. M. Hadjikyriacos Co. Ltd v. United Biscuits (UK) Ltd* 1 CLR 689 (1979); *Lakatamitis v. Theodorou* 1 CLR 520 (1983).
1101. *Acropol Shipping Co a.o. v. Rossis* 2 JSC 188 (1976).

341. In addition to said three conditions, it is well settled that the making of an interlocutory injunction is the outcome of the exercise of discretionary powers, as it is exercised when it appears to the court just or convenient to do so.[1102] At the same time, it is stressed that the remedy of interlocutory injunction should be kept flexible and discretionary and not be made the subject of strict rules.[1103]

342. Then the Supreme Court of Cyprus expressed its disagreement with the findings of the District Court. First, it stressed that the collaterals available to Commerzbank in respect to disputed agreements were to be taken into consideration under the third condition of interlocutory orders and not while deciding on the Court's discretion. Second, it highlighted the not unlikely possibility that the pledged shares would not fully secure the plaintiffs, as, for example, the value of the shares could drop or even plunge at the time of enforcing the award of the tribunal, or the shares themselves would be transferred to another entity. It further confirmed that the pawnor has a right, not a duty, to sell pledged shares and he shall decide, whether and when he is going to exercise it.[1104] Consequently, the Court underlined that the liability of the surety[1105] is distinct from the creditor's,[1106] especially in the present case, where the vendors surrendered possession and control of the bank and companies to the creditors, pending payment of consideration. The Supreme Court of Cyprus went on dismissing the finding of the District Court that Commerzbank did not come with 'clean hands'. It confirmed that the obligation of the applicants' full and honest disclosure, which summarizes the essence of the 'clean hands' doctrine, derives from the nature of ex parte interlocutory injunctions that are equity remedies.[1107] It affirmed that said disclosure applies to all material facts of the case, including laws and general principles, despite them possibly not being in favour of the applicants,[1108] along with communication conducted without prejudice.[1109] It then made a distinction between said disclosure obligation and submission of all documents without them being material to the case. Having said that and re-examining the documentation tabled before the ruling court, the Supreme Court of Cyprus was satisfied that Commerzbank had come with 'clean hands'. Hence, it is now undisputed that securities do not hinder the granting of interlocutory injunctions.

1102. *The Jonitexo Ltd v. Adidas Sportschufabrieken Adi Dassler KG* 1 CLR 263 (1984), citing *Karydas Taxi Co Ltd v. Komodikis* 1 CLR 321 (1975); *M & M Transport Co Ltd v. Eteria Astikon Leoforion Lemessou Ltd* 1 CLR 605 (1981).
1103. *The Jonitexo Ltd v. Adidas Sportschufabrieken Adi Dassler KG* 1 CLR 263 (1984), citing *Hubbart v. Vosper* 1 All ER 1023 (1972).
1104. Citing *Andreou v. Bank of Cyprus* 1A CLR 740 (2005); *Nikolaou v. Ellinas Finance Ltd a.o.*, Supreme Court of Cyprus Civil Appeal No. 373/09, Judgment of 22 Nov. 2013, not reported in CLR; *China and South Sea Bank Ltd v. Tan* 3 All ER 839 (1989).
1105. The term used in the judgment was 'πιστωτής'.
1106. The term used in the judgment was 'πρωτοφειλέτης'.
1107. Citing *Global Cruises SA a.o. v. Metro Shipping & Travel Ltd* 1 CLR 607 (1989); *Gregoriou v. Christoforou* 1 CLR 248 (1995); *Charalambous v. Petros Michael Exclusif Ltd* 1C CLR 1953 (2004).
1108. Citing *Swift Fortune Ltd (The Capaz Duckling) v. Magnifica Marine SA* 1 Lloyd's Rep. 54 (2008).
1109. Citing *Linsen International Ltd v. Humpuss Sea Transport Pte Ltd* EWHC 303 (2010).

343. Nevertheless, some comments are offered on the aforementioned judgment. First, it failed to explicitly distinguish the two separate securities protecting claims arising out of the agreements, that of pledge being separate and distinct from suretyship. Second, it misconstrued the nature of surety and pledge and confused it with award enforcement, as it ruled that '[t]he right of [Commerzbank] in the event of winning the arbitration was to be compensated for the amount of the suretyship in place … at the time of enforcing the arbitral award. The pledge of shares aimed to securing this obligation … '. Third, it is here purported that both the ruling court and the appellate court gravely misunderstood quantification of damages in international commercial arbitration. This is far from a straightforward and plain matter, including a range of issues of law, fact and procedure, involving not uncommonly a broad range of quality and quantity of evidence, problematic standards of proof,[1110] along with – naturally – arbitration costs (i.e., Article 40(2) of the UNCITRAL Arbitration Rules and Article 32 of the DIS Arbitration Rules). None of this was considered by the domestic courts.

§5. Pledge and Third Persons

344. Pledge does not have any impact on third persons, but for the aforementioned payments made by such persons to the pawnee, when the pawnor is in default (*see* paragraphs 217 and 218 above).

§6. Termination of Pledge

345. Pledge is ordinarily terminated upon payment of the debt or performance of the promise that it secures. It is further terminated, when the pawnor is in default and thereafter the pawnee decides to sell the pledged goods after giving notice to the pawnor (*see* paragraph 219 above).

1110. 'Part III: The Award, Chapter 14: Remedies and Interest', in Jeffrey Waincymer, Procedure and Evidence in International Arbitration (Kluwer Law International 2012) pp. 1119 et seq.

Chapter 10. Loans

346. Loans are not regulated by a special statute. Nevertheless, certain judgments have been discussing the issues of assigning bank loans and credits and loans in disguise. As these can offer some insight regarding issues of importance to the praxis, these judgments shall be portrayed below.

347. In *Papadopoulos v. Euroinvestment,*[1111] it has been ruled that loaning money is not prohibited by any statute. Further, it has been clarified that loaning money does not constitute per se a banking business, as this is defined in section 2 of Law on Banking Business,[1112] unless the money provided as a loan derives from taking on obligations in the form of deposits, securities or other proof of debt.[1113] In *Zervou v. Bank of Cyprus,*[1114] the claimants purported that the defendants issued an investment loan to the claimant for the sole aim of buying shares, without being members of the Stock Exchange of Cyprus, and that they were presented to claimants as stockbrokers and experts to matters of investments, convincing him to submit an application for a loan through increasing the limit of his existing account. These suggestions failed to convince the Court. It rather ruled that the contract in question was made with the free will of the parties without any unfair practice by the defendants.

348. Regarding interest, it has been decided that this is the return or compensation for the use or retention by one person of a sum of money belonging to or owed to another.[1115] It accrues *de die in diem* even if payable only at intervals, and is, therefore, apportionable in point of time between persons entitled in succession to the principal. Further, by the universal custom of bankers, a banker has the right to charge simple interest at a reasonable rate on all overdrafts.[1116] However, the interest that may lawfully be agreed to a loan contract is the one set out in the laws in force at the time that the relevant loan contract is made. This was clarified in *Evelthon Developments v. National Bank of Greece.*[1117] The court here decided that a contract to pay interest up to the date of repayment of the debt does not necessarily imply an agreement to pay interest beyond that date in the event of default in repayment, but in the situation interest (though not necessarily at the contract rate) can be awarded by way of damages. However, if the parties do agree to an interest that is higher than the statutory one, no rescission of the contract is caused. Merely

1111. *Papadopoulos v. Euroinvestment & Finance Ltd* 1 CLR 2091 (2011).
1112. Law on Banking Business ('ο περί Τραπεζικών Εργασιών Νόμος') No. 64 of 1997, OG I(I) No. 3168 of 18 Jul. 1997, p. 1253, as last amended by amending Law No. 103 of 2011, OG I(I) No. 4290 of 29 Jul. 2011.
1113. *Papadopoulos v. Euroinvestment & Finance Ltd* 1 CLR 2091 (2011), quoting *United Dominions Trust v. Kirkwood* 1 All ER 968 (1966). Confirmed in *Zervos v. Euroinvestment & Finance Public Ltd (ex Euroinvestment & Finance Ltd)* 1 CLR 688 (2013).
1114. *Zervou v. Bank of Cypris Public Company Ltd* 1 CLR 2192 (2011).
1115. *Turkish Bank of Nicosia Ltd v. Cukurova a.o.* 1 CLR 233 (1977), citing *Re Dunn Trust Ltd v. Feetham* 1 K.B. 22 (1936).
1116. *Ibid.*, citing *Crosskill v. Bower, Bower v. Turner* 32 LJ Ch. 540 (1863).
1117. *Evelthon Developments Ltd a.a. v. National Bank of Greece (Cyprus) Ltd* 1 CLR 2486 (2012).

the excessive interest, although agreed, is invalid.[1118] Any additional expenses, such as study expenses or real expenses, are conceived as such, that being excessive interest. Thus, they are illegal and therefore invalid.[1119]

1118. *Bank of Cyprus a.o. v. Coudounaris Food Products Ltd a.o.* 1 CLR 641 (1995).
1119. *Official Receiver v. National Bank of Greece S.A.* 1 CLR 38 (2005).

Chapter 11. Contracts with the Government

349. Contracts with the government are regulated in special statutes that implement Directives of the EU. These are: Law on Public Procurement[1120] (hereinafter 'Law No. 73(I)/2016'), which implements Directive 2014/24/EU;[1121] Law on Procurement by Entities Operating in the Water, Energy, Transport and Postal Services Sectors[1122] (hereinafter 'Law No. 140(I)/2016'), which implements Directive 2014/25/EU;[1123] and Law on Award of Certain Works in the Fields of Defence and Security[1124] (hereinafter 'Law No. 173(I)/2011'), which implements Directive 2009/81/EC.[1125] Law No. 73(I)/2016, which is the main statutory instrument shall be explained below in detail, whereas the rest shall be briefly described in the section referring to particular procurement regimes.

350. The scope of Law No. 73(I)/2016 is establishing rules on the procedures for procurement by contracting authorities with respect to public contracts as well as design contests, whose value is estimated to be not less than the thresholds laid down in a specific manner.[1126] Procurement ('διαδικασία σύναψης σύμβασης' or

---

1120. Law on Public Procurement and Relevant Matters ('ο περί της Ρύθμισης των Διαδικασιών Σύναψης Δημοσίων Συμβάσεων και για Συναφή Θέματα Νόμος') No. 73 of 2016, OG I(I) No. 4565 of 28 Apr. 2016, p. 835.
1121. Directive 2014/24/EU of the European Parliament and of the Council of 26 Feb. 2014 on public procurement and repealing Directive 2004/18/EC Text with EEA relevance, OJ L 94 of 28 Mar. 2014, p. 65, last amended by Commission Delegated Regulation (EU) 2017/2365 of 18 Dec. 2017 amending Directive 2014/24/EU of the European Parliament and of the Council in respect of the application thresholds for the procedures for the award of contracts, OJ L 337 of 19 Dec. 2017, p. 19.
1122. Law on Procurement by Entities Operating in the Water, Energy, Transport and Postal Services Sectors and Relevant Matters ('ο περί της Ρύθμισης των Διαδικασιών Σύναψης Συμβάσεων Φορέων που Δραστηριοποιούνται στους Τομείς του Ύδατος, της Ενέργειας, των Μεταφορών και των Ταχυδρομικών Υπηρεσιών και για Συναφή Θέματα Νόμος') No. 140 of 2016, OG I(I) No. 4586 of 23 Dec. 2016, p. 1296.
1123. Directive 2014/25/EU of the European Parliament and of the Council of 26 Feb. 2014 on procurement by entities operating in the water, energy, transport and postal services sectors and repealing Directive 2004/17/EC Text with EEA relevance, OJ L 94 of 28 Mar. 2014, p. 243, last amended by Commission Delegated Regulation (EU) 2017/2364 of 18 Dec. 2017 amending Directive 2014/25/EU of the European Parliament and of the Council in respect of the application thresholds for the procedures for the award of contracts, OJ L 337 of 19 Dec. 2017, p. 17.
1124. Law on the Coordination of Procedures for the Award of Certain Works Contracts, Supply Contracts and Service Contracts by Contracting Authorities or Entities in the fields of Defence and Security and Related Matters ('ο περί του Συντονισμού των Διαδικασιών Σύναψης Ορισμένων Συμβάσεων Έργων, Προμηθειών και Παροχής Υπηρεσιών που Συνάπτονται από Αναθέτουσες Αρχές ή Αναθέτοντες Φορείς στους Τομείς της Άμυνας και της Ασφάλειας και για Συναφή Θέματα Νόμος') No. 173 of 2011, OG I(I) No. 4313 of 23 Dec. 2011, p. 1388.
1125. Directive 2009/81/EC of the European Parliament and of the Council of 13 Jul. 2009 on the coordination of procedures for the award of certain works contracts, supply contracts and service contracts by contracting authorities or entities in the fields of defence and security, OJ L 216 of 20 Aug. 2009, p. 76, last amended by Commission Regulation (EU) 2017/2367 of 18 Dec. 2017 amending Directive 2009/81/EC of the European Parliament and of the Council in respect of the application thresholds for the procedures for the award of contracts, OJ L 337 of 19 Dec. 2017, p. 22.
1126. Section 3(1) Law No. 73(I)/2016, which corresponds to Art. 1(1) Directive 2014/24/EU.

'σύμβαση' in Greek, 'temin') here stands for the acquisition by means of a public contract of works, supplies or services by one or more contracting authorities from economic operators chosen by those contracting authorities, whether or not the works, supplies or services are intended for a public purpose.[1127] Public contracts ('δημόσιες συμβάσεις' in Greek, 'idari sözleşme' in Turkish) means contracts for pecuniary interest concluded in writing between one or more economic operators and one or more contracting authorities and having as their object the execution of works, the supply of products or the provision of services.[1128] Public work contracts ('δημόσιες συμβάσεις έργων' in Greek, 'kamu yapım sözleşmesi') means public contracts having as their object one of the following: the execution, or both the design and execution, of works related to specific activities;[1129] the execution, or both the design and execution, of a work; and the realization, by whatever means, of a work corresponding to the requirements specified by the contracting authority exercising a decisive influence on the type or design of the work.[1130] Public supply contracts ('δημόσιες συμβάσεις προμηθειών' in Greek, 'mal alımı sözleşmesi') means public contracts having as their object the purchase, lease, rental or hire purchase, with or without an option to buy, of products. Such contract may include, as an incidental matter, siting and installation operations.[1131] Public service contracts ('δημόσιες συμβάσεις υπηρεσιών' in Greek, 'hizmet sözleşmesi') means public contracts having as their object the provision of services other than those referred to under public work contracts.[1132] Finally, the manner of setting out said thresholds is the value net of value added tax (VAT) estimated to be equal or greater than the following:

- EUR 5,186,000 for public works contracts;[1133]
- EUR 134,000 for public supply and service contracts awarded by central government authorities and design contests organized by such authorities; where public supply contracts are awarded by contracting authorities operating in the field of defence, that threshold shall apply only to contracts concerning products covered by Annex III of the law;[1134,1135]

1127. Section 2 Law No. 73(I)/2016, which corresponds to Art. 1(2) Directive 2014/24/EU. *See T Systems Magyarország Zrt. and Others v. Közbeszerzési Hatóság Közbeszerzési Döntőbizottság and Others*, CJEU C-263/19, Judgment of 14 May 2020, digital ECR.
1128. Section 2 Law No. 73(I)/2016, which corresponds to Art. 2(1)(5) Directive 2014/24/EU. *See Ministrstvo za notranje zadeve v. Tax-Fin-Lex d. o. o.*, CJEU C-367/19, Judgment of 10 Sep. 2020, digital ECR.
1129. Said activities are specified in Annex II Law No. 73(I)/2016, which corresponds to Annex II Directive 2014/24/EU.
1130. Section 2 Law No. 73(I)/2016, which corresponds to Art. 2(1)(6) Directive 2014/24/EU.
1131. Section 2 Law No. 73(I)/2016, which corresponds to Art. 2(1)(8) Directive 2014/24/EU.
1132. Section 2 Law No. 73(I)/2016, which corresponds to Art. 2(1)(9) Directive 2014/24/EU.
1133. Section 9(1)(a) Law No. 73(I)/2016, which corresponds to Art. 4(a) Directive 2014/24/EU.
1134. Annex III Law No. 73(I)/2016 corresponds to Annex III Directive 2014/24/EU.
1135. Section 9(1)(b) Law No. 73(I)/2016, which corresponds to Art. 4(b) Directive 2014/24/EU.

- EUR 207,000 for public supply and service contracts awarded by subcentral contracting authorities and design contests organized by such authorities; that threshold shall also apply to public supply contracts awarded by central government authorities that operate in the field of defence, save for the reservation explained immediately above;[1136] and
- EUR 750,000 for public service contracts for social and other specific services.[1137]

§1. PARTIES TO PUBLIC PROCUREMENT

351. As evident from the definitions set out above, public contracts are made between one or more economic operators and one or more contracting authorities. Economic operator ('οικονομικός φορέας' in Greek 'istekli' in Turkish) means any natural or legal person or public entity or group of such persons and/or entities, including any temporary association of undertakings, which offers the execution of works and/or a work, the supply of products or the provision of services on the market.[1138] Contracting authorities ('αναθέτουσες αρχές' in Greek, 'ihale' in Turkish) stands for the state, regional or local authorities, bodies governed by public law or associations formed by one or more such authorities or one or more such bodies governed by public law.[1139]

§2. RULES ON THE FORMATION OF PUBLIC CONTRACTS

I. General Principles and Statutory Obligations

352. The law sets out specific provisions regarding principles of procurement and statutory obligations of the contracting authorities during the formation of public contracts. The general principles of procurement set out that contract authorities treat economic operators equally and without discrimination and act in a transparent and proportionate manner.[1140] In particular, the design of the procurement may not be made with the intention of excluding it from the scope of this law or of artificially narrowing competition. The latter is deemed to take place, where the design of the procurement is made with the intention of unduly favouring or disadvantaging certain economic operators.[1141]

1136. Section 9(1)(c) Law No. 73(I)/2016, which corresponds to Art. 4(c) Directive 2014/24/EU.
1137. Section 9(1)(d) Law No. 73(I)/2016, which corresponds to Art. 4(d) Directive 2014/24/EU. For the specific services *see* Annex XIV Law No. 73(I)/2016, which corresponds to Annex XIV Directive 2014/24/EU.
1138. Section 2 Law No. 73(I)/2016, which corresponds to Art. 2(1)(10) Directive 2014/24/EU.
1139. Section 2 Law No. 73(I)/2016, which corresponds to Art. 2(1)(1) Directive 2014/24/EU.
1140. On the equality of treatment, non-discrimination, proportionality and transparency *see Edra Costruzioni Soc. coop. and Edilfac Srl v. Comune di Maiolati Spontini*, CJEU Case C-140/16, Judgment of 10 Nov. 2016, digital ECR; *Spinosa Costruzioni Generali SpA and Melfi Srl v. Comune di Monteroduni*, CJEU Case C-162/16, Judgment of 10 Nov. 2016, digital ECR.
1141. Section 4(1) and (2) Law No. 73(I)/2016, which corresponds to Art. 18(1) Directive 2014/24/EU.

353. Thereafter, contracting authorities bear the duty to ensure that in the performance of public contracts economic operators comply with applicable obligations in the fields of environmental, social and labour law established by Union law, national law, collective agreements or by the international environmental, social and labour law provisions, as specified in the law.[1142,1143] Furthermore, contracting authorities take appropriate measures to effectively prevent, identify and remedy conflicts of interest arising in the conduct of procurement procedures so as to avoid any distortion of competition and to ensure equal treatment of all economic operators. The concept of conflicts of interest here covers at least any situation where staff members of the contracting authority or of a procurement service provider acting on behalf of the contracting authority who are involved in the conduct of the procurement procedure or may influence the outcome of that procedure have, directly or indirectly, a financial, economic or other personal interest which might be perceived to compromise their impartiality and independence in the context of the procurement procedure.[1144]

354. Especially for the World Trade Organisation Agreement on Government Procurement (GPA) and other international agreements, it is set out that, in so far as they are covered by Annexes 1, 2, 4 and 5 and the General Notes to the EU's Appendix I to the GPA and by the other international agreements by which the Union is bound, contracting authorities accord to the works, supplies, services and economic operators of the signatories to those agreements treatment no less favourable than the treatment accorded to the works, supplies, services and economic operators of the Union.[1145]

II. Available Procedures

355. Contracting authorities may further apply open or restricted procedures and innovation partnerships.[1146] In open procedures ('ανοικτή διαδικασία' in Greek, 'açık ihale usulü' in Turkish) any interested economic operator may submit a tender in response to a call for competition. Generally, the minimum time limit for the receipt of tenders is thirty-five days from the date on which the contract notice was sent, whereas the tender must be accompanied by the information for qualitative

On Art. 18 *see Kauno miesto savivaldybė, Kauno miesto savivaldybės administracija*, CJEU Case C-285/18, Judgment of 3 Oct. 2019, digital ECR; *Anodiki Services EPE v. GNA 'Evangelismos – Ofthalmiatrio Athinon – Poliklinikí', GNA 'Georgios Gennimatas', Geniko Onkologiko Nosokomio Kifisias – (GONK) 'Agioi Anargiroi'*, CJEU Case C-260/17, Judgment of 25 Oct. 2018, digital ECR.

1142. These are set out in Annex X Law No. 73(I)/2016, which corresponds to Annex X Directive 2012/24/EU.
1143. Section 4(3) Law No. 73(I)/2016, which corresponds to Art. 18(2) Directive 2014/24/EU.
1144. Section 6(1) Law No. 73(I)/2016, which corresponds to Art. 24 Directive 2014/24/EU.
1145. Section 22 Law No. 73(I)/2016, which corresponds to Art. 25 Directive 2014/24/EU.
1146. Section 23(1)(a) and (b) Law No. 73(I)/2016, which corresponds to Art. 26(2) and (3) Directive 2014/24/EU.

selection that is requested by the contracting authority.[1147] Restricted procedures ('κλειστή διαδικασία' in Greek, 'belli istekliler arasında ihale usulü' in Turkish) are differentiated from open procedures in the manner that any economic operator may submit a request to participate in response to a call for competition containing specific information[1148] by providing the information for qualitative selection that is requested by the contracting authority. Thereafter, only those economic operators invited to do so by the contracting authority following its assessment of the information provided may submit a tender.[1149] Generally, in such procedures minimum time limit for the receipt of tenders is thirty days from the date on which the invitation to tender was sent.[1150] In addition, contracting authorities have the power to apply a competitive procedure with negotiation or a competitive dialogue in the following situations with regard to works, supplies or services, when one or more of the following criteria are being fulfilled:

- the needs of the contracting authority cannot be met without adaptation of readily available solutions;
- they include design or innovative solutions;
- the contract cannot be awarded without prior negotiations because of specific circumstances related to the nature, the complexity or the legal and financial make-up or because of the risks attaching to them; and
- the technical specifications cannot be established with sufficient precision by the contracting authority with reference to a standard,[1151] European Technical Assessment,[1152] common technical specification[1153] or technical reference[1154] within the specific meaning set out in the law.[1155]

1147. Section 24(1), (2) and (6) Law No. 73(I)/2016, which corresponds to Art. 27(1) Directive 2014/24/EU.

1148. This information is set out in Annex V Parts B or C Law No. 73(I)/2016, which corresponds to Annex V Parts B or C Directive 2014/24/EU.

1149. Section 25(1) and (3) Law No. 73(I)/2016, which corresponds to Art. 28(1) and (2) Directive 2014/24/EU. *See Telecom Italia SpA v. Ministero dello Sviluppo Economico and Infrastrutture e telecomunicazioni per l'Italia SpA (Infratel Italia SpA)*, CJEU Case C-697/17, Judgment of 11 Jul. 2019, digital ECR.

1150. Section 25(2) Law No. 73(I)/2016, which corresponds to Art. 28(2) Directive 2014/24/EU.

1151. Standard ('πρότυπο' in Greek, 'standart' in Turkish) means a technical specification, adopted by a recognized standardization body, for repeated or continuous application, with which compliance is not compulsory, and which is one of the following: (a) 'international standard' means a standard adopted by an international standardization organization and made available to the general public; (b) 'European standard' means a standard adopted by a European standardization organization and made available to the general public; (c) 'national standard' means a standard adopted by a national standardization organization and made available to the general public. Annex VII(2) Law No. 73(I)/2016, which corresponds to Annex VII(2) Directive 2014/24/EU.

1152. European Technical Assessment ('ευρωπαϊκή τεχνική αξιολόγηση' in Greek, 'Avrupa teknik değerlendirme' in Turkish) means the documented assessment of the performance of a construction product, in relation to its essential characteristics, in accordance with the respective European Assessment Document, as defined in point 12 of Art. 2 of Regulation (EU) No. 305/2011. Annex VII(3) Law No. 73(I)/2016, which corresponds to Annex VII(3) Directive 2014/24/EU.

1153. Common technical specification ('κοινή τεχνική προδιαγραφή' in Greek, 'ortak teknik şartname') means a technical specification in the field of ICT laid down in accordance with Arts 13 and 14 of Regulation (EU) 1025/2012. Annex VII(4) Law No. 73(I)/2016, which corresponds to Annex VII(4) Directive 2014/24/EU.

356. A competitive procedure with negotiation ('ανταγωνιστική διαδικασία με διαπραγμάτευση' in Greek, 'pazarlik yapılan hallerde rekabet ihale usulü' in Turkish) constitutes of any economic operator having the option of submitting a request to participate in response to a call for competition containing specific information[1156] by providing the information for qualitative selection that is requested by the contracting authority.[1157] Here, the minimum time limit for receipt of requests to participate is thirty days from the date of the contract notice or, where a prior information notice is used as a means of calling for competition, the invitation to confirm interest was sent.[1158] Only those economic operators invited by the contracting authority following its assessment of the information provided may submit an initial tender which shall be the basis for the subsequent negotiations.[1159] A competitive dialogue ('ανταγωνιστικός διάλογος' in Greek, 'doğrudan temin' in Turkish) involves any economic operator submitting a request to participate in response to a contract notice by providing the information for qualitative selection that is requested by the contracting authority. Only those economic operators invited by the contracting authority following the assessment of the information provided may participate in the dialogue. In this procedure, the minimum time limit for receipt of requests usually is thirty days from the date on which the notice was sent.[1160]

357. Said procedures may equally be applied with regard to works, supplies or services, where, in response to an open or a restricted procedure, only irregular or unacceptable tenders are submitted. In such situations contracting authorities are not required to publish a contract notice where they include in the procedure all of, and only, the tenderers which satisfy the criteria for qualitative selection that are set out in sections 57–64 Law No. 73(I)/2016,[1161] and which, during the prior open or restricted procedure, submitted tenders in accordance with the formal requirements of the procurement procedure. In particular, tenders which do not comply with the procurement documents, which were received late, where there is evidence of collusion or corruption, or which have been found by the contracting authority to be

1154. Technical reference ('τεχνικό πλαίσιο αναφοράς' in Greek, 'teknik referans' in Turkish) means any deliverable produced by European standardization bodies, other than European standards, according to procedures adapted to the development of market needs. Annex VII(5) Law No. 73(I)/2016, which corresponds to Annex VII(5) Directive 2014/24/EU.

1155. Section 23(1)(c)(i)–(iv) Law No. 73(I)/2016, which corresponds to Art. 26(4)(a) Directive 2014/24/EU.

1156. Such information is specified in Annex V Parts B and C Law No. 73(I)/2016, which corresponds to Annex V Parts B and C Directive 2014/24/EU.

1157. Section 26(1) Law No. 73(I)/2016, which corresponds to Art. 29(1) Directive 2014/24/EU.

1158. Section 26(3) Law No. 73(I)/2016, which corresponds to Art. 29(1) Directive 2014/24/EU.

1159. Section 26(5) Law No. 73(I)/2016, which corresponds to Art. 29(2) Directive 2014/24/EU.

1160. Section 27(1), (2) and (3) Law No. 73(I)/2016, which corresponds to Art. 30(1) Directive 2014/24/EU.

1161. Sections 57–64 Law No. 73(I)/2016 correspond to Arts 57–64 Directive 2014/24/EU. With regard to Art. 57 *see Anodiki Services EPE v. GNA 'Evangelismos – Ofthalmiatrio Athinon – Polikliniki', GNA 'Georgios Gennimatas', Geniko Onkologiko Nosokomio Kifisias – (GONK) 'Agioi Anargiroi'*, CJEU Case C-260/17, Judgment of 25 Oct. 2018, digital ECR; *Meca Srl v. Comune di Napoli*, CJEU Case No. C-41/18, Judgment of 19 Jun. 2019, digital ECR.

abnormally low, are considered as being irregular. Further, tenders submitted by tenderers that do not have the required qualifications, and tenders whose price exceeds the contracting authority's budget as determined and documented prior to the launching of the procurement procedure shall be considered as unacceptable.[1162]

358. In specific cases and circumstances laid down in the law and explained immediately below, contracting authorities may award public contracts by a negotiated procedure without prior publication ('διαδικασία με διαπραγμάτευση χωρίς προηγούμενη δημοσίευση' in Greek, 'ilan yapılmayan hallerde pazarlık usulü' in Turkish).[1163] Said procedure may be used for public works contracts, public supply contracts and public service contracts in any of the following cases:

- where no tenders or no suitable tenders or no requests to participate or no suitable requests to participate have been submitted in response to an open procedure or a restricted procedure, provided that the initial conditions of the contract are not substantially altered and that a report is sent to the Commission where it so requests;[1164]
- where the works, supplies or services can be supplied only by a particular economic operator for any of the following reasons: (i) the aim of the procurement is the creation or acquisition of a unique work of art or artistic performance; (ii) competition is absent for technical reasons; (iii) the protection of exclusive rights, including intellectual property rights. The last two exceptions only apply when no reasonable alternative or substitute exists and the absence of competition is not the result of an artificial narrowing down of the parameters of the procurement;[1165]
- in so far as is strictly necessary where, for reasons of extreme urgency brought about by events unforeseeable by the contracting authority, the time limits for the open or restricted procedures or competitive procedures with negotiation cannot be complied with. However, the circumstances invoked to justify extreme urgency may not in any event be attributable to the contracting authority.[1166]

359. In addition to the aforementioned, the same procedure may be used for public supply contracts, in the following cases:

1162. Section 23(1)(c)(v) Law No. 73(I)/2016, which corresponds to Art. 26(4)(b) Directive 2012/24/EU.
1163. Section 29(1) Law No. 73(I)/2016, which corresponds to Art. 32(1) Directive 2014/24/EU.
1164. Section 29(2)(a) Law No. 73(I)/2016, which corresponds to Art. 32(2)(a) Directive 2014/24/EU. In same provision it is set out that a tender is considered not to be suitable where it is irrelevant to the contract, being manifestly incapable, without substantial changes, of meeting the contracting authority's needs and requirements as specified in the procurement documents. Further, a request for participation is considered not to be suitable where the economic operator concerned is to be or may be excluded due to the statutory exclusion grounds or does not meet the selection criteria set out by the contracting authority (*see* in this regard ss 57 and 58 Law No. 73(I)/2016, which correspond to Arts 57 and 58 Directive 2014/24/EU).
1165. Section 29(2)(b) Law No. 73(I)/2016, which corresponds to Art. 32(2)(b) Directive 2014/24/EU.
1166. Section 29(2)(c) Law No. 73(I)/2016, which corresponds to Art. 32(2)(c) Directive 2014/24/EU.

- where the products involved are manufactured purely for the purpose of research, experimentation, study or development; however, such contracts awarded shall not include quantity production to establish commercial viability or to recover research and development costs;[1167]
- for additional deliveries by the original supplier which are intended either as a partial replacement of supplies or installations or as the extension of existing supplies or installations where a change of supplier would oblige the contracting authority to acquire supplies having different technical characteristics which would result in incompatibility or disproportionate technical difficulties in operation and maintenance; the duration of such contracts as well as that of recurrent contracts may not, as a general rule, exceed three years;[1168]
- for supplies quoted and purchased on a commodity market;[1169] and
- for the purchase of supplies or services on particularly advantageous terms, from either a supplier which is definitively winding up its business activities, or the liquidator in an insolvency procedure, an arrangement with creditors, or a similar procedure under national laws or regulations.[1170]

360. Further, the same procedure may be used for public service contracts, where the contract concerned follows a design contest organized in accordance with this law and is to be awarded, under the rules provided for in the design contest, to the winner or one of the winners of the design contest. Mention deserves the provision that in the latter case, all winners must be invited to participate in the negotiations.[1171] Finally, the same procedure may be used for new works or services consisting in the repetition of similar works or services entrusted to the economic operator to which the same contracting authorities awarded an original contract, provided that such works or services are in conformity with a basic project for which the original contract was awarded pursuant to an open or close procedure (section 23(1) Law No. 73(I)/2016). The basic project has to indicate the extent of possible additional works or services and the conditions under which they will be awarded. As soon as the first project is put up for tender, the possible use of this procedure shall be disclosed and the total estimated cost of subsequent works or services shall be taken into consideration by the contracting authorities when calculating the threshold amounts. This procedure may be used only during the three years following the conclusion of the original contract.[1172]

III. Conduct of Procedure

361. Specific provisions regulate the conduct of the procedure, which involve issues such as: preliminary market consultations; prior involvement of candidates or tenderers; technical specifications; labels; test reports, certification and other

---

1167. Section 29(3)(a) Law No. 73(I)/2016, which corresponds to Art. 32(3)(a) Directive 2014/24/EU.
1168. Section 29(3)(b) Law No. 73(I)/2016, which corresponds to Art. 32(3)(b) Directive 2014/24/EU.
1169. Section 29(3)(c) Law No. 73(I)/2016, which corresponds to Art. 32(3)(c) Directive 2014/24/EU.
1170. Section 29(3)(d) Law No. 73(I)/2016, which corresponds to Art. 32(3)(d) Directive 2014/24/EU.
1171. Section 29(4) Law No. 73(I)/2016, which corresponds to Art. 32(4) Directive 2014/24/EU.
1172. Section 29(5) Law No. 73(I)/2016, which corresponds to Art. 32(5) Directive 2014/24/EU.

means of proof; variants; division of contracts into lots; setting time limits;[1173] and nomenclature;[1174] while at the same time ensuring and fostering publication and transparency.[1175]

IV. Criteria of Awarding Contracts

362. Specific importance is given to the criteria, on the basis of which contracts are awarded.

A. Necessary Conditions

363. However, for these criteria to be considered, first the following specific conditions need to be fulfilled. Initially, the tender has to comply with the requirements, conditions and criteria set out in the contract notice or the invitation to confirm interest and in the procurement documents, taking into account, where applicable, the provisions on variants.[1176] Equally important, the tender has to come from a tenderer that is not excluded and that meets the selection criteria set out by the contracting authority and, where applicable, the non-discriminatory rules and criteria.[1177] Further, the contracting authorities are at liberty to decide not to award a contract to the tenderer submitting the most economically advantageous tender where they have established that the tender does not comply with the applicable obligations in the fields of environmental, social and labour law established by Union law, national law, collective agreements or by the international environmental, social and labour law provisions.[1178] Especially in open procedures, contracting authorities may decide to examine tenders before verifying the absence of grounds for exclusion and the fulfilment of the selection criteria. Should they make use of

1173. Sections 37–45 Law No. 73(I)/2016, which correspond to Arts 40–47 and 19 Directive 2012/24/EU.

1174. Section 46 Law No. 73(I)/2016, which specifies that any references to 'Common Procurement Vocabulary (CPV)' are to be identified by reference to specific positions adopted by Regulation (EC) No. 2195/2002 of the European Parliament and of the Council of 5 Nov. 2002 on the Common Procurement Vocabulary (CPV), OJ L 340 of 16 Dec. 2002, p. 1, last amended by Regulation (EC) No. 596/2009 of the European Parliament and of the Council of 18 Jun. 2009 adapting a number of instruments subject to the procedure referred to in Article 251 of the Treaty to Council Decision 1999/468/EC with regard to the regulatory procedure with scrutiny – Adaptation to the regulatory procedure with scrutiny – Part Four, OJ L 188 of 18 Jul. 2009, p. 14. This is a hierarchically structured nomenclature, divided into divisions, groups, classes, categories and subcategories. *See also* para No. 119 to the preamble of Directive 2014/24/EU.

1175. Sections 47–55 Law No. 73(I)/2016, which correspond to Arts 48–55 Directive 2014/24/EU.

1176. Sections 56(1)(a) and 42 Law No. 73(I)/2016, which correspond to Arts 56(1)(a) and 45 Directive 2014/24/EU.

1177. Sections 56(1)(b), 57, 58 and 65 Law No. 73(I)/2016, which correspond to Arts 56(1)(b), 57, 58 and 65 Directive 2014/24/EU.

1178. Sections 56(1) and 4(3)(a) Law No. 73(I)/2016, which correspond to Arts 56 and 18(2) Directive 2014/24/EU.

this power, they have to ensure that the verification of absence of grounds for exclusion and of fulfilment of the selection criteria is carried out in an impartial and transparent manner so that no contract is awarded to a tenderer that should have been excluded or that does not meet the selection criteria set out by the contracting authority.[1179] Where information or documentation to be submitted by economic operators is or appears to be incomplete or erroneous or where specific documents are missing, contracting authorities may request the economic operators concerned to submit, supplement, clarify or complete the relevant information or documentation within an appropriate time limit, provided that such requests are made in full compliance with the principles of equal treatment and transparency.[1180]

B. Exclusion Criteria

364. As long as the aforementioned conditions are fulfilled, the criteria for qualitative selection, as explained below are applied by the contracting authorities. The first set of criteria relates to grounds, which upon their establishment they mandate the contracting authorities to exclude an economic operator from participation in a procurement procedure. Said grounds are mandatory and optional. The below-elaborated ones are mandatory and must be affirmed through a conviction of the economic operator by final judgment:

- participation in a criminal organization, as defined in Article 2 of Council Framework Decision 2008/841/JHA;[1181,1182]
- corruption, as defined in Article 3 of the Convention on the fight against corruption involving officials of the European Communities or officials of Member States of the EU[1183] and Article 2(1) of Council Framework Decision 2003/568/

1179. Sections 56(2)(a) and 57 Law No. 73(I)/2016, which correspond to Arts 56(2) and 57 Directive 2014/24/EU.
1180. Section 56(3) Law No. 73(I)/2016, which corresponds to Art. 56(3) Directive 2014/24/EU.
1181. Council Framework Decision 2008/841/JHA of 24 Oct. 2008 on the fight against organised crime, OJ L 300 of 11 Nov. 2008, p. 42. Article 2 states that the types of conduct related to a criminal organization and regarded as offences within the EU are: '(a) conduct by any person who, with intent and with knowledge of either the aim and general activity of the criminal organisation or its intention to commit the offences in question, actively takes part in the organisation's criminal activities, including the provision of information or material means, the recruitment of new members and all forms of financing of its activities, knowing that such participation will contribute to the achievement of the organisation's criminal activities; and (b) conduct by any person consisting in an agreement with one or more persons that an activity should be pursued, which if carried out, would amount to the commission of offences referred to in Art. 1, even if that person does not take part in the actual execution of the activity'.
1182. Section 57(1)(a) Law No. 73(I)/2016, which corresponds to Art. 57(1)(a) Directive 2014/24/EU.
1183. Council Act of 26 May 1997 drawing up, on the basis of Art. K.3(2)(c) of the Treaty on European Union, the Convention on the fight against corruption involving officials of the European Communities or officials of Member States of the European Union, OJ C 195 of 25 Jun. 1997, p. 1. Article 3 reads: '1. For the purposes of this Convention, the deliberate action of whosoever promises or gives, directly or through an intermediary, an advantage of any kind whatsoever to an official for himself or for a third party for him to act or refrain from acting in accordance with his duty or in the exercise of his functions in breach of his official duties shall constitute active corruption. 2. Each Member State shall take the necessary measures to ensure that conduct of the type referred to in paragraph 1 is made a criminal offence.'

JHA[1184] as well as corruption as defined in the national law of the contracting authority, or in the national law of the economic operator.[1185] It is here noted that corrupt transactions with agents under national law, that being section 3 Cap. 161,[1186] is statutory set out as one of the following three conducts: '(a) any agent corruptly accepts or obtains, or agrees to accept or attempts to obtain, from any person, for himself or for any other person, any gift, or consideration as an inducement or reward for doing or forbearing to do, or for having after the passing of Cap. 161 [that being 4 May 1920] done or forborne to do, any act in relation to his principal's affairs or business, or for showing or forbearing to show favour or disfavour to any person in relation to his principal's affairs or business; or (b) any person corruptly gives or agrees to give or offers any gifts or consideration to any agent as an inducement or reward for doing or forbearing to do, or for having after the passing of Cap. 161 [that being 4 May 1920] done or forborne to do, any act in relation to his principal's affairs or business, or for showing or forbearing to show favour or disfavour to any person in relation to his principal's affairs or business; or (c) any person knowingly gives to any agent, or if any agent knowingly uses with intent to deceive his principal, any receipt, account, or other document in respect of which the principal is interested, and which contains any statement which is false or erroneous or defective in any material particular, and which to his knowledge is interested to mislead the principal';

- fraud within the meaning of Article 1[1187] of the Convention on the protection of the European Communities' financial interests;[1188,1189]

1184. Council Framework Decision 2003/568/JHA of 22 Jul. 2003 on combating corruption in the private sector, OJ L 192 of 31 Jul. 2003, p. 54. Article 2(1) reads: 'Member States shall take the necessary measures to ensure that the following intentional conduct constitutes a criminal offence, when it is carried out in the course of business activities: (a) promising, offering or giving, directly or through an intermediary, to a person who in any capacity directs or works for a private-sector entity an undue advantage of any kind, for that person or for a third party, in order that that person should perform or refrain from performing any act, in breach of that person's duties; (b) directly or through an intermediary, requesting or receiving an undue advantage of any kind, or accepting the promise of such an advantage, for oneself or for a third party, while in any capacity directing or working for a private-sector entity, in order to perform or refrain from performing any act, in breach of one's duties.'
1185. Section 57(1)(b) Law No. 73(I)/2016, which corresponds to Art. 57(1)(b) Directive 2014/24/EU.
1186. The Prevention of Corruption Law of 4 May 1920, Ch. 161 of the Laws, London, 1959 edition, as amended.
1187. Therein fraud is defined as '(a) in respect of expenditure, any intentional act or omission relating to: the use or presentation of false, incorrect or incomplete statements or documents, which has as its effect the misappropriation or wrongful retention of funds from the general budget of the EU or budgets managed by, or on behalf of, the EU; non-disclosure of information in violation of a specific obligation, with the same effect; the misapplication of such funds for purposes other than those for which they were originally granted; (b) in respect of revenue, any intentional act or omission relating to: the use or presentation of false, incorrect or incomplete statements or documents, which has as its effect the illegal diminution of the resources of the general budget of the EU or budgets managed by, or on behalf of, the EU; non-disclosure of information in violation of a specific obligation, with the same effect; misapplication of a legally obtained benefit, with the same effect'.
1188. Council Act of 26 Jul. 1995 drawing up the Convention on the protection of the European Communities' financial interests, OJ C 316 of 27 Nov. 1995, p. 48.

- terrorist offences or offences linked to terrorist activities, as defined in Directive on combating terrorism,[1190] or inciting or aiding or abetting or attempting to commit an offence, as referred to in Article 14 of the same Directive. It is here noted that according to Article 3(1) of same Directive, terrorist offences are specified as the following intentional acts, which, given their nature or context, may seriously damage a country or an international where committed with specific aims: (a) attacks upon a person's life which may cause death; (b) attacks upon the physical integrity of a person; (c) kidnapping or hostage-taking; (d) causing extensive destruction to a government or public facility, a transport system, an infrastructure facility, including an information system, a fixed platform located on the continental shelf, a public place or private property likely to endanger human life or result in major economic loss; (e) seizure of aircraft, ships or other means of public or goods transport; (f) manufacture, possession, acquisition, transport, supply or use of explosives or weapons, as well as research into, and development of weapons; (g) release of dangerous substances, or causing fires, floods or explosions, the effect of which is to endanger human life; (h) interfering with or disrupting the supply of water, power or any other fundamental natural resource, the effect of which is to endanger human life; (i) illegal system interference;[1191] and (j) threatening to commit any of the acts listed in points (a) to (i). Said aims, according to Article 3(2) of the same Directive, are: seriously intimidating a population; unduly compelling a government or an international organization to perform or abstain from performing any act; and seriously destabilizing or destroying the fundamental political, constitutional, economic or social structures of a country or an international organization:
- money laundering or terrorist financing, as defined in section 4 Law No. 188(I)/2007 (*see* in this respect the European one, which has been implemented in national law, above at paragraph 88);[1192] and
- child labour and other forms of trafficking in human beings as defined in applicable national law.[1193,1194] It is here noted that the offence of trafficking consists of 'the recruitment, transportation, transfer, harbouring or reception of persons, including the exchange or transfer of control over those persons, by means of the

1189. Section 57(1)(d) Law No. 71(I)/2016, which corresponds to Art. 57(1)(d) Directive 2014/24/EU.

1190. Directive (EU) 2017/541 of the European Parliament and of the Council of 15 Mar. 2017 on combating terrorism and replacing Council Framework Decision 2002/475/JHA and amending Council Decision 2005/671/JHA, OJ L 88 of 31 Mar. 2017, p. 6. This directive has been implemented in Cyprus via the Law on Combating Terrorism and Protecting its Victims ('ο περί της Καταπολέμησης της Τρομοκρατίας και Προστασίας των Θυμάτων Νόμος') No. 75 of 2019, OG I(I) No. 4705 of 21 May 2019, p. 465.

1191. *See* in this respect Directive 2013/40/EU of the European Parliament and of the Council of 12 Aug. 2013 on attacks against information systems and replacing Council Framework Decision 2005/222/JHA, OJ L 218 of 14 Aug. 2013, p. 8.

1192. Section 57(1)(e) Law No. 73(I)/2016, which corresponds to Art. 57(1)(e) Directive 2014/24/EU.

1193. Law on Preventing and Combating Trafficking in Human Beings and Protecting its Victims ('ο περί της Πρόληψης και της Καταπολέμησης της Εμπορίας και Εκμετάλλευσης Προσώπων και της Προστασίας των Θυμάτων Νόμος') No. 60 of 2014, OG I(I) No. 4414 of 15 Apr. 2014, p. 352, which implements Directive 2011/36/EU of the European Parliament and of the Council of 5 Apr. 2011 on preventing and combating trafficking in human beings and protecting its victims, OJ L 101 of 15 Apr. 2011, p. 1.

1194. Section 57(1)(f) Law No. 73(I)/2016, which corresponds to Art. 57(1)(f) Directive 2014/24/EU.

threat or use of force or other forms of coercion, of abduction, of fraud, of deception, of the abuse of power or of a position of vulnerability or of the giving or receiving of payments or benefits to achieve the consent of a person having control over another person, for the purpose of exploitation'. In this context, a position of vulnerability means a situation in which the person concerned has no real or acceptable alternative but to submit to the abuse involved. Exploitation includes here, as a minimum, the exploitation of the prostitution of others or other forms of sexual exploitation, forced labour or services, including begging, slavery or practices similar to slavery, servitude, or the exploitation of criminal activities, or the removal of organs. Any consent of a victim of trafficking in human beings to the exploitation, whether intended or actual, is irrelevant where any of the means set forth above has been used. When the conduct referred to above involves a child, that being any person below 18 years of age, it is a punishable offence of trafficking in human beings even if none of the means set forth above has been used.[1195]

365. The aforementioned mandatory obligation to exclude an economic operator equally applies where the person convicted by final judgment is a member of the administrative, management or supervisory body of that economic operator or has powers of representation, decision or control therein.[1196]

366. Economic operators are further excluded from participation in a procurement procedure, where the contracting authority is aware that said operators are in breach of their obligations relating to the payment of taxes or social security contributions and where this has been established by a judicial or administrative decision having final and binding effect in accordance with the legal provisions of the country in which it is established or in Cyprus. Furthermore, such an exclusion may take place where the contracting authority can demonstrate by any appropriate means that the economic operator is in breach of the same obligations. However, no exclusion may be decided, when the economic operator has fulfilled its obligations by paying or entering into a binding arrangement with a view to paying the taxes or social security contributions due, including, where applicable, any interest accrued or fines.[1197]

367. Derogation from aforementioned mandatory exclusion may be decided by the contracting authorities on an exceptional basis, for overriding reasons relating to the public interest such as public health or protection of the environment. Similarly, derogation may be decided, where an exclusion would be clearly disproportionate, in particular where only minor amounts of taxes or social security

1195. Section 2 Law No. 60(I)/2014, which corresponds to Art. 2(1), (2), (3), (4), (5) and (6) Directive 2011/36/EU.

1196. Section 57(1) Law No. 73(I)/2016, which corresponds to Art. 57(1) Directive 2014/24/EU. On Art. 57 *see Vossloh Laeis GmbH v. Stadtwerke München GmbH*, CJEU Case C-124/17, Judgment of 24 Oct. 2018, digital ECR; *Meca Srl v. Comune di Napoli*, CJEU C-41/18, Judgment of 19 Jun. 2019, digital ECR.

1197. Section 57(2)(a), (b) and (c) Law No. 73(I)/2016, which corresponds to Art. 57(2) Directive 2014/24/EU.

contributions are unpaid or where the economic operator was informed of the exact amount due following its breach of its obligations relating to the payment of taxes or social security contributions at such time that it did not have the possibility of taking aforementioned measures before expiration of the deadline for requesting participation or, in open procedures, the deadline for submitting its tender.[1198]

368. The exclusion grounds, which are at the discretion of the contracting authorities and thus merely optional, are described below:

- where the contracting authority can demonstrate by any appropriate means a violation of applicable obligations referred to in section 18(3)(a) of this law;
- where the economic operator is bankrupt or is the subject of insolvency or winding-up proceedings, where its assets are being administered by a liquidator or by the court, where it is in an arrangement with creditors, where its business activities are suspended or it is in any analogous situation arising from a similar procedure under national laws and regulations;
- where the contracting authority can demonstrate by appropriate means that the economic operator is guilty of grave professional misconduct, which renders its integrity questionable. Admitting to facts or performing actions before the District Attorney or the competent Court in relation to one of the grounds set out in the first exclusion ground, explained above, constitutes grave professional misconduct;
- where the contracting authority has sufficiently plausible indications to conclude that the economic operator has entered into agreements with other economic operators aimed at distorting competition;
- where a conflict of interest within the meaning of section 6 of this law cannot be effectively remedied by other less intrusive measures;
- where a distortion of competition from the prior involvement of the economic operators in the preparation of the procurement procedure, as referred to in section 38 of this law, cannot be remedied by other, less intrusive measures;
- where the economic operator has shown significant or persistent deficiencies in the performance of a substantive requirement under a prior public contract, a prior contract with a contracting entity or a prior concession contract which led to early termination of that prior contract, damages or other comparable sanctions;
- where the economic operator has been guilty of serious misrepresentation in supplying the information required for the verification of the absence of grounds for exclusion or the fulfilment of the selection criteria, has withheld such information or is not able to submit the supporting documents required pursuant to section 59; or
- where the economic operator has undertaken to unduly influence the decision-making process of the contracting authority, to obtain confidential information that may confer upon it undue advantages in the procurement procedure or to

1198. Section 57(3)(a) and (b) Law No. 73(I)/2016, which corresponds to Art. 57(3) Directive 2014/24/EU.

negligently provide misleading information that may have a material influence on decisions concerning exclusion, selection or award.[1199]

369. Both mandatory and optional exclusion grounds may be applied by the contracting authorities at any time during the procedure, as long as the economic operator is, in view of acts committed or omitted either before or during the procedure, in one of the aforementioned situations.[1200] However, an economic operator has the statutory right to provide evidence to the effect that measures it took are sufficient to demonstrate its reliability despite the existence of a relevant ground for exclusion, save for the occasions of exclusions resulting from effective and final judgment. In order to make use of this right, the economic operator shall have to prove that it has paid or undertaken to pay compensation in respect of any damage caused by the criminal offence or misconduct, clarified the facts and circumstances in a comprehensive manner by actively collaborating with the investigating authorities and taken concrete technical, organizational and personnel measures that are appropriate to prevent further criminal offences or misconduct. The contracting authority exercises its discretion power in considering such evidence as sufficient, and it has to take into account the gravity and particular circumstances of said offences. Should it reach the conclusion that the undertaken measures are insufficient, it shall have to provide the economic operator with a statement of reasons.[1201] Specific implementing conditions of the aforementioned are set out in Regulations[1202] issued by the Council of Ministers.[1203]

C. Selection Criteria

370. Generally, the selection criteria may relate to: suitability to pursue the professional activity; economic and financial standing; and technical and professional ability. It is further set out that contracting authorities may impose those criteria, which are elaborated immediately below, on economic operators solely as requirements for participation. They are equally obliged to limit any requirements to those that are appropriate to ensure that a candidate or tenderer has the legal and financial

1199. Section 57(4) Law No. 73(I)/2016, which corresponds to Art. 57(4) Directive 2014/24/EU. On Art. 57(4) *see Delta Antrepriză de ConstrucŢii şi Montaj 93 SA v. Compania NaŢională de Administrare a Infrastructurii Rutiere SA*, CJEU Case C-267/18, Judgment of 3 Oct. 2019, digital ECR; *Indaco Service Soc. coop. sociale, Coop. sociale il Melograno v. Ufficio Territoriale del Governo Taranto,* CJEU Case C-552/18, Judgment of 20 Nov. 2019, digital ECR.

1200. Section 57(5)(a) and (b) Law No. 73(I)/2016, which corresponds to Art. 57(5) Directive 2014/24/EU.

1201. Section 57(6)(a), (b) and (c) Law No. 73(I)/2016, which corresponds to Art. 57(6) Directive 2014/24/EU. On Art. 57(6) and (7) *see Aannemingsbedrijf Norré-Behaegel v. Vlaams Gewest*, CJEU Case C-387/19, OJ C 270, 12 Aug. 2019, p. 19 (case pending).

1202. Regulations on Managing the Execution of Public Contracts and the Exclusion Procedures of Economic Operators ('οι περί της Διαχείρισης της Εκτέλεσης Δημοσίων Συμβάσεων και των Διαδικασιών Αποκλεισμού των Οικονομικών Φορέων από Διαδικασίες Σύναψης Δημοσίων Συμβάσεων Κανονισμοί') No. 138 of 2016, OG III(I) No. 4943 of 28 Apr. 2016, p. 1097, as amended.

1203. Sections 57(7)(a) and (b) and 93 Law No. 73(I)/2016, which correspond to Art. 57(7) Directive 2014/24/EU.

capacities and the technical and professional abilities to perform the contract to be awarded. All requirements have to be related and proportionate ('ανάλογες'-1 in Greek, 'ölçülü' in Turkish) to the subject matter of the contract.[1204] Required conditions of participation which may be expressed as minimum levels of ability, together with the appropriate means of proof, are to be indicated in the contract notice or in the invitation to confirm interest.[1205]

371. With regard to suitability to pursue the professional activity, contracting authorities may require economic operators to be enrolled in one of the professional or trade registers kept in their Member State of establishment or comply with any other request set out in the law.[1206] Particularly in procurement procedures for services, in so far as economic operators have to possess a particular authorization or to be members of a particular organization in order to be able to perform in their country of origin the service concerned, the contracting authority may require them to prove that they hold such authorization or membership.[1207]

372. With regard to economic and financial standing, contracting authorities may impose requirements ensuring that economic operators possess the necessary economic and financial capacity to perform the contract. For that purpose, contracting authorities may require the following: that economic operators have a certain minimum yearly turnover, including a certain minimum turnover in the area covered by the contract; that economic operators provide information on their annual accounts showing the ratios, for instance, between assets and liabilities; and an appropriate level of professional risk indemnity insurance. In any event, the minimum yearly turnover that economic operators are required to have, generally shall not exceed two times the estimated contract value, except in duly justified cases such as relating to the special risks attached to the nature of the works, services or supplies. The contracting authority shall indicate the main reasons for such a requirement in the procurement documents or the individual report set out in this law.[1208] Methods and criteria for considering the ration between assets and liabilities, if the contracting authority decides to consider it, have to be transparent, objective and non-discriminatory.[1209]

373. With regard to technical and professional ability, contracting authorities may impose requirements ensuring that economic operators possess the necessary human and technical resources and experience to perform the contract to an appropriate quality standard. In particular, contracting authorities may require that economic operators have a sufficient level of experience demonstrated by suitable

---

1204. Section 58(1)(a), (b), (c) and (d) Law No. 73(I)/2016, which corresponds to Art. 58(1) Directive 2014/24/EU.
1205. Section 58(5) Law No. 73(I)/2016, which corresponds to Art. 58(5) Directive 2014/24/EU.
1206. Both registers and requests are described in Annex XI Law No. 73(I)/2016, which corresponds to Annex XI Directive 2014/24/EU.
1207. Section 58(2) Law No. 73(I)/2016, which corresponds to Art. 58(2) Directive 2014/24/EU.
1208. The content of such individual reports is set out in s. 84 Law No. 73(I)/2016, which corresponds to Art. 84 Directive 2014/24/EU.
1209. Section 58(3) Law No. 73(I)/2016, which corresponds to Art. 58(3) Directive 2014/24/EU.

references from contracts performed in the past. A contracting authority may assume that an economic operator does not possess the required professional abilities where it has established that said operator has conflicting interests which may negatively affect the performance of the contract. Particularly, in procurement procedures for supplies requiring siting or installation work, services or works, the professional ability of economic operators to provide the service or to execute the installation or the work may be evaluated with regard to their skills, efficiency, experience and reliability.[1210]

V. The European Single Procurement Document

374. At the time of submission of requests to participate or of tenders, contracting authorities accept the European Single Procurement Document (ESPD), consisting of an updated self-declaration as preliminary evidence in replacement of certificates issued by public authorities or third parties confirming that the relevant economic operator fulfils the following conditions: (a) it is not in one of the aforementioned situations, which cause mandatory or optional exclusion;[1211] (b) it meets the relevant selection criteria, as explained above;[1212] (c) where applicable, it fulfils the objective rules and criteria.[1213] Should the economic operator rely on the capacities of other entities the ESPD further contains said information in respect of such entities.[1214]

375. The ESPD, which is drawn up on the basis of a standard form and is provided exclusively in electronic form, consists of a formal statement by the economic operator that the relevant exclusion ground does not apply and/or that the relevant selection criterion is fulfilled and provides the relevant information as required by the contracting authority. The ESPD further identifies the public authority or third party responsible for establishing the supporting documents and contains formal statement to the effect that the economic operator will be able, upon request and without delay, to provide those supporting documents. Where the contracting authority can obtain the supporting documents directly by accessing a database, the ESPD shall also contain the information required for this purpose. If an

1210. Section 58(4) Law No. 73(I)/2016, which corresponds to Art. 58(4) Directive 2014/24/EU. On Art. 58(4) *see Secretaria Regional de Saúde dos Açores v. Ministério Público*, CJEU Case C-102/17, Judgment of 25 Apr. 2018, digital ECR.

1211. Sections 59(1)(a) and 57 Law No. 73(I)/2016, which correspond to Arts 59(1)(a) and 57 Directive 2014/24/EU.

1212. Sections 59(1)(b) and 58 Law No. 73(I)/2016, which correspond to Arts 59(1)(b) and 58 Directive 2014/24/EU.

1213. Sections 59(1)(c) and 65 Law No. 73(I)/2016, which correspond to Arts 59(1)(c) and 65 Directive 2014/24/EU.

1214. Section 59(1) Law No. 73(I)/2016, which corresponds to Art. 59(1) Directive 2014/24/EU.

ESPD has already been used in a previous procurement procedure, economic operators may reuse it, provided that they confirm that the information contained therein continues to be correct.[1215]

376. At any moment during the procedure, a contracting authority may ask tenders and candidates to submit all or part of the supporting documents, where it is necessary to ensure the proper conduct of the procedure. Further, before awarding the contract, the contracting authority shall require the tenderer to which it has decided to award the contract to submit up-to-date supporting documents and may invite economic operators to supplement or clarify the certificates received.[1216] However, economic operators shall not be required to submit supporting documents or other documentary evidence, where this can be obtained by the contracting authority directly by accessing a national database in any Member State that is available free of charge, or it already possesses these documents.[1217] The means of proof that a contracting authority may require as evidence for the absence of exclusion grounds, for the fulfilment of the selection criteria, as proof of the economic operator's economic and financial standing and its technical abilities, along with the quality assurance standards and environmental management standards are specifically set out in the law.[1218]

VI. Contract Award Criteria

377. Without prejudice to national laws, regulations or administrative provisions concerning the price of certain supplies or the remuneration of certain services, contracting authorities base the award of public contracts on the most economically advantageous tender.[1219] A tender is identified as such on the basis of the price or cost, using a cost-effectiveness approach, such as life-cycle costing and may include the best price-quality ratio, which shall be assessed on the basis of criteria, including qualitative, environmental or social aspects, linked to the subject matter of the public contract in question. For instance, such criteria may comprise: quality, including technical merit, aesthetic and functional characteristics, accessibility, design for all users, social, environmental and innovative characteristics and trading and its conditions; organization, qualification and experience of staff assigned to performing the contract, where the quality of the staff assigned can have a significant impact on the level of performance of the contract; or aftersales service and technical assistance, delivery conditions such as delivery date, delivery process and delivery period or period of completion. The cost element may also take

1215. Section 59(2) and (3) Law No. 73(I)/2016, which corresponds to Art. 59(1) and (2) Directive 2014/24/EU.
1216. Sections 59(4), 60 and 62 Law No. 73(I)/2016, which corresponds to Arts 59(4), 60 and 62 Directive 2014/24/EU.
1217. Section 59(5) Law No. 73(I)/2016, which corresponds to Art. 59(4) Directive 2014/24/EU.
1218. Sections 60 and 62 Law No. 73(I)/2016, which corresponds to Arts 60 and 62 Directive 2014/24/EU.
1219. Section 67(1) Law No. 73(I)/2016, which corresponds to Art. 67(1) Directive 2014/24/EU.

the form of a fixed price or cost on the basis of which economic operators will compete on quality criteria only.[1220] However, contracting authorities may not use price only or cost only as the sole award criterion for awarding public contracts, unless reasoned grounds occur and are taken into account by contracting authorities.[1221] Obviously, in such cases, the administrative act shall have to be duly reasoned, as it is issued following the exercise of the discretionary powers of the administration and it affects negatively tenders. This is not set out in this law, but it derives from the General Principles of Administrative Law.[1222]

378. Award criteria are considered to be linked to the subject matter of the public contract, where they relate to the works, supplies or services to be provided under that contract in any respect and at any stage of their life cycle. They include factors involved in the specific process of production, provision or trading of those works, supplies or services or a specific process for another stage of their life cycle, even where such factors do not form part of their material substance.[1223] However, they may not have the effect of conferring an unrestricted freedom of choice on the contracting authority. To the contrary, they have to ensure the possibility of effective competition as well as be accompanied by specifications that allow the information provided by the tenderers to be effectively verified in order to assess how well the tenders meet the award criteria. In case of doubt, contracting authorities verify effectively the accuracy of the information and proof provided by the tenderers.[1224] The contracting authority further has the statutory duty to specify, in the procurement documents, the relative weighting which it gives to each of the criteria chosen to determine the most economically advantageous tender, except where this is identified on the basis of price alone. Should weighting be impossible for objective reasons, the contracting authority has to indicate the criteria in decreasing order of importance.[1225]

379. Life-cycle costing, to the extent relevant, covers parts or all of the following costs over the cycle of a product, service or works: costs, borne by the contracting authority or other users, such as costs of use and maintenance; and costs imputed to environmental externalities linked to the product, service or works during its life cycle, provided their monetary value can be determined and verified.[1226] Where contracting authorities assess the costs using a life-cycle costing approach, they indicate in the procurement documents the data to be provided by the tenderers and the

1220. Section 67(2) Law No. 73(I)/2016, which corresponds to Art. 67(2) Directive 2014/24/EU.
1221. Section 67(3) Law No. 73(I)/2016. The corresponding European provision, that being the last sentence to para. 2 of Art. 67 Directive 2014/24/EU, does not provide for any possibility of derogation.
1222. *See* in this regard s. 26 of Law on General Principles of Administrative Law ('ο περί των Γενικών Αρχών του Διοικητικού Δικαίου Νόμος') No. 158 of 1999, OG I(I) No. 3378 of 31 Dec. 1999, p. 478, as last amended by amending Law No. 99 of 2014, OG I(I) No. 4453 of 11 Jul. 2014.
1223. Section 67(4) Law No. 73(I)/2016, which corresponds to Art. 67(3) Law No. 73(I)/2016.
1224. Section 67(5) Law No. 73(I)/2016, which corresponds to Art. 67(4) Directive 2014/24/EU.
1225. Section 67(6) Law No. 73(I)/2016, which corresponds to Art. 67(5) Directive 2014/24/EU.
1226. Section 68(1)(a) and (b) Law No. 73(I)/2016, which corresponds to Art. 68(1)(a) and (b) Directive 2014/24/EU.

method that they shall use to determine said costs on the basis of the requested data. The method that the authorities choose to apply for the assessment of costs imputed to environmental externalities, needs to meet the following specific conditions: it must be based on objectively verifiable and non-discriminatory criteria; it must be accessible to all interested parties; and the data required can be provided with reasonable effort by normally diligent economic operators.[1227] Legislative acts making mandatory common methods for the calculation of life cycle[1228] are here applied.[1229]

380. Special mention is made on tenders appearing to be abnormally low in relation to the works, supplies or services. In such events, contracting authorities require economic operators to explain the price or costs proposed in the tender.[1230] Such explanations may in particular relate to:

- the economics of the manufacturing process, of the services provided or of the construction method;[1231]
- the technical solutions chosen or any exceptionally favourable conditions available to the tenderer for the supply of the products or services or for the execution of the work;[1232]
- the originality of the work, supplies or services proposed by the tenderer;[1233]
- compliance with obligations in the field of environmental, social and labour law;[1234]
- compliance with obligations on subcontracting;[1235] and
- the possibility of the tenderer obtaining state aid.[1236]

381. Any person, not necessarily an economic operator, having an interest in awarding a specific contract and already having sustained or shall possibly sustain damage by an act or decision of the awarding authority either prior to or after awarding a contract, may file a complaint ('προσφυγή' in Greek, 'iptal davası' in

---

1227. Section 68(2) Law No. 73(I)/2016, which corresponds to Art. 68(2) Directive 2014/24/EU.
1228. The only such legislative act is Directive 2009/33/EC of the European Parliament and of the Council of 23 Apr. 2009 on the promotion of clean and energy-efficient road transport vehicles, OJ L 120 of 15 May 2009, p. 5, which has been implemented in Cyprus via Law on the Coordination of Procedures for Making Public Contracts for Services, Works and Supplies and Related Matters (Amending) ('ο περί του Συντονισμού των Διαδικασιών Σύναψης Δημοσίων Συμβάσεων Προμηθειών, Έργων και Υπηρεσιών και για Συναφή Θέματα (Τροποποιητικός) Νόμος') No. 40 of 2011, OG I(I) No. 4275 of 24 Mar. 2011, p. 374.
1229. Section 68(3) Law No. 73(I)/2016, which corresponds to Art. 68(3) Directive 2014/24/EU.
1230. Section 69(1) Law No. 73(I)/2016, which corresponds to Art. 69(1) Directive 2014/24/EU.
1231. Section 69(2)(a) Law No. 73(I)/2016, which corresponds to Art. 69(2)(a) Directive 2014/24/EU.
1232. Section 69(2)(b) Law No. 73(I)/2016, which corresponds to Art. 69(2)(b) Directive 2014/24/EU.
1233. Section 69(2)(c) Law No. 73(I)/2016, which corresponds to Art. 69(2)(c) Directive 2014/24/EU.
1234. Sections 69(2)(d) and 4(3) Law No. 73(I)/2016, which correspond to Arts 69(2)(d) and 18(2) Directive 2014/24/EU.
1235. Sections 69(2)(e) and 71 Law No. 73(I)/2016, which correspond to Arts 69(2)(e) and 71 Directive 2014/24/EU.
1236. Section 69(2)(f) Law No. 73(I)/2016, which corresponds to Art. 69(2)(f) Directive 2014/24/EU.

Turkish). Necessary conditions, time frames, provisional injunctions and other matters are regulated in the Law on Complaints regarding Public Contracts.[1237]

§3. Content and Performance of Public Contracts

382. No provision refers to the content of public contracts. To the contrary, several provisions regulate their performance. In particular, contracting authorities may lay down special conditions relating to the performance of a contract, provided that they are linked to the subject matter of the contract and are indicated in the call for competition or in the procurement documents. Said conditions may relate to economic, innovation-related, environmental, social or employment-related considerations.[1238] Specific provisions also regulate subcontracting, providing for instance that the contracting authority may ask the tenderer to indicate in its tender any share of the contract it may intend to subcontract to third parties and any proposed subcontractors.[1239]

383. Contracts may be modified without a new procurement procedure in specific cases, as set out in this law. These cases are the following:

- where the modifications, irrespective of their monetary value, have been provided for in the initial procurement documents in clear, precise and unequivocal review clauses, which may include price revision clauses, or options. Such clauses have to state the scope and nature of possible modifications or options as well as the conditions under which they may be used. However, they may not provide for modifications or options altering the overall nature of the contract or the framework agreement;[1240]
- for additional works, services or supplies by the original contractor that have become necessary and that were not included in the initial procurement where a change of contractor: cannot be made for economic or technical reasons such as requirements of interchangeability or interoperability with existing equipment, services or installations procured under the initial procurement; and would cause significant inconvenience or substantial duplication of costs for the contracting authority. However, any increase in price shall not exceed 50% of the value of the original contract. Where several successive modifications are made, that limitation shall apply to the value of each modification. Such consecutive modifications shall not be aimed at circumventing this law;[1241]

1237. Law on the Procedure of Complaints in the Field of Awarding Public Contracts('ο περί των Διαδικασιών Προσφυγής στον Τομέα της Σύναψης των Δημοσίων Συμβάσεων Νόμος') No. 104 of 2010, OG I(I) 4259 of 19 Nov. 2010, p. 850, as last amended by amending Law No. 179 of 2017, OG I(I) No. 4631 of 15 Dec. 2017, p. 1147.

1238. Section 70 Law No. 73(I)/2016, which corresponds to Art. 70 Directive 2014/24/EU.

1239. Section 71 Law No. 73(I)/2016, which corresponds to Art. 71 Directive 2014/24/EU. On Art. 71 *see Vitali SpA v. Autostrade per l'Italia SpA*, CJEU Case C-63/18, Judgment of 26 Sep. 2019, digital ECR; *Direzione e coordinamento Vivendi SA v. Consip SpA, Ministero dell'Economia e delle Finanze*, CJEU C-395/18, Judgment of 30 Jan. 2020, digital ECR.

1240. Section 72(1)(a) Law No. 73(I)/2016, which corresponds to Art. 72(1)(a) Directive 2014/24/EU.

1241. Section 72(1)(b) Law No. 73(I)/2016, which corresponds to Art. 72(1)(b) Directive 2014/24/EU.

- where all of the following conditions are fulfilled: the need for modification has been brought about by circumstances which a diligent contracting authority could not foresee; the modification does not alter the overall nature of the contract; any increase in price is not higher than 50% of the value of the original contract or framework agreement. Where several successive modifications are made that limitation shall apply to the value of each modification. Such consecutive modifications shall not be aimed at circumventing this law;[1242]
- where a new contractor replaces the one to which the contracting authority had initially awarded the contract as a consequence of either: an unequivocal review clause or option in conformity with the aforementioned under modifications have been provided for in the initial procurement documents; universal or partial succession into the position of the initial contractor, following corporate restructuring, including takeover, merger, acquisition or insolvency, of another economic operator that fulfils the criteria for qualitative selection initially established provided that this does not entail other substantial modifications to the contract and is not aimed at circumventing the application of this law; or in the event that the contracting authority itself assumes the main contractor's obligations towards its subcontractors where this possibility is provided for under provisions in subcontracting;[1243] or
- where the modifications, irrespective of their value, are not substantial.[1244] A modification is substantial, where it renders the contract or the framework agreement materially different in character from the one initially concluded. In any event, a modification is considered to be substantial where one or more of the following conditions is met: the modification introduces conditions which, had they been part of the initial procurement procedure, would have allowed for the admission of other candidates than those initially selected or for the acceptance of a tender other than that originally accepted or would have attracted additional participants in the procurement procedure; the modification changes the economic balance of the contract or the framework agreement in favour of the contractor in a manner which was not provided for in the initial contract or framework agreement; the modification extends the scope of the contract or framework agreement considerably; or where a new contractor replaces the one to which the contracting authority had initially awarded the contract in other cases than those explained above.[1245]

384. Furthermore, contracts may equally be modified without a new procurement procedure being necessary, where the value of the modification is below both of the thresholds accounts that specify the applicability of this law[1246] and 10% of

1242. Section 72(1)(c) Law No. 73(I)/2016, which corresponds to Art. 72(1)(c) Directive 2014/24/EU.
1243. Section 72(1)(d) Law No. 73(I)/2016, which corresponds to Art. 72(1)(d) Directive 2014/24/EU.
1244. Section 72(1)(e) Law No. 73(I)/2016, which corresponds to Art. 72(1)(e) Directive 2014/24/EU.
1245. Section 72(4)(a), (b), (c) and (d) Law No. 73(I)/2016, which corresponds to Art. 72(4)(a), (b), (c) and (d) Directive 2014/24/EU.
1246. Sections 72(2)(a) and 9 Law No. 73(I)/2016, which correspond to Arts 72(2)(i) and 4 Directive 2014/24/EU.

the initial contract value for service and supply contracts and below 15% of the initial contract value for works contracts.[1247] In any event, the modification may not alter the overall nature of the contract or framework agreement. In cases where several successive modifications are made, the value shall be assessed on the basis of the net cumulative value of the successive modifications.[1248] Any other modification of the provisions of a public contract or a framework agreement during its term than those provided for above requires a new procurement procedure.[1249]

§4. Duties and Responsibilities of Economic Operators and Contracting Authorities

385. High regard is given to the confidentiality duty, to which the contracting authority is obliged to adhere. More specifically, it is set out that, unless otherwise provided in this law or in the laws of Cyprus, in particular legislation concerning access to information, and without prejudice to the obligations relating to the advertising of awarded contracts and to the information to candidates and tenderers,[1250] the contracting authority shall not disclose information forwarded to it by economic operators which they have designated as confidential, including, but not limited to, technical or trade secrets and the confidential aspects of tenders.[1251] Contracting authorities further have the power to impose on economic operators requirements aimed at protecting the confidential nature of information which same authorities make available throughout the procurement procedure.[1252]

386. Breach of said duty leads to imprisonment of no more than two years and/or monetary fine of up to EUR 4,000.[1253] In particular breach of confidentiality has one of the following forms: any person providing to any other person any information, in writing or orally, that has come into his knowledge during the exercise of his duties or his powers under this law and/or the Regulations issued under same law, is guilty of said offence, save for disclosure being done in relation to proper exercise of his or other person's duties under express order from a competent authority, or in relation to investigating any penal offence or within any procedure before any court;[1254] save for the immediately aforementioned, any person who without any lawful authority gives or receives any information regarding a contract award procedure;[1255] any person, who without any lawful authority, either personally himself, or through any other person, or on behalf of any other person, strives

1247. Section 72(2)(b) Law No. 73(I)/2016, which corresponds to Art. 72(2)(ii) Directive 2014/24/EU.
1248. Section 72(2) Law No. 73(I)/2016, which corresponds to Art. 72(2) Directive 2014/24/EU.
1249. Section 72(5) Law No. 73(I)/2016, which corresponds to Art. 72(5) Directive 2014/24/EU.
1250. *See* in this respect ss 49 and 54 Law No. 73(I)/2016, which correspond to Arts 50 and 55 Directive 2014/24/EU.
1251. Section 5(1) Law No. 73(I)/2016, which corresponds to Art. 21(1) Directive 2014/24/EU.
1252. Section 5(2) Law No. 73(I)/2016, which corresponds to Art. 21(2) Directive 2014/24/EU.
1253. Section 91(4) Law No. 73(I)/2016.
1254. Section 91(1)(a) and (b) *ibid.*
1255. Section 91(2) *ibid.*

or attempts to receive or elicit from any person, who acquired knowledge of information during his duties, any such information that may not be disclosed;[1256] and any person, who without any lawful authority, either personally himself, or through any other person, or on behalf of any other person, strives or attempts to influence the mind or decision, final or not, of any authority, corporate or officer, during the exercise of his duties or powers under this law regarding any procedure, examination, elaboration, evaluation, appreciation or anything done regarding a contract award procedure.[1257] However, any penal prosecution may only be initiated following the permission of the Attorney General of the Republic.[1258]

387. Pivotal position in ensuring that contracting authorities generally comply to their duties and responsibilities, from the perspective of the proper application of this law, has the Competent Authority of Public Contracts ('Αρμόδια Αρχή Δημοσίων Συμβάσεων' in Greek) has the power to supervise the contracting authorities with the aim of ensuring compliance with this law and the Regulations issued thereunder.[1259] It may further issue any recommendations to the contracting authorities for the proper application of the provisions of this law.[1260] In addition, it may ask and receive any information it deems proper with reference to the implementation of this law within a time frame set by itself.[1261] Furthermore, it has the power to issue circulars for the optimal application of this law and the Regulations issued thereunder.[1262] It also notifies to the contracting authorities the decisions of the European Commission.[1263] Finally, it has the competence to gather and submit the necessary statistical data to the European Commission within the relevant deadlines set out in this law.[1264]

388. In addition to the aforementioned powers and without prejudice thereto, the Competent Authority of Public Contracts has the following duties aiming at proper and effective application of this law, along with other rules and practices applied in public contracts. Its fundamental duty is monitoring the application of rules on the procedure of awarding public contracts.[1265] Should it note, on its own initiative or after receiving information, specific violations or systemic problems, it has the power to issue corrective recommendations to the contracting authorities.[1266] If the later does not comply, the Competent Authority for Public Contracts has the power, if it deems it proper, to refer the specifics of alleged violations of the use of the negotiated procedure without prior publication[1267] to the Tenders Review Authority ('Αναθεωρητική Αρχή Προσφορών' in Greek), a supervising public authority for

1256. Section 91(3)(a) *ibid.*
1257. Section 91(3)(b) *ibid.*
1258. Section 91(5) *ibid.*
1259. Section 92(a) *ibid.*
1260. Section 92(b) *ibid.*
1261. Section 92(c) *ibid.*
1262. Section 92(d) *ibid.*
1263. Section 92(e) *ibid.*
1264. Section 92(f) *ibid.*
1265. Section 83(1)(a) *ibid.*
1266. Section 83(1)(b) *ibid.*
1267. Section 29 *ibid.*

tenders with judiciary powers, with the request to issue a decision, when the interesting parties do not have access to appeal procedures.[1268] Specifics of other provisions being violated are being referred to the Attorney General of the Republic with the request to issue an opinion thereon, equally when the interesting parties do not have access to appeal procedures.[1269] Finally, it has the power to refer to the Council of Ministers through a relevant proposal of the Minister of Finance, systematic or other problems with the request to take appropriate measures, which it suggests following taking into consideration the opinion of the contracting authority.[1270] All results of the aforementioned monitoring activity are available to the public through proper communication means.[1271] Along with being the competent body for collaboration with and reporting to the European Commission[1272] and for keeping copies of public contracts of more than EUR 10,000 and of public contracts of services or supplies of more than EUR 1 million,[1273] it ensures providing free information and guidance for the interpretation and application of the legislation of the EU on public procurement in order to assist contracting authorities and the economic operators in correctly applying the relevant rules. Finally, it offers support to the contracting authorities regarding planning and conducting a procedure for awarding public contracts.[1274]

§5. Specific Provisions for Particular Procurement Regimes

389. This law sets out specifics for procurements regarding social and other services, and design contests. The specifics on procurement by entities operating in the water, energy, transport and postal services sectors as well as procurement by entities operating in the defence and security sector shall be equally portrayed here, in a brief manner.

I. Social and Other Services

390. The provisions explained here apply to public contracts regarding social and other services, as long as they have a value net of VAT estimated to be equal to or greater than the threshold of EUR 750,000.[1275] More specifically, these services include health and social services, administrative social, educational, healthcare and

1268. Section 83(1)(b)(i) *ibid.*
1269. Section 83(1)(b)(ii) *ibid.*
1270. Section 83(1)(b)(iii) *ibid.*
1271. Section 83(2) *ibid.*
1272. Section 83(1)(c) and (3) *ibid.*
1273. Section 83(4) *ibid.*
1274. Section 83(1)(e) and (f) *ibid.*
1275. Sections 74 and 9(1)(d) Law No. 73(I)/2016, which correspond to Arts 74 and 4(d) Directive.

cultural services, compulsory social security services, benefit services, other community, social and personal services, religious services, hotel and restaurant services, legal services, provision of services to the community, prison-related services, public security and rescue services, investigation and security services, international services and postal services.[1276]

391. In said cases, contract authorities intending to award a public contract make known their intention by means of a contract notice or by means of a prior information notice. Both of them have statutorily specified contents and underlie specific publication requirements.[1277] The results of the procurement procedure shall be made known by the contracting authorities by means of a contract award notice.[1278] However, such notices may be grouped on a quarterly basis and in such a case grouped notices shall be sent within thirty days of the end of each quarter.[1279]

392. In order to ensure that contracting authorities abide by the principles of transparency and equal treatment of the economic operators, awarding contracts falling into this category is performed in accordance with the following procedure. The contracting authority prepares the necessary documentation for the award procedure mentioning at least the exclusion grounds regarding taxes and social security (*see* in this respect paragraph 364 above).[1280] Said documentation may include the required technical standards, the evaluation process as well as any data or other information, as the contracting authority may think fit.[1281] Unless said documentation states otherwise, tenders have to be submitted until the set date and time mentioned therein.[1282] Contracting authorities may take into account the need to ensure quality, continuity, accessibility, affordability, availability and comprehensiveness of the services, the specific needs of different categories of users, including disadvantaged and vulnerable groups, the involvement and empowerment of users and innovation.[1283] The choice of the service provider shall be made on the basis of the tender presenting the best price-quality ratio, taking into account quality and sustainability criteria for social services, unless justified grounds for using the award criterion of price or cost exist, that the contracting authority takes into consideration while preparing the documentation for the award procedure. Further procedural rules may be issued by the Competent Authority of Public Contracts.[1284]

1276. These services are described in detail along with the corresponding CPV Code in Annex XIV Law No. 73(I)/2016, which corresponds to Annex XIV Directive 2014/24/EU.
1277. Section 75(1)(a) and (b) Law No. 73(I)/2016, which corresponds to Art. 75(1)(a) and (b) Directive 2014/24/EU.
1278. Sections 75(2) and 51 and Annex V Part J Law No. 73(I)/2016, which correspond to Arts 75(2) and 51 and Annex V Part J Directive 2014/24//EU.
1279. Section 75(2) Law No. 73(I)/2016, which corresponds to Art. 75(2) Directive 2014/24/EU.
1280. Sections 76(1)(a) and 57(2) Law No. 73(I)/2016. Ensuring compliance with the principles of transparency and equal treatment is a requirement set out in Art. 76(1) Directive 2014/24/EU.
1281. Section 76(1)(b) Law No. 73(I)/2016.
1282. Section 76(1)(c) *ibid.*
1283. Section 76(2) *ibid.*, which corresponds to Art. 76(2) Directive 2014/24/EU.
1284. Section 76(3)(a) and (b) Law No. 73(I)/2016, which implements last sentence of para. 2 to Art. 76 Directive 2014/24/EU.

393. The right to participate to public contracts exclusively for the award of health, social and cultural services covered by specific CPV codes,[1285] which may not have a duration longer than three years,[1286] may be reserved for specific organizations upon decision of the Council of Ministers.[1287] Such specific organizations need to fulfil all of the following conditions:

- have an objective to pursue a public service mission linked to the delivery of the services referred to above;[1288]
- reinvestment of profits with a view to achieving the organization's objective. Where profits are distributed or redistributed, this should be based on participatory considerations;[1289]
- the structures of management or ownership of the organization performing the contract are based on employee ownership or participatory principles, or require the active participation of employees, users or stakeholders;[1290] and
- the organization has not been awarded a contract for the services concerned by the contracting authority concerned pursuant to the applicable provision within the past three years.[1291]

II. Design Contracts

394. The provisions explained here apply to design contests organized as part of a procedure leading to the award of a public service contract and design contests with prizes or payments to participants. In the first set of cases the threshold (*see* in this regard paragraph 305 above) is calculated on the basis of the estimated value net of VAT of the public service contract, including any possible prizes or payments to participants. In the second set of cases the same threshold refers to the total amount of the prizes and payments, including the estimated value net of VAT of the public services contract which might subsequently be concluded, if the contracting authority has announced its intention to award such contract in the contest notice.[1292]

395. Notices of carrying out a design contest, awarding a subsequent service contract or of the results of the contest are specifically regulated.[1293] This equally

1285. These CPV codes are: 75121000-0, 75122000-7, 75123000-4, 79622000-0, 79624000-4, 79625000-1, 80110000-8, 80300000-7, 80420000-4, 80430000-7, 80511000-9, 80520000-5, 80590000-6, from 85000000-9 to 85323000-9, 92500000-6, 92600000-7, 98133000-4, 98133110-8.
1286. Section 77(3) Law No. 73(I)/2016, which corresponds to Art. 77(3) Directive 2014/24/EU.
1287. Section 77(1) Law No. 73(I)/2016, which corresponds to Art. 77(1) Directive 2014/24/EU.
1288. Section 77(2)(a) Law No. 73(I)/2016, which corresponds to Art. 77(2)(a) Directive 2014/24/EU.
1289. Section 77(2)(b) Law No. 73(I)/2016, which corresponds to Art. 77(2)(b) Directive 2014/24/EU.
1290. Section 77(2)(c) Law No. 73(I)/2016, which corresponds to Art. 77(2)(c) Directive 2014/24/EU.
1291. Section 77(2)(d) Law No. 73(I)/2016, which corresponds to Art. 77(2)(d) Directive 2014/24/EU.
1292. Sections 78, 9, 29(4), 50, 51 and Annex V Parts E and F Law No. 73(I)/2016, which correspond to Arts 78, 4, 32(4), 51(2)–(6) and 52 and Annex V Parts E and F Directive 2014/24/EU.
1293. *See* in this respect s. 79 Law No. 73(I)/2016, which corresponds to Art. 79 Directive 2014/24/EU.

applies to the organization of design contests and the selection of participants. Generally, when organizing design contests, contract authorities have to apply procedures adapted to the aforementioned on thresholds and exclusion grounds (*see* in this respect paragraphs 307 and 321 et seq. above) and to the therein provided. In particular, the admission of participants to design contests may not be limited by reference to the territory or part of the territory of Cyprus, or on the grounds that, under the law of Cyprus, they would be required to be either natural or legal persons.[1294] Should design contests be restricted to a limited number of participants, the contracting authorities underlie the statutory duty to lay down clear and non-discriminatory selection criteria. In any event, the number of candidates invited to participate shall be sufficient to ensure genuine competition.[1295]

396. The jury to reach a decision on the award of contracts is composed exclusively of natural persons who are independent of participants in the contest. Should a particular professional qualification be required from participants in a contest, at least a third of the members of the jury need to have that qualification or an equivalent one.[1296] The jury is autonomous in its decisions or opinions and examines the plans and projects submitted by the candidates anonymously and solely on the basis of the criteria indicated in the contest notice. It further records its ranking of projects in a report, signed by its members, made according to the merits of each project, together with its remarks and any points that may need clarification. The quality of anonymity needs to be observed until the jury has reached its opinion or decision. If deemed necessary, the jury has the power to invite candidates to answer questions that the jury has recorded in the minutes in order to clarify any aspect of the projects. Finally, complete minutes of the dialogue between jury members and candidates have to be made.[1297]

III. Procurement by Entities Operating in the Water, Energy, Transport and Postal Services Sectors

397. The procurement related to the water, energy, transport and postal services sectors, which is explained thereunder, is regulated in Law No. 140(I)/2016. Said sectors, which naturally define the application of this law, are specified in a detailed manner therein. The threshold amounts[1298] are generally the same as the ones set out under public contracts (*see* in this respect paragraph 350 above).

1294. Section 80(1) and (2)(a) and (b) Law No. 73(I)/2016, which corresponds to Art. 80(1) and (2)(a) and (b) Directive 2014/24/EU. On Art. 80(2) *see Parsec Fondazione Parco delle Scienze e della Cultura v. Ministero delle Infrastrutture e dei Trasporti, Autorità nazionale anticorruzione (ANAC)*, CJEU Case C-219/19, Judgment of 11 Jun. 2020, digital ECR.

1295. Section 80(3) Law No. 73(I)/2016, which corresponds to Art. 80(3) Directive 2014/24/EU.

1296. Section 81 Law No. 73(I)/2016, which corresponds to Art. 81 Directive 2014/24/EU.

1297. Section 82 Law No. 73(I)/2016, which corresponds to Art. 82 Directive 2014/24/EU.

1298. Section 10 Law No. 73(I)/2016, which corresponds to Art. 15 Directive 2014/24/EU.

398. As far as gas and heat are concerned, this law applies to the provision of operation of fixed networks intended to provide a service to the public in connection with the production, transport or distribution of gas or heat and the supply of gas or heat to such networks.[1299] However, the supply, by a contracting entity other than a contracting authority, of gas or heat to fixed networks which provide a service to the public is not considered to be a relevant activity within the aforementioned meaning, where all of the following conditions are met: the production of gas or heat by that contracting entity is the unavoidable consequence of carrying out an activity other than those referred to above and in electricity, water and transport services;[1300] and the supply to the public network is aimed only at the economic exploitation of such production and amounts to not more than 20% of the contracting entity's turnover on the basis of the average for the preceding three years, including the current year.[1301] Further to the sector of gas, this law applies to activities relating to the exploitation of a geographical area for the purposes of extracting oil or gas and exploring for, or extracting, coal or other solid fuels.[1302]

399. As far as electricity is concerned, this law applies to the provision or operation of networks intended to provide a service to the public in connection with the production, transport or distribution of electricity; and the supply of electricity to such networks.[1303] Nevertheless, the supply, by a contracting entity other than a contracting authority, of electricity to fixed networks which provide a service to the public shall is not considered to be a relevant activity within said meaning, where all of the following conditions are met: the production of electricity by that contracting entity takes place because its consumption is necessary for carrying out an activity other than those referred to above and in gas and heat, water and transport services.[1304]

400. As far as water is concerned, this law applies to the provision or operation of fixed networks intended to provide a service to the public in connection with the production, transport or distribution of drinking water and the supply of drinking water to such networks.[1305] This law also applies to contracts or design contests awarded or organized by contracting entities which pursue an activity referred to above and which are connected with one of the following: hydraulic engineering projects, irrigation or land drainage, provided that the volume of water to be used for the supply of drinking water represents more than 20% of the total volume of water made available by such projects or irrigation or drainage installations; or the

1299. Section 13(1)(a) and (b) Law No. 140(I)/2016, which corresponds to Art. 8(1)(a) and (b) Directive 2014/25/EU.
1300. Sections 13(2)(a), 14, 15 and 16 Law No. 140(I)/2016, which correspond to Arts 8(2)(a), 9, 10 and 11 Directive 2014/25/EU.
1301. Section 13(2)(b) Law No. 140(I)/2016, which corresponds to Art. 8(2)(b) Directive 2014/25/EU.
1302. Section 19 Law No. 140(I)/2016, which corresponds to Art. 14(a) and (b) Directive 2014/25/EU.
1303. Section 14(1)(a) and (b) Law No. 140(I)/2016, which corresponds to Art. 9(1)(a) and (b) Directive 2014/25/EU.
1304. Sections 14(2)(a), 13, 15 and 16 Law No. 140(I)/2016, which correspond to Arts 9(2)(a), 8, 10 and 11 Directive 2014/25/EU.
1305. Section 15(1)(a) and (b) Law No. 140(I)/2016, which corresponds to Art. 10(1)(a) and (b) Directive 2014/25/EU.

disposal or treatment of sewage.[1306] In any event, the supply, by a contracting entity other than a contracting authority, of drinking water to fixed networks which provide a service to the public are not considered to be a relevant activity within the meaning stated above, where all of the following conditions are met: the production of drinking water by that contracting entity concerned takes place because its consumption is necessary for carrying out an activity other than gas and heat, electricity, water and transport services; and the supply to the public network depends only on that contracting entity's own consumption and has not exceeded 30% of that contracting entity's total production of drinking water, on the basis of the average for the preceding three years, including the current year.[1307] It is specified that the notion of *supply* ('τροφοδότηση' in Greek, 'temin' in Turkish) mentioned above includes generation (production), wholesale and retail sale, but for production of gas in the form of extraction.[1308]

401. As far as transport services are concerned, this law applies to activities relating to the provision or operation of networks providing a service to the public in the field of transport by railway, automated systems, tramway, trolley bus, bus or cable. With reference to transport services, a network is considered to exist where the service is provided under operating conditions laid down by a competent authority of Cyprus, such as conditions on the routes to be served, the capacity to be made available or the frequency of the service.[1309] This law equally applies to activities relating to the exploitation of a geographical area for the purpose of the provision of airports and maritime or inland ports or other terminal facilities to carriers by air, sea or inland waterway.[1310] It also applies to activities relating to the provision of postal services,[1311] as well as other services than postal services,[1312] on condition

1306. Section 15(2)(a) and (b) Law No. 140(I)/2016, which corresponds to Art. 10(2)(a) and (b) Directive 2014/25/EU.
1307. Section 15(3)(a) and (b) Law No. 140(I)/2016, which corresponds to Art. 10(3)(a) and (b) Directive 2014/25/EU.
1308. Section 12 Law No. 140(I)/2016, which corresponds to Art. 7 Directive 2014/25/EU. The term supply used in this law is wider than the term supply ('προμήθεια' in Greek, 'temin' in Turkish), as defined in Art. 2(19) Directive 2009/72/EC, which does not include production.
1309. Section 16(1) and (2) Law No. 140(I)/2016, which corresponds to Art. 11 Directive 2014/25/EU.
1310. Section 17 Law No. 140(I)/2016, which corresponds to Art. 12 Directive 2014/25/EU.
1311. Postal services mean services consisting of the clearance, sorting, routing and delivery of postal items. This term includes both services falling within and services falling outside the scope of the universal service set up in conformity with Directive 97/67/EC. Section 18(2)(b) Law No. 140(I)/2016, which corresponds to Art. 13(2)(b) Directive 2014/25/EU. On Arts 13 and 6 *see Irideos S.p.A. v. Poste Italiane S.p.A.*, CJEU Case C-419/19, OJ C 328, 30 Sep. 2019, p. 5 (case pending).
1312. This term means services provided in the following areas: mail service management services (services both preceding and subsequent to despatch, including mailroom management services) and services concerning postal items not included under the aforementioned, such as direct mail bearing no address. Section 18(2)(c) Law No. 140(I)/2016, which corresponds to Art. 13(2)(c) Directive 2014/25/EU.

that such services are provided by an entity which also provides postal services provided that the condition of the specific activity being directly exposed to competition on markets to which access is not restricted is not satisfied in respect of said services.[1313]

402. Turning to the rules on the formation of contracts, the general principles set out for public contracts (*see* in this respect paragraphs 309 et seq. above) equally apply here.[1314] The procedures available in procurement by entities operating in the sectors explained here are open procedure, restricted procedure, negotiated procedure with prior call for competition competitive dialogue, innovation partnership and use of the negotiated procedure without prior call for competition. Open procedure ('ανοικτή διαδικασία' in Greek, 'açık ihale usulü' in Turkish),[1315] competitive dialogue ('ανταγωνιστικός διάλογος' in Greek, 'doğrudan temin')[1316] and innovation partnership ('σύμπραξη καινοτομίας' in Greek, 'yenileşim ortaklığı' in Turkish)[1317] are the same as the ones explained above under public contracts (*see* in this respect paragraphs 355 et seq. above).

403. The procedures with contents that differentiate from the one in public contracts are the following. Restricted procedure ('κλειστή διαδικασία' in Greek, 'belli istekliler arasında ihale usulü' in Turkish) stands for a procedure, during which any economic operator submits a request to participate in response to a call for competition by providing the information for qualitative selection that is requested by the contracting entity. As a general rule, the minimum time limit for the receipt of requests to participate is fixed at no less than thirty days from the date on which the contract notice or the invitation to confirm interest was sent and, in any event, it may be no less than fifteen days.[1318] Only those economic operators invited to do so by the contracting entity following its assessment of the information provided may submit a tender.[1319] Similarly, in negotiated procedures with prior call for competition ('διαδικασία με διαπραγμάτευση με προηγούμενη προκήρυξη διαγωνισμού' in Greek, 'ilan yapılan hallerde pazarlık usulü' in Turkish), any economic operator may submit a request to participate in response to a call for competition by providing the information for qualitative selection that is requested by the contracting entity. The minimum time limits are the ones already set out above for restricted

1313. Sections 18(1) and 35(1) Law No. 140(I)/2016, which correspond to Arts 13(1) and 34(1) Directive 2014/25/EU.
1314. Sections 4 and 6 Law No. 140(I)/2016, which correspond to Arts 36 and 42 Directive 2014/25/EU.
1315. Section 39 Law No. 140(I)/2016, which corresponds to Art. 45 Directive 2014/25/EU.
1316. Section 42 Law No. 140(I)/2016, which corresponds to Art. 48 Directive 2014/25/EU.
1317. Section 43 Law No. 140(I)/2016, which corresponds to Art. 49 Directive 2014/25/EU.
1318. Section 40(1) and (2) Law No. 140(I)/2016, which corresponds to Art. 46(1) Directive 2014/25/EU.
1319. Section 40(3) Law No. 140(I)/2016, which corresponds to Art. 46(2) Directive 2014/25/EU.

procedures.[1320] Also, only those economic operators invited by the contracting entity following its assessment of the information provided may participate in the negotiations.[1321]

404. Finally, the negotiated procedure without prior call for competition ('διαδικασία με διαπραγμάτευση χωρίς προηγούμενη προκήρυξη διαγωνισμού' in Greek, 'ilan yapılmayan hallerde pazarlık usulü' in Turkish) may be used by contracting agencies in the following cases:

- where no tenders or no suitable tenders or no requests to participate or no suitable requests to participate have been submitted in response to a procedure with a prior call for competition, provided that the initial conditions of the contract are not substantially altered;[1322]
- where a contract is purely for the purpose of research, experiment, study or development, and not for the purpose of securing a profit or of recovering research and development costs, and insofar as the award of such contract does not prejudice the competitive award of subsequent contracts which do seek, in particular, those ends;[1323]
- where the works, supplies or services can be supplied only by a particular economic operator for any of the following reasons: the aim of the procurement is the creation or acquisition of a unique work of art or artistic performance; competition is absent for technical reasons; and the protection of exclusive rights, including intellectual property rights. The last two exceptions apply only when no reasonable alternative or substitute exists and the absence of competition is not the result of an artificial narrowing down of the parameters of the procurement;[1324]
- in so far as is strictly necessary where, for reasons of extreme urgency brought about by events unforeseeable by the contracting entity, the time limits laid down for open procedures, restricted procedures and negotiated procedures with prior call for competition cannot be complied with. The circumstances invoked to justify extreme urgency shall not in any event be attributable to the contracting entity;[1325]
- in the case of supply contracts for additional deliveries by the original supplier which are intended either as a partial replacement of supplies or installations or as the extension of existing supplies or installations, where a change of supplier would oblige the contracting entity to acquire supplies having different technical characteristics which would result in incompatibility or disproportionate technical difficulties in operation and maintenance;[1326]

1320. Section 41(1) and (2) Law No. 140(I)/2016, which corresponds to Art. 47(1) Directive 2014/25/EU.
1321. Section 41(3) Law No. 140(I)/2016, which corresponds to Art. 47(2) Directive 2014/25/EU.
1322. Section 44(a) Law No. 140(I)/2016, which corresponds to Art. 50(a) Directive 2014/25/EU.
1323. Section 44(b) Law No. 140(I)/2016, which corresponds to Art. 50(b) Directive 2014/25/EU.
1324. Section 44(c) Law No. 140(I)/2016, which corresponds to Art. 50(c) Directive 2014/25/EU.
1325. Section 44(d) Law No. 140(I)/2016, which corresponds to Art. 50(d) Directive 2014/25/EU.
1326. Section 44(e) Law No. 140(I)/2016, which corresponds to Art. 50(e) Directive 2014/25/EU.

- for new works or services consisting in the repetition of similar works or services assigned to the contractor to which the same contracting entities awarded an earlier contract, provided that such works or services conform to a basic project for which a first contract was awarded according to the statutory choice of procedures;[1327]
- for supplies quoted and purchased on a commodity market;[1328]
- for bargain purchases, where it is possible to procure supplies by taking advantage of a particularly advantageous opportunity available for a very short time at a price considerably lower than normal market prices;[1329]
- for purchases of supplies or services under particularly advantageous conditions from either a supplier which is definitively winding up its business activities or the liquidator in an insolvency procedure, an arrangement with creditors or a similar procedure under national laws or regulations;[1330] and
- where the service contract concerned follows a design contest organized in accordance with this law and is to be awarded, under the rules provided for in the design contest, to the winner or to one of the winners of that contest; in the latter case, all the winners shall be invited to participate in the negotiations.[1331]

405. Contracting entities have the discretionary power to apply the same exclusion grounds and the selection criteria applicable to public contracts (*see* in this respect paragraphs 365 et seq. and 371 et seq. above).[1332] Further, they have the same confidentiality duties, as the ones already explained above under public contracts (*see* in this respect paragraphs 386 et seq. above).[1333] Breach of duties leads to same penalties described above regarding public contracts.[1334]

IV. Procurement by Entities Operating in the Defence and Security Sector

406. Procurement in the defence and security sector is regulated in Law No. 173(I)/2011. Defence and security, which are decisive in the application of this law, are specified therein, as it is explained below. The threshold amounts, which constitute a further concurrent condition for the application of this law, are a value excluding VAT estimated to be no less than the following: EUR 387,000 for supply and service contracts and EUR 8,845,000 for works contracts.[1335] Said amounts are calculated in a statutory defined manner.[1336]

1327. Section 44(f) Law No. 140(I)/2016, which corresponds to Art. 50(f) Directive 2014/25/EU.
1328. Section 44(g) Law No. 140(I)/2016, which corresponds to Art. 50(g) Directive 2014/25/EU.
1329. Section 44(h) Law No. 140(I)/2016, which corresponds to Art. 50(h) Directive 2014/25/EU.
1330. Section 44(i) Law No. 140(I)/2016, which corresponds to Art. 50(i) Directive 2014/25/EU.
1331. Section 44(j) Law No. 140(I)/2016, which corresponds to Art. 50(j) Directive 2014/25/EU.
1332. Section 77 Law No. 140(I)/2016, which corresponds to Art. 80 Directive 2014/25/EU.
1333. Section 5 Law No. 140(I)/2016, which corresponds to Art. 39 Directive 2014/25/EU.
1334. Section 105(1), (2), (3), (4) and (5) Law No. 140(I)/2016.
1335. Section 9(a) and (b) Law No. 173(I)/2011, which corresponds to Art. 8 Directive 2009/81/EC. Albeit the European provision provides for thresholds of EUR 443,000 and EUR 5,548,000 respectively.
1336. Section 10 Law No. 173(I)/2011, which corresponds to Art. 9 Directive 2009/81/EC.

407. In said law, it is specified that this law applies, subject to Articles 36, 51, 52, 62 and 346 TFEU, to contracts awarded in the fields of defence and security for: the supply of military equipment, including any parts, components and/or subassemblies thereof; the supply of sensitive equipment, including any parts, components and/or subassemblies thereof; works, supplies and services directly related to the equipment referred to above for any and all elements of its life cycle; and works and services for specifically military purposes or sensitive works and sensitive services.[1337] The term classified information ('διαβαθμισμένες πληροφορίες' in Greek, 'gizli bilgiler' in Turkish) stands here in the foreground, as it assigns the quality of sensitivity to equipment, works and services, and hence causes the application of this law. Specifically, it means any information or material, regardless of the form, nature or mode of transmission thereof, to which a certain level of security classification or protection has been attributed, and which, in the interests of national security and in accordance with the laws, regulations or administrative provisions in force in Cyprus, requires protection against any misappropriation, destruction, removal, disclosure, loss or access by any unauthorized individual, or any other type of compromise.[1338] Further, military equipment ('στρατιωτικός εξοπλισμός' in Greek, 'askerî ekipmanları' in Turkish) means equipment specifically designed or adapted for military purposes and intended for use as an arm, munitions or war material.[1339]

408. In any event, some specific contracts explicitly set out in the law, such as contracts for the purposes of intelligence activities and contracts awarded by a government to another government relating to the supply of military equipment or sensitive equipment, works and services directly linked to such equipment or works and services specifically for military purposes, or sensitive works and sensitive services, are excluded from the material application of this law.[1340] Such exception is equally foreseen for contracts awarded pursuant to international rules and reserved contracts.[1341]

409. The general principles governing procurement equally mandate contracting authorities and entities treat economic operators equally and in a non-discriminatory manner, as well as to act in a transparent way.[1342] The procedures to be applied are the restricted procedure, the negotiated procedure with publication of a contract notice and, under circumstances, the competitive dialogue or a negotiated procedure without publication of a contract notice.[1343] In the negotiated procedures with publication of a contract notice ('διαδικασία διαπραγμάτευσης με δημοσίευση

1337. Section 3 Law No. 173(I)/2011, which corresponds to Art. 2 Directive 2009/81/EC.
1338. Section 2 Law No. 173(I)/2011, which corresponds to Art. 1(8) Directive 2009/81/EC.
1339. Section 2 Law No. 173(I)/2011, which corresponds to Art. 2(6) Directive 2009/81/EC.
1340. Section 13(a)–(j) Law No. 173(I)/2011, which corresponds to Art. 13(a)–(j) Directive 2009/81/EC.
1341. Sections 12 and 14 Law No. 173(I)/2011, which correspond to Arts 12 and 14 Directive 2009/81/EC.
1342. Section 5 Law No. 173(I)/2011, which corresponds to Art. 4 Directive 2009/81/EC.
1343. Section 25 Law No. 173(I)/2011, which corresponds to Art. 25 Directive 2009/81/EC.

προκήρυξης της σύμβασης' in Greek, 'ilan yapılan hallerde pazarlık usulü' in Turkish) contracting authorities or entities negotiate with tenderers the tenders submitted by them in order to adapt them to the requirements they have set in the contract notice, the contract documents and supporting documents, if any, and to seek out the best tender in accordance with the contract award criteria.[1344] Competitive dialogue ('ανταγωνιστικός διάλογος' in Greek, 'doğrudan temin' in Turkish) is used in the case of particularly complex contracts.[1345] Contracts are deemed to be particularly complex when contracting authorities and entities are objectively not in a position to determine the technical means that could satisfy their needs and aims and/or they are not able to determine the legal and/or financial organization of a plan.[1346] In this regard, mention deserves the well-founded German principle of law ('Vorbehalt des Gesetzes'), according to which failure of public administration to determine the legal grounds on which it operates, equals for it acting beyond its statutory assigned powers and, hence, disregard the rule of law. Said German principle is applicable in Cyprus, due to Cypriot case law allowing for judgments of German courts to unfold the effect of precedent in Cyprus.[1347] Thus, any use of this provision should be discouraged. Further to competitive dialogue, contracting authorities and entities publish a contract notice setting out their needs and requirements, which they define in that notice and/or in a descriptive document.[1348] They then open with the candidates selected a dialogue, the aim of which is to identify and define the means best suited to satisfying their needs, during which they may discuss all aspects of the contract with the chosen candidates.[1349] While conducting said dialogue, they further bear the duty of equality of treatment among all tenderers and of not disclosing solutions proposed or other confidential information communicated by a participating candidate, without the agreement of that candidate.[1350] In this procedure, a contract is awarded on the sole basis of the award criterion for the most economically advantageous tender.[1351] The negotiated procedure without publication of a contract notice ('διαδικασία διαπραγμάτευσης χωρίς δημοσίευση προκήρυξης της σύμβασης' in Greek, 'ilan yapılmayan hallerde pazarlık usulü' in Turkish) may only be used in cases explicitly set out in this law that differentiate among works contracts,[1352] supply contracts,[1353] service contracts[1354] and contracts related to the

1344. Sections 26(1) and 48 Law No. 173(I)/2011, which correspond to Arts 26(1) and 47 Directive 2009/81/EC.
1345. Section 28(1) Law No. 173(I)/2011, which corresponds to Art. 27(1) Directive 2009/81/EC.
1346. Section 28(1)(a) and (b) Law No. 173(I)/2011. No definition of *particularly complex contracts* is offered in Directive 2009/81/EC.
1347. *Stelios Morsis v. Cyprus* 1 JSC 12 (1965).
1348. Section 28(3) Law No. 173(I)/2011, which corresponds to Art. 27(2) Directive 2009/81/EC.
1349. Section 28(4)(a) Law No. 173(I)/2011, which corresponds to Art. 27(3) Directive 2009/81/EC.
1350. Section 28(4)(b) and (c) Law No. 173(I)/2011, which corresponds to Art. 27(3) Directive 2009/81/EC.
1351. Section 28(2) Law No. 173(I)/2011, which corresponds to Art. 27(1) Directive 2009/81/EC.
1352. Section 27(a) and (d) Law No. 173(I)/2011, which corresponds to Art. 28(1) and (4) Directive 2009/81/EC.
1353. Section 27(a), (b) and (c) Law No. 173(I)/2011, which corresponds to Art. 28(1), (2) and (3) Directive 2009/81/EC.
1354. Section 27(a) and (b) Law No. 173(I)/2011, which corresponds to Art. 28(1) and (2) Directive 2009/81/EC.

provision of air and maritime transport services.[1355] One of these statutory cases, which is characteristic for the defence and security sector, is when the periods laid down for the restricted procedure and negotiated procedure with publication of a contract notice, are incompatible with the urgency resulting from a crisis.[1356] Crisis ('κρίση' in Greek, 'kriz' in Turkish) means any situation in a Member State or third country in which a harmful event has occurred which clearly exceeds the dimensions of harmful events in everyday life and which substantially endangers or restricts the life and health of people, or has a substantial impact on property values, or requires measures in order to supply the population with necessities. A crisis is also deemed to have arisen if the occurrence of such a harmful event is deemed to be impending. Finally, armed conflicts and wars equally fall under the notion of crisis.[1357]

410. The contract award criteria are explicitly set out in this law. It is foreseen that these are either various criteria linked to the subject matter of the contract in question, such as quality, price, technical merit, functional characteristics, environmental characteristics, running costs, life-cycle costs, cost-effectiveness, aftersales service and technical assistance, when the award is made to the most economically advantageous tender from the point of view of the contracting authority or entity; or the lowest price only.[1358] In the first case, the contracting authority or entity has to specify in the contract documentation the relative weighting which it gives to each of the criteria chosen to determine the most economically advantageous tender. The weightings can be expressed by providing for a range with an appropriate maximum spread. Should, however, in the opinion of the contracting authority or entity, weighting not be possible for demonstrable reasons, the contracting authority or entity indicates in the contract documentation the criteria in descending order of importance.[1359]

411. With reference to confidentiality, this law protects not only confidential information, which includes, in particular, technical or trade secrets and the confidential aspects of tenders, through imposing non-disclosure duties to contracting authorities and entities.[1360] Furthermore, it protects classified information by enabling contracting authorities and entities to impose on economic operators requirements aimed at protecting such information, which is communicated throughout the tendering and contracting procedure. Contracting authorities and entities may also request these economic operators to ensure compliance with such requirements by their subcontractors.[1361] With reference to security of information, it is further set out that, when contracts involve, require and/or contain classified

1355. Section 27(e) Law No. 173(I)/2011, which corresponds to Art. 28(5) Directive 2009/81/EC.
1356. Section 27(a)(iii) Law No. 173(I)/2011, which corresponds to Art. 28(1)(c) Directive 2009/81/EC.
1357. Section 2 Law No. 173(I)/2011, which corresponds to Art. 1(10) Directive 2009/81/EC.
1358. Section 48(1) Law No. 173(I)/2011, which corresponds to Art. 47(1) Directive 2009/81/EC.
1359. Section 48(2) and (3) Law No. 173(I)/2011, which corresponds to Art. 47(2) Directive 2009/81/EC.
1360. Section 7 Law No. 173(I)/2011, which corresponds to Art. 6 Directive 2009/81/EC.
1361. Section 8 Law No. 173(I)/2011, which corresponds to Art. 7 Directive 2009/81/EC.

information, the contracting authority or entity shall specify in the contract documentation the measures and requirements necessary to ensure the security of such information at the requisite level.[1362] To this end, the contracting authority has the discretionary power of requiring that the tender contains, *inter alia*, the following particulars:

- a commitment from the tenderer and the subcontractors already identified to appropriately safeguard the confidentiality of all classified information in their possession or coming to their notice throughout the duration of the contract and after termination or conclusion of the contract, in accordance with the relevant laws, regulations and administrative provisions;[1363]
- a commitment from the tenderer to obtain the commitment provided above from other subcontractors to which it will subcontract during the execution of the contract;[1364]
- sufficient information on subcontractors already identified to enable the contracting authority or entity to determine that each of them possesses the capabilities required to appropriately safeguard the confidentiality of the classified information to which they have access or which they are required to produce when carrying out their subcontracting activities;[1365] and
- a commitment from the tenderer to provide the information required immediately above on any new subcontractor before awarding a subcontract.[1366]

412. Breach of said duties constitutes a crime, as per the aforementioned under public contracts and procurement in the water, energy, transport and postal services sectors. However, the penalties that may be imposed are harsher, when the committed crimes involve classified information. The monetary fine is up to EUR 20,000 along with imprisonment for the maximum period of five years.[1367]

§6. Termination of Public Contracts

413. Contracting authorities have the power under the following circumstances and under the conditions set out in the Law of Contracts, Cap. 149, to set out in the documentation of the procedure of awarding contracts, the option of terminating a public contract during its term. This is possible, as long as it is evidenced, that: the contract has undergone a substantial modification, which would have required a new procurement procedure;[1368] the contractor has, at the time of contract award, been in one of the statutory situations of exclusion and should therefore have been

1362. Section 22(1) Law No. 173(I)/2011, which corresponds to Art. 22 Directive 2009/81/EC.
1363. Section 22(2)(a) Law No. 173(I)/2011, which corresponds to Art. 22(a) Directive 2009/81/EC.
1364. Section 22(2)(b) Law No. 173(I)/2011, which corresponds to Art. 22(b) Directive 2009/81/EC.
1365. Section 22(2)(c) Law No. 173(I)/2011, which corresponds to Art. 22(c) Directive 2009/81/EC.
1366. Section 22(2)(d) Law No. 173(I)/2011, which corresponds to Art. 22(d) Directive 2009/81/EC.
1367. Section 56(1), (2), (3), (4) and (5) Law No. 173(I)/2011.
1368. Sections 73(a) and 72 Law No. 73(I)/2016, which correspond to Arts 73(a) and 72 Directive 2014/24/EU.

excluded from the procurement procedure;[1369] and the contract should not have been awarded to the contractor in view of a serious infringement of the obligations under the Treaties and this directive that has been declared by the Court of Justice of the EU in a procedure pursuant to Article 258 TFEU.[1370]

1369. Sections 73(b) and 57(1) Law No. 73(I)/2016, which correspond to Arts 73(b) and 57(1) Directive 2014/24/EU.

1370. Section 73(c) Law No. 73(I)/2016, which corresponds to Art. 73(c) Directive 2014/24/EU. Article 258 TFEU reads '[i]f the Commission considers that a Member State has failed to fulfil an obligation under the Treaties, it shall deliver a reasoned opinion on the matter after giving the State concerned the opportunity to submit its observations. If the State concerned does not comply with the opinion within the period laid down by the Commission, the latter may bring the matter before the Court of Justice of the European Union'.

Chapter 12. Contract of Partnership

414. Partnerships are regulated in the Law on Partnerships[1371] (hereinafter 'Cap. 116'). Partnership ('συνεταιρισμός' in Greek, 'kollektif şirket' in Turkish) is the relation, which subsists between persons carrying on a business in common with a view of profit.[1372] But the relation between members of any company or association which is registered as a company under any Law relating to the registration of limited liability companies, or formed or incorporated by or in pursuance of any other Law, is not a partnership within the meaning of this Law.[1373] Partnership may be general or limited.

§1. Parties to Partnership

415. General partner ('ομόρρυθμος συνεταίρος' in Greek, 'genel ortak' in Turkish) is any partner who is not a limited partner as defined by this Law. Limited partner ('ετερόρρυθμος συνεταίρος' in Greek, 'sınırlı ortak' in Turkish) is a person, who during the time of joining the partnership or later, contributes an amount of money as capital for the limited partnership or asset, and who does not have responsibility for the debts or the obligations of the partnership beyond the amount of his contribution.[1374]

416. In addition to the above definitions, there are numerical limitations to parties to partnership. A partnership may be formed for the purpose of carrying on any business that has for its object the acquisition of gain by the partnership or by the individual members thereof, under the condition that it consists of 100 persons or less.[1375] Especially for the purpose of carrying on the business of banking, said limitation is ten persons.[1376]

§2. Formation of Partnership

417. Whether or not a given venture falls within the definition of partnership is a question of mixed law and fact depending on the circumstances of the particular case.[1377] In addition, in determining whether a partnership does or does not exist, the following rules are regarded. Joint tenancy, tenancy in common, joint property, common property, or part ownership does not of itself create a partnership as to anything so held or owned, whether tenants or owners do or do not share any profits

1371. Partnership of 12 May 1928, Ch. 116 of the Laws, London, 1959 edition, as amended.
1372. Section 5(1) Cap. 116. *See* in this regard *Tamassos Tobacco Suppliers and Co. v. The Republic of Cyprus* 3A CLR 219 (1989).
1373. Section 5(2) Cap. 116.
1374. Section 2 *ibid.*
1375. Section 3(2) *ibid.*
1376. Section 3(1) *ibid.*
1377. *Kurt Kingsfield v. The Republic of Cyprus* 3 CLR 45 (1966).

made by the use thereof.[1378] The sharing of gross returns does not in itself create a partnership, whether the persons sharing such returns have or have not a joint or common right or interest in any property from which or from the use of which are derived.[1379] The receipt by a person of a share of the profits of a business is prima facie evidence that he is a partner in the business, but the receipt of such a share, or of a payment contingent on or varying with the profits of a business does not of itself make him a partner in the business.[1380] In particular, the receipt by a person of a debt or other liquidated amount, by instalments or otherwise, out of the accruing profits of a business does not of itself make him a partner in the business or liable as such.[1381] Equally, a contract for the remuneration of a servant or agent of a person engaged in a business by a share of the profits of the business does not of itself make the servant or agent a partner in the business or liable as such.[1382] In addition, a person being the widow or child of a deceased partner, and receiving by way of annuity a portion of the profits made in the business in which the deceased person was a partner, is not, by reason only of such receipt, a partner in the business or liable as such.[1383] Further, the advance of money by way of loan to a person engaged or about to engage in any business on a contract with that person that the lender shall receive a rate of interest varying with the profits, or shall receive a share of the profits arising from carrying on the business, does not make the lender a partner with the person or persons carrying on the business or liable as such.[1384] Similarly, a person receiving, by way of annuity or otherwise, a portion of the profits of a business in consideration of the sale by him of the goodwill of the business is not, by reason only of such receipt, a partner in the business or liable as such.[1385] Finally, especially in cases of co-owners of an estate or interest in any land, not being itself partnership property, who are partners as to profits made by the use of that land or estate and purchase other land or estate out of the profits to be used in like manner, the land or estate so purchased belongs to them as co-owners and not as partners. However, aside from this statutory provision, they are free to reach an agreement to the contrary.[1386]

418. Aside from the aforementioned on establishing the essence of a partnership in a negative manner, the following typical conditions are applicable. First, every partnership whether general or limited carrying on business in Cyprus has to be registered in the statutory directed manner.[1387] The registration of a partnership is effected by sending by post or delivering to the Registrar, within one month of the date of its establishment, a statement in the prescribed form signed by all the partners and containing the following particulars: the name of the house; the general

1378. Section 6(a) Cap. 116.
1379. Section 6(b) *ibid.*
1380. Section 6(c) *ibid.*
1381. Section 6(c)(i) *ibid.*
1382. Section 6(c)(ii) *ibid.*
1383. Section 6(c)(iii) *ibid.*
1384. Section 6(c)(iv) *ibid.*
1385. Section 6(c)(v) *ibid.*
1386. Section 23(2) *ibid.*
1387. Section 50(a) *ibid.*

nature of the business; the principal place of the business; the current name(s) and surname, the nationality and the usual residence of each of the individuals, who are partners, whether general or limited, and the corporate name and registered or principal office of every corporation which is a partner.[1388] Said statement further contains the term, if any for which the partnership is entered into, and the date of its commencement, a statement, if such be the case, that the partnership is limited, the sum or the stocks already contributed or shall be contributed to and/or by each limited partner and whether paid in cash or how otherwise, along with the names of the general partners who are authorized to administer the affairs of the partnership, to manage it and to sign for it.[1389] Where the business of the firm is carried on under two or more names, each of those names must be stated.[1390] Any change made or occurred to said particulars has to be communicated to the Registrar within seven days.[1391]

419. The Registrar has discretion regarding the registration of the name of the partnership[1392] and he is therefore obliged to properly and lawfully exercise his discretion.[1393] On receiving any statement made in pursuance to the aforementioned the Registrar causes the same to be filed and registered if satisfied that the provisions of this law have been complied with. He then sends to the firm or person from whom such statement has been received a certificate in the prescribed form of the registration thereof.[1394] It has been held that the registration of a partnership does not create any rights additional to those deriving from the partnership contract. Neither the keeping of a register nor its availability for inspection can possibly alter the character of the act of registration.[1395] Further, the Registrar publishes this entry in the Official Gazette, as his duty for every entry made on the register under the provisions of this law. Nonetheless, the Registrar has the authority to replace the publication in the Official Gazette with publication in an electronic gazette operated by himself, as long as the Council of Ministers has authorized him to do so.[1396]

420. Especially limited partnerships must consist of one or more persons called general partners, who shall be liable for all debts and obligations of the firm, and one or more persons to be called limited partners, who shall at the time of entering into such partnership contribute thereto a sum or sums as capital or property valued at a stated amount and for which a specific amount of shares may be issued, and who shall not be liable for the debts or obligations of the firm beyond the amount so contributed.[1397] Along with this material element, the law sets out an additional

1388. Section 51(1)(a), (b), (c) and (d) *ibid.*
1389. Section 51(1)(e), (f), (g) and (h) *ibid.*
1390. Section 51(2) *ibid. See* in this regard *Tamassos Tobacco Suppliers and Co. v. The Republic of Cyprus* 3A CLR 214 (1989).
1391. Section 54 Cap. 116.
1392. Section 55 *ibid. Papacharalambous a.o. v. The Republic of Cyprus* 3A CLR 342 (1989).
1393. *Fashions House v. The Republic of Cyprus* 3 CLR 231(1973).
1394. Section 56(1) Cap. 116. *Takis Photiades v. The Republic of Cyprus* 3 CLR 460 (1986).
1395. *Photiades v. Photiades* 3 CLR 2084 (1988).
1396. Section 59 Cap. 116.
1397. Section 47(2) *ibid.*

typical one. Every limited partnership must be registered as such in accordance with the provisions of this law. In default thereof, the unregistered limited partnership is deemed to be a general partnership, and every limited partner is deemed to be a general partner.[1398] Especially with reference to limited partners, who may not be a legal person,[1399] they may not during the continuance of the partnership, either directly or indirectly, draw out or receive back any part of their contribution. Should they do so, any such part shall be liable for the debts and obligations of the firm up to the amount so drawn out or received back.[1400] A limited partnership may have capital and be of limited liability via shares.[1401] However, such a partnership, regardless of it having a capital or not, is not considered to be a legal person with a distinct legal personality.[1402]

§3. Content of Partnership

421. The partnership agreement along with the purposes of the partnership mandate the manner in which partnership property is held and applied by the partners. Partnership property ('περιουσία συνεταιρισμού' in Greek, 'kollektif şirket malları' in Turkish) stands for all property and rights and interests in property originally brought into the partnership stock or acquired, whether by purchase or otherwise, on account of the firm, or for the purposes and in the course of the partnership business; provided that the legal estate or interest in any land belongs to the partnership shall devolve according to the nature and tenure thereof and the general rules of the law thereto applicable, but in trust, so far as necessary, for the persons beneficially interested in the land under this section.[1403] In addition, it is deemed that property bought with money belonging to the firm, has been bought on account of the firm, unless the contrary intention appears.[1404]

422. The partnership agreement may provide for an agreed fixed term for the duration of the partnership.[1405] Where such a partnership is continued after the term has expired, and without any express new agreement, the rights and duties of the partners remain the same, as they were at the expiration of the term, so far as is consistent with the incidents of a partnership at will.[1406] A continuance of the business by the partners or such of them as habitually acted therein during the term, without any settlement or liquidation of the partnership affairs, is presumed to be a continuance of the partnership.[1407]

1398. Section 48 *ibid.*
1399. Section 47(4) *ibid.*
1400. Section 47(3) *ibid.*
1401. Section 47(5) *ibid.*
1402. Section 47(6) *ibid.*
1403. Section 23(1) *ibid.*
1404. Section 24 *ibid.*
1405. Section 28(1) *ibid.*
1406. Section 29(1) *ibid.*
1407. Section 29(2) *ibid.*

423. The mutual rights and duties of parties, whether ascertained by agreement or defined by Cap. 116, may be varied by the consent of all partners. Such consent may be either express or inferred from a course of dealing.[1408] Finally, the partnership agreement may set out the power of majority of partners to expel any partner. In the event that such an explicit provision is absent, this may not be decided.[1409]

§4. The Parties' Duties and Responsibilities

424. Specific provisions regulate the effects of partners' acts onto the firm, such as representation, and relevant liability issues. Every partner is an agent of the firm and his other partners for the purpose of the business of the partnership. Similarly, the acts of every partner, who does any act for carrying on in the usual way business of the kind carried on by the firm of which he is a member bind the firm and his partners. This, however, does not apply, when the partner so acting has in fact no authority to act for the firm in the particular matter, and the person with whom he is dealing either knows that he has no authority or does not know or believe him to be a partner.[1410] Any pledge of the credit of the firm for a purpose apparently not connected with the firm's ordinary course of business does not bind the firm, unless the partner doing so is in fact specially authorized by the other partners. However, this does not affect any personal liability incurred by an individual partner.[1411] Further, an agreed restriction to the power of any partner to bind the firm results into no act done in contravention of the agreement to be binding on the firm. Yet, this effect is restricted solely to persons having notice of the agreement.[1412] Especially an act or instrument relating to the business of the firm and done or executed in the firm name, or in any other manner showing an intention to bind the firm, by any person thereto authorized, whether a partner or not, is binding on the firm and all the partners. Provided that this does not affect any general rule of law relating to the execution of deeds or negotiable instruments.[1413] Finally, a provision on liability by 'holding out' ('παραστάσεις' in Greek, 'gizleyenler' in Turkish) is set out. Everyone who, by words spoken or written, or by conduct, represents himself, or who knowingly suffers himself to be represented, as a partner in a particular firm, is liable as a partner to anyone who has, on the faith of any such representation, given credit to the firm, whether the representation has or has not been made or communicated to the person so giving credit by or with knowledge of the apparent partner making the representation or suffering it to be made. Provided that where after a partner's death the partnership business is continued in the old firm name, the continued use of that name or of the deceased partner's name as part thereof shall not make his executors or administrators estate or effects liable for any partnership debts contracted after his death.[1414]

1408. Section 22 *ibid.*
1409. Section 27 *ibid.*
1410. Section 8 *ibid.*
1411. Section 10 *ibid.*
1412. Section 11 *ibid.*
1413. Section 9 *ibid.*
1414. Section 17 *ibid. See* in this respect *Voniatis v. Koureas a.a.* 1 CLR 492 (1979).

425. The interests of partners in the partnership property and their rights and duties in relation to the partnership may be determined in any express or implied agreement between the parties. If such an agreement is not reached, the following set of statutory rules apply:

- All the partners are entitled to share equally in the capital and profits of the business, and must contribute equally towards the losses, whether of capital or otherwise, sustained by the firm.[1415]
- The firm must indemnify every partner in respect of payments made and personal liabilities incurred by him in the ordinary and proper conduct of the business of the firm, or in or about anything necessarily done for the preservation of the business or property of the firm.[1416]
- A partner making, for the purposes of the partnership, any actual payment or advance beyond the amount of capital which he has agreed to subscribe, is entitled to interest at the right of nine per centum per annum from the date of the payment or advance.[1417]
- A partner is not entitled, before the ascertainment of profits, to invest in the capital subscribed by him.[1418]
- Every partner may take part in the management of the partnership business.[1419]
- No partner shall be entitled to remuneration for acting in the partnership business.[1420]
- No person may be introduced as a partner without the consent of all existing partners.[1421]
- Any difference arising as to ordinary matters connected with the partnership business may be decided by a majority of the partners, but no charge may be made in the nature of the partnership business without the consent of all existing partners.[1422]
- The partnership books are to be kept at the place of business of the partnership (or the principal place, if there are more places than one), and every partner may, when he thinks fit, have access to and inspect and copy any of them.[1423]

426. With reference to partners' liability issues, it is set out that every partner in a firm is liable jointly with the other partners for all debts and obligations of the firm incurred while he is a partner. In the event of a partner's death, his estate is also severally liable in a due course of administration for such debts and obligations, so far as they remain unsatisfied but subject to the prior payment of his separate debts.[1424] This liability does have time limits. In particular, a partner is not liable to

---

1415. Section 26(a) Cap. 116.
1416. Section 26(b)(i) and (ii) *ibid.*
1417. Section 26(c) *ibid.*
1418. Section 26(d) *ibid.*
1419. Section 26(e) *ibid.*
1420. Section 26(f) *ibid.*
1421. Section 26(g) *ibid.*
1422. Section 26(h) *ibid.*
1423. Section 26(i) *ibid.*
1424. Section 12 *ibid.*

the creditors of the firm for anything done prior to him being admitted as a partner.[1425] Similarly, a partner retiring from a firm does not cease to be liable for partnership debts or obligations incurred before his retirement.[1426] A retiring partner may, however, be discharged from any existing liabilities, by an agreement to that effect between himself and the members of the firm as newly constituted and the creditors. This agreement may be either express or inferred as a fact from the course of dealing between the creditors and the firm as newly constituted.[1427] Further limits are set by improperly ('αντικανονικά' in Greek, 'usulsüz' in Turkish) employing trust property in the business or on the account of the partnership by a partner, being a trustee. In such an event, no other partner is liable for the trust property to the persons beneficially interested therein.[1428] This, however, does not affect any liability incurred by any partner by reason of his having notice of a breach of trust.[1429] Equally, it does not prevent trust money from being followed and recovered from the firm, if still in its possession or under its control.[1430]

427. Every partner is accountable towards other partners. In particular, he has the statutory duty to account to the firm for any benefit derived by him, without the consent of the other partners, from any transaction concerning the partnership or from any use by him of the partnership property, name or business connection.[1431] This also applies to transactions undertaken after a partnership has been dissolved by the death of a partner and before the affairs thereof have been completely wound up, either by any surviving partner or by the representatives of the deceased partner.[1432] He further equally bears a statutory duty to account for and over to the firm all profits made by him, when he, without the consent of the other partners, carries on any business of the same nature as and competing with that of the firm.[1433] Finally, partners are under the statutory duty to render true accounts and full information of all things affecting the partnership to any partner or his legal representatives.[1434]

428. Turning to firm's liability issues, it is specified that where, by any wrongful ('παράνομη' in Greek, 'haksız' in Turkish) act or omission of any partner acting in the ordinary course of business of the firm, or with the authority of his co-partners, loss or injury is caused to any person not being a partner in the firm, or any penalty is incurred, the firm is liable therefor to the same extent as the partner so acting or omitting to act.[1435] The firm is liable to make good the loss in the following cases:

1425. Section 20(1) *ibid.*
1426. Section 20(2) *ibid.*
1427. Section 20(3) *ibid.*
1428. Section 16 *ibid.*
1429. Section 16(a) *ibid.*
1430. Section 16(b) *ibid.*
1431. Section 31(1) *ibid.*
1432. Section 31(2) *ibid.*
1433. Section 32 *ibid.*
1434. Section 30 *ibid. See* in this regard *In re Ellinas* 1 CLR 106 (1989).
1435. Section 13 Cap. 116.

- where one partner, acting within the scope of his apparent authority, receives the money or property of a third person and misapplies it;[1436] and
- where a firm in the course of its business receives the money or property of a third person, and the money or property so received is misapplied by one or more of the partners while it is in the custody of the firm.[1437]

429. When a firm is liable according to the aforementioned, every partner is liable jointly with his co-partners and also severally for everything, while he is a partner therein.[1438]

430. Especially, where a firm required to furnish statements of particulars has failed to do so, then the rights of such firm under or arising out of any contract made or entered into by or on behalf of same in relation to the business requiring such particulars to be furnished at any time while he is in default are not enforceable by action or other legal proceeding either in the firm or business name or otherwise.[1439] Provided always as follows:

- the defaulter may apply to the Court for relief against said imposed disability. The Court, on being satisfied that the default was accidental, or due to inadvertence, or some other sufficient cause, or that on other grounds it is just and equitable ('δίκαιο και σύμφωνο με τις αρχές της επιείκειας' in Greek, 'doğru ve hakkaniyet' in Turkish) to grant relief, may grant such relief either generally, or as respects any particular contracts. The Court is at liberty of imposing the condition of the costs of the application being paid by the defaulter along with any other conditions in its power. However, such a relief is not granted except on such service and such publication of notice of the application as the Court may order. Equally, relief shall not be given in respect of any contract, if any party to the contract proves to the satisfaction of the Court that, if this Law had been complied with, he would not have entered into the contract;[1440]
- rights of any other parties against the defaulter in respect of such contract are not affected from the aforementioned;[1441] and
- if any action or proceeding is commenced by any other party against the defaulter to enforce the rights of such party in respect of such contract, the aforementioned do not preclude the defaulter from enforcing in that action or proceeding, by way of counterclaim set-off or otherwise, such rights as he may have against that party in respect of such contract.[1442]

1436. Section 14(a) *ibid.*
1437. Section 14(b) *ibid.*
1438. Section 15 *ibid.*
1439. Section 62 *ibid. Fruit and Vegetable Industry v. Halco Ltd a.a.* 1 CLR 302 (1975).
1440. Section 62(a) Cap. 116.
1441. Section 62(b) *ibid.*
1442. Section 62(c) *ibid.*

431. A specific statutory provision regulates issues arising from change in the constitution of the firm and guarantees. It is provided that a continuing guarantee[1443] or cautionary obligation given either to a firm or to a third person in respect of the transactions of a firm or to a third person in respect of the transactions of a firm is revoked as to future transactions by any change in the constitution of the firm to which, or of the firm in respect of the transactions of which, the guarantee of obligation was given. Albeit, said regulation is not mandatory and an agreement to the contrary may be reached among the partners.[1444]

432. In addition, the firm has statutory obligations related to making specific information public. This duty relates to the following information: the current first name(s) or the initials thereof and current surnames of all partners in the firm; in the event that an entity is a partner, its present name, but for a limited partner; and in the event of a limited partnership, in addition to the information already stated above, whether this partner is of limited liability. Said mention must be made in all trade catalogues, trade circulars and business letters, on or in which the firm name appears and which are issued or sent by the firm to any person in any place.[1445] In case of default, every partner of the firm is liable on summary conviction for each offence to a fine not exceeding CYP 25 (EUR 42.75).[1446]

433. Further, the firm has the duty to keep books of account. Such books are properly kept, when they can exhibit or explain their transactions and financial position in their trade or business, including book(s) containing entries from day to day in sufficient detail of all cash received and cash paid. Where the trade or business have involved dealings in goods, also accounts have to be kept of all goods sold including a description in sufficient detail of all goods sold and purchased, whether for cash or credit, as will enable such goods to be identifiable and also particulars of the name and address of the supplier or purchaser of such goods. Equally, statements of annual stocktakings have to be made showing the basis upon which such stocktakings are made.[1447] Anyone failing to do so is liable to summary conviction to a fine not exceeding EUR 1,710 and/or imprisonment for a term not exceeding one year.[1448] In the event that the only or all of the general partners are limited liabilities companies established under Cap. 113, companies of a Member State of the EU, companies of a third state, which have a form similar to the one described, partnerships established under this law, or partnerships of a Member State of the EU, such a partnership has to prepare financial statements.[1449] Such financial statements are to be prepared in the predefined form according to sections 118–122 Cap. 113. They are further publicly available,[1450] present a true and fair picture of the

1443. *See* in this regard s. 87 *ibid.*
1444. Section 21 *ibid.*
1445. Section 65(1)(a) *ibid.*
1446. Section 65(2) *ibid.*
1447. Section 64(1) *ibid.*
1448. Section 64(2) *ibid.*
1449. Section 64A(1)(a), (b), (c), (d) and (e) *ibid.*
1450. Section 150 Cap. 113.

partnership[1451] and are submitted to a general assembly, where all partners or legally appointed representatives are attending.[1452,1453] Failure to comply with these duties is a criminal offence and a fine of up to EUR 17,000 and/or imprisonment of up to one year may be imposed.[1454] In addition to said penal liability, the Registrar has the authority to impose to any firm failing to timely submit its financial statements administrative fine of EUR 50 plus EUR 1 for each day of said failure during the first six months; thereafter each day of failure to comply is fined with EUR 2. Still this administrative fine may amount up to EUR 500.[1455] The introduction of this administrative measure in December 2018 is most certainly welcome. Still, it is highly questionable, whether it shall have an effective, proportionate and dissuasive effect.

434. Lastly, the certificate or a certified copy of registration of the partnership, issued by the Registrar, has to be kept exhibited in a conspicuous position at the principal place of business of the firm, individual or corporation. Failure to do so gives rise to liability of the firm to a fine of no more than EUR 171.[1456]

§5. Partnership and Third Persons

435. Third persons may give notice to any partner as this operates as a notice to the firm. The served partner must, however, habitually act in the partnership business of any matter relating to partnership affairs. Yet, this is not effective in the case of a fraud on the firm committed by or with the consent of that partner.[1457]

436. Specific provisions regulate the rights of third persons dealing with a firm against apparent members of firm. More specifically, it is set out that, where a person deals with a firm after a change in its constitution, he is entitled to treat all apparent members of the old firm as still being members of the firm until he has notice of the change.[1458] A statement in the Official Gazette or in the electronic gazette operated by the Registrar (*see* in this respect paragraph 419 above) as to a firm whose principal place of business is in Cyprus operates as notice to persons, who had no dealings with the firm before the date of the dissolution with the firm before the date of said publication.[1459]

1451. Sections 142–143 *ibid.*
1452. Section 156 *ibid.*
1453. Section 64A(2) Cap. 116.
1454. Section 64A(4) *ibid.*
1455. Section 64A(5) *ibid.*
1456. Section 56(2) *ibid.*
1457. Section 19 *ibid.*
1458. Section 38(1) *ibid.*
1459. Sections 38(2) and 59 *ibid.*

§6. Termination of Partnership

437. A partnership is dissolved by expiration of notice. In particular and subject to any agreement between the parties, it is set out that this takes place:

- if entered into for a fixed term, by the expiration of that term;[1460]
- if entered into for a single adventure or undertaking, by the termination of that adventure or undertaking;[1461] and
- if entered into for an undefined time, by any partner giving notice to the other(s) of his intention to dissolve the partnership.[1462] Where the partnership has originally been constituted by deed, a notice in writing, signed by the partner giving it, is sufficient for this purpose.[1463]

438. Death or bankruptcy of any partner equally dissolves a partnership, save for agreement to the contrary.[1464] Separate debt of a partner may have the same effect, at the option of the other partners, when any partner suffers his share of the partnership to be charged ('επιβάρυνση' in Greek, 'mükellefiyet' in Turkish) under the Partnerships Law.[1465] Said effect is further caused by the happening of any event, which makes it unlawful ('παράνομο' in Greek, 'yasaya aykırı' in Turkish) for the business of the firm to be carried on or for the members. This is absolute and no agreement to the contrary may be reached in this regard.[1466]

439. Fraud ('απάτη' in Greek, 'hile' in Turkish) or misrepresentation ('ψευδής παράσταση' in Greek, 'sahtekârlık' in Turkish) of a party to a partnership contract, as explained above under paragraphs 71 et seq., causes a partnership contract to rescind.[1467] Similarly, a partnership is dissolved, when the formal conditions, the conditions of substantive validity or other conditions of validity already explained above, are not fulfilled.

440. A Court may decree a dissolution of the partnership on application by a partner, in the following cases, which are explicitly and restrictively set out in the law:

- when a partner is shown, to the satisfaction of the Court, to be of permanently unsound mind ('μόνιμο κλονισμό του λογικού' in Greek, 'daimi akıl hastası' in Turkish), in which case the application may be made as well on behalf of that partner by his next friend, or person having to intervene as by any other partner;[1468]

1460. Section 34(1)(a) *ibid.*
1461. Section 34(1)(b) *ibid.*
1462. Sections 34(1)(c) and 28(1) *ibid.*
1463. Section 28(2) *ibid.*
1464. Section 35(1) *ibid.*
1465. Section 35(2) *ibid.*
1466. Section 36 *ibid.*
1467. Section 43 *ibid.*
1468. Section 37(a) *ibid.*

- when a partner, other than the partner suing, becomes in any other way permanently incapable of performing his part of the partnership contract;[1469]
- when a partner, other than the partner suing, has been guilty of such conduct as, in the opinion of the Court, regard being had to the nature of the business, is calculated to prejudicially affect the carrying on of the business;[1470]
- when a partner, other than the partner suing, wilfully or persistently commits a breach of the partnership agreement or otherwise so conducts himself in matters relating to the partnership business that it is not reasonably practicable for the other partner or partners to carry on the business in partnership with him;[1471]
- when the business of the partnership can only be carried on at a loss;[1472]
- whenever in any case circumstances have arisen which, in the opinion of the Court render it just and equitable that the partnership be dissolved;[1473] and
- in the event of petition for dissolution without liquidation due to merger of a partnership with one or more limited liability companies or division of a partnership into one or more limited liability companies, registered especially with this object under the Companies Law, as amended.[1474]

441. The Registrar has power to remove a firm from the register, under the following conditions. Where he has reasonable cause ('εύλογη αιτία' in Greek, 'makûl sebep' in Turkish) to believe that any firm is not carrying on business, he may send to the firm by registered post a notice that, unless an answer is received to such notice within one month from the date thereof, the firm may be removed from the register.[1475] Such entry in the register, like all entries, is also published in the Official Gazette.[1476]

442. The procedure following dissolution of a partnership is described below. First, upon dissolution any partner may publicly notify the same and may require the other partner or partners to concur for that purpose in all necessary or proper acts, if any, which cannot be done without his or their concurrence.[1477] The partners bear the statutory duty to send by post or deliver to the Registrar a statement in the prescribed form that the firm has ceased to carry on business, within one month thereof.[1478] On receiving such statement, the Registrar files and registers the same and removes the firm from the register.[1479]

443. The authority of each partner to bind the firm, and the other rights and obligations of the partners, continue. If the partnership is dissolved by a Court order,

1469. Section 37(b) *ibid.*
1470. Section 37(c) *ibid.*
1471. Section 37(d) *ibid.*
1472. Section 37(e) *ibid.*
1473. Section 37(f) *ibid.*
1474. Section 37(g) *ibid.*
1475. Section 57(3) and (4) *ibid. Hyatt International Corporation of Delaware, USA, v. Cyprus* 3 CLR 337 (1985).
1476. Section 59 Cap. 116.
1477. Section 39 *ibid.*
1478. Section 57(1) *ibid.*
1479. Section 57(2) *ibid.*

notwithstanding the dissolution, said authority continues so far as may be necessary to wind up the affairs of the partnership, and the complete transactions begun but unfinished at the time of the dissolution, but not otherwise, unless the Court directs otherwise. Provided that the firm is in no case bound by the acts of a partner who has become bankrupt but this proviso does not affect the liability of any person who has, after the bankruptcy, represented himself or knowingly suffered himself to be represented as a partner of the bankrupt.[1480] Further, every partner is entitled, as against the other partners in the firm and all persons claiming through them in respect of their interests as partners, to have the property of the partnership applied in payment of the debts and liabilities of the firm, and to have the surplus assets after such payment applied in payment of what may be due to the partners respectively, after deducing what may be due from them as partners to the firm. For that purpose, any partner or his representatives may, on the termination of the partnership, apply to the Court to wind up the business and affairs of the firm.[1481]

444. In the specific case of a partner paying a premium to another on entering into a partnership for a fixed term and the partnership is dissolved before the expiration of that term, the first partner may apply to the Court for repayment of the premium. The Court, having regard to the terms of the partnership contract and to the length of time during which the partnership has continued, may order repayment in full or of such part thereof as it thinks fit.[1482] No payment shall be ordered, when the dissolution is, in the opinion of the Court, wholly or chiefly due to misconduct of the partner who paid the premium.[1483] This also applies, when the partnership has been dissolved by an agreement containing no provision for a return of any part of the premium.[1484]

445. When partnership is dissolved due to fraud or misrepresentation, the innocent party, which is entitled to do so, without prejudice to any other right, is entitled: (a) to a lien on, or right of retention of, the surplus of the partnership assets, after satisfying the partnership liabilities, for any sum of money paid by him for the purchase of a share in the partnership and for any capital contributed by him; (b) to stand in the place of the creditors of the firm for any payments made by him in respect of the partnership liabilities; and (c) to be indemnified by the person guilty of the fraud or making the representation against all the debts and liabilities of the firm.[1485]

446. Where any member of a firm has died or otherwise ceased to be a partner, and the surviving or continuing partners carry on the business of the firm with its capital or assets without any final settlement of accounts as between the firm and the outgoing partner or his estate, then the outgoing partner or his estate is entitled, at the option of himself or his representatives to share of the profits. An agreement

1480. Section 40 *ibid.*
1481. Section 41 *ibid.*
1482. Section 42 *ibid.*
1483. Section 42(a) *ibid.*
1484. Section 42(b) *ibid.*
1485. Section 43 *ibid.*

to the contrary may be reached among the partners. The precise share of the profits made is the one the Court may find to be attributable to the use of his share of the partnership assets, or to the interest at the rate of nine per centum per annum on the amount of his share of the partnership assets. However, if in the partnership contract an option is given to surviving or continuing partners to purchase the interest of a deceased or outgoing partner and this option is duly exercised, then there is no right to further or other share of profits. But, if any partner assuming to act in exercise of the option does not in all material respects comply with the terms thereof, he is liable to account under the aforementioned.[1486] Yet, the estate of a partner, who dies, is not liable for partnership debts contracted after the date of the death. This also applies to partners, who become bankrupt, or a partner, who, not having been known to the person dealing with the firm to be a partner, retires from the firm.[1487]

1486. Section 44 *ibid.*
1487. Section 38(3) *ibid.*

Chapter 13. Quasi-Contracts

§1. *Negotiorum Gestio*

447. No specific provision on *negotiorum gestio* is set out in laws in Cyprus. Rather, in such cases, the provisions explained immediately below, under enrichment without cause, are applicable.

§2. Enrichment Without Cause

448. Where a person lawfully ('νόμιμα' in Greek, 'yasal' in Turkish) does anything for another person not intending to do so gratuitously, and such other person enjoys the benefit thereof, the latter is bound to make compensation ('αποζημίωση' in Greek, 'tazminat' in Turkish) to the former in respect of the thing so done. This equally applies to delivering anything to the former. In such an event, the latter is bound to make compensation or to restore the thing so done.[1488] It has been established that for this section to apply, the following conditions have to be met: (i) the act in question has to be lawful; (ii) same act has to be performed for another person; (iii) same act has to be done by a person, who does not intend to act gratuitously; and (iv) the person in favour of which same act is done, must enjoy benefit therefrom.[1489]

449. In *A. I. Karpasitis & Ioi (Biomichania) Ltd v. Karafoka*,[1490] where reference to sections 70, 71 and 72 Cap. 149 was made, it was ruled that unjust enrichment – still – does not constitute an independent cause of action. The Court clarified that it rather lays in the centre of and supports restitution claims, whereas as an institution it has its roots in civil law.[1491]

450. In *Orphanides v. Michaelides*,[1492] payment, alleged to be due as agent's commission on the sale of land, was claimed. The facts of the case were briefly as follows: The appellant, an estate agent, visited the shop of the respondent and enquired whether he was willing to sell his property. The respondent, who was acquainted with the appellant, replied that he was willing to sell his land provided that he would get a good price, of the amount of CYP 30,000 (EUR 51,300). During this meeting, nothing was said about a commission being paid to the appellant and no contract was signed appointing the appellant to be the agent of the respondent for the purpose of effecting a sale of his land. A third party then visited the land of the respondent and, after some negotiations as to the price of such land, he offered CYP 25,000 (EUR 42,750) that the respondent did not accept while adding that he would be willing to sell his land for the sum of CYP 26,000 (EUR 44,460).

1488. Section 70 Cap. 149.
1489. *Ismini Kyriacou HjiLoizi a.o. v. Irini Iona* 2 CLR 11 (1962).
1490. 1 CLR 1980 (1991).
1491. *Ibid.*, citing *Orakpo v. Manson Investments* 3 All ER 1 (1977).
1492. 1 CLR 309 (1967).

These negotiations did not result in an agreement between them. A further offer of the same third party was rejected after consideration from the respondent and negotiations between them ceased. The following month the Respondent met with other third parties and after some bargaining the respondent accepted to sell his land for the price of CYP 24,000 (EUR 41,040). When the whole agreement was concluded, this other third party in the presence of the respondent rang up the first third party, who had contacted him earlier and agreed to purchase in partnership the land of the respondent. First third party also said to the other third party that the appellant was the middleman for the sale of this property. On the day that the contract of sale was signed, the appellant visited the respondent and asked for his commission. The respondent alleged that he had sold the property privately and without the services of any commission agent.

451. The ruling court held that the plaintiff constituted an agent of the defendant with a view to finding a ready and willing purchaser who would enter into a binding contract with the defendant. After construing section 70 Cap. 149 in favour of the plaintiff the Court assumed further that the plaintiff would be paid reasonable commission on the sale price. The Supreme Court was satisfied with the totality of the evidence that it was reasonably open to the Court to reach such a conclusion. The court further adopted and applied the reasoning that *if the relation of buyer and seller is really brought about by the act of the agent, he is entitled to commission although the actual sale has not been effected by him.*[1493] The court citing further English principles[1494] decided that the applicant's act remained the efficient cause of the sale taking place and thus, in the absence of any express payment, a reasonable remuneration was payable.

452. The issue of personal services rendered upon the faith of a promise to leave property by will was discussed in *Evripidou v. Demosthenous.*[1495] The facts of this case summarize in the following. The appellant was the administrator of the estate of a deceased person. It was the case of the respondent that under an arrangement with the deceased, made at the latter's suggestion, the plaintiff rendered personal and household services to the deceased over a period of more than three years on the promise of a bequest of her immovable property. In fact, the deceased had executed a will benefiting the plaintiff, but sometime later, when the good relations between the parties had broken down, the deceased revoked her said will and eventually terminated the plaintiff's services in question. Several months later the deceased died leaving no will. The Supreme Court dismissed the finding of the trial Court that remuneration on the ground of section 70 Cap. 116 had to be awarded. It rather held that where services are rendered upon the faith of a promise to leave property by will, which the testator fails to perform, an action may be maintained against his representatives to recover compensation for the services in the shape of

---

1493. *Ibid.*, citing *James T. Burchell v. Gowrie and Blockhouse Collieries Ltd* AC 614 (1910).

1494. *Orphanides v. Michaelides* 1 CLR 309 (1967), citing *Jack Windle Ltd v. Brierley* 1 All ER 398 (1952); *Coles v. Enoch* 3 All ER 327 (1939).

1495. 1 CLR 112 (1971).

damages for breach of the previous promise.[1496] It further noted that in such cases, the success of the claim depends on whether the plaintiffs could satisfy the Court that a legally enforceable agreement between the parties, had been broken by the defendant. In the present case, it found that on a fair reading of the statement of claim and upon the evidence before him, the trial judge's finding that the services of the plaintiff were rendered to the deceased on the basis of the alleged agreement between them is well justified. The breach of the agreement by the deceased is likewise sufficiently established. Finally, it took the view that the plaintiff is entitled to the amount awarded as damages for breach of the agreement under which she rendered her services to the deceased and not as quasi-contract.

453. Section 70 Cap. 149 equally is the statutory basis of the *quantum meruit* principle ('η αρχή της λογικής αμοιβής' in Greek, 'Quantum Meruit prensip' in Turkish). This principle dictates that, where a person offers services to another under circumstances demonstrating that he would do that under remuneration although no precise amount had been agreed, it is assumed that there is a promise of paying reasonable amount. It is the court's duty to define according to the evidence adduced, a reasonable remuneration.[1497] To this effect previous negotiations among the parties may be taken into consideration.[1498] In addition, it was decided that for calculating a reasonable remuneration the prices set out in the last agreement between the parties for providing services of the same nature had to be taken into account.[1499]

454. When enrichment has the form of finding goods belonging to another and taking them into custody, it is set out that the finder is subject to the same responsibility as a bailee.[1500] Hence, said provisions (*see* paragraphs 196 et seq. above) apply in analogy here.

455. In addition, specific provisions regulating contracts with persons, incapable of entering into a contract, when they are supplied with necessaries suited to his condition in life, are foreseen. According to these, the person who has furnished such supplies is entitled to be reimbursed ('αποζημίωση' in Greek, 'geri alma' in Turkish) from the property of such incapable person. This equally applies to persons supplying with necessaries any one, whom they are legally bound to support.[1501]

1496. *Ibid.*, citing *M' Gugan v. Smith* 21 SCR 263 (1892).

1497. *Basilaras a.a. v. A/phoi Thrasou & Synergates* 1 CLR 1754 (2003); *Hadjipanayiotou v. Cyprus Airways (Duty Free Shops) Ltd* 1 CLR 173 (2009); *Hadjizacharia v. Armeutis*, Supreme Court of Cyprus, Civil Appeal No. 374/2010, Judgment of 28 Sep. 2015, not published in CLR.

1498. *Hadjipanayiotou v. Cyprus Airways (Duty Free Shops) Ltd* 1 CLR 173 (2009), citing *Way v. Latilla* 3 All ER 759 (1937).

1499. *Stavrou v. G. Roditis & Partners* 1 CLR 477 (2008), citing *S.O.R.E.L. Limited v. Nicos Servos* 1 CLR 123 (1968).

1500. Section 71 Cap. 149.

1501. Section 68 *ibid.*

§3. MONEY PAID BUT NOT DUE

456. A person to whom money has been paid by mistake ('πλάνη' in Greek, 'yanlışlık' in Turkish) or under coercion ('εξαναγκασμός' in Greek, 'baskı' in Turkish) bears the statutory duty to repay it. Equally, when a person has anything delivered again by mistake or under coercion must return it.[1502] In *Portsmouth v. Cyprus Inland Telecommunications Authority*,[1503] it has been established that the term mistake refers to a payment which was not legally due and which could not have been enforced; thus this statutory provision covers both a mistake of fact and a mistake of law.[1504] Thus, it ruled that the respondents, who had been paying a cost-of-living allowance to the appellant from 1956 to 1960, through a mistake of fact, were entitled to recover whatever amount they had paid in this respect under section 72 of Cap. 149, as long as evidence proving a mistake would be adduced. The relevant burden of establishing a mistake was on the respondents. In view of the respondents failing to discharge the onus of establishing by preponderance of evidence, or by the balance of probabilities, the Court dismissed the claim.[1505]

457. In *Chomatenios v. Stavrinou*,[1506] where evidence for making of a contract between the parties was not adduced, although it was both purported and established that money was paid, section 72 in relation to section 70 Cap. 149 was discussed. The factual surrounding involved payment for acquisition of joint ownership of a plot. Money was paid in advance, whereas the rest was agreed to be paid upon transfer of the land. The written agreement was not submitted to the land registry due to alleged ignorance of the law. The trial court was not convinced that a contract was concluded between the parties and thus, it did not order the enforcement thereof. Albeit, it accepted that paid money constituted undue enrichment and on the grounds of both sections 70 and 72 Cap. 149, it ordered for it to be repaid. The Supreme Court based on the points of facts as established by the trial court, it reaffirmed said findings of law.[1507]

458. Finally, a person who is interested in the payment of money which another is bound by law to pay, and who therefore pays it, is entitled to be reimbursed ('αποζημίωση' in Greek, 'geri alma' in Turkish) by the other.[1508]

1502. Section 72 *ibid.*
1503. 1 CLR 87 (1967).
1504. *Ibid.*, citing *Sir Shiba Prasad v. Maharaja Srish Chandra*, AIR PC 297 (1949). It was further established that s. 72 Cap. 149 is in every aspect identical with s. 72 of the Indian Contract Act 1878. The finding that mistake covers both a mistake of fact and a mistake of law has been equally found in *C.T.C. Consultants v. Grindlays Bank* 1 CLR 294 (1988).
1505. *Portsmouth v. Cyprus Inland Telecommunications Authority* 1 CLR 87 (1967).
1506. Supreme Court of Cyprus Civil Appeal No. 62/2011, Judgment of 17 Dec. 2015, not published in CLR.
1507. *Ibid.*
1508. Section 69 Cap. 149.

Selected Bibliography

Phillipe Jougleux. *Elements of Cypriot Law of Obligations* (in Greek) (Sakkoulas Publications 2011).

Euripides Hadjinestoros and Giorgos Charalambous. *Cyprus Law on Sale of Goods and Consumer Protection* (in Greek) (Nomiki Bibliothiki 2016).

Andreas Neocleous & Co LLC. *Handbook of Cypriot Laws* (in Greek) (2nd ed., Nomiki Bibliothiki 2013).

Andreas Neocleous. *Neocleous's Introduction to Cyprus Law* (C. Melides et al. eds, 3rd ed., Andreas Neocleous & Co LLC 2011).

Louis Parlas (ed.). *Contracts Cap. 149* (in Greek) (2012).

Alekos Patsalides. *Specimens of Modern Legal Contracts and Documents* (in Greek) (Othon Press Ltd 2012).

Polyvios G. Polyviou. *The Law of Contracts* (in Greek) (Chrysaphinis and Polyviou Publications 2014).

Polyvios G. Polyviou. *Contract in Cyprus Law: Theory and Praxis* (in Greek) (Chrysaphinis and Polyviou Publications 2017).

Tatiana Synodinou. *Cypriot Private Law* (in Greek) (Sakkoulas Publications 2014).

Eleni Troba and Panayiotis Skouris. *The European Law on Public Contracts* (in Greek) (Sakkoulas Publications 2009).

Table of Cases

The numbers here refer to paragraph numbers.

A.A. Pilottos Ltd and another v. George Houghton and another 1 CLR 783 (2007), 264
A. Athinodoros (Antiprosopeies) Asphalion Ltd v. Marketrends Financial Services Ltd 1 CLR 1205 (2008), 120, 208
A.B.C. Ltd v. Koiliaris a.a. 1 CLR 41 (1996), 130
A.G. v. Blake 1 All ER 933 (1998), 169
A. I. Karpasitis & Ioi (Biomichania) Ltd v. Karafoka 1 CLR 1980 (1991), 449
A.N. Stasis Estates Co Ltd v. Waldner a.a. 1 CLR 250 (1998), 152
A. Panayides Contracting Ltd v. M & M Frangos Engineering & Contracting Ltd, Supreme Court of Cyprus, Civil Appeal No. 301/2008, Judgment of 31 May 2012, not published in CLR, 32, 35, 175, 285
Aannemingsbedrijf Norré-Behaegel v. Vlaams Gewest, CJEU Case C-387/19, Judgment of 14 January 2021, digital ECR, 369
Acropol Shipping Company Ltd a.o. v. Rossis 1 CLR 38 (1976), 340
Acropol Shipping Co a.o. v. Rossis 2 JSC 188 (1976), 340
Agathocleous a.a. v. Lappa 1 CLR 2202 (1998), 90, 94
Agrotou a.a. v. Agrotou, Supreme Court of Cyprus, Civil Appeal No. 288/2010, Judgment of 31 May 2016, not published in CLR, 41, 190
Ahapittas v. Poc-chik Ltd 1 CLR 1 (1968), 310
Aimilios Thoma and others v. Iacovos Eliades 1 CLR 1263 (2006), 173
Ajero J Kristoffer Castardo 1 CLR 1165 (2006), 271
Alexander v. Gardner 4 LJ CP 223 (1835), 239
Alexandrou v. Komodromou 1 CLR 576 (1997), 129, 130, 288
Alexiadi v. Robinson 2 F & F 679 (1861), 75
Ali Selim v. The Heirs of Emete Filo Ali 17 CLR 143, 174
Allcard v. Skinner 36 Ch D 145 (1887), 41, 70, 73, 74, 75
Alpan Furnishings v. Demades 1E CLR 170 (1989), 120
Alpha Bank Cyprus Ltd v. A.G. Demetriou Metafores Ltd and another, District Court of Limassol, Action No. 1048/2007, Judgment of 16 April 2013, not reported in CLR, 263, 266
Alpha Bank Cyprus Ltd v. Miller a.a., District Court of Paphos, Civil Case No. 2014/2008, Judgment of 31 October 2017, not published in CLR, 183
Amethyst Distributors Ltd v. Ieras Monis Kykkou 1 CLR 199 (2011), 129
Anastasiou v. Stylianou 1 CLR 62 (1974), 282
Anchorage Management Services Ltd v. 465404 BC Inc BCCA 771 (1999), 35
Anderson Ltd v. Daniel 1 KB 138 (1924), 93, 113

Table of Cases

Andreas Kasianos & Sons Ltd v. Filitsas D. Vasileiou Ltd 1B CLR 1337 (2006), 93
Andreou v. Bank of Cyprus 1A CLR 740 (2005), 342
Andris Spanou v. Christinas Vasileiou a.o., District Court of Larnaca Action No. 3522/2012, Judgment of 22 January 2018, not published in CLR, 172
Anodiki Services EPE v. GNA 'Evangelismos – Ofthalmiatrio Athinon – Polikliniki', GNA 'Georgios Gennimatas', Geniko Onkologiko Nosokomio Kifisias – (GONK) 'Agioi Anargiroi', CJEU Case C-260/17, Judgment of 25 October 2018, digital ECR, 352, 357
Anorthosis v. Apollon 1 CLR 518 (2002), 288
Antenna Ltd v. Arhis Radiotileorasis Kyprou 3 CLR 29 (2010), 271
Antoniadou v. Laiki Kypriaki Trapeza (Chrimatodotiseis) Ltd 1(A) CLR 530 (2003), 155
Antoniou v. Gestami & Co Ltd 1 CLR 1070 (2002), 82
Antriani Haralambous v. Marias Haralambous 1 CLR 1298 (2008), 17
Apaisioti v. Rayia 1 CLR 882 (1993), 160
Archangelos Domain Ltd v. Adriatica Societa per Azione di Navigatione 1 CLR 439 (1978), 47
Argyri v. Chrysostomou 1 CLR 1362 (2006), 323
Aristotelous v. General Insurance Co. 1 CLR 582 (1981), 178
Astro Vendeor Compania Naviera S.A. v. Mabanaft GmbH 2 Lloyd's Rep 267 (1970), 126
Atesli a.a. v. Bank of Cyprus Public Company Ltd 1 CLR 2222 (2013), 37
Attorney-General v. Ellis 2 QB 466 (1895), 114
Attorney-General of the Republic v. Etaireia Technikon Ergon Ltd 1 CLR 94 (1993), 171
Attorney-General v. Pentaliotis Papapetrou Estates Limited a.o. 1 CLR 1931 (1988), 242
Aulesford (Earl) v. Morris 8 Ch App 484 (1873), 51
Austrian Airlines v. Genikes Asfaleies Kyprou Ltd 1 CLR 764 (1991), 213
Ayia Napa Nissi Ltd a.o. v Papamichail 1 CLR 549 (1992), 92
Bakeview Properties Ltd v. Charalambous, District Court of Limassol Action No. 2642/2012, Judgment of 18 September 2019, not published in CLR, 176
Balfour v. Balfour 2 KB 571 (1919), 36
Balkancarimpex Fto v. Leasco Ltd 1 CLR 815 (1994), 126
Bank of Credit and Commerce International SA v. Aboody 1 QB 923 (1990), 74
Bank of Cyprus a.o. v. Coudounaris Food Products Ltd a.o. 1 CLR 641 (1995), 155, 156, 348
Bank of Cyprus (London) Ltd v. Markou a.a. 2 All ER 707 (1999), 319
Bank of Cyprus Public Company Ltd, District Court of Nicosia, Civil Case No. 6394/04, Judgment of 2 August 2013, not reported in CLR, 40
Bank of Montreal v. Stuart AC 120 (1911), 319
Barclays Bank Plc v. Boulter a.a. 4 All ER 513 (1994), 64
Barclays Bank Plc v. O'Brien a.a. All ER 417 (1993), 64, 319
Baudains v. Richardson AC 169 (1906), 77
Bauer v. Diogenis Erodotou & Yioi Ltd 1 CLR 325 (1994), 149, 178
Basilaras a.a. v. A/phoi Thrasou & Synergates 1 CLR 1754 (2003), 453
Bater v. Bater 2 All ER 458 (1950), 51, 80

Bentsen v. Taylor Sons & Co 2 QB 274 (1893), 239
Billage v. Southee 9 Hare 534 (1852), 70
Biometal Ltd v. Hawaii Hotels Ltd 1 CLR 281 (1998), 30
Bradford Building Society v. Borders 2 All ER 205 (1941), 17
Bristol, Cardiff, and Swansea Aerated Bread Co. v. Maggs 44 Ch D 616 (1890), 30
British Columbia (Minister of Transportation and Highways) v. Reon Management Services Inc BCCA 679 (2001), 35
Brooks v. Beirnstein 1 KB 98 (1909), 262
Brown v. Gould 2 All ER 1505 (1971), 88
Brown v. Percy Dalton Ltd 2 All ER 844 (1957), 83
Bullock v. Lloyds Bank Ltd Ch. 317 (1955), 75
Burnard v. Haggis 14 CBNS 45 (1863), 74
Bushwell Properties v. Vortex Properties 2 All ER 283 (1976), 88
C. Malathouras & Sons Ltd v. Popular Insurance Company Ltd 1 CLR 1233 (2004), 35
C.I.B.C. Mortgages Plc v. Pitt a.a. 1 AC 200 (1994), 319
C.T.C. Consultants v. Grindlays Bank 1 CLR 294 (1988), 456
Capital Tour (Cyprus) Ltd and D & CH Travel & Tours Ltd v. Gesoma Estates Ltd, District Court of Famagusta Action No. 703/2011 Judgment of 25 July 2018, not published in CLR, 175
Carter v. Silber 2 Ch. 278 (1892), 114
Cassel & Co Ltd v. Broone 1 All ER 801 (1972), 19
Centra (Holdings) Ltd. v. Reuters Ltd. 1(A) CLR 298 (1999), 175
Central London Property Trust Ltd v. High Trees House Ltd KB 130 (1947), 171, 240
Centrovincial Estates plc v. Merchant Investors Assurance Co. Ltd. Com LR 158 (1983), 32
Ch.P.Th. Alexandrou Ltd v. Symvouliou Apoheteuseon Leukosias 1 CLR 630 (1999), 129, 287
Chalhoub v. the Police 2 CLR 153 (1988), 32
Chambers v. Goldthorpe 1 KB 638 (1901), 286
Chaplin & Co. Ltd. v. Brammail 1 K.B. 233 (1908), 63, 319
Charalambous v. Aristotelous 1 CLR 750 (2001), 74
Charalambous v. Krystallis 1 CLR 656 (1984), 57
Charalambous a.o. v. Liberty Life 1 CLR 1739 (2011), 179
Charalambous v. Petros Michael Exclusif Ltd 1C CLR 1953 (2004), 342
Charalambous v. Solomou 1 CLR 1058 (2001), 41
Charalambous and another v. Stefanou JSC 223 (1987), 261
Charles Clay & Sons Ltd v. B. R. Board 1 All ER 1007 (1971), 88
Charles Rickards Ltd v. Oppenhaim 1 K.B. 616 (1950), 239
Chillingworth v. Esche 1 Ch. 97 (1924), 36
China and South Sea Bank Ltd v. Tan 3 All ER 839 (1989), 342
Chloe Andrea Patatsou v. Ahmet Hilmi a.o. Civil Appeal No. 300/2011, Judgment of 31 May 2017, not reported in CLR, 70
Chomatenios v. Stavrinou Supreme Court of Cyprus Civil Appeal No. 62/2011, Judgment of 17 December 2015, not published in CLR, 457
Chr. Tornari & Co. & F. Vassiliades v. Savva JSC 389 (1974), 94, 265

Chrineste Holdings Ltd v. Zavos Race-City Co. Ltd, District Court of Limassol, Civil Case No. 5905/2011, Judgment of 29 June 2018, not published in CLR, 154
Christodoulides v. Kymisi and Ekastica Kymisis Ltd 1 CLR 635 (2009), 85
Christodoulides v. Mehmed Pasha 10 (1) CLR 82, 141, 142
Christodoulou and Lindsay v. Antonius H.F.M. Vraets 1 CLR 802 (2009), 86
Christodoulou v. C.H.R. Othonos Homes Ltd, District Court of Paphos Action No. 3291/2010, Judgment of 30 August 2019, not published in CLR, 150
Christofides v. Moustafa Ahmet Aliye Kadis 18 (1) CLR 1,49
Christodoulou v. Kazafaniotis 1 CLR 325 (1988), 282
Christofides v. Kotzanaggasi 1 CLR 718 (1993), 159
Christoforou v. Christoforou 1 CLR 1551 (1998), 41, 207
Christophe a.a. v. Phetokaki 1 CLR 1208 (2009), 288
Christopher Scottis Ltd a.a. v. Scottish & Newcastle International Ltd a.a., Supreme Court of Cyprus, Civil Appeal No. 179/2011, Judgment of 20 September 2017, not published in CLR, 184
Christophorou v. Iakovou 1 CLR 33 (2002), 41, 73
Christopoulou a.o. v. Christopoulou 1 CLR 437 (1971), 51
Christou v S.D. Clinic Co Ltd 1 CLR 2039 (2000), 92
Chrysostomou v. G.S. Chalkousi & Sons 1 CLR 10 (1978), 139
Chrystalla Demetriou a.a. v. Savvas Ioannides 1 CLR 16 (1982), 304
Chrystalla Stylianoudes v. Sportking Limited, District Court of Limassol Action No. 4569/11, Judgment of 12 September 2012, not reported in CLR, 149
Clunis v. Camden and Islington Health Authority 3 All ER 180 (1998), 86
Coles v. Enoch 3 All ER 327 (1939), 451
Commerzbank Auslandsbanken Holding AG a.a. v. Adeona Holdings Ltd, Supreme Court of Cyprus, Civil Appeal No. E6/2014, Judgment of 27 February 2015, not published in CLR, 339–342
Constantinides v. Pitsillou a.a. JSC 279 (1980), 19
Constantinou v. Attorney-General 1 CLR 741 (1997), 302
Constantinou v. Firm S. Mamas & Co 9 JSC 1098 (1973), 258, 262
Constantinou v. Panayi a.a. 1 CLR 191 (1968), 112
Cope v. Rowlands 2 M & W 149 (1836), 93
Cornell v. Harrison a.a. All ER Rep 1827 (1916–1917), 114
Costas Chr. Karacis Ltd v. Doritis Makaroni Factory Ltd 1 CLR 251 (2001), 204
Costas Panayi and Eleftherios Costa Artemiou and Others, District Court of Famagusta, Civil Action No. 3299/73, Judgment of 30 March 1974, not published in CLR, 258
Coudounaris v. Coudounaris 1 CLR 581 (1980), 313
Courtis a.a. v. Iasonides 1 CLR 83 (1972), 136
Craythorne v. Swinburne 14 Ves. Jun. 160 (1807), 322, 325
Credit Lyonnais Bank Nederland NV v. Burch 1 All ER 144 (1997), 72
Crosskill v. Bower, Bower v. Turner 32 LJ Ch. 540 (1863), 348
Cyprus v. Hossam Taleb Yaacoub, District Court of Limassol, Criminal Case No. 17714/12, Judgment of 28 March 2013, not published in CLR, 99–103
Cyprus Cinema & Theatre Co. Ltd. v. Christodoulos Karmiotis 1 CLR 42 (1967), 153
Cyprus Import Corporation Ltd v. Kaisis 1 CLR 16 (1974), 136

Cyprus Phassouri Plantations Co. Ltd v. Adriatica di Navigazione SP of Venice 1 CLR 290 (1985), 126
Cyprus Popular Bank Ltd v. General District Attorney 1 CLR 83 (2004), 328
Cyprus Popular Bank Ltd v. T.G. & Sons Importing Ltd a.o. 1 CLR 180 (2004), 321
Cyprus Popular Bank Public Co. Ltd v. Otis Elevators (Cyprus) Ltd, Supreme Court of Cyprus, Civil Appeal No. 371/2009, Judgment of 16 February 2015, not published in CLR, 190
Cyprus Popular Bank (Leasing) Ltd v. Konstantinou a.o. 1 CLR 1432 (2001), 37
Cyprus Popular Bank (Leasing) Ltd v. Konstantinou a.a. 1 CLR 2067 (2002), 37
Cyprus Popular Bank (Leasing) Ltd v. Michael 1 CLR 41 (2012), 37
Cyprus Trading Corporation Ltd v. ZIM Israel Navigation Co. Ltd a.a. 1 CLR 1335 (2000), 137
D I Demades Sons Ltd v. Kaoullas a.a. JSC 270 (1972), 95, 265
Damtsas a.o. v. Ouzounian M. Sultanian and Company (Cars) Ltd, Supreme Court of Cyprus, Civil Appeal No. 133/11, Judgment of 24 March 2016, not reported in CLR, 179
Day Morris Associates v. Voyce All ER (D) 368 (2003), 29
De Brassac v. Martyn 9 LT 287 (1863), 160
Decro Wall International S.A. v. Practitioners in Marketing 2 All ER 216 (1971), 204, 240
Delta Antrepriză de ConstrucŢii şi Montaj 93 SA v. Compania NaŢională de Administrare a Infrastructurii Rutiere SA, CJEU Case C-267/18, Judgment of 3 October 2019, digital ECR, 368
Demetriou v. Andorkas 21 (1) CLR 187, 154
Demetriou v. Bank of Cyprus Public Company Ltd, Supreme Court of Cyprus, Civil Appeal No. 167/2010, Judgment of 21 October 2015, not published in CLR, 323
Demetriou a. o. v. Konstantinides a.a. 1 CLR 1503 (2002), 41
Demetriades v. Caxton Publishing Co Ltd 1 CLR 35 (1973), 241, 245
Demetris Souglis and another v. Elias Papadopoulos and another, District Court of Limassol Action No. 4390/2009, Judgment of 24 June 2015, not published in CLR, 176
Demosthenous and another v. Unicars Limited and another, District Court of Limassol Action No. 5488/2009, Judgment of 9 August 2019, not published in CLR, 176
Denny, Mott & Dickson, Ltd. v. James B. Fraser & Co. Ltd. 1 All ER 678 (1944), 152
Diaheiristiko Symvoulio Emporikis Sholis Mitsi Lethymou v. Petraki 1 CLR 941 (1998), 107
Direzione e coordinamento Vivendi SA v. Consip SpA, Ministero dell'Economia e delle Finanze, CJEU C-395/18, Judgment of 30 January 2020, digital ECR, 382
Dita Danosa v. LKB Līzings SIA, CJEU Case No. C-232/09, Judgment of 11 November 2010, ECR I-11405 (2010), 297
Drane v. Evangelou 2 All ER 437 (1978), 86
Dryades a.a. v. Kalispera 1 CLR 881 (1998), 169, 177
Duncan v. Dixon 44 Ch D 211 (1890), 310
Duncan, Fox & Co. v. North and South Wales Bank 6 App. Cas. 1 (1880), 322, 325
Dunlop Pneumatic Tyre Co Ltd v. Selfridge & Co Ltd AC 847 (1915), 38

Edra Costruzioni Soc. coop. and Edilfac Srl v. Comune di Maiolati Spontini, CJEU Case C-140/16, Judgment of 10 November 2016, digital ECR, 352
Edwards v. Carter AC 360 (1893), 114
Edwards v. Halliwell 2 All ER 1064 (1950), 173
Efthymiou v. M. & T.H. Petrou & Sons Developers Ltd, District Court of Ammochostos Action No. 98/2010, Judgment of 9 March 2018, not published in CLR, 150
Egerton v. Brownlow All ER Rep. 970 (1843–1860), 106
Electromatic Const. v. Azov 1 CLR 768 (1988), 107
Eleftheriades v. Cyprus Hotels Ltd 1 CLR 677 (1985), 312
Eleni Andrea Avgousti v. Niovi Papadamou a.a. 1 CLR 66 (1968), 161
Eleni Christofides v. Moustafa Ahmet Aliye Kadis 18 (1) 1 CLR, 49
Eliza Christodoulou v. Christos Papadopoulos & Yioi Ltd., District Court of Paphos Action No. 1040/2011, Judgment of 5 April 2016, not published in CLR, 178
Elli Meitz a.a. v. Andreas Pelengaris 1 CLR 226 (1977), 304
Ellinas and others v. Zartarian, Court of Rent Control of Nicosia, Case No. E209/2011, Judgment of 19 October 2015, not published in CLR, 154
Elliniki Trapeza Ltd and another v. Nikos Tsartellis 1 CLR 246 (2003), 266
Elliniki Trapeza Ltd v. Lextalionis Investments Ltd and others, District Court of Larnaca, Action No. 3172/99 Judgment of 25 January 2007, not reported in CLR, 271
Ellinopoulou v. Demetriades 1 CLR 709 (1995), 41
Eracleous v. Pitrou 1 CLR 239 (1994), 176
Eraclis Michaelides Ltd. v. G & C. Exhaust Systems Ltd. 1(A) CLR 500 (2001), 175
Erotokritou v. Theodorou a.a. 1I CLR 1800 (1997), 19, 161, 180
Etaireia Diatheseos Tsimenton Basilikou Apollon Ltd v. Akthitzioti 1 CLR 687 (1998), 318
Euaggelos Charalambous v. Yiannaki Lysioti 1 CLR 409 (1991), 149
Euro-Diam Ltd v. Bathurst 1 QB 1 (1990), 86
Eurogal Surveys Ltd v. D. Trade International Ltd, Supreme Court of Cyprus, Civil Appeal No. 348/2009, Judgment of 17 October 2014, not published in CLR, 138, 197
Evaggelides v. Kosma a.a. 1 CLR 932 (1998), 197
Evelthon Developments Ltd a.a. v. National Bank of Greece (Cyprus) Ltd 1 CLR 2486 (2012), 348
Evripidou v. Demosthenous 1 CLR 112 (1971), 452
Fadil Izzet v. Kypriaki Et. Apothikeusis Petreleoeidon Ltd 1(A) CLR 11 (2009), 153
Fairways (Limassol) Ltd v. A. Petsa & Yioi Ltd 1B CLR 1387 (2000), 175
Fakonti v. Vryoni 1 CLR 1404 (2004), 81
Fashions House v. The Republic of Cyprus 3 CLR 231(1973), 419
Fender v. Mildmay 3 All ER 402 (1937), 106
Fetokakis a.a. v. Cyprus Trading Corporation Plc, Joined Civil Appeals Nos. 328/2010 and 431/2011 of 31 March 2017, not reported in CLR, 141
Filiki Asfalistiki Etaireia Ltd v. Demetri 1 CLR 551 (1999), 183, 201
Financings Ltd v. Stimson 3 All ER 386, 391 (1962), 261
Firippis v. Elvimag Ltd, District Court of Nicosia Action No. 1661/04 Judgment of 10 April 2006, not published in CLR, 175

Fisher v. Bridges 3 E & B 642 (1854), 94, 113
Flecha Contracting Ltd v. M. C. Michael Development Ltd 1A CLR 263 (2003), 93
Foreman v. Great Western Railway 38 LT 851 (1878), 74
Foss v. Harbottle 67 ER 189 (1843), 173
Frangos v. Limited Liability Partnership 'Prasino Livadhi' JSC 48 (1978), 95
Freeman and Lockyer v. Buckhurst Properties All ER 630 (1964), 183
Frost v. Knight Law Rep. 7 Ex. 111 (1872), 152
Fruit and Vegetable Industry v. Halco Ltd a.a. 1 CLR 302 (1975), 430
G.I.P. Constructions Ltd v. Assiotis 1 CLR 535 (1982), 130
G.K. Theonell Building & Construction Ltd v. AIG Cyprus Limited, District Court of Limassol Action No. 2743/2013, Judgment of 7 March 2017, not published in CLR, 172
G.M. Platritis & Co a.o. v. Computer Patent Annuities a.o. 1 CLR 135 (1988), 93
Garnac Grain Co., Inc. v. H.M.F. Faure and Fairclough, Ltd. and Bunge Corporation 2 All ER 353 (1967), 150
General Attorney v. G.T.P. Electrical Products Ltd 1 CLR 2326 (1998), 184
Geo. M. Hadjikyriacos Co. Ltd v. United Biscuits (UK) Ltd 1 CLR 689 (1979), 340
George Charalambous Ltd v. Kalos Kafes Ltd a.o. 1 CLR 199 (1997), 119, 175
Georghiades v. Cyprus 1 CLR 239 (1989), 310, 312
Georghiades v. Georghiades 1 CLR 623 (1985), 288, 268
Georgiades v. Bernoulli Trading Co. Ltd 1 CLR 629 (1994), 197
Georgiades v. Georgiades 1 CLR 428 (1988), 288, 310, 311
Georgios Ppatsia and another v. K. & M. (Famagusta) Developers & Constructions Ltd, District Court of Famagusta, Action No. 634/10 Judgment of 24 May 2011, not published in CLR, 175
Georgiki Etaireia D.G. Phoutas v. Etaireia Vasos, Emporoi Georgikon Proionton Ltd 1 CLR 168 (1993), 130, 133
Georgiou a.a. v. Alpha Concrete Ltd 1 CLR 1049 (2009), 65
Georgiou v. Constantinides 1 CLR 62 (1976), 310
Georgiou v. Kypriakon Aerogrammon Ltd 1C CLR 1794 (1998), 30, 32
Gerolemou and another v. Giovani Developers Ltd and others, District Court of Ammohostos Civil Action No. 801/2012, Judgment of 8 January 2018 not published in CLR, 153
Gibson v. Manchester City Council 1 WLR 294 (1979), 32
Gilchrist Watt and Sanderson Pty Ltd v. York Products Pty Ltd (1970) 3 All ER 825 (1970), 207
Glamor Development Ltd v. Christodoulou 1 CLR 444 (1984), 106, 107
Global Cruises SA a.o. v. Metro Shipping & Travel Ltd 1 CLR 607 (1989), 342
Glynn & Co v. Margetson All ER Rep 693 (1891–1894), 130
Goldsworthy v. Brickell Ch. 378 (1987), 78
Gorringe v. Irwell India Rubber and Gutta Percha Works 34 Ch D 128 (1886), 139
Gort Processing Centre Ltd v. Cyprus 1 CLR 442 (1997), 129
Governor of the Bank of Ireland v. McCabe 4 J.I. B.L. 9 (1995), 321
Gray and another v. Demari Kronos Ltd, District Court of Ammochostos, Civil Case No. 748/2009, Judgment of 16 June 2014, not published in CLR, 153
Greenock v. Caledonian Ry (1917) A.C. 556, 153
Gregoriades v. Cyprus 3 CLR 2178 (1986), 267

Gregoriou a.a. v. Christoforou a.a. 1 CLR 248 (1995), 159, 342
Hadjiantoni v. Matsis 1 CLR 260 (1979), 166
Hadjikypris and others v. Sanifix Agencies Ltd and others 1 CLR 447 (1993), 175
Hadjipanayiotou v. Cyprus Airways (Duty Free Shops) Ltd 1 CLR 173 (2009), 453
HadjiYannis v. Attorney-General 1 CLR 32 (1970), 160, 171
Hadjizacharia v. Armeutis, Supreme Court of Cyprus, Civil Appeal No. 374/2010, Judgment of 28 September 2015, not published in CLR, 453
Haji Kypri Constantinides and Sons v. The King's Advocate 10 (1) CLR 29, 29, 35
Hamade v. Anthimos Demetriou Ltd a.o. 1 CLR 443 (1994), 210
Hamilton v. Watson 12 Cl. & F. 109 (1845), 320
Harrow Trading Ltd a.a. v. ADM Investor Services International Ltd 1 CLR 161 (2004), 318
Hartley v. Hymans 3 K.B. 475 (1920), 239
Hellenic Bank Ltd v. Polydorides a.o. 1 CLR 68 (1993), 156, 321
Hellenic Lines v. Artemis Co Ltd 1 CLR 139 (1969), 133
Hely-Hutchinson v. Brayhead Ltd a.a. 3 All ER 98 (1967), 183
Henderson & Co v. Williams 1 QB 521 (1895), 215
Heyman and another v. Darwins, Limited AC 356 (1942), 150
Hill v. South Staffordshire Railway 12 LT Rep 63 (1865), 122, 286
Hochster v. De la Tour 22 L.J. (Q.B.) 455 (1853), 150
Holman v. Johnson 1 Cowp 341 (1775), 83, 86
Hornal v. Neuberger Products Ltd 3 All ER 970 (1956), 51, 80
Horrocks v. Forray 1 All ER 737 (1976), 88
Hossam Taleb Yaacoub v. Cyprus, Supreme Court of Cyprus, Criminal Appeal No. 72/2013, Judgment of 19 March 2014, not published in CLR, 93
Howard v. Shirlstar Container Transport Ltd 1 WLR 1292 (1990), 86
Hubbart v. Vosper 1 All ER 1023 (1972), 341
Huntington v. Attrill AC 150 (1893), 107
Hussey v. Horne-Payne AC 311 (1879), 30
Hyatt International Corporation of Delaware, USA, v. Cyprus 3 CLR 337 (1985), 441
Iakovou a.a. v. Zapri 1 CLR 926 (2008), 190
ICS v. West Bromwich BS 1 All ER 98 (1998), 156
lderslade v. Hendon Laundry Ltd. QB Div 149 (1945), 178
In re Charalambous 1 CLR 736 (1985), 310
In re Ellinas 1 CLR 106 (1989), 427
In re Empress Engineering Company 16 Ch. D. 125, 137
In re Macartney 1 Ch. 522 (1921), 107
Inche Noriah v. Shaik Allie Bin Omar All ER Rep 189 (1928), 72
Indaco Service Soc. coop. sociale, Coop. sociale il Melograno v. Ufficio Territoriale del Governo Taranto, CJEU Case C-552/18, Judgment of 20 November 2019, digital ECR, 368
ING Re (UK) Ltd v. R & V Versicherung AG All ER (Comm) 870 (2006), 183
Inland Revenue Commissioners v. Electric and Musical Industries Ltd 1 All ER 120 (1949), 139
Inter Depol Ltd v. Kyriacos Papavassiliou Ltd 1 CLR 769 (1984), 340
Ioannis Kokkalos & Sons Ltd v. Karayiannis 1 CLR 377 (1975), 124, 178

Ioannou v. Charalambidou 1 CLR 555 (1998), 51, 75
Ioannou v. Karageorgiades 1 CLR 2240 (1998), 318
Ioannou v. Kounnides 1C CLR 1215 (1998), 207
Ioannou a.a. v. Siakalli a.o. 1 CLR 1877 (2013), 59
Ioannou a.a. v. Laiki Kypriaki Trapeza (Chrimatodotiseis) Ltd 1 CLR 91 (2011), 155
Iordanou v. Anyftos 1 CLR 97 (1958), 179
Iosifakis a.o. v. Mohammed Abdul Ghani 1 CLR 190 (1967), 40, 90
Irideos S.p.A. v. Poste Italiane S.p.A., CJEU Case C-419/19, OJ C 328, 30 September 2019, p. 5 (case pending), 401
Ismini Kyriacou HjiLoizi a.o. v. Irini Iona 2 CLR 11 (1962), 448
Isseyegh v. Cyprus 4 CLR 956 (1992), 198
Izzet v. Kypriaki Etaireia Apothukeusis Petrelaioeidon Ltd 1 CLR 11 (2009), 152
J. Evans & Son (Portsmouth) Ltd v. Andrea Merzario Ltd 2 All ER 930 (1976), 45
J. S. (a minor) 1 All ER 1061 (1980), 340
J T Stratford & Son Ltd v. Lindley 3 All ER 102 (1964), 340
Jack Windle Ltd v. Brierley 1 All ER 398 (1952), 451
Jacobson v. Frachon 138 LT 386 (1928), 107
James Miller and Partners Ltd v. Whitworth Street Estates (Manchester) Ltd 1 All ER 796 (1970), 129
James T. Burchell v. Gowrie and Blockhouse Collieries Ltd AC 614 (1910), 451
Janissa Trading Ltd v. Tikhonov a.o., District Court of Paphos, Civil Case No. 214/16, Judgment of 12 February 2016, not published in CLR, 98, 191
Jean Mackenzie v. Royal Bank of Canada AC 468 (1934), 63, 319
Jennings v. Hammond 9 QB 225 (1882), 94
Johnson v. Agnew 1 All ER 883 (1979), 175
Johnstone v. Milling 16 Q.B.D. 460 (1886), 150
Jupiter Electrical (Overseas) Ltd v. Savvas Costa Christides 1 CLR 144 (1975), 20
Kakoullou v. Kakoulli 1 CLR 355 (1985), 176
Kalisperas v. Dryadi 1 CLR 867 (1998), 175
Kallice Holding Co. Ltd v. MTR Metals (Overseas) Ltd (No. 2) 1B CLR 946 (1996), 83, 137
Kanaris v. Tosoun 1 CLR 637 (1969), 93, 95, 113
Karaoli a.o. v. Laouri a.a. 1 CLR 225 (2008), 43, 129, 130, 132
Karatsiolis v. Royal Sports Betting Ltd 1 CLR 669 (2008), 318
Karydas Taxi Co Ltd v. Komodikis 7 JSC 1101 (1976), 340, 341
Kastanos a.o. v. Cyprus Popular Bank (Leasing) Ltd 1 CLR 1374 (2009), 37, 174
Katafygiotis v. Chrysostomis 1 CLR 1746 (1997), 172
Katsikides v. Constantinides 1 CLR 31 (1969), 304
Katsikides v. Constantinides 1 CLR 147 (1970), 304
Kauno miesto savivaldybė, Kauno miesto savivaldybės administracija, CJEU Case C-285/18, Judgment of 3 October 2019, digital ECR, 352
Kefalas a.o. v. Cyprus 3 CLR 1011 (1993), 41
Kefalas v. Nicola 1 CLR 1226 (2000), 70, 72, 73
Kier (Cyprus) Ltd v. Trenco Constructions Ltd 1 CLR 30 (1981), 152, 174,181, 182
Kimon Tutorial Centre (Idiotika Frontistiria) Ltd v. Gabriel 1 CLR 2069 (1998), 116
Kirkness v. Lord Hudson & So Ltd 2 All ER 345 (1955), 234

Kish v. Taylor 1 KB 625 (1911), 131
Klemke Mining Corporation v. Shell Canada Ltd ABQB 176 (2007), 35
Kokkinos v. Pissarides 1 CLR 967 (1995), 156
Kolokasides v. Epitropis Ekpaideutikis Ypiresias 4 CLR 1063 (1996), 34
Kolokasides v. Michael Theodosiou Ltd 1 CLR 1671 (1997), 172
Konstantinou a.o. v. National Bank of Greece (Cyprus) Ltd 1 CLR 1327 (2007), 321
Konteades v. Yusukjian 15 (1) CLR 122, 286
Komodromou v. A.Th. Shikkis Motors Ltd a.a. 1 CLR 481 (1999), 172
Koropouli & Demetriou v. Abraham 1 CLR 78 (1987), 93
Koropoulis v. Pelides, Supreme Court of Cyprus, Civil Appeal No. 324/2009, Judgment of 14 November 2014, not published in CLR, 57
Kostonia v. Photos Photiades Distributors Ltd 1 CLR 670 (2012), 29
Kotsara v. The Official Receiver and Registrar, Trustee in Bankruptcy 1 CLR 119 (1966), 142
Kounnas and Sons Ltd v. Zim 1 CLR 181 (1966), 15
Kountourou v. Cyprus Bank of Development Ltd 1A CLR 322 (2008), 319
Kounouna and others v. Kostas Kyriakou & Yios Ltd and others 1(C) CLR 2126 (2001), 176
Kourris v. Alpo Ltd a.o. 1 CLR 217 (1981), 137, 207
Koutas v. Dimos Lefkosias 1E CLR 516 (1989), 76
Ktimatiki Etaireia Hadjikyriakou Demosia Ltd v. A. & Chr. Agapiou Imports Ltd and others, District Court of Nicosia Action No. 6408/2006, Judgment of 4 October 2012, not published in CLR, 175
Kurt Kingsfield v. The Republic of Cyprus 3 CLR 45 (1966), 417
Kypriaki Epitropi Sitiron v. Zako Ltd 1 CLR 1046 (1990), 197
Kyriakides v. Kyriakides 1 CLR 76 (1976), 129
Kyrillis Masouri & Bro v. the Employers' Liability Assurance Corporation Ltd 1 CLR 517 (1969), 124
KYRIO (I.T.H.) Company v. Kassapi 2 JSC 259 (1980), 49, 178
Laiki Kypriaki Trapeza (Chrimatodotiseis) Ltd v. Christou Iordanous and another, District Court of Nicosia Action No. 13803/03, Judgment of 20 May 2008 not reported in CLR, 261
Laiki Kypriaki Trapeza (Chrimatodotises) Ltd v. Konstantinou and another 1 CLR 1432 (2001), 261
Laiki Kypriaki Trapeza (Chrimatodotiseis) Ltd. v. Thomas Liobay Developments Ltd. and others, District Court of Nicosia Action No. 369/01, Judgment of 31 May 2007, not published in CLR, 268
Lakatamitis v. Theodorou 1 CLR 520 (1983), 340
Lambrianides a.o. v. The Electricity Authority of Cyprus 1 CLR 466 (1968), 35, 52, 179
Lambrou v. Paraschou a.o. 1 CLR 397 (1993), 130
Langley Lo-Cost Builders Ltd v. 474835 BC Ltd BCCA 365 (2000), 35
Larcos v. Attorney-General 1 CLR 510 (1995), 302
Laurence v. Lexcourt Holdings Ltd 1 WLR 1128 (1978), 65
Lazouras v. Skyllouriotou 1A CLR 168 (1992), 131
Leduc v. Ward QBD 475 (1888), 47
Lee a.a. v. Jones English Reports 144 (1864), 63

Lefkaritis a.o. v. Beach Hotels Ltd 1 CLR 194 (2000), 129
Leniana Tourist Services Ltd. v. Andrea Chr. Karpaspi & Yioi (Biomihania) Ltd. 1 CLR 75 (1991), 150
Level Tachexcars Ltd. v. Kargotis 1 CLR 163 (1970), 304
Levison v. Patent Steam Carpet Cleaning 3 All ER 498 (1977), 178
Lindos Constructions Ltd v. Dieufthintis Tmimatos Kinonikon Asfaliseon 1 CLR 17 (1993), 184
Linsen International Ltd v. Humpuss Sea Transport Pte Ltd EWHC 303 (2010), 342
Liopetri Transport Co. v. Constantinou 1 CLR 424 (1971), 183
Litonor Financial Ltd. v. R.G.I. Residential Holdings Ltd., District Court of Nicosia Action No. 3073/2014, Judgment of 29 December 2016, not published in CLR, 173
Lloyds Bank Ltd v. Bundy 3 WLR 501 (1974), 51, 70, 319
Loizidou v. Georgiou 9 JSC 1219 (1973), 49
London General Omnibus Company Ltd. v. Holloway 2 KB 72 (1912), 63, 319
Louka v. Eurolife Ltd 1 CLR 1524 (2009), 139
Luxor (Eastbourne) Ltd. a.o. v. Cooper 1 All ER 33 (1941), 120, 129
Lymperopoulou v. Christodoulou a.o. 22 (1) CLR 186,143
M' Gugan v. Smith 21 SCR 263 (1892), 452
M & M Transport Co Ltd v. Eteria Astikon Leoforion Lemessou Ltd 1 CLR 605 (1981), 341
M. Moniati & Sons Ltd v. Neophytou 1 CLR 1096 (2008), 84
M.C.A. Hotels Ltd v. Sartas Ltd, District Court of Larnaca, Civil Case No. 1662/04, Judgment of 29 March 2007, not reported in CLR, 90
Magdalene Theodoulou Kalogerou v. A. Zakheos Estates Ltd., District Court of Famagusta Action No. 411/2002, Judgment of 21 June 2006, not published in CLR, 176
Magistrato Gardens Limited v. Attorney-General 1 CLR 220 (2012), 242
Maison Jenny Ltd v. Krashias Footwear Industry Ltd 1 CLR 1156 (2002), 152, 153
Maltezou a.a. v. Louka a.a. 16 CLR 88, 179
MARCEGAGLIA SpA and another v. m/v VYSOKOGORSK, Naval Court of Cyprus, Naval Action No. 31/2013 Judgment of 25 September 2017, not published in CLR, 175
Marfin Popular Bank Public Co Ltd v. Demos Hadjineocleous and others 1 CLR 595 (2013), 268
Marketrends Finance Ltd v. Perdikou a.o. 1 CLR 1042 (2006), 49
Marketventures Ltd v. Dikomites 1 CLR 383 (2009), 45
Marketventures Ltd v. Kallika 1 CLR 48 (2010), 183
Markides v. Ellinas Finance Public Company Ltd, Supreme Court of Cyprus, Civil Appeal No. 97/2011, Judgment of 5 May 2017, not published in CLR, 200, 206
Markidou v. Hellenic Bank Ltd 1 CLR 2069 (2001), 64
Markidou v. Kiliaris a.a. 1 CLR 392 (1983), 139, 161, 177, 179
Martin-Baker Aircraft Co Ltd v. Canadian Flight Equipment 2 All ER 722 (1955), 204
Markitsis v. Thanos Hotels Ltd 1 CLR 449 (2005), 153
Maskell v. Horner 3 KB 106 (1915), 76
Matthews v. Munster 20 QBD 141 (1887), 310

Mavromoustaki v. Yeroudes 1 CLR 176 (1965), 90
Mavroskoufi v. Piraeus Bank (Cyprus) Ltd, Supreme Court of Cyprus, Civil Appeal No. 352/2008, Judgment of 16 April 2014, not published in CLR, 319
Mavrou v. Theodorou 1 CLR 635 (1984), 49
McCutcheon v. David Macbrayne Ltd. 1 Lloyd's Rep. 16 (1964), 32
Meca Srl v. Comune di Napoli, CJEU Case No. C-41/18, Judgment of 19 June 2019, digital ECR, 357, 365
Men Mar Ltd v. CLP Catering Ltd, District Court of Larnaca Action Nos 891/06 & 874/06, Judgment of 1 December 2011, not published in CLR, 175
Melaisi v. M & M Georgiki Eteria 1 CLR 748 (1979), 167
Mercantile Bank of Sydney v. Taylor AC 317 (1893), 49
Merkis v. Intertobacco (Cyprus) Ltd 1 CLR 1091 (2003), 137, 215
Metaxas Loizides Syrimis & Co a.o. v. L.K. Globalsoft Com. Ltd 1 CLR 54 (2007), 117, 172
Miaris v. Cyprus Popular Bank Ltd 1 CLR 1625 (2011), 329
Michaelides a.o. v. Chatziirodotou 1 CLR 1609 (2003), 92 *Mills v. Bayley* 133 RR 579 (1863), 286
Ministrstvo za notranje zadeve v. Tax-Fin-Lex d. o. o., CJEU C-367/19, Judgment of 10 September 2020, digital ECR, 350
Modern Light Cars Ltd. v. Seals 1 KB 32 (1934), 262
Mogul Steamship Co v. McGregor, Gow & Co AC 25 (1982), 106
Mohori Bibee v. Dhurmodas Ghose 19 Times Law Reports 295, 58
Molivo Ltd a.a. v. Hudaverdi Mustafa Hudaverdi a.a. 1 CLR 278 (2013), 136
Morley v. Loughnan 1 Ch D 736 (1893), 72, 75
Mosilioti v. Panayi a.a. JSC 384 (1979), 95
Mountis v. Papachristophorou 1 CLR 2637 (2012), 66
Mourtzinos v. tou ploiou Galaxias a.o. 1 CLR 80 (1997), 51, 80
Murray v. Cohen 9 LR (NSW) Eq 124 (1888), 286
Muskita Aluminium Industries Ltd a.o. v. Alsako Aluminium Ltd a.o. 1 CLR 1481 (2009), 45
Mutual Finance Ltd v. Wetton 2 KB 389 (1937), 74
Myroforas John Seago v. Thoma Athanasiou and another, District Court of Larnaca, Action No. 1730/2005, Judgment of 19 September 2007, not reported in CLR, 149
Nadine Paquay v. Société d'architectes Hoet + Minne SPRL, CJEU Case No. C-460/06, Judgment of 11 October 2007, ECR I-08511 (2007), 297
Najem Houry and Sons v. Ex-King Hussein 13 (1) CLR 49, 35
Nash v. Inman 2 KB 1 (1908), 310
National Westminster Bank plc v. Morgan 1 All ER 821 (1985), 78
Nemitsas Industries Ltd v. S & S Maritime Ltd. a.o. 10 JSC 1542 (1976), 340
Neophytos Neophytou v. Elma Holdings Ltd 1 CLR 1807 (2013), 150
Neophytou v. Kyriakides (No. 3) 1 CLR 299 (1999), 155
Neophytou and others v. Ttaba 1 CLR 1352 (2012), 153
Nicolaides v. The Chartered Bank of Famagusta 1 CLR 56 (1966), 63, 68, 319
Nicolas Droushiotis (Import-Export) Ltd v. L'Union Des Assurances De Paris a.o. 1 CLR 19 (1983), 322, 325

Nikolas Genethliou and another v. G. Kofteros Industries Ltd., District Court of Nicosia Action No. 1060/2011, Judgment of 5 September 2017, not published in CLR, 178
Nikolaou v. Ellinas Finance Ltd a.o., Supreme Court of Cyprus Civil Appeal No. 373/09, Judgment of 22 November 2013, not reported in CLR, 342
Nippon Yusen Kaisha v. Karageorgis a.a. 3 All ER 282 (1975), 340
Noriah v. Omar AC 127 (1929), 77
Odysseos v. Pieris Estates a.o. 1 CLR 557 (1982), 340
Official Receiver v. National Bank of Greece S.A. 1 CLR 38 (2005), 348
Oikonomou a.a. v. Ttofini a.a. 1 CLR 436 (1993), 88, 131
Olds Discount Co. Ltd. v. John Playfair Ltd. 3 All ER 275 (1938), 268
Orakpo v. Manson Investments 3 All ER 1 (1977), 449
Orlando Development Ltd v. Lante Enterprises Ltd, District Court of Larnaca Civil Case No. 871/2011, Judgment of 30 November 2018, not published in CLR, 153
Orphanides v. Michaelides 1 CLR 309 (1967), 450, 451
Oterom Ltd v. Christodoulides 1 CLR 1081 (2002), 127
Oxynou v. Nikolaides a.o. 1 CLR 351 (2001), 156
P.A. Panagoulas Trading Ltd v. Aggelas Oikonomidou, District Court of Paphos Action No. 144/2011, Judgment of 3 October 2017, not published in CLR, 175
Paikkos v. Kontemeniotis 1 CLR 50 (1989), 183
Pamborides v. Michaelides 1 CLR 685 (1984), 312
Pampos Zenios Trading Ltd a.o. v. Hadjipavlou & Ios Ltd a.o. 1C CLR 2322 (2011), 143
Panagiasis a.o. v. Spyros Stavrinides Chemicals Ltd 1 CLR 232 (1993), 179
Panasoft AE v. Xenos Travel Ltd, District Court of Nicosia Action No. 4828/2005, Judgment of 28 February 2011, not reported in CLR, 149
Panayiotou v. Bank of Cyprus Ltd, Supreme Court of Cyprus, Civil Appeal No. 276/2009, Judgment of 9 July 2014, not published in CLR, 320
Panayiotou v. Island Beach Development Ltd 1 CLR 623 (1985), 179
Panayiotou v. Solomou CLR 779 (1979), 106
Panoutsos v. Raymond Hadley Corporation of New York 2 K.B. 473 (1917), 239
Panpa Estates & Investments Ltd a.o. v. Rodou Charalambous & Son Ltd 1 CLR 1897 (2013), 323
Pantzaris v. Cyprus 3A CLR 861 (1989), 234
Pantziari v. Aquarian Container Lines Ltd a.a. 1 CLR 748 (1993), 172, 175, 180
Papacharalambous a.o. v. The Republic of Cyprus 3A CLR 342 (1989), 419
Papadopoulos v. Christophorou 1 CLR 204 (2002), 51
Papadopoulos v. Euroinvestment & Finance Ltd 1 CLR 2091 (2011), 347
Papadopoulou v. Polycarpou 1 CLR 352 (1968), 58, 114, 131, 174, 310
Papakleovoulou v. Elia a.a. 1 CLR 222 (1972), 130
Papakokkinou v. Kanther 1 CLR 65 (1982), 176, 180
Papapetrou v. Laiki Factors Ltd, Supreme Court of Cyprus, Civil Appeal No. 180/2010, Judgment of 20 February 2015, not published in CLR, 49
Papargyrou v. Michaelides, Supreme Court of Cyprus, Civil Appeal No. 215/2010, Judgment of 27 September 2016, not published in CLR, 167
Papavasiliou v. Kleanthous a.a. 1 CLR 200 (1984), 242
Paraskeva a.o. v. Lantas 1 CLR 285 (1988), 167, 180

Parsec Fondazione Parco delle Scienze e della Cultura v. Ministero delle Infrastrutture e dei Trasporti, Autorità nazionale anticorruzione (ANAC), CJEU Case C-219/19, Judgment of 11 June 2020, digital ECR, 395
Partridhe v. Crittenden I WLR 1204 (1968), 32
Paschalis v. Proodeutikis Asphalistikis Etaireias Ltd 1A CLR 69 (2008), 33
Patatsou v. Hilmi a.a., Supreme Court of Cyprus, Civil Appeal No. 300/2011, Judgment of 31 May 2017, not published in CLR, 41
Pattis v. Pari, District Court of Nicosia Action No. 60/2015, Judgment of 18 October 2017, not published in CLR, 175
Patsalidou v. Kyriakides 1 CLR 71 (1979), 51, 70, 75, 77
Paul Smith Ltd v. H & S. (International) Holdings Inc. 2 Lloyd's Rep 127 (1991), 126
Peak Hotels And Resorts Limited v. Tarek Investments Limited EWHC 3048 (2015), 173
Pell Frishmann Consultants Ltd v. Cyprus 1A CLR 33 (2001), 128, 130
Pelidou-Kalli a.a. v. Golden Star Supermarket Ltd 1 CLR 1624 (2010), 305
Perestrello e Companhia Limitada v. United Paint Co Ltd. 1 WLR 570 (1969), 176
Perihan Mustafa Korkut v. Georgiou 1 CLR 905 (2008), 106
Petrotim Ltd v. Itera International Energy LLC a.o. 1 CLR 260 (2007), 71
Pharmaceutical Society v. Boots I QB 401 (1953), 32
Philippou v. Philippou 1 CLR 689 (1986), 271
Philippou Ltd. v. Josephy Hoyle and Son Ltd. 1 CLR 625 (1982), 175, 282
Photiades v. Photiades 3 CLR 2084 (1988), 419
Photiou Bros. Co. Ltd. a.a. v. Autolifts and Engineering Co Ltd 1 CLR 422 (1984), 240
Photo-Staff Consultants Ltd. v. Michael Geades and others, District Court of Nicosia Action No. 645/1977, Judgment of 19 May 1980, not published in CLR, 178
Pierides v. Youlielmou 1 CLR 470 (1985), 305
Pilavachi & Co Ltd v. International Chemical Co Ltd 1 CLR 97 (1965), 107
Pilkington United Kingdom Limited v. CGU Insurance Plc EWCA Civ 23 (2004), 172
Pirillou v. Konnari 1 CLR 1153 (2000), 137, 176
Pittalis a.o. v. Ianira Enterprises Ltd a.o. 1 CLR 814 (1997), 51
Pitts v. Hunt 1 QB 24 (1991), 86
Poly G. Knitwear Ltd v. Loukos Trading Co. Ltd a.a. 1 CLR 96 (2007), 318
Polycast Panels Ltd v. Alpha Trapeza Ltd 1 CLR 1396 (2009), 32
Polycarpou v. Polycarpou 1 CLR 182 (1982), 49, 81
Poosathurai v. Kannappa Chettiar LR 47 Ind. App.1 (1919), 78
Portsmouth v. Cyprus Inland Telecommunications Authority 1 CLR 87 (1967), 51, 61, 120, 121, 456
Potter v. Sanders 6 Hare 1 (1846), 160
Pourikkos v. Savva a.o. 1 CLR 507 (1991), 189
Poyiatzis v. Pilavakis a.a. 1 CLR 411 (1988), 305
Powell v. Powell 1 Ch D 243 (1900), 72
Prenn v. Simmonds 3 All ER 237 (1971), 129
Preston v. Luck 27 Ch D 497 (1884), 340
Prince v. Alico American Life Insurance Company 1A CLR 280 (2005), 33

Prokopiou v. Adelfoi Tymvioi Ltd 1 CLR 903 (2007), 200
Prolific Insurance Consultants Ltd v. Liberty Life Insurance Public Co Ltd 1 CLR 1069 (2010), 194
Property Discount Corpn. v. Lyon Group 1 All ER 33 (1980), 161
Protopappa v. Protopappa a.a. 1 CLR 1329 (2002), 188
Prudential Assurance Ltd v. Newman Industries Ltd & Others (No.2) Ch. 204 (1982), 173
PT Kiani Kertas v. Interorient Navigation Company Ltd a.o. 1 CLR 967 (1999), 126
Rabin v. Mendoza 1 WLR 271 (1954), 310
Raffles v. Wichehaus 2 H & C 906, 29
Raif v. Dervish 1 CLR 158 (1971), 40
Ramez Karanouh v. Maros Agapiou and another 1(E) CLR 377 (1989), 175
Raptopoulos a.o. v. Alpha Bank Ltd, Supreme Court of Cyprus, Civil Appeal No. 337/2011, Judgment of 11 April 2017, not reported in CLR, 59, 67
Re Brocklehurst (deceased) Hall and Another v. Roberts 1 All ER 767 (1978), 51
Re Craig (Deceased) Ch. 95 (1971), 51
Re D'Angiban 15 Ch D 228 (1880), 74
Re Dunn Trust Ltd v. Feetham 1 K.B. 22 (1936), 346 *Re Wells Boyer v. MacLean* 1 Ch D 848 (1903), 310
Redgrave v. Hurd 20 Ch D 1 (1881), 65
Resola (Cyprus) Ltd v. Christou 1 CLR 598 (1998), 340
Riley v. Troll 1 All ER 966 (1953), 36
Roland Preston & Partners v. Markheath Securities 2 EGLR 23 (1988), 36
Romanos v. Chrysanthou 1 CLR 991 (1991), 39
Ron Ghitter Property Consultants Ltd v. Beaver Lumber Company Ltd ABCA 221 (2003), 35
Rookes v. Barnard 1 All ER 367 (1964), 19
Roussos v. Cyprus 3 CLR 517 (1996), 41
Royal Bank of Scotland v. Etridge (No.2) All ER 449 (2001), 64, 319
Saab a.o. v. The Holy Monastery of Ayios Neophytos 1 CLR 499 (1982), 88, 131, 175, 177
Said Hamade v. Anthimos Demetriou Ltd a.o. 1 CLR 443 (1994), 15
Salgrove Properties Inc v. Amro Consultants Ltd a.o. 1 CLR 2171 (2012), 174
Satyabrata Ghose v. Mugneeram Bangur and co. SCR 31 (1954), 151, 152
Savides v. Haji Stavrinou, Haji Sava and Yannadji 13 (1) CLR 29, 142
Savvides v. Christofides 1 CLR 303 (1978), 261
Savoy Overseers v. Art Union of London AC 296 (1896), 114
Savva v. Laiki Asfalistiki Etaireia Ltd 1(B) CLR 1609 (2009), 119
Scammell & Nephew Ltd v. Ouston AC 251 (1941), 29, 35
Scarpetta v. Lowenfeld 27 TLR 509 (1911), 107
Scholefield Goodman & Sons v. Zyngier 3 All ER 105 (1985), 321
Secretaria Regional de Saúde dos Açores v. Ministério Público, CJEU Case C-102/17, Judgment of 25 April 2018, digital ECR, 373
Sergidou v. Dimos Lefkosias a.a. 4 CLR 211 (1993), 198
Shacolas v. Michaelides a.a. 1 CLR 290 (1967), 239, 282

Silver Trust Commercial Ltd v. Genikes Asphalies Kyprou Ltd a.o., District Court of Limassol, Civil Case No. 4837/08, Judgment of 15 April 2016, not published in CLR, 33
Sir Shiba Prasad v. Maharaja Srish Chandra A.I.R. P.C. 297 (1949), 61, 456
Skattou v. M/V 'KOREIZ' a.a. 1 CLR 804 (1982), 310
Smally v. Smally 1 Eq Cas Abr 283 (1700), 74
Smeaton Hanscomb & Co. Ltd. v. Sassoon I. Setty Son & Co. (No. 1), 1 WLR 1468 (1953), 149
Smith v. Hamilton 2 All ER 928 (1950), 167
Smith v. Hughes LR 6 QB 597 (1871), 32
Smith v. Mawhood 14 M & W 452 (1845), 93
Socratous v. Siviranides 1 CLR 1602 (1998), 51
Sokratous v. Emenby Company Ltd, District Court of Limassol, Civil Case No. 1534/2012, Judgement of 7 September 2018, not published in CLR, 153
Sokratous v. Tsivanides 1 CLR 1602 (1998), 41,72, 73, 64
Solomou a.o. v. Marfin Popular Bank Public Co. Ltd 1 CLR 36 (2011), 37
Solomou v. Solomou a.o. 1 CLR 1058 (2001), 41
Solon Piitarides Developers Ltd a.o. v. Markoullis a.o., District Court of Famagusta, Civil Case No. 47/2008, Judgment of 30 April 2015, not published in CLR, 45
Sonco Canning Ltd v. 'Adriatica' (Societe Per Azioni Di Navigazione) 1 CLR 127 (1973), 137
S.O.R.E.L. Limited v. Nicos Servos 1 CLR 123 (1968), 453
Spinosa Costruzioni Generali SpA and Melfi Srl v. Comune di Monteroduni, CJEU Case C-162/16, Judgment of 10 November 2016, digital ECR, 352
Spyrou a.a. v. Kosta Kyriakou & Sons Ltd a.o. 1 CLR 663 (1992), 189
St. George (G.N.W.) Ltd v. National Bank of Greece (Cyprus) Ltd 1 CLR 337 (2010), 210
St. John Shipping Corporation v. Joseph Rank Ltd 1 QB 267 (1957), 90, 93, 113
State of Gujarat v. Memon Mohammad 3 SCR 938 (1967), 207
Stavrou v. Demetriou 1 CLR 304 (1991), 71, 180
Stavrou v. G. Roditis & Partners 1 CLR 477 (2008), 453
Steamer Shipping Co Ltd v. Sibyl Trading & Shipping Ltd 1 CLR 106 (1996), 127
Stefanos & Andreas Cold Stores Trading Ltd. v. Etaireias Anapsyktikon KEAN Ltd. 1 CLR 2335 (1998), 178
Stelios Morsis v. Cyprus 1 JSC 12 (1965), 409
Stock v. Frank Jones 1 All ER 948 (1978), 130
Storer v. Manchester City Council 1 WLR 1403 (1974), 32
Stylianides v. British American Insurance Co. Ltd 1C CLR 1722 (2003), 35, 36
Stylianides v. Hadjipiera 1 CLR 1056 (1992), 39
Stylianou v. Iliada Hotels Ltd, District Court of Famagusta, Joint Civil Cases Nos. 1293/2010 and 1294/2010, Judgment of 8 June 2015, not published in CLR, 183
Stylianou v. Lalakis 1 CLR 287 (1982), 282
Stylianou a.o. v. Papacleovoulou a.a. 1 CLR 542 (1982), 156
Suisse Atlantique Societe D'armement Maritime SA v. N V Rotterdamsche Kolen Centrale 2 All ER 61 (1966), 149

Swift Fortune Ltd (The Capaz Duckling) v. Magnifica Marine SA 1 Lloyd's Rep. 54 (2008), 342
Synergatiki Kentriki Trapeza Ltd v. The Ship 'Elegance' of Belize 1 CLR 981 (2005), 126
Synergatiki Pistotiki Etaireia Agias Fylaksews v. Poulla a.a. 1B CLR 961 (2004), 78, 319
Synergatiki Pistotiki Etaireia Konteas v. Nikos Larkos 1 CLR 369 (1998), 17
Synergatiki Pistotiki Etaireia Makrasykas v. Kapetaniou, Supreme Court of Cyprus, Civil Appeal No. 200/2009, Judgment of 9 January 2014, not published in CLR, 323
Syrimi v. Organismos Chrimatodotiseos Pagkypriaki Ltd 1 CLR 1131 (2010), 116
T Systems Magyarország Zrt. and Others v. Közbeszerzési Hatóság Közbeszerzési Döntőbizottság and Others, CJEU C-263/19, Judgment of 14 May 2020, digital ECR, 350
Takis Photiades v. The Republic of Cyprus 3 CLR 460 (1986), 419
Tamassos Tobacco Suppliers and Co. v. The Republic of Cyprus 3A CLR 219 (1989), 414, 419
Tams Beit v. Elias Ioanni Papa and another 1 CLR 172 (1971), 150
Tamplin S.S. Co. v. The Anglo Mexican Petroleum Products Co 2 AC 397 (1916), 152
Taylor v. Stibbert 2 Ves 437 (1794), 160
Tecoma Travel & Tours Ltd v. Basos Ioannou Ltd 1 CLR 399 (2007), 197
Telecom Italia SpA v. Ministero dello Sviluppo Economico and Infrastrutture e telecomunicazioni per l'Italia SpA (Infratel Italia SpA), CJEU Case C-697/17, Judgment of 11 July 2019, digital ECR, 355
Tennent v. Earl of Glascow 2 Macq. (H.I.) 22 (1864), 153
The Antclizo 2 Lloyd's Rep. 130 (1987), 32
The El Amria 2 Lloyd's Reports 119 (1981), 126
The Eleftheria 2 All ER 641 (1969), 126
The 'Hoegh Apapa' 2 Lloyd's Law Reports 9 (1983), 76
The Jonitexo Ltd v. Adidas Sportschufabrieken Adi Dassler KG 1 CLR 263 (1984), 340, 341
The Sennar 2 All ER 104 (1985), 126
The Ship Dama v. Georghiades SA 1 CLR 368 (1980), 15
The Ship Yayasan Satu v. Welsen Shipping Co. Ltd. 1 CLR 1115 (1998), 20
Theocharous v. Pastelli 1 CLR 240 (1993), 131
Theodoulou v. Aspis Pronia Asphalistiki Etairia Zois 1 CLR 1551 (1997), 288
Theodorou v. Sekkeris 1 CLR 337 (1971), 150
Theologou a.a. v. Ktimatikis Etaireias Nemesis Ltd 1 CLR 407 (1998), 59, 129, 132, 156
Thomas and James Bernard Ltd v. Lanitis 13 (1) CLR 43, 333
Thomas Bates & Son v. Wyndhams Ltd 1 WLR 505 (1981), 156
Three Rivers DC v. Bank of England 4 All ER 312 (1995), 139
Thunder Shipping Co Ltd v. Lloyd Triestino, Di.Nav.S.p.A. 1 CLR 135 (1984), 197
Tinsley v. Milligan 1 AC 340 (1994), 86
To Ploio 'Panayia Myrtidiotissa' v. Sidiropoulou a.a. 1 CLR 1000 (1998), 76

Tomaridou-Eliadou v. Dimou Paphou, District Court of Paphos, Civil Case No. 3093/2007, Judgment of 28 July 2011, not published in CLR, 154
Torquay Hotel Co Ltd v. Cousins 2 Ch. 106 (1969), 19
Touloumi a.a. v. Militadou 1 CLR 129 (1982), 311
Tradax v. Gueensea Marine Co 1 CLR 559 (1986), 127
Trapeza Kyprou Dimosia Etaireia Ltd v. K&M Famagusta Developers and Constructions Ltd, District Court of Larnaca-Famagusta Action No. 736/2012, Judgment of 22 September 2016, not published in CLR, 178
Trendtex Trading corpn.v. Credit Suisse 3 All ER 721 (1980), 139
Trifonides v. Alpan/(Taki) Bros 1 CLR 224 (1988), 160
Tseriotis v. Christodoulou 19 CLR 216, 179
Tufton v. Sperni 2 TLR 516 (1952), 74
Turkish Bank of Nicosia Ltd v. Cukurova a.o. 1 CLR 233 (1977), 155, 348
Turner v. Collins 7 Ch App 329 (1871), 66
Tziepra v. Savva a.a. 1 CLR 2410 (2013), 143
U Drive Company Ltd v. Panayi a.a. 1 CLR 544 (1980), 137
United Dominions Trust v. Kirkwood 1 All ER 968 (1966), 347
Universe Tankships Inc of Monrovia v. International Transport Workers' Federation 2 All ER 67 (1982), 76
Unknown v. unknown, Supreme Court of Greece (Areios Pagos) Civil Case No. 172/2013, Judgment of 8 January 2013, not published, 153
Vandervell's Trusts (No. 2) 3 All ER 205 (1974), 86
Vartholomeou v. Kannaourou 1 CLR 221 (1978), 114
Veniera Navigation Co. Ltd. v. Sertina Shipping Co. Ltd. 1 CLR 742 (1985), 175
Vetalia Clothing Manufacturers Ltd v. Cyprus 4 CLR 453 (2000), 41
Vincent Della Tolla v. Kyriakides 20 (1) CLR 89, 152
Vitali SpA v. Autostrade per l'Italia SpA, CJEU Case C-63/18, Judgment of 26 September 2019, digital ECR, 382
Voniatis v. Koureas a.a. 1 CLR 492 (1979), 424
Vossloh Laeis GmbH v. Stadtwerke München GmbH, CJEU Case C-124/17, Judgment of 24 October 2018, digital ECR, 365
Walford v. Miles 2 AC 128 (1992), 26
Watkins v. Vince 2 Stark 368 (1818), 74
Waugh a.o. v. H.B. Clifford & Sons 1 All ER 1095 (1982), 310
Way v. Latilla 3 All ER 759 (1937), 453
Whitehouse v. Jordan a.a. 1 All ER 650 (1980), 51, 80
Whittaker v. Campbell QB 318 (1984), 32
Winn v. Bull 7 Ch D 29 (1877), 36
Xenopoulos v. Makrides 1 CLR 488 (1969), 160, 161
Xenopoulos v. Thomas Nelson (Insurance) Ltd a.o. 1 CLR 674 (1982), 49, 130
Xenophondos v. Anastasiadou 4 JSC 578 (1974), 19
Xenophontos v. Tyrimou 1 CLR 23 (1984), 151, 152
Xenos Travel Ltd v. Panasoft AE, Supreme Court of Cyprus, Civil Appeal No. 116/2011, Judgment of 21 February 2017, not reported in CLR, 149
xxx Georgiades and Tahudomi Ltd and xxx Theodotou, District Court of Larnaca Action No. 2008/2011, Judgment of 25 April 2019, not published in CLR, 172

xxx Zachariades v. Universal Life Insurance Ltd, Civil Appeal No. 144/2013, Judgment of 16 April 2019, not reported in CLR, 19
Yalta Sea Trade Port v. Emed Chartering Ltd a.o. 1 CLR 7 (2001), 126
Yiannakouri a.a. (No. 3) v. Cyprus Sea Cruises (Limassol) Ltd 1 CLR 397 (1965), 197 *Zacharias Stavrou Zachariades Ltd v. Tax Department* 3 CLR 445 (2000), 93
Zamet v. Hyman 3 All ER 933 (1961), 51
Zervos a.o. v. Bank of Cyprus Public Company Ltd 1 CLR 38 (2013), 40
Zervos v. Euroinvestment & Finance Public Ltd (ex Euroinvestment & Finance Ltd) 1 CLR 688 (2013), 347
Zervou v. Bank of Cyprus Public Company Ltd 1 CLR 2192 (2011), 347
Zinonos a.o. v. Cyprus Popular Bank (Financing) Ltd 1 CLR 927 (2002), 129

Index

The numbers here refer to paragraph numbers.

Accident, 72, 430
Accident, major, 299
acta iure imperii, 314
Advantage, 62, 70, 114, 117, 174, 176, 181, 297, 359, 363, 368, 377–378, 404, 409–410
Advertisement, 32, 230
Agency, 11, 12, 27, 136, 138, 183–205, 253
Arbitration, 11, 110
Arbitration, clause of, 110, 126–128, 343
Arbitration, international commercial, 127, 339 et seq.
Authorization, 98, 196, 228, 305

Bailment, 11, 12, 27, 206–253, 258, 331
Bill of exchange, 250, 253
Bill of lading, 15, 47, 83, 250, 253, 334

CISG (*see* international trade of goods)
Civil uprising, 293
Classified information, 407, 411–411
Clean hands, 98, 342
Coercion, 61, 69–70, 76–77, 115, 364, 456
Collateral agreement, 45
Collateral security, 262, 338
Common law – deviation from, 39–40
Compensation, 14, 18, 40, 52, 83, 151, 155, 166–167, 172, 174, 179, 190, 195, 203–204, 214, 219–220, 245, 282, 307, 340, 348, 369, 448, 452
Confidentiality, 315, 385–386, 405, 411
consensus ad idem, 35–36
Constitution, 3, 5, 108, 301, 364, 431, 436
Corporate veil, piercing, 200
Corruption, 357, 364
Crisis, 71, 409

Damages, exemplary, 19, 180
Damages, indirect, 172, 190
Damages, nominal, 52
Damages, remote, 172
Damages, punitive, 180
Damages, quantification, 177, 343
Defect of consent, 16, 59–78, 114–118, 158–182
Death, 14, 25, 146–147, 205, 221, 278, 301, 330, 364, 424, 426–427, 438, 446
depositum, 207
Diligence, ordinary, 62, 66, 263
Diligence, reasonable, 151, 190, 219
Discrimination, gender, 292, 301, 352, 363, 372, 379, 395, 409
Discrimination, nationality, 301, 352, 363, 372, 379, 395, 409

Enforcement, 2, 107, 145, 159, 343, 457
English law, 4, 152, 160, 172, 179
Environment, 2, 298–299, 353, 367, 376, 377, 379–380, 382, 410
Estoppel, 65, 171, 183, 312
European Union, 1, 7, 28, 97, 108, 289, 301, 354, 364, 388
Equal payment, 292
Equity, 3, 5, 76, 139, 160, 167, 171, 271, 321–322, 325, 342
Evidence, documentary, 349
Evidence, extrinsic, 45, 49, 130
Evidence, hearsay, 101
Evidence, parol, 49
Evidence, preliminary, 374
ex turpi causa non oritur action, 86

German Civil Code, 12, 339
Gratuitous, 41, 210, 218, 221, 448

Index

Fictitious contracts, 37, 174–175
Force majeure, 153-154, 293
Forgery, 85
Fraud, 14, 17, 51, 72, 80–85, 90, 96–103, 116–117, 122, 141–143, 173, 193, 201, 228, 261, 263, 286, 334, 339, 364, 435, 439, 445

Human health, 299
Husband (& wife), 14, 63–64, 72, 75, 301, 319

Illegality, 70, 83–86, 89–112, 113, 116, 155, 230, 265, 288, 294, 305, 348, 364
Immorality, 86, 90, 105–107, 305
Impossibility, 40, 111, 116, 134–136, 151–152, 340, 378
Imprisonment, 14, 102, 223–226, 228–229, 267, 272, 292, 294, 297, 386, 412, 433
Indemnity, 12, 24, 27, 83, 372
Indian Contract Law, 152
Injunction, interlocutory, 340–342
Insurance, 14, 33, 67, 124, 260, 272–273, 372
Insurance premium, 33
Intention, 32, 35–37, 45, 49, 58, 76, 80, 83, 86, 88, 90, 93, 97, 120–121, 126, 129, 131, 141, 145–147, 156, 167, 178, 183, 240–241, 250, 352, 363, 391, 394, 421, 424, 437
International sale of goods, 233
Interpretation, 4, 12–14, 24, 93, 127–133, 301, 311, 388

Just, 304
Just and convenient, 341
Just and equitable, 430, 440

Loan, 2, 24, 37, 64, 66–67, 71, 170, 218, 268, 271, 318–319, 339, 346–348, 417
Loss, 15, 24, 52, 83, 152, 162, 166–167, 172, 175–176, 179, 188, 190, 201, 212–213, 217–218, 245, 249, 252, 263, 282, 307, 364, 407, 425, 428, 440

Minors, 74, 174, 226, 230–231
Misrepresentation, 62–68, 72, 83–84, 115, 201, 261, 319–320, 368, 439, 445
Mistake, 49, 51, 59–62, 115, 117, 156, 456
Merchant, 15, 63, 197
Military equipment, 407–408
Monetary fine, 223–226, 228, 230–231, 272, 279, 291, 294–295, 297, 386, 412
Money laundering, 97–103, 364
Mortgage, 22, 64, 142, 206, 335

Negotiations, 26, 55, 83, 129, 355–356, 360, 403–404, 450, 453

Offences, criminal, 103, 180, 224, 293–294, 334, 364, 369, 386, 432–433
Oil trade, 71

Penalty, 179, 428
Penalty clauses, 125
Precedent, 3, 6, 409
Promissory note, 71, 206, 262, 335
Public policy, 89–112, 155, 315

Quasi-contracts, 21, 27, 61, 138, 181, 447–458
  quantum meruit, 453

Reasonableness, 5, 12, 33, 35, 52, 83, 88, 103, 110, 119, 125, 132, 148, 151, 168, 175, 178–179, 190, 199, 203–205, 219, 236, 242–243, 245–247, 249–250, 263, 282, 291, 293, 297, 303, 305, 307, 334, 338, 348, 358, 379, 404, 441, 451, 453
Rescission, 43–44, 67, 117, 172, 181, 288, 348
  restitio in integrum, 181
Rights in personam, 11, 22, 161
Rights in rem, 11, 22, 139, 275
Risk, 33, 217, 252, 281, 299, 355, 372
Rule of law, 3, 120, 409, 423

Undue influence, 51, 69–71, 73–75, 77–78, 115, 313, 319

Security (*see also guarantee*; *suretyship*) 63, 67, 113, 216, 262, 268, 303, 324, 331, 335, 338
Security and defence, 349, 389, 405–412
Security, social, 366–367, 390, 392
Shares, 66–67, 206, 212, 233, 335, 339–340, 342–343, 347, 420
Silence, 33, 80, 320
Sound mind, 11, 57, 202, 205, 440
Spouse (see husband)
Substances, dangerous, 299, 364
Suretyship (*see also guarantee*; *security*), 11, 316–330, 343

Terrorism, 99, 100–101, 364
Trafficking in human beings, 364

Validity conditions, 56–113, 158, 439

War, 407
Warranty, 119, 206, 239, 241, 242, 282, 334–335
Witness testimony, 64
Wrongful, 250, 282, 305, 319, 322, 428

Index